To Ken,

with our very best wishes,

Joe + Clon

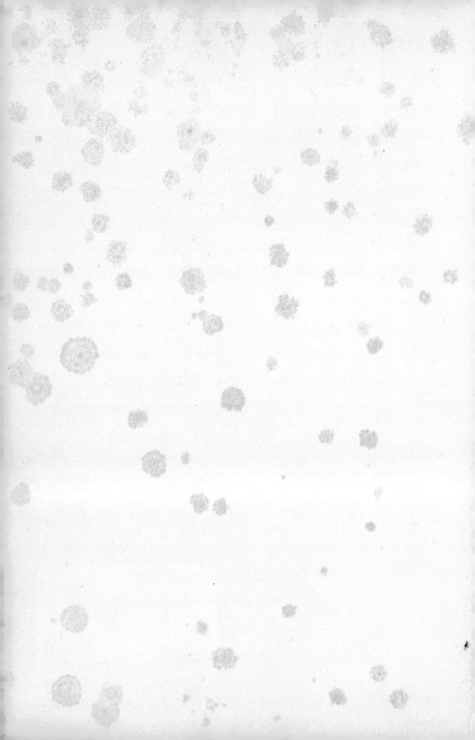

Whether you have a large garden or a small one, shrubs should be allowed to contribute their part

De La Mare Garden Books

THE BOOK OF
Shrubs

Alfred Carl Hottes

WITH A SUPPLEMENT OF LATEST
DEVELOPMENTS BY HOWARD W. SWIFT

DODD, MEAD & COMPANY
NEW YORK   1958

Printed in the United States of America

SUPPLEMENT OF
LATEST DEVELOPMENTS

THE BOOK OF SHRUBS has been used as a standard text over a long period of years and is very deserving of its continued popularity. The book serves as a guide to better choice of plants for specific situations, offers valuable cultural advice, and has been a very commendable influence on landscape design in this country. Not discounting my sincere appreciation for THE BOOK OF SHRUBS through many years of horticultural work, I attempt in this preface to correct a few obvious errors and to bring its subject-matter as up-to-date as possible without altering the Sixth Edition text. I hope that a subsequent edition may include hardiness zones, as no other feature would so greatly increase the book's value for both amateur and professional. Hardiness zones, as supplied by Alfred Rehder's MANUAL OF CULTIVATED TREES AND SHRUBS and Donald Wyman's SHRUBS AND VINES FOR AMERICAN GARDENS, even though they need interpreting according to one's knowledge of climatic variations within a zone area and the exposure to which a plant is subjected, are of great assistance in the intelligent selection of plants.

It will be noted in the Sixth Edition that many plants were added to those found in older editions. The majority of these shrubs are usable only in warmer sections of the country. If hardiness zones were indicated, either by number or in the text, this would be immediately and helpfully apparent.

In the Preface to the First Edition, Dr. Hottes states that STANDARDIZED PLANT NAMES has been used as far as the writer found it feasible for determining the plant names to be used. Evidently he did not find it feasible, however, to make many changes recommended by STANDARDIZED PLANT NAMES. Included among these are some which involve generic name changes which have now quite generally been adapted and should be called to the reader's attention:

LATEST DEVELOPMENTS

Benzoin aestivale	:	Lindera benzoin
Calycanthus praecox	:	Chimonanthus praecox
Citrus trifoliata	:	Poncirus trifoliata
Fatsia papyrifera	:	Tetrapanax papyriferum
Laburnum adami	:	Laburnocytisus adami
Laurocerasus caroliniana	:	Prunus caroliniana
L. lusitanica	:	P. lusitanica
L. officinalis	:	P. laurocerasus
Meratia fragrans	:	Chimonanthus praecox
Rhus cotinus	:	Cotinus coggygria
R. cotinoides	:	Cotinus americanus
Veronica (species in text)	:	Hebe (specific epithets the same)
Zanthorhiza apiifolia	:	Xanthorhiza simplicissima

Figures given under the heading of "Budget Your Planting" (p. 18-19) should be increased at least a third to be in line with prices in 1957.

Dr. Hottes, on page 27, advises that all shrubs should be pruned at transplanting time to balance top growth with a diminished root system. This would surely not apply to a deciduous shrub moved in the fall after its leaves have become inactive. Often, pruning had best be left until the following spring after transplanting late in the fall, particularly in colder climates where some die-back from freezing temperatures is inevitable.

The recommendation of a moving crew consisting of three men and pair of horses (p. 34) is hardly applicable in many places today, but the attachments available to make large tractors efficient assistants in moving trees and for accomplishing equally heavy tasks are readily available; even a small tractor or jeep may take the place of horses.

Figures given on page 35 should probably be doubled to be in line with man-power costs in 1957.

Use of dormant lime-sulphur or miscible oil spray may surely precede such drastic action as cutting out even major infestations of scale on shrubs (p. 37).

Parathion, TEPP, Malathion and Lindane for the control of aphids might well be added to those spray materials recommended by Dr. Hottes (p. 43). Specific recommendations are offered by texts such as THE GARDENER'S BUG BOOK by Dr. Cynthia Westcott on the control of insects on plants.

As controls for red spider (p. 43-4), new miticides such as Aramite and Malathion are in common use today and will usually be found more effective than the author's recommendations. The use of forcefully-applied water from a hose is often resorted to in dislocating red spider from sturdy plants.

Keeping plants in good health is the first and perhaps best insurance against borers (p. 44). DDT is frequently sprayed on trunks of woody plants and effectively kills young borers on emergence from eggs which adults have left there.

The most effective and practical treatment of soil to prevent damping-off (p. 45) is sterilization by the use of steam, heat or chloropicrin. The organic mercury compounds are often only partially effective.

In speaking of golden- and purple-leaved shrubs as well as variegated varieties (p. 46), I am sure the author had no intention of restricting his comment (by implication) to mockoranges, lilacs and weigelias, but meant shrubs generally, the varieties of which have golden or purple foliage or which have variegated foliage. Cutleaf varieties, dwarf sorts and pyramidal forms which the author claims will come quite true from seed are also meant to include shrubs generally which can be so described.

Chloropicrin should again be mentioned as one of the most effective means of sterilizing soil to prevent damage to seedlings by fungus which might be present in a seed-bed (p. 54). This method of sterilization is particularly adaptable for treating soil outside.

In his chapter on propagation (p. 46-82), most of the suggestions offered by Dr. Hottes on the handling of seed and woody cuttings are very dependable. They are particularly applicable for the amateur who wishes to experiment with propagation projects. New practices for more rapid rooting have been devised within the last few years, however, which change considerably some propagation practices given in the Sixth Edition. This is particularly true for large-scale operations where time and efficiency are important. Knowledge of latest experimental work in propagation methods is essential to anyone propagating plants on a commercial scale. To the amateur, knowledge of new methods is often stimulating—and may frequently save time in obtaining results. To compare methods of only a few years ago with methods used today teaches us that there is never only one method of procedure to achieve success with plant propagation, and that there may be better ways of doing things even though they violently oppose principles that have been standard in the past.

Those interested in modern propagating methods and recently-concluded experiments may wish to check the following texts, as well as material supplied in periodical literature: PLANT PROPA-GATION PRACTICES by James S. Wells (The Macmillan Co., 1955), PLANT PROPAGATION by Professors P. Mahlstede and E. S. Haber (John Wiley and Sons, Inc., 1957), and a freer-styled text with many helpful illustrations called PROPAGATION IN PICTURES by Montague Free (The American Garden Guild, Inc. and Doubleday and Company, 1957).

Two giant steps have been made in improving propagation techniques. These are due to a wide use of polyethelene film (polythene apparently its British equivalent), and the improved use of mist systems which supply intermittently and automatically very fine sprays of water over cuttings inserted in proper media. Polyethelene is much-used to preserve a high humidity in the immediate area of cuttings inserted for rooting, as an improvement over older materials used in airlayering, and in the protection of cions and cuttings being held in storage or during a rest period induced by low temperatures. It is very valuable as covering for growing-houses in warmer climates, and in some cases as a lining material for standard greenhouses. Incidentally, when cut into narrow strips, it makes an excellent wrap for grafts.

Both use of improved mist systems and polyethelene (which aids in the retention of high humidity within the space which it encompasses) have influenced the recommended appearance of cuttings prepared for insertion. Cuttings may often be longer and with more foliage left intact. Cutting stock is in many cases younger and softer, and cuttings made from this stock often root more quickly than harder-wood cuttings which were best for techniques used before. It might be interesting to add to the author's paragraph on shading results of recent propagation work in Florida. Frames of cuttings are subjected to an all-day mist treatment where cuttings are successfully grown without being shaded.

LATEST DEVELOPMENTS

For detailed propagation practices which have proven to be successful and, in some instances, improvements over methods employed previously, reference may be made to charts by Wells and by Mahlstede and Haber. To root cuttings of some plants, stronger concentrations of root-inducing substances than those readily available in powder form are recommended. Procedures with several kinds are given in Mr. Wells' PLANT PROPAGATING PRACTICES.

On page 71 the author includes a paragraph on vitamins. A number of years ago vitamins were given much publicity as being important in the culture of plants. So successful was the campaign that often amateurs expected vitamins (supplied in soluble capsules) to be a miraculous cure-all for any ailing plant. One notes that little is heard about dosages of vitamins for plants today—either in propagation practices or in ordinary plant culture.

The use of "inherit" (p. 161:2) in speaking of the character of plants grown from cuttings of Japanese Barberry is incorrect. The verb continue might be substituted.

As a control for box leaf miner (p. 166), use of DDT in wettable powder form is now recommended in preference to the molasses and nicotine prescribed by the text.

The statement (p. 172) that "no shrub has such waxy flowers and leaves" as the camellia is untrue. Numerous shrubs might accurately be described as more "waxy." Comment regarding the popularity of camellias by florists is certainly not applicable in 1957. In many parts of the country, camellias are as popular or more popular than gardenias. Reasons are that many of our contemporaries object to the odor of gardenias and that they are extremely perishable. Camellias have gained in popularity because of more recently-developed hybrids which do not shatter as easily as many older varieties, a greater use of color—particularly in corsages and funeral tributes, and a wider distribution of cut flowers due to improved transportation facilities and modern packing techniques.

Gardenias should not be restricted by the term "boutonniere flowers" (p. 246).

Plumbago (p. 324) is not "commonly seen as part of most plantings in Southern Florida"—but is popular as an outdoor

LATEST DEVELOPMENTS

plant in many parts of the Southern United States and in California.

Correction should be made in Dr. Hottes' statement regarding the use of Pyracantha as a hedge plant (p. 334). Pyracanthas do make attractive hedges for areas where their hardiness is unquestionable.

The last sentence on page 340 might best be omitted.

Making cuttings (as mentioned on page 341) would not be particularly difficult for amateurs, but rooting them might.

Eleagnus pungens (p. 420) flowers in October and not in June.

HOWARD W. SWIFT
Assistant to the Curator
of Education and Horticulturist,
The New York Botanical Garden

New York, N. Y.
January, 1958

CONTENTS

THE BOOK OF SHRUBS

LIST OF ILLUSTRATIONS

LIST OF ILLUSTRATIONS

PREFACE TO FIRST EDITION

What are shrubs? Shrubs are such woody plants as branch freely from the soil. How vast is the number of these desirable plants ! This book aims to describe the best in the language of all.

The author has necessarily drawn upon Bailey's *Manual of Cultivated Plants* and Rehder's *Manual of Cultivated Trees and Shrubs* for standard descriptions of species. Without these two books, his work would have been much more difficult.

Standardized Plant Names, as compiled by nurserymen, landscape architects and botanists, has been used as far as the writer has found it feasible. Other names which have been in common use in catalogs, even though they are not accepted, are included in parenthesis at the head of the description of the shrub.

This is the first American attempt to give the uses, objections, soils and complete propagation notes in one book. Scores of plantsmen have helped to make the facts complete. At nursery schools in five sections of Ohio the author gleaned many gems from the storehouse of experience of long-time plantsmen. He is grateful to all who realize that they have helped.

ALFRED C. HOTTES

PREFACE TO SIXTH EDITION

The author has profited by some years criticism of "The Book of Shrubs." Residents of the great regions of the Pacific Coast and the Gulf States will find their range of plants more adequately discussed. Descriptions of many additional plants have been included, more copious notes on culture have been added, the lists of shrubs for various purposes have been supplemented, and many new illustrations have been included. All these features, the writer hopes, will serve to increase the interest of the readers.

ALFRED C. HOTTES

VISION IN A GARDEN

"The landscape planting is a picture; it must have a canvas. This canvas is the greensward. Upon this, the artist paints with tree and bush and flower, the same as the painter does upon his canvas with brush and pigments. The opportunity for artistic composition and structure is nowhere so great as in the landscape garden, because no art has such a limitless field for the expression of its emotions. There can be no rules for landscape gardening, any more than there can be for painting. The operator may be taught how to hold the brush or plant the tree, but he remains the operator; the art is intellectual and emotional and will not confine itself in precepts."

—L. H. BAILEY

"WHERE there is no vision the people perish." Without vision no garden can be thoroughly satisfactory. A garden is not a problem in mathematics nor is it a puzzle. It should be a vision to be realized from the soil. It is built of grass, trees, flowers and stone but must also be fabricated by means of the head, the hands and the heart.

It is simple to have your planting done for you. However, it is more interesting to plan your garden to suit your own taste and in accordance with the situation which presents itself.

If it be true, as Bacon has said, that "men come to build stately sooner than to garden finely, as if gardening were the greater perfection," then gardens should be studied conceptions or inspirations in the mind of the landscape architect or gardener. Each spot in such a garden should aim to be as much a matter of inspiration as a poem, a play, a novel, a statue or a symphony. Each group of trees should suggest an idea, each clump of shrubs a consummation of thought, each bank of color in perennials or annuals an opportunity to bring nature to our dooryard.

The work of most artists is stable; not so that of the gardener The sculptor chisels his marble; today it is the same Venus de Milo that he made centuries ago. The painter mixes his colors and, in an inspired moment, produces a Mona Lisa. The psychological poet

writes; a play such as Hamlet is the result. The heart of the musician
is stirred; he gives us "Die Walküre" for all time. The landscape artist
dreams a dream, but the winters destroy it and rains do not fall. But
if neither the sculptor, the painter, the poet, the musician nor the
landscape architect dreams, who shall be the wiser? Surely not we!

The joy which may be derived from a planting depends upon un-
derstanding it, knowing that one is attempting definite effects—carrying out a vision—making a picture of each little spot in the landscape.
The true artist never finishes his picture. Each year, by pruning and
planting, the combination approaches his ideal in mind. One year he
cuts back the foreground plants because they hide the background;
another year he clothes the foreground with a ground cover plant.
Some years he allows a planting to grow as it will; another year his
mood changes and he tidies the planting by pruning to a little more
confined lines.

PLANT KNOWLEDGE

With study, the gardener comes to know his plants, their habits
and likes, their faults and virtues. He plans his plantings to the best of
his ability and changes such plants each year as are not as well adapted
to the situation or to an effect he desires to produce. So the housewife
changes her furniture from room to room and place to place.

Each sort of shrub may be aptly suited to some definite use. We
need to have a growing knowledge of what material will perpetually
produce this picture of our mind. Plants either grow or they languish;
they are the proper texture or they just do not adapt themselves.
There are places in gardens for Sunflowers, weeping trees and variegated shrubs, just as there is propriety in tears and homely truth.

Many persons are lovers of plants for their own sake. Some landscape architects carry the idea of the pictorial effect too far and neglect
the materials they use to produce that effect. We do care to know
what plants we grow. Variety is the spice of the garden as it is of life.
The short list of plants often used by some professional landscape
architects and nurserymen gives monotony to plantings. Such plantings appear as though made by the mile or gross; they lack the touch
of genius and the charm which personal interest lends—something,
at least, which the most incongruous amateur garden does not lack.
However, it must be admitted that whereas some landscape architects
err in the use of plants for their own sakes, most amateur plant lovers
make museums of their gardens by chosing plant material for individual

merit rather than absolute need to carry out the picture they have in their minds.

Some cities are Spirea mad; others specialize in Peegee Hydrangeas to the exclusion of the many shrubs carried by nurserymen. This book will be criticized by some amateurs and nurserymen who will say that many shrubs are listed which are not obtainable from nurseries. Only a demand for the unusual things will increase the supply of available plant materials. If the public demands the bug-ridden common Snowball, and pays as much for it as it does for the lovely Japanese Snowball which is more difficult to propagate and transplant, who is to be blamed? In northern regions California Privet is not hardy but is demanded from nurserymen, whereas the Ibolium, the Amur River and the Ibota Privets, all hardier sorts, languish in the nursery rows and are often relegated to the bonfire before they are sold.

Each plant has its individual use, value and need. Sumacs are wild, suckering and common; they are not adapted to the confined beds about the foundations of a small house, yet they are admirable upon steep, barren slopes where they can spread at will and take on their intense Autumnal colors which they do not do so well in cultivated and manured soil. So also, the Itea is a beautiful denizen of moist, naturalistic places but unsatisfactory in cultivation. Gaudy, variegated plants are too showy for some plantings, but each of them may be used with good taste in some spot. When a woman at a flower show asked me for a list of plants with golden foliage I wondered whether she had a bronze statue set on a yellow sandstone base.

TWENTY POINTS OF PLANTING

In planning a planting bear in mind the following:

1. Select the site of the house with an eye to good soil, surface drainage, desirable views and perhaps a few large trees.

2. Make a plan, drawn to scale. showing dimensions and including in detail the exact location of each tree, shrub, vine and flower bed, besides the buildings, walks, drives, fences and terraces. It is well to indicate the permanent features in ink—such plantings and accessories as you do not care to change; in pencil, mark the features which are removable — shrubs, trees and walks which have outlived their usefulness. Indicate the size and kind of plants to be removed. Mark on the plan the desirable views, the directions north and south, and the slope of the land.

3. Grade the yard to avoid unnecessary terraces and banks. Use gentle, natural slopes, with drainage away from the house. Save topsoil for lawns; lifeless subsoil will not grow lawns, shrubs nor flowers, therefore, manure heavily; spade or plow, harrow and level.

4. Determine whether the planting is to be laid out formally or informally.

5. In locating the walks and drives, remember the fuel supply. Avoid excessive use of concrete except where absolutely needed. Plan the walks far enough away from house so that a planting may be used at the base of the house, if possible. Walks and drives may be curved slightly but should be as direct as possible. Avoid steps in walks. Pleasing, sinuous curves are desirable, but the artistic eye distinguishes between monotonous scallops and pleasing curves.

6. Locate and develop lawn areas. Seed at proper time with the right kind of grass seed. Use best seed available. Fertilize with chemicals yearly. Roll every Spring; mow regularly. Keep lawns open; do not obstruct with trees, shrubs or flower beds. Do not lime or manure established lawns.

7. Select the desirable views to be seen from porch, living room, dining room and kitchen. Avoid shutting out these vistas. Frame the view from the house as well as the view of the house as seen from a distance.

8. Select and locate shade trees. Use long-lived, hardwood trees. Plant irregularly as frame, background and shade for house. Save ten to twenty years by planting large trees with 2- to 4-in. trunks.

9. Do not expect a beautiful planting unless the soil is prepared properly and fed yearly. What has become of the millions of trees, shrubs, Roses and evergreens sold by nurserymen? They have not been properly planted and then have been allowed to starve to death in many cases.

10. Locate shrub groups and exact placing of each shrub. Give them room to grow. Avoid monotonous sky lines. Use a few accents in height. For informal plantings avoid straight lines. Use a variety of shrubs. Be original. Don't copy your neighbors. Don't overplant. Do not scatter shrubs all over the lawn. Such shrubs assume the appearance of having been dropped from an aeroplane. A planting of this kind does not make allowance for a good lawn area. The lawn should serve as the canvas for your picture.

11. The foundation planting should tie the house and grounds together. Plant at least 2 to 3 ft. from the house with specimens 3 to 6 ft. apart, depending on size. Avoid excessively tall shrubs around small houses. Never plant a shrub that will get so tall it will have to be

pruned back constantly. Avoid conspicuous shrubs and plants, such as Koster Blue Spruce and Umbrella Catalpa, in front lawn and foundation plantings. Use low shrubs or perennials in front of low windows. and porches.

12. Screen plantings are often necessary to shut out neighbors. Use tall, quick growing forms. Feed heavily.

13. Boundary plantings serve to break straight property lines. Use flowers, vines, shrubs and trees.

14. Select and locate vines for porches, bare spots on the house, trellises, arbors and small buildings. Use vines adapted to each place, selecting a variety of them. Cover bare or steep banks with vines or shrubs. Feed well. Keep cultivated.

15. Plan and locate shrub beds as background for the flowers.

16. Plan and locate arches, arbors, trellises, seats, pools, birdbaths, sandbox. A small number of these features add to any yard or garden. Make the back of the house and yard as attractive as the front. Stake out location of each shrub before planting. Learn to know all your trees, shrubs, flowers and vines. Add a few new ones each year to complete the picture.

17. Make a list of all shrubs, vines, trees and flowers needed. Avoid strange agents; order your stock direct from a reliable nursery.

18. Encourage your neighbors and friends to beautify their homes, and develop your community into one of the most beautiful in your state. Every home should be beautified.

19. Satisfaction of any planting depends on the care and thought given to its planning.

20. Order early, plant properly, spade deeply, manure liberally.

THREE ESSENTIAL DIVISIONS OF THE YARD

Helen Field Fischer in *Ten Important Points in Planning Your Landscape*, tells us that every yard has three main divisions. The dividing line may be achieved in various ways, but the areas are for certain definite uses no matter how large or how small your grounds.

First of all you have your public yard between the house and the street. To be correct this must be dignified and strictly tailormade. The only way in which it can excel that of your neighbor's is in the absolute perfection of its stretch of smooth green lawn. No striking shrub or flower should be in view to attract attention from the house with its foundation planting.

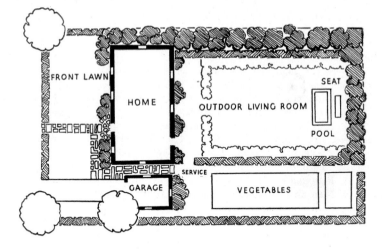

The second division is the service yard. This is on the kitchen side
of the house usually and is designed to hide the clothesline, ash can,
and all the necessary but unbeautiful accumulations of busy home life.
It should be screened from public view with shrubbery or a vine-covered
lattice. It often includes the vegetable garden and the annual garden
for cut flowers.

The third section—the intimate garden can be a part of an outdoor
living room, and to be ideal it should connect with the living room
of the house. While it is screened from the street with shrubbery, there
should always be a gateway or arch through which one may catch a
vista the full length of the lot, but keep in mind that though we love
long vistas, we also want to know definitely where they end. Be sure
to have an attractive feature at the end of this long vista to arrest and
satisfy the eye. A pretty lawn seat answers nicely for this and adds the
idea of hospitality.

In your intimate garden conventionality is laid aside and the
family may revel in outdoor hobbies. Pools, rock gardens, bird feeding
stations, unusual and striking flower novelties, all may be enjoyed in
privacy. There should be an open lawn in the middle, but stepping
stones, set low enough for the lawn mower to override them, can lead
enticingly from one point of interest to another until the round of the
garden is made and one is back at the gate. Handy benches and a
table in a shady corner will tempt one to do as much as possible of
the kitchen work out of doors.

FOUNDATION PLANTING EXAMPLES

We use lawns, shrubs and evergreens about our homes for one purpose—to set off the architecture, either to enhance its lines of beauty or to hide architectural mistakes. The wise home builder employs an architect and builds a home which follows some definite architectural style or period. Good English, Norman, Early American Colonial, Ranch, and Spanish Californian are always in style but the fads of building become as absurd as the hats of another day.

OUR CHANGING ARCHITECTURE

At one time our homes were built without regard to these more standard periods, the fad of the Victorian age carried ornamentation and gingerbread work to absurd lengths. Today we have shifted to the other extreme in the boxlike severity of the so-called Modern house.

Many old houses are built high above the level of the soil. Obviously such homes on stilts need to be brought down to earth with shrubs. However, do not hide the foundations without reason. The tendency now is to set the house close to the level of the grass. Each home needs an individual treatment. Stock plans can never completely solve your individual problem. The artistic eye chooses abundance of planting in one case and repression in others. Poor foundation planting may undo the best efforts of an architect.

CONIFEROUS EVERGREENS

The tendency in planting is toward the wider use of coniferous evergreens. Granting that these are all-season plants, that the proper sorts are slow growing and give a permanent effect, even so, they are often poorly adapted to city conditions and subject to insects and Winter injury, and only those persons who are willing to replace a few each year should use them. Shrubs are cheaper and generally more lasting. They do not, as a rule, hold their leaves through the Winter, but the flowers and fruits which they bear will give a change in the pictorial effect from season to season. The argument is not that conifers are

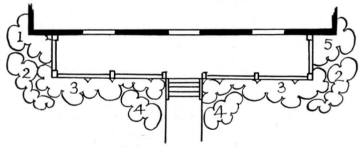

Front porch planting plan

SIX COMBINATIONS AROUND A FRONT PORCH

(The figure following each shrub indicates planting distance)

Combination 1
1. French Hybrid Lilac.......4 ft.
2. Anthony Waterer Spirea...2 ft.
3. Vanhoutte Spirea.........3 ft.
4. Japanese Barberry........2 ft.
5. Virginal Mockorange......4 ft.

Combination 2
1. Japanese Cranberrybush...4 ft.
2. Japanese Barberry........2 ft.
3. Pink Weigela.............4 ft.
4. Slender Deutzia..........3 ft.
5. Snowhill Hydrangea.......3 ft.

Combination 3
1. Vanhoutte Spirea.........3 ft.
2. Regel Privet.............3 ft.
3. Morrow Honeysuckle......3 ft.
4. Japanese Barberry........2 ft.
5. Snowberry...............3 ft.

Combination 4
1. Shrub-althea............4 ft.
2. Slender Deutzia..........2 ft.
3. Snowhill Hydrangea......3 ft.
4. Anthony Waterer Spirea...2 ft.
5. Arrowwood..............4 ft.

Combination 5
1. Showy Goldenbells.......4 ft.
2. Snowhill Hydrangea......3 ft.
3. Ibota Privet.............3 ft.
4. Regel Privet.............3 ft.
5. Coral Dogwood..........4 ft.

Combination 6
1. Magnifica Deutzia.......4 ft.
2. Froebel Spirea...........2 ft.
3. Lemoine Deutzia.........3 ft.
4. Slender Deutzia..........2 ft.
5. Pride of Rochester Deutzia.4 ft.

bad and that shrubs are perfect; but for economy's sake and the possibility of seasonal changes, shrubs are more interesting and less monotonous.

COMBINATIONS

Another tendency among landscapists is to plant shrubs in such large clumps as to appear monotonous, clumpy and lacking in naturalness. In the naturalistic method of planting the clumps of various sorts should be well planned to give a series of effects as the season advances. A clump of Lilacs may be made more interesting by using a few of the Hydrangea paniculata type in front, to give a late Summer effect. A plant of Tamarix at the back of a Mockorange will redeem its monotony. The more or less intermittent blooming Spirea Anthony Waterer will cheer a foundation planting of Weigela. The feathery masses of the Tree-spirea, *Sorbaria arborea*, will detract the attention from a non-blooming Vanhoutte Spirea clump. So in front of tall Spruces and Larches we may plant Flowering Dogwood, Cornelian-cherry or Shadblow, because such small trees are thrown into relief by an adequate foliage background. Let us visualize Azaleas in front of Hemlocks and Goldenbells drooping over a high stone foundation wall.

The grayish horizontal branching of the various Hawthorns will add much to a planting otherwise too usual in Winter. The various colored twigs will serve to add life to the Winter vistas. Fruiting shrubs scattered among the others will bring birds and generally add interest to a planting.

Fremontias are natives of California and Mexico. The woolly leaves and clear butter-yellow flowers are distinctive

New England Colonial House

THE NEW ENGLAND COLONIAL

Those who enjoy the neat primness of homes representing the New England stability of character will enjoy the austere dignity of the typical New England Colonial. It is an ever popular style which seems to fit our landscape equally well, be it in Massachusetts, Ohio, or elsewhere. The foundation planting needed should be of the character of the house itself—rather severe, formal, restrained. This type of house must not be overplanted and the shrubbery should not make it seem taller than normal.

The doorways are usually architectural gems which must not be masked with too much foliage. Sometimes a small front porch is a feature of this style, then a Wisteria may be used, but so trained that the pillars or their capitals are not completely hidden.

Hedges and characteristic picket fences are in keeping with the New England Colonial style.

In the upper sketch (page 10) of the New England Colonial the planting brings out the character of the house and complements the architecture. The doorway is flanked by rather formal shrubs or evergreens clipped to neat form to emphasize the doorway rather than dwarf it. The facade of the home is seen as a whole. A hedge surrounds a low terrace and gives a foundation on which the house stands firmly. Between the large shrubs at the foundations, an area back of the walk is to be filled with ground cover plants. To confine the area a hedge not over 6 in. high is suggested. Note the value of the vine at the left corner in tying the house to the lawn area.

For planting this home the plants listed on page 12 are advised for various sections of the country.

In the lower sketch the planting consists of a startling series of points and globes. Often the planter has used large evergreens such as Spruces, Firs, and similar cone-shaped trees which completely hide the house, obscure the view from the windows and shut out the light. The plants used give a false perspective to the facade of the house. It hardly seems as if the artist had drawn the houses in the same proportions. In each sketch showing the foundation planting examples for various styles of architecture, the lower sketch shows undesirable plantings.

In this series of pictures it is not the desire of the author to show absurd plantings, even in the less desirable lower pictures. In this case we might have shown the good architectural lines of the house smothered with shrubbery or evergreens. The most common mistakes with the New England Colonial would result from planting horticultural freak varieties with gaudy foliage.

No. on the plan	Deciduous Shrubs for Midwest and Northeastern States	Hardy Evergreens	The South	California
1	Euonymus alatus (Winged Euonymus)	Canaert Juniper	Lagerstroemia (Crape-myrtle)	Ilex cornuta (Chinese Holly)
2	Lonicera tatarica (Tartarian Honeysuckle)	Column Juniper	Ligustrum lucidum (Wax Privet)	Chamaelaucium uncinatum (Geralton Waxflower)
3	Deutzia gracilis (Slender Deutzia)	Prostrate Juniper	Ilex crenata (Japanese Holly)	Fuchsia in shade or Correa in sun
4	Ampelopsis tricuspidata (Boston Ivy) or Chinese Wisteria	Euonymus vegetus (Bigleaf Wintercreeper)	English Ivy	Chinese Wisteria
5	Cotoneaster acutifolia (Peking Cotoneaster)	Ilex crenata var. macrophylla (Japanese Holly)	Boxwood	Coprosma baueri (Mirror-plant)
6	Ligustrum regelianum (Regel Privet)	Taxus cuspidata (Japanese Yew)	Boxwood	Eugenia myrtifolia (Australian Brushcherry)
7	Periwinkle or Sedum (such as S. sarmentosa) or Thyme, edged with Box Barberry	Pfitzer Juniper or Pachysandra if lower growth is desired	English Ivy	Salvia leucantha, edged with Small-leaf Japanese Euonymus
8	Ibota or Amur River Privet hedge	American Arborvitae hedge	Ligustrum lucidum (Wax Privet)	Eugenia myrtifolia (Australian Brushcherry) Myrtus microphylla (Rosemary Myrtle)

THE ENGLISH
TYPE HOUSE

See page 14 for planting plan
of the upper sketch

The English style house need not be of plaster and lath but it is one of the more informal houses. It is perhaps less economical of space than the square houses such as the New England Colonial. The style is characterized by long, sweeping roof lines which carry the eye pleasantly from the soil to the sky. Chimneys are often over-emphasized, sometimes so much so as to almost overpower the house. It is

No. on plan	Hardy Deciduous Shrubs for Midwest and North-eastern States	Hardy Evergreens	The South	California
1	French Hybrid Lilac	Canaert Juniper	Oleander	Pittosporum tobira
2	Lemoine Deutzia	Japanese Yew	Azaleas	Fuchsia
3	Japanese Barberry	Ilex glabra (Inkberry) or Pfitzer Juniper	Wilson Barberry	Polygala dalmaisiana
4	Boston Ivy	Bigleaf Wintercreeper	English Ivy	Climbing Fig
5	Flowering Dogwood or Japanese Crab	Sweetbay (Magnolia glauca)	Crapemyrtle	Acacia baileyana
6	Regel Privet	Ilex crenata (Japanese Holly)	Ligustrum lucidum (Wax Privet)	Coprosma baueri (Mirror-plant)
7	Rhamnus frangula (Glossy Buckthorn)	Ilex opaca (American Holly)	Ilex vomitoria (Yaupon)	Arbutus (Strawberry-tree)
8	Hypericum aureum (Gold-en St. Johnswort)	Mugho Pine	Rhododendron	Abelia grandiflora

generally picturesque, an ideal home of a flower lover, for its very air demands flowers and shrubs in profusion and variety. Such rambling structures must be treated informally in contrast to the more sedate New England Colonial houses. The typical English house relies on planting to bring out its true character and finish. There is always a corner to fill, a roof to wreathe or bring down to the greensward. Some gay color may be introduced into the planting. All stiffness must be avoided except to add an emphatic note.

The upper sketch (page 13) is a house by Fernando Carrere and adapted from a sketch in "51 Prize-Winning Small Homes." It shows some Norman influence as well as English. The planting has been planned in sufficient variety so that it seems a spot for garden enthusiasts to develop their tastes to their heart's content.

To execute the planting shown, we suggest the plants listed on page 14.

In the lower sketch the owner has planned a setting for his home which is too stiff and formal. There are too many restless accents, each of which attracts attention itself. The house seems divided into definite sections and the shrubs do not contribute toward making a picture as a whole. As Professor M. E. Bottomley would express it: "Exclamation points often become interrogation points in the landscape." The chimney is beautiful and should not be entirely clothed in vines, yet the low evergreens here used intrude this over-large feature upon our attention. The reader will readily note how different the proportions of the house seem in the two pictures.

THE SPANISH HOUSE

Through the South and on the West Coast the Spanish house has become popular. It is, of course, a home designed for warm, subtropical climates and brilliant sunshine. Such houses seem foreign in certain Northern cities but yet they are built by those whose sentiment is tied closely to Spain or California and are tempted to get what they want.

The plants used in these frostless climates are luxuriant in growth, bright in color, and likely to be unique in form. Such plants are difficult to harmonize together because such plants stand out as individuals.

Their abundant growth necessitates frequent pruning. The Northern visitor to subtropical gardens is conscious of a certain unbelievable quality in them—plants which he finds only as greenhouse pot plants are here trees. Sometimes he is a bit thankful that frosts destroy his garden mistakes whereas the gardens of Florida and California, without freezes, often take on the appearance of a jungle hiding lovely archi-

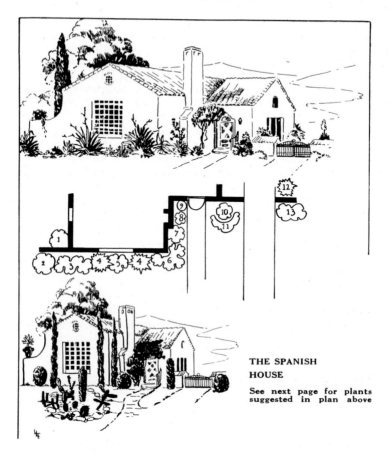

**THE SPANISH
HOUSE**

See next page for plants
suggested in plan above

tecture in a mass of over-vigorous shrubbery and snarled vines. In such
regions, even the meanest shack soon becomes a bower of foliage and
bloom whereas, unfortunately, many typical Spanish homes are hidden
at the end of the second year.

The Spanish house in the upper sketch is surrounded by a har-
monious array of plants. The semi-formal plan demands some order
in the planting. For this reason similar masses of foliage are arranged
on each side of the large front window. A vine is trained over the
entrance, but it is kept within bounds so that the interesting shape of
the archway is not obscured.

In the list below for plants hardy in the Midwest and Northeastern States, perennials rather than shrubs are suggested inasmuch as there is a scarcity of woody material with luxuriant foliage.

No. on plan	Hardy Plants for Midwest and Northeastern States	Tender Plants especially for California and Florida
1	Lombardy Poplar	Italian Cypress
2	Kansas Gayfeather (*Liatris*)	Blue Lily-of-the-Nile (*Agapanthus*)
3	Artemisia (some gray sort)	Breath-of-heaven (*Diosma*)
4	Devils-walkingstick or Ravenna Grass	New Zealand Flax (*Phormium tenax*)
5	Statice (*Limonium latifolium*)	*Statice perezi*
6	Goldflower (*Hypericum moserianum*)	Goldflower (*Hypericum moserianum*)
7	Laland Firethorn (*Pyracantha lalandi*)	Graber Firethorn (*Pyracantha crenato-serrata*)
8	Spreading Euonymus (*E. patens*)	Australian Bluebell Creeper (*Sollya*)
9	Jackman Clematis	Lovevine (*Antigonon*)
10	Siebold Viburnum	Fatsia (*Aralia*)
11	Fountain Grass (*Pennisetum*)	Princessflower (*Tibouchina semidecandra*)
12	Tree-spirea (*Sorbaria arborea*)	Yucca, various
13	Globethistle (*Echinops ritro*)	Breath-of-heaven (*Diosma ericoides*)

The owner of the house in the lower sketch (page 16) is a cactus lover who has intruded a bed of these strange forms in the front lawn area.

Three Italian Cypresses are planted in bean-pole regularity in front of the house. As commonly seen in such positions they are bound together with heavy cord, or stand at strange angles, or are clipped flat on top. Everyone who plants them improperly seems to know something is wrong. The Italian Cypress in the upper sketch is planted where it may tower to lofty heights to form a contrasting note to the otherwise horizontal lines of the home.

In our poorly conceived planting an incongruous plant tops the lefthand wall in contrast to the use of a billowy vine in the upper good planting.

Several severe globes and columns, religiously pruned monthly, are unfortunately too showy and out of harmony. Had the pruning shears been used wisely, the vines that hide the lovely archway would have been thinned and trained away from the doorway.

COST OF PLANTING

Whenever we plant our home grounds, most of us do it rather gradually and we hardly realize how much time we have spent upon the work and how much we have saved by doing the planting and care ourselves. Then, too, some of us prefer to buy large plants which will give an immediate effect, while others enjoy seeing the babies grow up to adult shrubhood. Naturally, the nurserymen cannot sell big specimen plants at bargain prices, but, conversely, it takes more plants to fill a similar area if they are small.

The wise home owner puts aside ten percent of the construction cost of the house for his budget for grading, walks, walls if needed, lawn, trees, shrubs, and gardens. Undue skimping on soil preparation will prove expensive in the end. Good lawns and flower beds need some 3 to 6 inches of fertile soil. When building have the topsoil removed before the excavation starts.

AVOID PUNY PLANTS

Don't plant shrubs and trees which are too small. The nursery, with ideal growing conditions, is the place to train plants into healthy, symmetrical specimens. It's a pity to plant weakling shrubs and trees supported by broomsticks and stakes because they should have stayed a year or two under the expert care of a nurseryman. With puny plants there's always a temptation to overcrowd for immediate effect; this results in a crowded, overgrown planting. There is a proper spacing for all plants, depending somewhat on the effect desired, and regardless of size, this spacing should be adhered to.

BUDGET YOUR PLANTING

If you must economize let your plans extend over a period of three or four years. I am indebted to George Siebenthaler for the following facts.

First year: The most immediate need is to establish a lawn and the foundation planting around the house, with the approximate costs for the lawn:

	Per square foot
Preparation of sub-grade	$0.00½
Fine grading	.00¾
Plant food	.00¾
Seeding, raking, and rolling	.02
Total per square foot	$0.04

For foundation planting around the home for a 55x120 foot lot you will need approximately the following list of plants:

```
2 Dwarf evergreens, 2 feet tall, at $7.50.............$15.00
4 Dwarf spreading evergreens, 2 feet spread, at $6.00.. 24.00
6 Dwarf evergreen shrubs, 1½ feet, at $4.50.......... 27.00
2 Specimen shrubs, 4 feet at $3.00................... 6.00
8 Flowering shrubs, 3–4 feet, at $2.00............... 16.00
2 Climbing vines, 2 year, at $1.50.................. 3.00
3 cubic yards topsoil spread 6 feet deep............. 24.00
```

          Total...................................$115.00

Second year: If you can't plant trees the first year, set them as soon as possible so that they can develop and enhance your picture. Trees, according to size, will cost from $4.00 up.

Third year: This year give thought to increasing the grounds with shrub borders and hedges, for privacy is one of the essentials of enjoyment. The hedge will cost approximately 70c. a foot whether it be Barberry, 18 inches high, spaced 2 feet apart, or Privet, spaced 10 inches apart.

The shrub border cost will be approximately as follows:

```
Flowering Shrubs (spaced 3–4 feet)..................$0.20
Topsoil—3 inches deep.............................. .03
Plant food........................................ .02
```

          Per square foot...........................$0.25

For the full planting there will be about 800 square feet of area in which shrubs should be planted which, at 25c. per square foot, would amount to $200.

Fourth year: After you have attained the desired privacy turn to the luxuries of a flower border or a small garden. This does not mean that you would not have some flowers before, but it is a great mistake to spend money putting on the finishing touches before the essentials are planned and in their places. Let's do the first things first. How often the plea is made that you can't afford to do the thing right. Doing a thing wrong always costs more in the end.

Perennial borders will cost approximately as follows:

```
                                    Per square foot
Perennials, assorted 2-year-old (spaced 18 inches)......$0.30
Topsoil, 6 inches deep, spread...................... .08
Plant food........................................ .02
```

          Per square foot...........................$0.40

A high degree of economy and appearance is achieved by careful planting, and the nurseryman's slogan, "It's not a home until it's planted" should be revised to read, "It's not a home until it's *properly* planted."

ACID, NEUTRAL AND ALKALINE SOILS

Plants, as they range themselves over the surface of the earth, have definite soil preferences as to moisture, texture and chemical analysis. Each plant adapts itself to its natural habitat. When we cultivate plants away from their natural haunts, it behooves us to determine their optimum soil needs.

CHEMICAL CLASSIFICATION*

Acid soils are sour soils; alkaline soils are the opposite and a solution of the soil tastes soapy; neutral soils are those in which the acid present exactly balances the alkali. The sap within a plant has a definite reaction at which best growth is maintained; anything which changes this reaction causes the plant to dwindle and die. Improper soils, then, contain minerals which in solution affect plants adversely.

As the thermometer measures temperature which we express in degrees, so the soil technologist has devised a method of expressing the relative amounts of acidity or alkalinity which the soil contains. It is not enough to say that a soil is slightly acid. It is preferable to give definite expression to the degree of acidity or alkalinity. The symbol pH is used to express these units; thus we say that a soil testing pH 3.1 is superacid, 4.1 is mediacid, 5.1 is subacid, 6.1 is minimacid, 7.0 is neutral, 7.1 is minimalkaline, 8.0 is subalkaline, 9.0 is medialkaline.

WHERE SUCH SOILS ARE FOUND IN NATURE

SUPERACID, pH 3.1–4.0. Peat bogs in which the chief plant is sphagnum moss.

MEDIACID, pH 4.0–5.0. Various peat bogs. Swamps where soil lacks lime. Thickets of Rhododendrons and plants of the Heath family. Woods where Hemlock, Spruce and Oak are common. Accumulations of peat, rotting wood. Mountain peaks and sand hills where the subsoil lacks lime.

---

*Readers should refer to the source of the information here presented: Edgar T. Wherry, *Soil Reaction in Relation to Horticulture*. American Horticultural Society Bulletin 4 (1926).

SUBACID, pH 5.0–6.0. Many marshes, meadows, swamps and upland woods. Long-abandoned fields and gardens in regions lacking lime.

MINIMACID, pH 6.0–7.0. Humus-rich meadows, swamps, woods in limestone regions. Fields and gardens under standard cultivation.

MINIMALKALINE, pH 7.0–8.0. Marshes and swamps permeated by water carrying lime. Woods where there is an accumulation of black leafmold. Ledges of limestone. Piles of manure, compost and similar materials.

CIRCUMNEUTRAL, pH 6.0–8.0. A general term applied to the last two classes. Far the greater share of plants prefer circumneutral conditions.

TESTING SOIL

Soils may be tested for acidity in various ways by the amateur, but it is better to send samples of your soil to the State College or Experiment Station for a report. Most home methods of testing soil require practice and an interest in chemistry.

Without pretending to be an accurate test or one that gives the degree of acidity, Nitrozene and litmus paper may be used. This paper can be purchased at the druggist. Place a piece of it on the moist soil. If the paper is blue and changes red, the soil is acid; conversely if the red paper changes to blue, the soil is neutral or alkaline. Red paper does not change color when applied to an acid soil; blue does not change when used to test alkaline soils.

Several other tests are purchasable. The Kenny Indicator Field Set and the Morgan Soil Testing Set may be obtained from the La Motte Chemical Products Company of Baltimore. A number of Agricultural Colleges distribute soil testing sets at a nominal price.

BUILDING AN ACID SOIL*

HOW SOIL BECOMES ACID IN NATURE. In nature acid nourishment is provided by the accumulation, on the surface of the ground, of a layer of half-rotted leaves, twigs, and rootlets. Such an accumulation when it occurs in a Sphagnum bog is called bog peat, or simply peat. On well-drained, sandy or gravelly soils, it is called upland peat. Under good conditions upland peat is laced into a tenacious mat, a few inches in thickness, by the roots of the ericaceous plants that accompany it, and this mat persists year after year, continually renewing itself through each year's leaf-fall and the penetration of new roots into the decaying mass. Upland peat is normally brown, but is often blackened by ground fires. On limestone soils or on soils which for any reason have an alkaline chemical reaction upland

---

*From an article by Dr. Frederick V. Coville, botanist, U. S. D. A., in *The Florists Exchange and Horticultural Trade World*, Dec. 10 and 17, 1927.

The condition of Rhododendrons after three years in an ordinary (alkaline) garden soil

peat does not form. The lime and other alkaline substances in the soil greatly hasten the decomposition of the leaves. Each year's leaf-fall is decomposed, much of it passing in liquid form into the underlying soil, prior to the leaf-fall of the following year. Fully decomposed leaves form a true leafmold, black in color and neutral or alkaline in reaction, in which Rhododendrons and other acid-soil plants will not grow. In soils derived from granite, sandstone, sand, and gravel, acid conditions are usually maintained with little difficulty by the addition of upland peat, half-rotted Oak leaves, or decayed wood or bark.

USE OF SAWDUST AND TANBARK. Sawdust and spent tanbark are acid materials useful as mulch for acid-soil plants. They should be applied experimentally at first, however, to test the safety and suitability of the particular kind that is available. Some kinds of sawdust, notably Redcedar and Pitch Pine, contain, when fresh, substances that are directly injurious. Other kinds, such as Basswood, Maple, and Birch, are free from these substances. In general, it is best to use sawdust that is weathered and somewhat decayed.

EXCAVATION NEEDED. When an attempt is to be made to grow Rhododendrons or other acid-soil plants in a place in which the soil is neutral or

How Rhododendrons of the same batch grew in an acid soil during the same three years (see illustration at top of page)

alkaline, such as a limestone soil, the bottom land of a river valley, the ordinary fertile garden, or a prairie or arid-region soil, it is necessary to prepare holes or trenches and make up a special soil mixture. This should consist of one part of clean sand to one or two, or even four parts of upland peat or its equivalent. To keep earthworms from bringing up the underlying soil the bottom of the hole should be lined with a 2 in. layer of soft-coal cinders. The depth of the peat and sand mixture need not be more than 8 in. to 12 in. If the materials for the mixture are available in quantity a bed may be laid down over the whole surface of the ground. A permanent mulch of Oak leaves will help maintain a proper degree of moisture and by decomposition will supplement the peat supply.

PEATS VARY. In choosing peat for the culture of acid-soil plants two mistakes should be avoided. First, certain swamps contain a deposit that looks like peat but is neutral or alkaline in chemical reaction. The soil of such swamps, to which the name muck should be applied, is well suited to the culture of Onions, Celery, and Lettuce, but altogether unsuited to the culture of Rhododendrons and other acid-soil plants. Second, the much decomposed peat in the submerged lower layers of deep bogs, such as is used for fuel in Europe, or the lighter kinds for stable bedding, is not suitable, by itself, for acid-soil plants. It is many years, often centuries, old and although it may furnish the needed acidity it is deficient in plant food. When such a peat is used, nourishment for the plant must be supplied in some other component of the soil mixture. A very light peat of this kind, imported from Europe, consisting chiefly of brown fragments of Sphagnum Moss, is much used in the United States as a mulch, as an ingredient of potting mixtures, and in propagating beds, for acid-soil plants. It is well suited to these purposes, but being deficient in plant food it should not be used alone, or with sand only as a potting soil.

LEAFMOLD. A sharp distinction should be made between half-rotted Oak leaves and the ordinary compost of leaves with manure, garden soil, and garden trash. Such a compost is neutral or alkaline in reaction and should not be used on acid-soil plants. Sugar Maple, Elm, and Linden leaves rot rapidly and so soon reach the alkaline stage that they also are not desirable for application to an acid-soil planting. Oak leaves, especially Red Oak leaves, rot slowly, and in two or three years, if the pile is turned over several times, make a good substitute for upland peat.

FERTILIZERS. No manure, lime, or wood ashes should be applied to Rhododendrons or other plants that require an acid soil, for all these substances tend to neutralize the necessary acidity. Cottonseed meal, ground soy beans, and spent malt, all of which contain a large amount of nitrogen in organic and acid form, are excellent fertilizers for acid-soil plants. Experiments with fertilizers made by the writer show that skimmed milk and buttermilk are useful as fertilizers for acid-soil plants. Undoubtedly, the partially dried forms of these products now marketed for poultry feed are also serviceable as fertilizer for such plants. The warning should be given, however, that skimmed milk contains about ten times as much lime as cottonseed meal and that the possible cumulative effect of repeated applications may require remedial measures, such as the application of aluminum sulphate to remove the excess lime.

In very sandy soils for which so little peat is available that the plants suffer for nourishment, the following special acid fertilizer devised for Blueberries and Cranberries will probably do well for Rhododendrons, applied at the rate of an eighth to a fourth of a pound per square yard:

	Pounds
Cottonseed meal	10
Acid phosphate	4
Sulphate of potash	2

WATER. Hard water, which is alkaline in reaction, will ultimately injure an acid-soil planting. Rainwater or some other water that is neutral or even acid in reaction should be used if practicable. If only alkaline water is available for sprinkling purposes it can be made neutral or slightly acid by dissolving in it a suitable amount of aluminum sulphate. The proper amount can be determined by adding to a teaspoonful of the treated water in a white dish a fraction of a drop of the dye known as bromthymol blue. If the amount of aluminum sulphate added to the water was just sufficient to make it neutral, its color under this test will be green; if it has become acid, yellow; if it is still alkaline, blue.

Ornamental plants vary in the degree of soil acidity or alkalinity to which they are best adapted. The preparation of authentic lists of species on this basis will necessarily be a slow procedure, the outcome of careful experimentation. European gardeners have learned from long and cumulative experience that certain plants thrive best when supplied with peat, and this knowledge has been handed down to us in garden literature, and in garden practice when conducted intelligently, but never apparently with any suggestion that the essential quality of the peat was its acidity. The statement in any reliable work on gardening that a particular species requires peat may be taken as good evidence that this species is an acid-soil plant. In very many cases, however, especially in American works, even this evidence is lacking.

AIDS TO MAINTAINING ACIDITY

When a planting of acid-loving trees and shrubs is wanted in an alkaline soil, we can help to keep the soil on the acid side by the use of several materials as follows:

1. *Aluminum sulfate.* This is the commercial form of alum which is less refined. The amount needed will depend on the pH of the soil and the water which is applied to it. It is also important to know just what degree of acidity the plants you desire to grow will need. There is no danger in using it if an excess of phosphorus is added to the soil, otherwise free aluminum is toxic.

2. *Dusting sulfur* is slower acting but more lasting than aluminum sulfate. Common powdered sulfur should not be used as it takes 3 to 6 months to produce results.

3. *Iron sulfate* is also useful at the same rate as aluminum sulfate.

How Aluminum Sulphate cured a sickly Rhododendron

Both these plants were sickly on June 3 after having been grown in ordinary soil since May 3. The one at the right thereupon was dosed with aluminum sulphate and a second application was given July 27, the one at the left being left untreated. The photograph, taken Aug. 31 shows the beneficial effect of the doses

The Ohio Experiment Station advises that aluminum sulfate and sulfur should be used as follows:

To Change pH from	to	Use Aluminum Sulfate per 100 square feet	Use Dusting Sulfur per 100 square feet
8	7	4.5	2
8	6.5	7	2
8	6	10	4
8	5.5	13.5	5.5

4. *Tannic acid.* Edward Gilette suggest 1 part commercial tannic acid to 50 parts of water.

The J. D. Heald Co. of Lynchburg, Va., puts out a Hemlock extract, about which they say:

"Weekly applications of Hemlock extract, one part to 50 parts of water, seem to render any common soil a proper medium in a comparatively short time. Where extracts are dissolved in water, a further production of acid goes on for two reasons. Firstly, the so-called tannic acid content undergoes a splitting up of sugars which forego fermentation, and under favorable circumstances develop a marked amount of acid. This would probably occur when an extract was mixed with a soil which was moist. So, inferentially, under what are commonly called growing temperatures, we can assume that a soil irrigated with dilute extract, may shortly arrive at a condition similar to that produced under nature, without the lengthy period following the breakdown and dissolution of tannin-containing vegetable tissues."

5. See also discussion under Rhododendrons, page 340.

PLANTING
AND TRANSPLANTING

Shrubs may be transplanted in either Fall or Spring, although the former time is generally preferable. The ideal date in Fall is after a heavy freeze; earlier or later than that may be successful, however, much depends upon the climatic conditions prevalent in your section of the country.

ADVANTAGES OF FALL PLANTING

1. The soil is warm and easily worked. Plenty of moisture is available, but the soil is not as soggy as in the Spring.

2. Long season of planting. Spring comes with a rush; Autumn lingers into Winter. Transplant after the leaves have had a hard frost and the growth has been checked or made dormant. One often waits for some weeks in Spring for a good transplanting day.

3. Nurseries are very busy in Spring. They must fill their orders in rotation. Sometimes you are ready for your stock earlier than they can dig it; sometimes they ship it too early so that it lies about and dries out. Shrubs in full leaf of early Spring are not ideal for planting.

4. Rare plants are always sold out by Springtime. The nurseries are always short of certain items in Spring. It is disappointing to be forced to leave vacancies in our plantings. It is always a case of "first come, first served" with the best.

5. The shrubs are established and ready to grow when Spring arrives. The roots having grown some in the warm soil of the Autumn will force the tops into immediate growth.

DISADVANTAGES OF FALL PLANTING

1. Alternate freezing and thawing in heavy, lifeless clays break roots and heave plants from soil unless mulched.

2. Winter winds loosen plants which are not fibrous rooted nor furnished with a number of stems coming from the soil.

3. Too late transplanting, using frozen soil, results in clods which cause air spaces. When ground freezes hard, stop transplanting.

DO NOT TRANSPLANT IN FALL

In spite of the admonition to plant in the Fall, experience dictates that the following shrubs are exceptions:

Azalea

Benzoin (Spicebush)

Buddleia (Butterflybush)

Calycanthus (Sweetshrub)

Colutea (Bladder-senna)

Cornus florida (Flowering Dog-wood)

"If the plants are thoroughly dormant they transplant best in Autumn because the sap is more dilute in Spring."—Horvath.

Crataegus (Hawthorn)

Hibiscus syriacus (Shrub-althea)

Kalmia latifolia (Mountain-laurel)

Magnolia (See page 297)

Rhododendron (See page 339)

Rhus (Sumac)

Stephanandra

Tamarix (Tamarisk)

Viburnum tomentosum plicatum (Japanese Snowball)

PLANTING INSTRUCTIONS

The planting of shrubs is not attended with difficulties if the following points are remembered:

1. Buy from a nearby nursery so that the shrubs will not suffer from long shipments.

2. Having received shrubs from the nursery, plant them as soon as possible, so that the roots may not be exposed to the sun or dry out. If received too early to plant or at an unfavorable season, heel them in a convenient place, being sure that the roots are well covered. When shrubs have dried in transit bury them, tops and all, in moist soil for several days.

3. Dig the holes large enough, generally 15 inches to 18 inches deep and often larger in diameter, so that roots are not too crowded and twisted. It is a mistake to dig a hole in the sod to plant shrubbery; better prepare a bed for them.

4. Use good topsoil around the roots rather than at the surface. The builders often leave much rubbish or bad soil next to the cellar walls so that in foundation plantings some of this should be removed.

5. After planting apply a liberal amount of decayed manure to each shrub and spade it into the soil.

6. Pack the soil thoroughly about the roots.

7. Water after planting using a root-promoting substance such as discussed on page 71.

8. Prune the branches at planting so as to balance the loss of roots which would result from their being dug. Heavy pruning at planting

is generally advisable. This point is contended by some who insist that when the roots are not severely injured in transplanting there is little need to shorten the tops to a great degree.

9. Mulch shrubbery for the first year after planting, using decayed manure, marsh hay or straw. Sometimes, however, the soil is naturally lacking in drainage so that a mulch holds the water in a dish-like hard-pan.

CONSIDERATIONS

The question perhaps which comes to the mind of the planter is what distance apart to set the shrubs. Each planter will have a different ideal in mind. Some will impatiently desire immediate effects; on the other hand, others will be too patient and will not have a good planting because the grouping will not be perfected until after a period of years. Aristotle told us years ago that "medium" is a synonym for "right." Consequently, we shall consider that the shrubs should be planted at such distances apart that they will be at their best the beginning of the third year.

Vigorous young plants are better than old, decrepit ones which have grown to great height because they have been allowed to become too crowded in nursery rows. Nurserymen grade shrubs in sizes 12 in. to 18 in., 2 ft. to 3 ft., and 3 ft. to 4 ft. Sometimes they are branchy for their height and often they are tall and leggy with a feather-duster-like mass of twigs at the top. Large shrubs must be pruned soon after establishing themselves or they will appear less handsome than young stock 2 to 3 ft. tall. Some nurseries prune young shrubs to the soil to make them branch from the base; such shrubs, irrespective of height, are the best. Old, hardwooded, gnarly shrubs are not worth trans-planting, much less buying. Nevertheless, the landscape architect and the home gardener often need a few tall shrubs for background plantings and nurserymen should recognize this need by raising a quantity of specimen shrubs. The public would gladly pay the price.

COLLECTING NATIVE MATERIAL

Many shrubs of great usefulness and beauty are native to the wood-lots and roadsides of our country. The visitor to a Mountain-laurel region is apt to tear up a shrub from the hillside so that he may remove it to his home. This effort is often without success. Plants in the wild must compete with other vegetation, and in so doing, often send their feeding roots a great distance for moisture and food. Such root systems, then, are not compact, balanced, or fibrous. Nursery-grown stock is often root pruned, and is at least, cultivated to produce a balanced

Rhododendron plant balled and burlapped

root system. It is a perversity of Nature that the shrubs most desirable for collecting from our wild places, such as Rhododendrons, Kalmias, Flowering Dogwood and Bayberry, are the most difficult to transplant. Such shrubs are best moved in the Fall and severely pruned. Young stock only should be collected. Tremendous and surprising root systems usually accompany large woodland shrubs. Be sure to use root-promoting substances.

Figuring labor, time and disappointment, it is far better to buy stock from a reputable nursery, except in the case of the easily transplanted shrubs, such as Coral Dogwood, Indian Currant, Snowberry, Sumac and Elders. Some persons make too much fuss about the use of native materials collected from the wild. Each shrub has certain qualities suiting certain conditions. Whether it comes from Japan, China, Ohio, Michigan or Chicago should not be the primary consideration. The question should be, "Which shrub best suits the situation?"

BALL AND BURLAP

Certain shrubs are difficult to transplant. In that case they are safely moved when root pruned the year previous to transplanting. When such shrubs are dug, a large ball of earth should also be taken. Nurserymen who sell shrubs balled and burlapped must charge more for them. Such shrubs have been frequently transplanted in the nursery and the handling of the ball and the labor of putting on the burlap involve expense. But, it is only by this method that successful transplanting is assured. If the shrubs are long in transit from the nursery, the ball of soil will become dry. In this case, soak the ball before planting. It is as well to plant the shrub, burlap and all, unless there has been too much burlap used. In that case cut off some of it at the top or at least loosen the burlap. Such stock often dies because water does not penetrate to the center of the ball. Give careful watering at first.

The following shrubs are considered difficult to transplant.

Abelia grandiflora (Glossy Abelia)
Comptonia (Sweetfern)
Cotoneaster (Dwarf sorts; buy pot plants)
Ceanothus (Jersey-tea)
Corylus (Hazel)
Exochorda (Pearlbush)
Hibiscus syriacus (Shrub-althea)
Ilex glabra, verticillata (Holly)
Magnolia (See page 297)
Mahonia bealei especially
Myrica (Bayberry)
Pyracantha (Firethorn)
Rhamnus (Buckthorn)
Tamarix (Tamarisk)
Viburnum tomentosum plicatum (Japanese Snowball)
And all broad-leaved evergreens. (See page 118)

SUMMER TRANSPLANTING

Nurserymen are gradually working out methods whereby shrubs may be moved during full growth. Usually these shrubs are lifted in the Spring and planted in containers of some sort. Walter Hillenmyer, of Louisville, Ky., has devised a method of moving shrubs at all seasons, using wire baskets, not unlike ox-muzzles, but larger. (See illustration, page 31.) Some dig the shrubs with a ball and wrap with chicken wire; others use tin or metal containers. Such shrubs may be heeled into sand beds, slag or set in a protected place in the open ground.

Dowax is a commercial product designed to be used for spraying on the branches to assist in easy transplanting. Henry Hicks remarks:

"Shrubs used to be little sticks to plant in the Spring or Fall and wait for them to grow and bloom. You had to employ a landscape architect or know a long list of Latin names or be satisfied with a few things you knew, as Lilacs or Privet. Now you can come to some nurseries and see many of the kinds and pick out most of them for Summer planting."

Wire baskets are used by Walter Hillenmyer for Summer transplanting.
The roots easily make contact with the surrounding soil, so that this method is preferable
to the use of metal containers

If one desires to move a shrub from one place to another on one's own home grounds, it may be dug with a large ball, moved, carefully watered for a few weeks, pruned back by removing a quantity of leaves and some branches, and it will go right on growing as though hardly disturbed.

HEELING-IN GROUNDS FOR NURSERYMEN

In order to extend the planting season in the Spring, nurserymen store their shrubs in a storage house, or else heel them in out-of-doors.

H. V. Lawrence, before the New England Nurserymen's Association, described a good method of heeling-in shrubs:

"For deciduous shrubs, we open trenches in the heeling-in ground, which, by the way, should be conveniently located where water is easily available for use as needed. These trenches are about two feet in width and a little deeper than we would open for ordinary lining out; a space two to three feet is left between them according to the size of stock to go in. About the time the foliage begins to start we carefully dig (or buy) good, well-rooted shrubs of the varieties most likely to be needed, in what we believe to be proper proportions. The stock is set upright in the trenches as one would plant a hedge, as near together as the size of the plants will allow without crowding and so that one or two of a variety may be lifted without disturbing two or three others. The roots are covered with soil carefully but loosely, so as not to quite fill the trenches; it is not tramped at all. If rain does not come within a day or two we put the hose on and thoroughly wet down the stock. This watering naturally puddles the loose soil around the roots and new fiber begins to form very soon; however, these shrubs, being checked by digging, come along more slowly than those undisturbed in the field. So, of course, we plant from the field and ordinary heeling-in ground as long as we can.

"We all know that plants which are shingled* in the heeling-in ground soon spoil after they begin to grow and must be lined out or lost. Not so with the prepared stock. By this time it is well out in leaf, possibly in flower, but if the soil around the roots has been kept moist, practically every piece (being in an upright and accessible position) will lift easily with some soil adhering to the roots. Careful handling will retain much of this and all the roots.

"In severely dry weather we sometimes puddle, but not often, for if the puddle is a bit too thick, it is apt to break the new roots, and if too thin it will wash off more than it puts on.

"In loading we shingle the stock on the trucks, which have some loose earth or moss (no hay or straw) in the bottom. A little of this is also sprinkled on each layer of roots, and the load is *carefully watered—not washed—* and covered with canvas; it is then good for a 20 or 30 mile trip. Of course it is not possible to carry a large load, for it will dry out too quickly if piled high. Naturally, it is important that the minimum of time elapse between digging and final planting."

LATE SPRING TRANSPLANTING

Often landscape architects cannot plant in the Spring until a house is finished by the builder, or the nurseryman may desire to hold back stock for late planting. H. N. Horvath has used a method of puddling which is serviceable in such cases. Make a puddle of heavy clay and water. Dip the roots in it and while wet dust them with a mixture of pulverized dry clay and ¼ dried cow manure. Use a shovel and put as much of this dry dust on as will adhere to the mud-covered roots. Nursery stock so treated may be planted weeks after the normal season.

MIDWINTER PLANTING

If one desires to move shrubs of great size, he often resorts to Midwinter planting. The nurseryman and landscape architect practice it because they must extend their planting season or they would be unable to complete the large amount of work which demands their attention in early Spring and Fall.

The main point of Winter planting is to insure proper conditions and preparation of the beds where shrubs are to be planted. Mulch the shrubs to be dug and the area to be planted, using any available cornstalks, straw or even leaves. Let the mulch be deep so that the soil beneath is not frozen deeply. Dig the plants, moving them with a ball.

---

*By shingling is meant, lapping one row of shrubs over another, in which case the shrubs are put in at an angle approaching horizontal.

Prepare the hole and tramp fine earth about the ball. Large clods of frozen soil cannot be used if the transplanting is to be successful.

Large sods of ground cover plants can be moved successfully in Midwinter, namely Bearberry, Sandmyrtle, Sweetfern, Vinca and Pachysandra.

MOVING LARGE SHRUBS IN WINTER*

Transplanting very large shrubs often becomes a necessity, either as a means of obtaining immediate effects or to avoid overcrowding which when small, was planted closely for the very purpose of giving quick results.

Large shrubs (that is, shrubs more than six or seven years old) will require considerable pruning to make up for a reduced root system if transplanted by ordinary methods, unless great care is taken to preserve a very large root ball while moving them. In light soils this is practically impossible, and Winter moving with a frozen ball of earth must be resorted to. In heavy clay soils, however, the following method may be pursued whenever the soil is dry and stiff enough to hold together, especially if the clay root-ball is filled with a network of fibrous roots.

For Winter transplanting, work is begun in November or early December. Before tying in the straggling branches of the shrubs to be moved, it is well to look them over carefully and drive a stake close to the butt of each on the side that it seems best to have "to the front" in the new location. This makes it unnecessary to untie the limb to be sure that the shrub is faced properly when planting.

Trench around the shrub to be moved to a depth of about 2 ft., leaving a ball of earth from 5 to 10 ft. in diameter, according to the size of the shrub. A Box plant or a specimen evergreen 8 ft. tall and 6 to 8 ft. in diameter will require a ball about 5 ft. across. Plants with fibrous roots can be handled with smaller balls than do those with coarser roots.

The soil below the root ball is taken out, except for about 2 ft. under the center—thus leaving the plant with its root system perched on a 2-ft. pivot. One-half of the outside of the trench bank is sloped away to facilitate removing the shrub from the hole. A 6 in. covering of hay is placed in the very bottom of the trench to keep the root-ball from freezing to the ground so firmly that it cannot be moved when the time comes.

The holes that are to receive the shrubs may be dug at this time, and the soil covered with hay, but it usually works out better if the ground is covered a foot deep with hay where the holes are to go, and the holes dug later, when the plants are moved.

Except for overhauling and collecting the necessary tools, and removing from the root-balls any blanket of snow heavy enough to exclude the frost, nothing more is done until after the balls are thoroughly frozen. Several

*An article by Carl Stanton in *Garden Magazine and Home Builder*, October, 1924, pages 117 and 118.

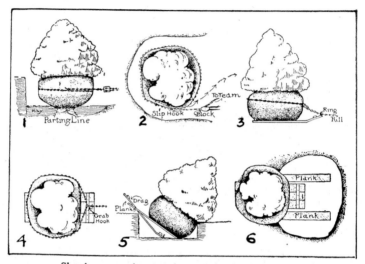

Showing successive steps in transplanting large shrubs

First trench around the shrub (Fig. 1) to a depth of about 2 ft. leaving ball of earth 5 to 10 ft. in diameter according to size of plant; take out soil below, leaving 2 ft. under the center, and cover bottom of trench with 6 in. of hay (as directed in text). Slip a chain around root ball (Figs. 2, 3, 4) and it can be readily shifted by a pair of horses with the aid of block and fall. Figures 5 and 6 show method of lowering into new hole as described in text. (*From Garden Magazine and Home Builder*)

pieces of strong chain from 6 to 12 ft. in length, blocks and tackle of 1 in. rope, crowbars, two 5-ton lifting jacks, planks of assorted sizes, plenty of small pieces of board for blocking, and some pieces of burlap for use around tree trunks to which are attached the blocks for pulling, will be all the apparatus required.

For the moving, a crew of three men and a pair of horses, with perhaps two men to dig the new holes, will prove to be economically efficient.

To avoid overcrowding, where plants are only moved a few feet, the hole to receive them is connected with the trench around them so that they need only be drawn across, without lifting from the hole. If a chain be slipped around the root-ball a pair of horses, with the aid of blocks and tackle, can easily move a very large shrub by a series of twisting pulls.

If the shrub is to be moved any distance it is jacked up on one side with two jacks, spaced so that a stone-drag may be slid between them and under the ball. The jacks are removed and, if the ball sits far enough onto the drag, a chain is fastened around it with one end slipped through the ring of the drag so that the pull of the team will come on the ball and not on the drag—thus preventing the latter from sliding out from under the ball. A twisting pull with the chain on the ball, while the drag is held stationary with crowbars will slide the ball farther onto the drag if it seems desirable.

On arriving at the new hole, the drag is swung around end on to it, and two short pieces of plank are laid, one end of each on the bottom of the hole, and one beneath the ball—one plank each side of the drag, to receive the ball. A twisting pull with the blocks and tackle will turn the shrub so that the good side is toward the front, as it slips into the hole on the planks. These planks carry the ball clear across the hole instead of allowing one side to drop straight down so as to throw the plant on its side. The drag and the planks are then withdrawn, the ball pried or jacked up if necessary to straighten the plant, and a stone or two wedged under it to hold it so.

Water is applied as the earth is thrown back and tamped, thus "puddling" the plant and insuring a firm footing for it as the water soaks away.

A warm covering of hay prevents winterkilling due to drying winds, but if plants are moved from a sheltered spot to one open to strong winds a temporary windbreak will be required until the plants become acclimated.

Success should follow if these three precautions are heeded:

There is no reason why one hundred per cent success should not follow such Winter planting if the three precautions below are heeded:

1. Do not leave the plants too long before moving them, after the soil has become frozen.

2. Be sure that no frost is in the floor of the new hole below the plant, and that no frozen earth is thrown back into the hole next to the roots. If only a little unfrozen soil is securable at planting time, it is better to "puddle" that in and surround the ball with hay to prevent its drying out until such time as loose soil is obtainable.

3. Cover the ground to prevent its freezing after the plants are in, and erect a temporary windbreak if necessary, leaving both until the middle of April or the first of May.

As to the cost of doing this sort of work, figuring men at $4.50, a team at $10, and a foreman (if necessary) at $10 a day, each large shrub could be transplanted for an average of $8 to $10. Hemlocks 20 ft. high, or Cedars, or Pines of this size could be transplanted under good conditions for from $10 to $20. Smaller specimens, say from 10 to 15 ft., not very heavy, could be moved for approximately $8 each.

PLANT FOODS

In order that they may thrive, all plants need food of some sort. Any plant which grows for a long time in one place is likely to exhaust the soil.

When we discuss the scores of shrubs planted in all sections of the country, we cannot lay down very definite rules for fertilization, inasmuch as some need an abundance of fertilizer and others thrive for a century without it.

In preparing the beds for shrub planting, it will be wise to use a liberal quantity of manure on the soil, because the nitrogen in the manure will tend to cause immediate and healthy growth and the bulkiness of the manure will make the soil more porous for the penetration of the roots.

Too frequently the planter does not realize the conditions of the soil about the foundations of new homes. The concrete wall has been built, and when the forms are removed, the space is filled in with mortar, bricks and clods of soil, all of which is not conducive to shrub growth. Such areas should be investigated and when necessary good soil added to that which is found. Entire excavation of the area is rarely necessary, but each shrub should be supplied with several bushels of good soil.

Each year the shrubs may be lightly mulched in Winter with decayed manure. In the Spring, some of the coarsest litter may be removed and a great share of it spaded in. Large shrubs according to size, may be fed with from one to three pounds of a high test complete fertilizer. Vigorous shrubs are less subject to insects and disease. Obviously, starved shrubs do not bloom as profusely.

Such fertilizers as bonemeal and superphosphate increase the hardiness of shrubs, whereas excess applications of nitrate of soda, ground blood, and other nitrogen-carrying fertilizers will promote great growth and less hardiness.

Each shrub mentioned in the pages which follow will have remarks about soil when the definite fertilizer requirements are known. Acid loving plants are discussed on pages 20 to 25, 90 and 91.

PRUNING

Is pruning necessary? Any one who desires well-formed shrubs must give some care to pruning them. The very nature of a shrub indicates that pruning is necessary. Shrubs are plants which renew themselves by new growth from the base of the plant; trees grow by producing the new wood near the top, growing ever upward. Therefore we prune shrubs:

1. To renew the wood, taking out the oldest branches every year or two, even before they die.

2. To increase the profusion of bloom.

3. To keep the ornamental twig sorts attractive. It is only the younger wood of the red and yellow twigged Dogwoods that is beautiful; severe pruning is essential.

4. To remove scale on such shrubs as Lilacs and Dogwoods. It is easier to eliminate an infestation of scale by cutting it out than by spraying it.

5. To make them treelike by pruning them to a single stem. Many of our shrubs are quite attractive when all the branches are removed but one, so that the growth is forced into a treelike head. The Japanese Snowball, the Spindle-tree, the Shrub-althea, the Tamarix, Peegee Hydrangea, Rose-acacia, the Goldenrain-tree, Lilacs, and Privets can be so trained. Even the Weeping Goldenbells (*Forsythia suspensa*) can be carefully tied to a stake 3 to 6 ft. tall and encouraged to produce one trunk which is not allowed to branch until it attains the desired height. The gracefully drooping branches wreathed in bloom in early Spring will make this a most useful addition to the specimens of the garden.

When one desires to train an established shrub to standard or tree form, cut away all shoots but the straightest one and, if none are straight, cut them all out and force the growth of an upright cane.

In the case of Lilacs, which sucker so freely, it is always wise to train the French sorts to tree form, inasmuch as they flower better and keep their allotted place instead of spreading year by year from a space 3 ft. in diameter to large unmanageable clumps.

In training shrubs to tree form, they may be pruned to make them informal, or for certain definite uses they may be sheared into standards or formal objects.

6. To make them formal in outline, producing globular Privets, Barberries, Boxwoods and Golden Mockoranges for formal gardens. Pruning for hedges, walls of green and living arches come under this category. Such pruning is known as shearing.

7. To make young shrubs bushy. To attain this the nurseryman prunes back the growth from hardwood cuttings at the end of the first year. Such shrubs are cut to the soil, whereupon they produce an abundance of strong shoots from the crown of the plant.

8. To rejuvenate old established and unsightly Snowballs, Lilacs and Mockoranges. These are best trimmed back to the soil and allowed to spring up anew from the base. As S. N. Baxter said, "Such pruning leads to the spring which Ponce de Leon sought in vain and prevents the frowziness of age."

9. To offset the loss of roots at planting time. The writer strongly believes in cutting back newly transplanted shrubs severely. Only by this method do the shrubs give a good appearance in the near future. They become bushier and, although not as showy the first year, develop into the proper shapes the second year.

10. To make shrubs more everblooming. If Weigelas, Spirea Anthony Waterer and Buddleias are pruned immediately after one set of flowers is passed, they will bloom again. Prune back the flower stems of some branches of Weigelas and head in the strong growths. In a few weeks prune back the strong growths again and a scattering of bloom all Summer and Fall will result.

WHAT TO AVOID IN PRUNING

1. Avoid pruning shrubs in late Fall so that they appear dehorned in Winter.

2. Do not prune shrubs flat on top by cutting all the shoots to the same height; such shrubs appear unnatural and give a broom-like effect—the model for the brush cut of the barber shop.

3. Do not prune early Spring blooming shrubs before they bloom; wait until afterward. All pruning of Forsythia, *Spiraea thunbergi*, Japanese Quince and other vernal flowering shrubs should be pruned after their floral effect is passed. See list on page 39.

4. Ornamental fruited sorts should be pruned moderately before and after they bloom, but not vigorously, either in early Spring or in Summer.

5. Do not prune shrubs too severely at any one time, nor cut back the strong growth at the top only. This would result in the production of upright, strong canes lacking grace. When shrubs become old and unsightly, it is often necessary, however, to cut them to the soil.

TO BE PRUNED AFTER FLOWERING

Includes shrubs which bloom very early and have their flowers produced upon wood of last year. This automatically removes the unsightly seed pods.

* *Amelanchier* (Shadblow)
* *Amygdalus* (Flowering Almond)
* *Aronia* (Chokeberry)
‡*Azalea
* *Calycanthus* (Sweetshrub)
* *Camellia*
* *Caragana* (Pea-shrub)
* *Cercis* (Redbud)
* *Chionanthus* (Fringetree)
  Coronilla (Scorpion-senna)
  Cydonia (Flowering Quince)
* *Cytisus* (Broom)
* *Deutzia* (Deutzia)
* *Exochorda* (Pearlbush)

* *Forsythia* (Goldenbells)
‖ *Hydrangea opuloides* (House H.)
‡*Kalmia (Mountain-laurel)
‡ *Lilac*
‡ *Magnolia* (Prune as little as possible)
  Philadelphus (Mockorange)
* *Pieris* (Andromeda)
‡*Rhododendron
* *Ribes* (Currants)
  Roses, Climbers
  Spiraea (Spirea) (See page 369)
  Tamarix, early flowered sorts. Severe pruning desirable.
* *Viburnum carlesi, lantana*

TO BE PRUNED A LITTLE AFTER FLOWERING AND A LITTLE IN EARLIEST SPRING

Includes shrubs with ornamental fruits and those which may be more everblooming when so treated.

§*Cornus* (Dogwood), ornamental twig sorts
*Cotoneaster
*Halesia (Silverbell)
*Laburnum (Goldenchain)
  Lonicera (Honeysuckle)

*Mahonia (Hollygrape)
  Sambucus (Elder)
§*Spiraea bumalda* and varieties
  Symphoricarpos (Snowberry)
  Viburnum
  Weigela

---

*Shrubs which need no pruning except to remove old wood.

‡Shrubs which should have developing seeds removed.

†Shrubs in which the tips freeze each winter and need to be pruned for appearance sake.

§Prune back to a few eyes on each shoot every spring.

‖Any pruning after July ruins the possibility for bloom the next year. It is the bud formed in the Fall which blooms the next Spring. If these Winter buds are not protected and are injured, the shrub will not bloom. Cut out entire shoots and prune back others.

TO BE PRUNED IN EARLIEST SPRING OR EVEN LATE WINTER

Includes all shrubs flowering on new wood and those with dead twigs in Spring (marked with †).

† *Abelia* (Arbutus-shrub)
* *Acanthopanax* (Angelica-tree)
§ *Amorpha* (False-indigo)
* *Baccharis* (Groundsel shrub)
* *Berberis* (Barberry)
§†‡*Buddleia* (Butterflybush)
§†*Callicarpa* (Beautyberry)
§†*Caryopteris* (Bluebeard)
§ *Ceanothus* (Jersey-tea)
‡ *Clethra* (Summersweet)
§ *Colutea* (Bladder-senna)
‡ *Hibiscus* (Bush-althea)
§ *Hydrangea* (except *H. opuloides*)
§ *Hypericum* (St. Johnswort)
§†*Indigofera* (Indigo)

†*Kerria* (Kerrybush)
Lagerstroemia (Crapemyrtle)
§†*Lespedeza* (Bushclover)
Leycesteria
Ligustrum (Privet)
Lonicera (except *L. fragrantissima*)
§ *Neillia* (Neillia)
§†*Rhus* (Sumac)
Roses
§ *Salix vitellina* (Golden Willow)
Spiraea (Spirea)
Staphylea (Bladdernut)
‡ *Stephanandra*
§ *Tamarix* (Tamarisk)
§†*Vitex* (Chaste-tree)

HOW TO PRUNE

1. Do not shear shrubs but reach in and take out old branches at the base. Year by year the shrubs become more choked with old stems, so that new shoots cannot get the light to grow. They start at the top of the bush rather than at the bottom where they should. Renew the whole plant—not only the top of it. Such cutting saves time because one cut is made, saving a half dozen to remove smaller branches.

2. If possible avoid stubs by cutting all shoots above an eye, especially when the eyes are far apart. This is not as essential for alternate leaved shrubs as for those having opposite leaves.

3. When one desires to keep a shrub low he must constantly prune it so that it never gets large. If a shrub grows near a porch and once becomes 6 ft. tall, it cannot be kept at 3 ft. unless the roots are pruned. Vigorous tops produce vigorous roots and the more pruning we do, the more the tops will grow if once the roots have been allowed to become large. This applies to hedges especially. Take a spade and cut off a circle of roots around the shrub.

Instead of trying to work against the natural height of a shrub, take it out and plant one of lower natural growth.

4. The treatment of the Vanhoutte Spirea may be seen in the cut on the opposite page. The same would apply to the pruning of

many of the shrubs which bloom in early Spring. Sketch number 4
shows the progressive development of the plants. The flower clusters are produced upon short branchlets borne upon the wood of
the previous season's growth. After flowering, growth starts from a
little below the flower clusters (at "*a*") and also beyond them. The
seed vessels begin to ripen and weigh down the branches. If the shrub
in the upper sketch is pruned back to the point marked "*a*" (that is,
to a shoot from near the center of the plant), it prevents the growth
marked by the dotted line. The plants do not become top-heavy but
develop gracefully as shown in sketch number 5. Each year the shrub
should be headed in to encourage the growth of long, willowy shoots.
In the sketches, compare the difference in the growth resulting from
pruning, marked by the double lines.

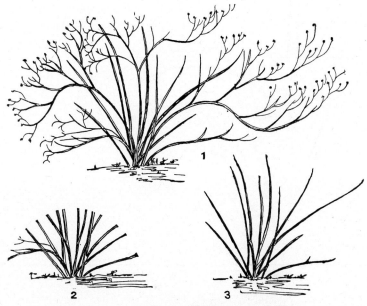

Pruning Shrubs

1, Unpruned; 2, pruned so that branches are of equal length, thus making the shrub too
formal, common but improper; 3, correct method, growths thinned and shortened.
In each case 1, 2, and 3 we are dealing with the same shrub

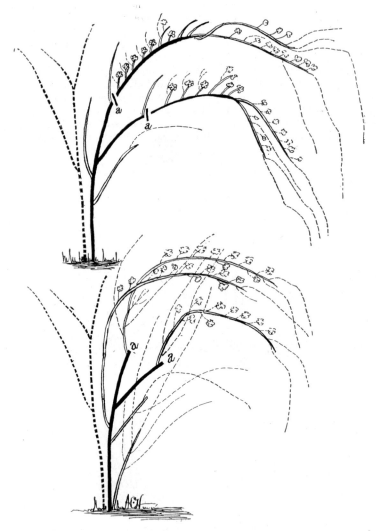

See text, "How to Prune", page 40

SHRUB TROUBLES—INSECTS AND DISEASES

Shrubs, like cats, birds and men, have their troubles. We must expect these things and not bemoan our fate. It is useless to plant without informing ourselves about the simple fundamentals of insect and disease control.

Every gardener needs a small medicine box for his shrubs which will surely need some spraying or dusting for insects and diseases.

INSECTS

SCALE. Of the insects, few are as common as the various kinds of scale. They are tiny insects which hide beneath a scaly covering which they secrete as a protection against our sprays. Nevertheless, they are not too formidable and may be killed if they are sprayed during a vulnerable period of their lives. Just before the shrubs start to grow in Spring is the best time to spray Lilacs, Japanese Quince, Dogwoods, Crabs and such as are infested with the tiny San José scale. We use miscible oils which do not discolor the foliage. Commercial sprays are more effective if a Winter spray is also given. At this time the solutions may be stronger because the leaves have been shed. When the whole shrub is covered with scale, rather than attempt to control it, prune the shrub to the soil and let it start anew.

LICE, APHIDES. Certain shrubs, notably Anthony Waterer Spirea, Vanhoutte Spirea, Crabs, Flowering Currant, Euonymus and others, become infested with tiny lice which cover the tips of the growing branchlets. These are killed by a nicotine, pyrethrum, or rotonone solution. Soap may be added as a sticker. We may use a pyrethrum or a rotenone extract. Aphides are soft bodied and feed by puncturing the plant tissues and sucking the juices. Remember the effectiveness of the control depends upon hitting the bugs hard and hitting everyone of them. Needless to say, a spray pump is essential.

RED SPIDER. The shrubs planted beneath overhanging eaves, those which are subjected to too dry growing conditions and those which are planted in a situation allowing of but little circulation of air about them become grayish in appearance because of infestation with a subtle little mite called Red Spider. It spins a web but the insect itself is too tiny to be noticeable. It has foiled our efforts to control it for some years but at last we have learned that it can be controlled in three ways—first, by spraying with water; second, by dusting with sulphur, using dusting sulphur, a product more finely ground than the ordinary flowers of sulphur; third, by spraying with "Volck," a proprietary material which has recently come into almost universal use. It is of the nature of a miscible oil. The plants are cleaned by the spray, and one must surely admit that its use is so varied and valuable as to be truly a boon to the gardener out of doors or in the greenhouse.

BORERS. Of course, borers which get into the stems of shrubs are not easy to control. That cannot be expected. Nevertheless, we can find their burrows and inject carbon bisulfide therein with a medicine dropper. This forms a gas heavier than air which travels along their burrows and kills the insects.

Calcium cyanide is a powder which may be injected in large holes. Moisture in the air or of the wood generates the poisonous hydrocyanic acid gas which kills.

Digging out the borers is thoroughly satisfactory but laborious.

Lilacs, Pussy Willows, Flowering Dogwoods and the Prunus group are especially susceptible to borers.

MISCELLANEOUS WORMS, SLUGS, CATERPILLARS. Anything one sees in the shape of a worm eating the foliage needs to be given a good meal of rotenone, DDT, or arsenate of lead solution, whereupon it will become a thing of the past. Even the bagworm which makes cocoons on your plants may be sprayed in early May before it hides itself. Do not gossip with your neighbors about the prevalence of worms; just spray them.

SUMMARIZATION ON INSECTS. When an insect sucks the juices from the plant but does not eat holes in the leaves, spray with nicotine, pyrethrum, rotenone, or a miscible oil, hitting the insect

When an insect eats the foliage, spray with arsenate of lead, DDT, or rotenone.

When the foliage becomes grayish, it needs red spider treatment.

DISEASES

Briefly, diseases are not common upon plants in proper growth. Improve the culture, and the disease cannot ruin your plants.

When golden-leaved shrubs become brown around the edge, they are not diseased but sunburned. Golden sorts are anemic; they cannot stand adversity nor full sunshine. Do not spray them; move them next Fall.

When Lilacs become covered with mildew they are starved, growing in an improper place, or else the season is too wet. Dust with sulphur or move the shrubs.

It is better to cut out disease than attempt to control it. Spraying the plants with Bordeaux mixture, the most widely used fungicide, prevents disease.

DAMPING-OFF. A serious trouble of all seedlings and softwood cuttings is the disease known as "damping-off." Several fungi are concerned so that truly it is not one disease but a combination of many different fungi. It attacks the small plants near the surface of the soil.

Conditions favorable to disease:
1. Close, humid atmosphere.
2. Overwatering, especially having the plants damp at night.
3. Plants weakened because of insufficient air, food or light.
4. Sand or soil too low in frames, flats or pots so that there is poor air circulation.
5. Seedlings too thickly sown.
6. Temperature too high.

Preventive means:
1. Sterilize soil or sand with heat, mercuric compounds or formalin.
2. Use fresh, uninfested soil or sand.
3. Ventilate.
4. Do not overwater.

Control:
1. Improve growing conditions.
2. Sterilize the seeds, the seedlings or cuttings by dusting, spraying or soaking in one of the organic mercury compounds, such as Semesan, Cuprocide, zinc oxide, Spergan, and Arasan. Such products are a great boon to the nurseryman, florist and gardener. Write to the manufacturers of these products for the latest information about their use. Most careful gardeners treat all seed of questionable subjects.
3. Seedlings or cuttings which are infested should be removed as well as some of the soil or sand. Then apply hot sand to the area.

PROPAGATION

The plant lover knows inherently how to propagate his plants. Nevertheless, there is always a right way to do things. Through the years of practical experience, propagators have followed the ways of Nature and supplemented them with the improvements of practical experience.

In the following pages it will be shown where Science has stepped in to expedite and assist. The graduates from the school of hard knocks may call certain of these scientific deductions theoretical and entirely impracticable. On the other hand, there will be those who recognize that, with perhaps a modification of these theoretical ideas, the methods recommended by Science become practical.

The absolutely correct procedure may not be known; your opinion, good reader, may differ from that of the writer.

SHRUBS FROM SEED

Seeds are used to propagate plants in great quantity cheaply, although usually this cannot be done as quickly as by cuttings. Often seedlings have great vigor, generally seedling grown stock is more uniform in growth.

Certain species of Viburnums, Honeysuckles and Mockoranges hybridize with one another so freely in gardens that plants of these grown from seed do not breed true. The plants are often intermediate in character between two parents, so that frequently we see Honeysuckles which are not truly Morrow or Tatarian.

The named varieties of Mockoranges, Lilacs, Weigelas and Spireas do not come true from seed. Usually golden and purple leaf sorts and variegated varieties produce but a small percentage of seedlings true to color. Cutleaf varieties, dwarf sorts and pyramidal forms produce quite true from seed.

Double-flowered shrubs such as Kerria, *Spiraea prunifolia*, and varieties of Hibiscus and Lilac produce no seed. Varieties of Hydrangeas and Viburnums which have only sterile flowers, of course, produce no seed. Many shrubs have either male or female flowers, but not both on the same plant. Such plants are known as *dioecious*. Examples are Shepherdia, Skimmia, Hollies, and White Fringetree. Berry dis-

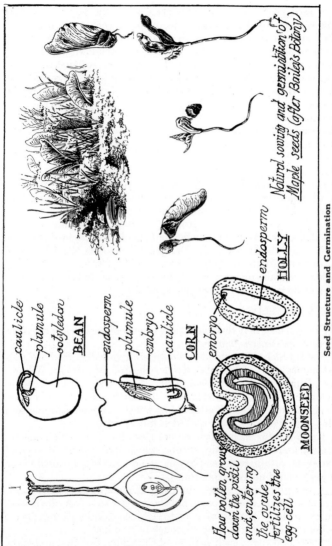

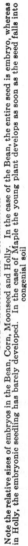

Seed Structure and Germination

Note the relative sizes of embryos in the Bean, Corn, Moonseed and Holly. In the case of the Bean, the entire seed is embryo, whereas in Holly, the embryonic seedling has barely developed. In the case of Maple the young plant develops as soon as the seed falls into congenial soil

play or seed production only takes place when the plants are set in clumps with one male, or staminate, plant to each three female, or pistillate, plants. Some gardeners graft both sexes on the same plant.

Isolated plants do not produce as good seed of Flowering Dogwood as do those in clumps. For example, Dr. Opal Davis found that 90 to 100 per cent of the seeds from plants growing alone were infertile. Evidently, this Dogwood is self-sterile; that is, it cannot produce good seed unless pollenized by a plant other than itself. Dogwoods growing in clumps had less than 10 per cent of the seeds empty.

We are just beginning to know a few real facts about shrub seeds, due to the work conducted by Dr. William Crocker of the Boyce-Thompson Institute.

When seed does not germinate we merely say that we have purchased or collected poor seed. But until recently we did not know fully what we meant by "poor" seed. Furthermore, we are but touching the hem of knowledge about seed germination.

Seed develops in the ovules from egg cells when they are fertilized by a pollen grain. We have thought that ripe fruit contained ripe seed but this is not always true, says Dr. Crocker. In Soft Maple the seed ripens and deteriorates quickly, whereas in Ginkgo often the seed is not ripe when the fruits mature; in fact, the egg cell has not been fertilized as yet and there is no embryonic plant within.

CLASSES OF SEEDS

We realize now that there are many classes of seeds, each requiring a different treatment, namely:

1. Seeds which ripen and have a large embryo within ready to grow almost immediately. Examples, besides the Soft Maple, are Willows, Poplars, Elms and many tropical plants. Such seeds must be sown as soon as ripe or kept in cold storage with a high humidity; otherwise, the seed becomes worthless after a few weeks. Japanese Maple seed can dry more but should be soaked before sowing.

2. Certain seeds with which we are more familiar, such as beans, peas, most annuals and many shrubs, which have a fully developed embryo plant within, will stand drying and are easy to germinate even when kept under adverse conditions.

3. The bulk of some seeds (the Holly being a notable example) is made of stored food, or *endosperm*, but the embryo has hardly developed. In American Holly it takes from one to eighteen months after the berry is ripe before the seed is developed enough to germinate.

4. Some seed coats, such as those of Caragana, Robinia, and many other legumes, have hard seed coats, impervious to water and air. These coats must be softened before they sprout. Soaking in hot water, acid,

Germination test of Rosa rubiginosa seeds, showing the effective stratification temperature to be 5 deg. C. or 41 deg. F.

The check row was stored dry and the others in moist sand at the temperatures shown. After six months all were planted in a flat in a greenhouse. (From Boyce Thompson Institute)

or filing the seed coats is necessary. Dr. Crocker remarks that the Lotus, *Nelumbium*, seed has been often found to lie at the bottom of an old lake for 200 or more years without germinating, because the stony seed coat would not let the water in. After filing the coat, or cracking the seeds, they grew. In some seeds, the freezing of the seeds serves to crack the bony coverings.

5. Strangely, certain seeds need a certain temperature for ripening properly, and will not germinate when given a supposedly normal temperature for growth. The scientists say that these seeds need a period of *after-ripening*. It is a stage in the development of seeds which goes on at a low temperature, generally 40 or 41 degrees F. (5 degrees C.). To this class belong such seeds as we usually say need to be frozen and also those requiring two years for germination. Generally, it is not that the seeds need freezing or a certain time, but a low temperature for a longer period than normal. Here then belong the Rose, Cotoneaster, Peach, Plum, Apple, Cherry, Hawthorn, Hard, Norway and Japanese Maples (not Soft Maple), Basswood, Viburnum, Dogwood and Barberry. These are the seeds we stratify.

By *stratification*, we mean mixing the seed with sand or peat moss shortly after the fruits are ripe so that they may be given a low temperature without lack of water or exposure to too rapid alternate freezing and thawing. Such seeds may be frozen without detriment, whereas the same seeds remaining on the bushes would be killed. Nurserymen have stratified seed for years; now we know why seed germinated better when so treated.

We are ready for definite facts.

Apple seed after-ripens in 75 days at a temperature of 41° F.

Rosa multiflora after-ripens in 60–90 days at a temperature of 32° to a few degrees above.

Rosa hugonis after-ripens in 90 days at a temperature of 41°.

Rosa rubiginosa after-ripens in 90 days at a temperature of 41°.

Cornus florida after-ripens in 120–130 days at a temperature of 41°.

Cornus nuttalli* after-ripens in 145–165 days at a temperature of 33°.

Cotoneaster after-ripens in 150–180 days at a temperature of 40°.

Peach after-ripens in 45-90 days at a temperature of 40°, down to freezing.

Birch after-ripens in 90–150 days at a temperature from freezing to 5° or 10° above.

Cherry after-ripens in 60–90 days at a temperature of 40°.

Sorbus aucuparia after-ripens in 75-80 days at a temperature of 32°–41°.

---

*Cornus nuttalli is the Western representative of our Flowering Dogwood. Note the difference and that the temperature is only 1° above freezing.

Basswood (*Tilia americana*) after-ripens in 90 days at a temperature of 41° (break the seed coat.)

Norway and Sugar Maples after-ripens in a short period at a temperature of 41°.

Japanese Maples after-ripens in a long period at a temperature of 32°–50°. There is great variation in the Japanese Maple varieties; some after-ripen in three months, others six months.

Barberries and Elderberries after-ripen when in a fluctuating temperature between 40° and 80°, so that sowing the seed in the Fall gives this variation.

Viburnum opulus has an interesting three-stage period of development. (See page 402.)

Other seeds requiring an after-ripening period are *Cydonia*, *Malus*, *Pyrus*, *Prunus*, *Rhodotypos*, *Arctostaphylos*, *Sambucus*, *Halesia* and *Juniperus*.

WORTHLESS SEED

We must carry this matter a few steps further. There are several reasons why we say that seed is poor, namely:

1. When we do not understand how to handle it.

2. When, like in the case of the Flowering Dogwood noted on page 48, the seeds are empty and we cannot tell by superficial examination.

3. Seed is poor when it is infested with fungus. It was found that in the case of one lot of Yew seed 50 per cent of the seed had a fungus all through it and 50 per cent had disease upon the seed coats, so that the young plants became infected as soon as they attempted to grow. It is not uncommon for seeds with fleshy seed coats to be infested with fungus. It is, therefore, advisable to remove the pulp from all seeds and disinfect the seeds with some organic mercury compound, such as Semesan, Cuprocide, zinc oxide, Spergan and Arasan. Never sow rare seeds without using some seed disinfectant.

4. Seed is frequently infested with insects. A certain lot of Hawthorn, *Crataegus oxyacantha*, was badly infested with ichneumon fly; 75 per cent contained larvae, 10 per cent of the seeds were without embryos. This leaves 15 per cent as being the greatest possible percentage of germination.

5. Seed is not viable when it is too old, too dry or the many other things that may happen to seeds.

PRACTICAL METHODS OF STORING SEEDS

1. Store seeds in bottles, cans or some container that will not allow drying out.

2. Store other seeds in sand or peat moss, especially those which must be kept moist and need after-ripening.

3. Sow the seeds in the proper medium. Peat moss is generally better than sand because it retains moisture. Cotoneasters do not like the acidity of the peat moss. For those seeds needing an after-ripening period, sow the seed in sand or peat moss and place in cold storage or refrigerator at the proper temperature for the proper length of time. They may remain for a longer time than noted on page 50, but not for a shorter period; otherwise the seeds may need to after-ripen all over again. Freezing near the end of this after-ripening period may kill the seeds. When the after-ripening period is up, the seeds may be sown, as is described below.

SEED BEDS*

When seedling shrubs are raised on a large scale, seed beds are necessary, but for small quantities flats or abbreviated soap boxes, 3 to 4 inches deep, may be used. Fill the flats with soil to within ½ inch of the top; press it down firmly; sow the seed and mulch. Such flats can be stacked in a cool cellar or coldframe.

In arranging for seed beds, spare no pains. Make them properly so that they may be permanent. Follow these suggestions:

1. Select a location sheltered from heavy east and northeast winds, and provide windbreaks in the form of hedges, plantings, fences, etc., where natural protection is missing.

2. A well-drained, sandy loam is the best soil. Naturally heavy soils should have sand added to them and too sandy soils are improved by mixing some loam with them.

3. The soil should be worked to a depth of at least 12 inches, should be free from stones and weeds and it should be brought to as fine a mechanical condition as is humanly possible, by repeated raking or harrowing.

4. The earlier the preparation of a seed bed is begun, the better results may be expected. Green manuring is very beneficial.

5. Well-rotted cow manure or compost can be used but fresh manure, and particularly stable manure, should be avoided.

6. If the seed beds can be kept under a hoe crop for a season it will help to destroy weeds which might give much trouble later on.

---

*The main facts are derived from suggestions of O. Katzenstein in a talk before the Southern Nurserymen's Association, Sept. 8, 1926.

7. The length of a seed bed depends upon the local conditions. The width may range from 3½ to 5 feet. Beds wider than 5 feet are handled under difficulties only.

8. The beds may be crowned very slightly to assist in drainage, and in heavier soils they may be elevated a few inches above the dividing paths.

HOW TO SOW

1. Sowing may be made in drills or broadcast. Both methods have their advantages and disadvantages. Much depends upon local conditions. Seeds of conifers are quite frequently sown broadcast and particularly small quantities are generally sown across the bed. Seeds of deciduous trees and shrubs are more often sown in drills which run lengthwise the beds. No hard and fast rule can be stated covering sowing in drills or broadcast.

2. The depth of sowing depends upon the size of the seeds. Many good seeds are needlessly sacrificed by improper handling. Fundamentally it is better to err by sowing too shallow rather than too deep. It is about correct to cover the seeds to their own thickness. Seeds of conifers require very light covering. Seeds of nuts, acorns, Honeylocusts, Kentucky Coffeetree and some others come up best from a depth of 2 or 3 ins.

3. When sown in drills, allow for a distance of 4 to 5 ins. between the rows for slow-growing plants, like conifers, and 9 to 12 ins. for fast-growing kinds, especially for most shrubs. Where cultivation by power is preferred the distance between the drills should be 40 ins. and the field is then not laid off in beds.

4. Before sowing, smooth and firm the soil.

5. For an experienced planter the sowing by hand is the best method, as the seeds can then be distributed evenly. It may also be done with the aid of mechanical devices or with a seeding machine. There are a good many practical devices in use.

6. Very fine seed may be mixed with sand or earth to give it more consistency. Do not sow too thickly. Seeds should not touch each other or the danger of damping-off will be multiplied. After sowing the soil should be firmed again with a board, or the back of a spade or a very light roller.

7. A light mulch will be found very beneficial. Peat moss, chopped Sphagnum moss, lawn grass refuse, pine needles, thoroughly rotted and pulverized cow manure, such as mushroom manure, where obtainable, make satisfactory mulches. Coverings of parchment paper also have given good results. Sawdust is not advised because it may

rot, causing pernicious fungi to enter the seedlings. Leafmold may contain weed seeds and is to be avoided. The mulch must be removed gradually as the seedlings appear. The beds, particularly of conifers, should be kept shaded during the first Summer. This is not so important for beds containing acorns or nuts.

8. Handy screens are prepared by the use of building laths, by nailing burlaps on frames or by rolling canvas over the beds on elevated frames.

9. The screens should be placed 18 ins. above the beds, the posts being raised gradually as the seedlings become accustomed to the light. Finally, they are removed.

10. Water cautiously, remembering that the beds being kept shaded and mulched will not need much water. When very dry, water early in the morning or late in the evening.

11. After the seedlings are up the beds should be cultivated carefully but lightly so as not to disturb the growth of the seedlings. The closest attention must be given now to judicious shading. The seedlings of shrubs are kept in the seed beds until they are large enough to be moved into nursery rows during the next planting period.

DAMPING-OFF

Not only is it necessary to use a mercuric compound, such as Semesan, for sterilizing seed but this substance can be dusted or sprayed upon the seed beds. Previous to the advent of this substance, seed sowing was more of a gamble than at present. The cost of material and labor is negligible when the benefits to be derived are considered. See page 45 for details.

SHRUBS FROM CUTTINGS

It has been a common observation that any part of a plant severed has the ability to reproduce the missing parts. Cuttings, then, may be made of stems, roots and leaves, providing that we know just how to treat each particular plant.

Cuttings do not vary but reproduce the plants exactly. They generally make a larger plant and more quickly than from seed.

HARDWOOD CUTTINGS

For making hardwood cuttings one year old branches are used. The wood should be without leaves and gathered before freezing weather, or at least at a time during the late Autumn or Winter when the branches are not actually in a frozen condition.

For economy of material cuttings 8 ins. long are sufficient, but cuttings even 2 ft. long might root. When rooted, short cuttings dry out more quickly and cannot be properly firmed in the soil. Each cutting should have two or three eyes, or nodes. The very sappy growth is not as good as that which has grown just good and strong. Too slender wood has little food stored in it.

Cut near a node at top and bottom if the nodes are far apart; if close together, this is not so important. It is, however, especially necessary to have an eye at the top.

The object should be to keep these cuttings as nearly dormant as possible during the Winter. Some growers are anxious to have the cuttings produce a good sized callus at the base but many successful plant propagators point out that the callus is soft and quickly dries out in the air when removed from the Winter storage and laid out on the soil preparatory to planting. Therefore, as soon as the cuttings are made pack them in boxes, bins, frames or some place which is cool (40°–45°) but not freezing.

This storage must not be too moist. The material in which the cuttings are packed should consist of sand, shingletow or peat moss of such a degree of moisture that neither the cuttings will absorb water from the storage material nor the storage material absorb water from the cuttings. Generally, the cuttings are placed right side up. Some difficult subjects are buried upside down. There is always a flow of sap upward, so that even when the cuttings are inverted, the sap rises and, perhaps, induces callus more quickly. In easily rooted subjects sometimes growth starts at the wrong end. To be safe, set cuttings right side up.

Hardwood Cuttings

A, Weigela; B, Golden Currant; C, Mockorange; D, Climbing Rose. Note that the cuts are near the nodes, or buds

When Spring comes, the cuttings are set in the field, in beds or in frames. In beds the cuttings are less disturbed by cultivation. The rows in the field may be made far enough apart for proper cultivation according to the method one intends to use. Mark the rows, using the beam of the plow only, or for small areas use a spade.

The ideal way is to throw out a V-shaped trench. Set the cuttings so that the top pair of eyes is above the soil; then pack the soil carefully about the cuttings and tramp with the feet. When the soil is in good friable condition the soil can be merely cut with an "opener" and the cuttings inserted but not packed. Sometimes when packing is not carefully done, the tramping at the surface or the use of a heavy wheel only serves to cause an air pocket about the base of the cutting. In good soil the fine soil will wash down about the base of the cutting after the first rain. The success of hardwood cuttings depends upon the storage, the field conditions and the moisture available from the start.

SOFTWOOD CUTTINGS

Hardwood cuttings are less under control than the tender, half-ripe, green wood or softwood cuttings which may be taken in Summer. The writer uses the term "softwood" throughout the discussions, which does not necessarily mean juicy, very immature shoots, but the opposite of woody cuttings. With experience the propagator learns just how soft each cutting roots best. (See page 60.)

The advantages of this Summer propagation are:

1. There is a wealth of material, every little shoot 3 inches to 6 inches long, making a potential new plant. Only straight, canelike growth may be used for hardwood cuttings.

2. Such cuttings root rapidly.

3. Difficult subjects can be handled more easily under the glass of propagating frames. Such pithy wood as *Kerria japonica* and slender wood as *Stephanandra incisa* are more difficult by other methods.

4. Established root systems are immediately made so that when the cuttings are transplanted they go forward quickly.

5. Economy of field space. Hardwood cuttings are always a gamble.

FRAME ROOTED CUTTINGS

The commonest method of rooting softwood cuttings is to place them in frames outdoors in July, August and September, these months being considered the most favorable.

However, Dr. Zimmerman has propagated the Nanking Cherry, *Prunus tomentosa*, by very soft wood, 6 inches to 8 inches long, cut to its base. This was done in early May. These cuttings rooted much better than those made of harder wood. The same results apply to *Viburnum opulus, Ulmus pumila,* and *Sambucus canadensis aurea* (Golden Elder), especially, also *Lespedeza formosa, Hydrangea arborescens grandiflora,* and other difficult subjects. W. B. Cole thinks that early propagation of many shrubs would be desirable were it not for the fact that the nurseryman is too busy in late Spring.

EQUIPMENT. No elaborate equipment is necessary. Build frames 3 feet x 6 feet or larger, according to the sash to be used. Slant to the north or west not to the south. This is a propagating frame from which we prefer to exclude the direct sun, but not the light. Hotbeds are built facing south to catch the maximum amount of sunshine.

Many nurseries use a double frame sloping both north and south because there is better protection against the wind which, on the single frame, often gets under the shade and sash and carries them away. The watering, syringing and shading of such frames are more easily handled.

The frames may be built of concrete for permanency or of wood for lessening the first cost. Concrete frames should have a strip of

Prunus tomentosa cuttings root well in sand
These were placed well down and struck in three or four weeks, the photograph being taken after five weeks (From Boyce Thompson Institute)

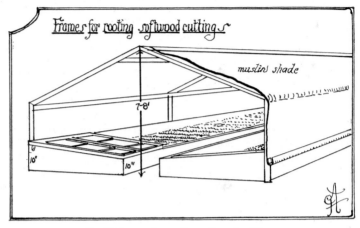

Frames for rooting softwood cuttings

muslin shade

7-8'

10"

10"

Double frames for rooting softwood cuttings

The frames are wide enough for a sash run lengthwise and as long as desired. A framework above is covered with muslin which may be rolled up when shade is not desired. The frames are 16 in. high at back and 10 in. high in front

wood along the top so that it may fit the sashes better. Select good sash, kept in almost airtight repair.

HEAT OR NONE. Some growers prefer electric cables or manure as a source of heat. A higher temperature in the sand than in the air hastens rooting and serves as a source of increased humidity. Others do not use manure, believing that the temperatures of Summer are excessive enough and that too great humidity is injurious to cuttings which become charged with more water than they can transpire through their reduced leaf surface. Generally 8 inches to 12 inches of fresh manure is necessary to furnish the heat.

SHADING. Some method of shading is desirable, a shade elevated above the frame for convenience in working and to give bright conditions within, but not the direct rays of the sun. The shade will tend to keep up the humidity which is its main value. Muslin purchased in 50-yard bolts, is usually the best material to use. Heavy canvas is too dense. Each section should be lapped in such a way that the wind does not get under the shade. The muslin is usually attached to a piece of wood and shades should be rolled down in the morning before the heat becomes too great and removed again when the sun has passed. If the shades are not used, burning of the foliage results, especially when the cuttings have been accustomed to the shade.

Rooting Media. The cuttings are inserted in some medium which holds them in place and supplies them with moisture.

Sand is commonly used. Select a sharp, coarse sand which gives good drainage and packs firmly. Hacker advises finer sand for difficult subjects, as Golden Mockorange and such sorts, and these should not be syringed too frequently. When Golden Mockorange goes through the night with moist foliage it becomes blackened quickly. Certain cuttings, when once wilted, do not revive. Some growers use the same sand for years, changing it only for difficult subjects. Old sand may be sterilized (See page 45). Cover the sand after treatment with paper and let it stand, working it thoroughly afterward.

Peat Moss. This is coming into common use as a rooting medium. It is especially advised for the broad-leaf evergreens, Azaleas and the ericaceous plants which especially need an acid rooting medium (See illustration below).

Slag. Agricultural slag, a by-product of blast furnaces, has been widely tried around Youngstown, Ohio. It is a porous material, light

Azalea amoena cuttings do best in pure peat moss
These were taken in June, with the old wood attached. The photograph was taken after six weeks in the moss (From Boyce Thompson Institute)

in weight, crumbly in texture, limey in reaction and in its process of manufacture becomes perfectly sterile. In some sections of the United States it is cheaper than sand. Its faults are: When first purchased and not exposed to the air it contains sulphur fumes which are injurious to plants; it is often too coarse in texture and may need screening or crushing.

The root growth of cuttings of many kinds is phenomenal. The roots enter the pores of such material as Vermiculite and Perlite so that when cuttings are removed they bring a ball of the material with them. Cuttings may apparently be left indefinitely in this material.

Pfitzer's Juniper rooted in agricultural slag

A rather large cutting was used. This plant is fourteen months old. Cutting in slag six weeks

Vermiculite, Terra-Lite, or *Mica-Grow* is an expanded mica which because of its thin layers is retentive of moisture yet allows for good drainage because the particles are far apart. Vermiculite is sold as insulation material and may be known by such trade names as Terralite and Agralite. It must not be packed firmly as is sand.

Perlite or *Sponge Rock.* This is a snow white product which is very porous so that it retains vast quantities of water in the pores of each particle. Due to its lightness in weight it is difficult to water inasmuch as it floats away easily. It seems wise to mix about one-third sand or peat with it.

AGE OF WOOD TO USE

Half-ripened wood is best for most sorts. Experience leads the propagator to know just the condition of ripeness for each sort. Unfavorable conditions in the rooting medium are more serious for very soft wood, but when frames are perfectly controlled, the young wood roots more quickly. Too green wood blackens, so that such cuttings are best stuck shallowly. Take into consideration the experience, advising very soft wood, as noted on page 56. Nevertheless, the riper wood is less exacting in controlled conditions but takes longer to root.

Series of cuttings made from a Weigela shoot three weeks after being taken
All would presumably have rooted if given enough time (From Boyce Thompson Institute)

Dr. P. W. Zimmerman, remarking upon the age of wood, writes:

"The age of stem tissue which is best able to form roots varies. Heliotrope cuttings if cut *just one inch* back of the growing tip, will root in seven days. If the base of the cutting is three inches below the tip it will root in 14 days, while a cutting made six inches below the tip requires three to five weeks.

"If a growing cane of American Pillar Rose be cut up into a series of three-inch cuttings, each provided with a leaf, cutting number five from the tip will root much quicker and stronger than any other cuttings. When

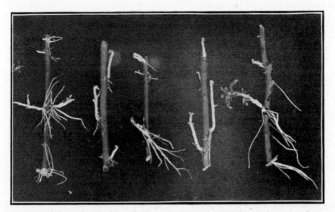

Cuttings of Dorothy Perkins Rose with roots arising from the new shoots
High humidity alone can bring out this response (From Boyce Thompson Institute)

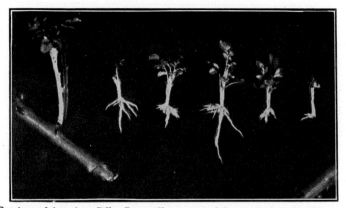

Cuttings of American Pillar Rose will not root while attached to the old canes
A "heel" or "mallet" might thus be detrimental to such cuttings (From Boyce Thompson Institute)

I select another similar cane, but one which is growing more slowly, cutting number three from the tip may root quickest. It seems to be determined by the rate at which the cane grows.

"Similarly, if a shoot of Weigela (see cut, page 61) is made up into a series of cuttings a particular cutting roots easier than the rest. Here again the number of the best cutting (i.e. its position on the stem) varies with the rate of growth of the shoot. We are now making anatomical and microchemical studies of the quick responding points to see how they might differ from other points. We hope by this method to learn something about the factors which control root growth.

"Again if we study new shoots of Dorothy Perkins as compared with American Pillar Rose (see illustrations) we find that the young shoots of the former root *while still attached to the old cane*, but the latter do not. The young inch-long shoot from the Pillar cane will root readily when removed and placed in the rooting medium. What must be the difference between these two forms? Dorothy Perkins shoots need no stimulus other than high humidity while still attached to the old stem. We are now studying the corresponding points on these two forms hoping again to find out what might be the fundamental differences between the two types."

Recent experiments at the California Agricultural Experiment Station seem to show that the ease of rooting in Grapes is dependent upon the amount of starch found in the cuttings. Potassium iodide (iodine) is used to test for starch. The cuttings, when immersed to a depth of 1 in. for one minute in a 2 per cent solution, show various colorations due to their starch content. Absence of color change or faint coloration is indicative of insufficient starch.

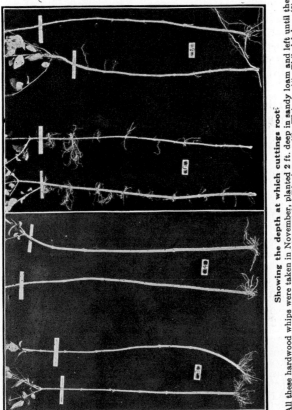

Showing the depth at which cuttings root

All these hardwood whips were taken in November, planted 2 ft. deep in sandy loam and left until the following July. The species are, from left to right, Rhodotypos (3), Weigela (4), Philadelphus (6), and Lonicera (5). (From Boyce Thompson Institute)

The following brief table will show the differences:

	Rooting	Vigorous Rooting
1. Well stained	62.5%	30.0%
2. Faint stain	35.3	9.3
3. No stain	16.9	1.8

This was tried for a number of varieties and in every case the rooting was in favor of the cuttings which showed the staining. From a practical standpoint, the method is of immense value. By its use, the operator is enabled to reduce the mortality among the planted cuttings, to save space and time and in addition gain in vigor of his plants.

MAKING CUTTINGS. One year differs from another in growing conditions, so that some years cuttings root well because the stock plants produce proper material for cuttings. The stock plants should be well cared for and kept free from insects and disease.

Generally, the tips (3 in. to 8 in.) of the shoots are selected for cuttings. In such cuttings as Japanese Snowball, the nodes are 4 in. apart. With most sorts we can easily have three to five nodes to a cutting, but in the case of those in which the nodes are far apart, the node at the base is more important than one at the top.

In the *Nursery Manual*, Bailey says that in most cuttings the tip can be cut off the cutting, but in others it seriously injures the cutting. Weigela, *Cercis japonica, Spiraea japonica, S. trilobata, S. cantoniensis* and *S. blanda* are "end growers" and can not be beheaded. Hacker says that when the tips are cut from a Weigela cutting they produce larger callus and fewer roots.

DEPTH AT WHICH CUTTINGS ROOT. Dr. Zimmerman attempted an experiment to find out at what depth of soil aeration was proper for rooting. The illustration on page 63 shows cuttings with their bases 2 ft. below the surface of the soil.

"Note that Rhodotypos, Weigela, Plum, and Sour Cherry rooted *only at the base*, which was two feet below the surface of the soil. Lonicera, Philadelphus, Salix and Ribes, rooted *all the way* from an inch below the soil level to a point two feet below the surface. These facts make me question the old idea that cuttings root best where they have good aeration near the surface. Certainly some oxygen is necessary but, is a large supply as important as is generally thought? Propagators often allow the tops to dry out by placing the cuttings so that the cut end can be well aerated.

"The appearance of callus does not insure rooting. Many propagators are happy when they see callus appear. To be sure it does indicate that the cutting is in a favorable condition, but roots do not necessarily follow callousing. In the majority of cases roots do not arise from the callus; they push through the bark somewhere above it. In the case of Sour Cherry and Blue Plum, roots, in all probability, arise in the callus. Here I have seen

Viburnum opulus cuttings, showing a tendency toward root growth at the nodes
(From Boyce Thompson Institute)

the roots appear on the callus after it had grown a quarter of an inch beyond the back of the cutting.

"The exact position from which roots arise varies with different plant
forms. The variation is from roots at the node, to above, below, or between
the nodes. Above cut shows how uniformly roots arise about the nodes of
Viburnum opulus. In the case of Quince and often in Apple cuttings, roots
arise in the axils of the buds. Some forms show strong polarity, rooting
only at the base, while others form roots along the stems as well as at the
base."

If aeration of the roots is not so important as was once believed, it
is peculiar that when potted the young roots immediately go to the
outside of the ball of earth and circle around the sides of the pot where
aeration is more perfect.

REMOVING LEAVES.   It has been the practice to remove a good
share of the leaves by holding the cutting in the hand with the leaves
bunched together; the leaves are then cut off to uniform length. Dr.
Zimmerman points out that as few leaves as possible should be
removed. Illustration, on page 66, shows two sets of Black Currant cuttings; where the cuttings had leaves they rooted in two weeks and without leaves they were unable to produce roots. As Autumn approaches,
a time is reached when leaves can be dispensed with. In a trial with
Prunus tomentosa, the Nanking Cherry, when all leaves were removed
they did not root. A small leaf might pull them through but it would
take some time. Three leaves can bring out the roots in four weeks.
The larger the number of leaves that can be kept in good condition,
the better will be the root growth. In some experiments all leaves
were allowed to remain, some being even buried. Commercial propa-

gators remove the leaves to conserve space. It is wise to remove as few leaves as possible.

W. B. Cole has tried cuttings with no leaves removed and no shading. They rooted splendidly with less care as to ventilation and watering but were more difficult to insert.

INSERTING CUTTINGS. Insert the cuttings into the sand and firm them in, the distance between rows depending upon the size of the leaves of the cuttings. The rows should be so close that the sand is scarcely visible. It is well to partition off the sections of the frames as filled.

WATERING AND SYRINGING. Give a thorough watering when the cuttings are inserted; then water often enough to keep them from wilting. However, the less they are watered the better, depending upon the weather—perhaps every four days in dry weather and once a week in a humid season. Syringe often on sunny days so that they may dry before the sun goes down. If syringed normally and the cuttings droop, it is a sign that the sand is too dry.

Leave the sash on the frames at all times until the cuttings are rooted; then gradually give them air.

GREENHOUSE ROOTING

1. WINTER. Softwood cuttings may be made in the late Winter or early Spring, taking the wood from stock plants which are benched or potted. Such plants are stored in frames first and then brought indoors, in December. These cuttings are soft and sappy, more like the cuttings of house plants. Golden Mockoranges, Azaleas, Cotoneasters

Black Currant cuttings after 21 days, showing how the presence of leaves stimulates rooting (From Boyce Thompson Institute)

and many broad-leaved evergreens are well rooted at this season. In concrete benches the sand is sometimes cooler than the air, in which case rooting is retarded.

2. SUMMER. Sometimes greenhouses are available for Summer propagation of softwood cuttings of unusual sorts. Princeton Nurseries and Henry A. Dreer keep the houses cool in Summer by shading the glass with burlap or bamboo, a spray of water playing upon the roof and running down to the gutter, which absorbs the heat. Such houses are 10° to 15° cooler than houses not sprayed, and are ideal because the air is cool overhead and not hot and dry.

The cuttings are inserted in flats or sand benches. Flats may be more easily moved from place to place.

POTTING

Many propagators do not pot the rooted cuttings but leave them in the frame until Spring, thus saving the labor of potting and conserving the space.

However, rooted cuttings are more easily established out of doors in the Spring if they are potted into 2¼ in. pots as soon as the roots are about ½ in. to ¾ in. long. It is well to wait until they are well-rooted, but they are more easily potted when the roots are not so large as to be broken and wadded when placed in the tiny pots.

Young potted stock will need the protection of glass at first and little air. Gradually remove the shade and the glass when the roots come toward the outside of the ball of earth.

WINTER PROTECTION

Whether in the sand frames or in pots, which should be plunged into sand or peat moss, many of the cuttings, especially the tenderer subjects such as Snowballs, Forsythia and Weigela will need Winter protection. Cover with cornstalks or tree branches. Do not use straw because of mice. Forest leaves will be good to use but are best scattered upon tree branches so that they will not pack and ferment. Take pains to stir the mulch in early Spring, otherwise mold starts and the young cuttings would have been better wintered without protection.

SETTING IN THE FIELD

The young plants are either set in the field the following Spring or else grown in beds for a year.

In the field the rows may be marked with a home devised marker, making them 20 ins. to 3 ft. apart, or any width suiting convenience for cultivation. In the row the plants may be set 1 in. to 4 ins. apart.

depending upon the sort of stock one desires to produce. Some set the plants 15 in. to 18 in. apart and do not transplant until sold. Kerrias make about 18 in. of growth the first year. Cutleaf Elder makes light 18 in. to 24 in. plants, but merchantable stock is usually two or three years old.

During the Fall of the first year the plants may be cut to the soil as a source of hardwood cuttings. This will cause the plants to stool out, producing good, branchy plants. Stock grown from softwood cuttings naturally has more stems, but it has less height than that grown from hardwood cuttings, because it is handled differently.

CHEMICALS AS AN AID TO ROOTING

During the last few years the experimenters have been trying out a great many different types of chemical treatments for cuttings. Certain chemicals (1) shorten the rest period of hardwood cuttings; (2) supply oxygen; (3) change the balance in the food supply—for example, starch may be changed to sugar; (4) deter harmful bacteria and increase beneficial ones; (5) increase the supply of carbon dioxide; and (6) change the chemical analysis of the rooting medium.

Perhaps the whole idea was started from Dr. James Small's *Textbook of Botany* when he said that plants have acid roots and alkaline shoots. This led Sir I. B. Balfour of Edinburgh to test the value of acid in propagation. Accordingly, he soaked peat moss in water and used this to water Oak cuttings. The result was a large increase in the percentages of success and a reduction of the time for rooting. In his case, he attempted to root cuttings by watering with tap water or a dilute solution of acetic acid. Dr. Small, in the *Gardener's Chronicle* (England) III series, 73 (1923), page 244, writes "According to the theory of acid root and alkaline shoot, this difference in reaction of the opposite ends of the plant is mainly due to the difference in carbon dioxide balance. The green shoot uses up the carbon dioxide gas to make sugars and starch during the day, while the root in respiring below ground is always producing but never using up, the same acidic gas."

Dr. Small conducted his experiments with Aucuba cuttings and bubbled carbon dioxide once a week for four weeks through the water in which were dipped the lower ends of the cuttings. Five out of six callused, and two produced four roots. Similar results were obtained with other plants.

Various other substances were tried, such as potassium permanganate, sugar, vinegar, and peat moss, but it remained for Dr. P. M. Zimmerman, Dr. F. C. Went, Dr. Vernon Stoutemyer, and others to

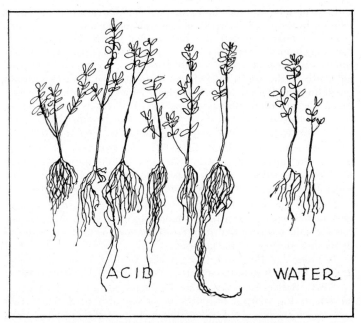

Showing the value of acid in rooting cuttings of Privet
(Sketched from photograph in *Gardener's Chronicle*)

perfect a practical method of treating cuttings to increase their speed
and ability to root.

HORMONES OR PLANT GROWTH SUBSTANCES

In recent years, many of the cuttings which have been considered
impossible or very slow to root have been treated with various chemicals, especially in the greenhouses of the United States Department of
Agriculture at Beltsville, Md. and in the California Institute of
Technology in Pasadena.

Plants manufacture hormones which regulate stem, bud, fruit, and
root development. In the last few years some fifty chemical substances
for plant hormones have been found. Among these substances are
indoleacetic acid, indolebutyric acid, naphthaleneacetic acid, and nap-
thylacetimide acid. These are just a few of the root promoting substances, but fortunately the amateur will not need to concern himself
with these long jaw-breaking names, for on the market are now several
commercial products, some liquids and others powders, in which the

cuttings may be dipped. The growth promoting substance is put in solution in water, or incorporated with powdered talc. As a general thing, the amateur prefers the dust method for he does not need to make up a solution every time he wishes to insert a cutting. With these commercial products come careful directions, for cuttings respond differently to the length of treatment and to the value of these growth promoting substances. But it has been found that such cuttings as Magnolias and many other hardwood trees and shrubs have submitted to the treatments and rooted successfully. On the other hand, many of the softwooded plants root just as readily without the treatment

There seems to be some evidence to show that these growth promoting substances work a little better in a medium of sand to which is added some substance such as peat moss, leafmold, or even a soil which does not contain disease spores or too much organic material.

Most of the leaves are allowed to remain on the cutting for they manufacture enough growth substances to start roots; furthermore, there is some evidence that longer cuttings may be used when growth promoting substances are employed.

In order that the powder may adhere to the base of the cuttings it is best to dip them in water so that the base of each cutting is moist.

Seeds. Besides the value of these growth promoting substances as an aid in the rooting of cuttings, it has also been found that seeds which are dusted not only germinate faster but they make a more rapid root development. Some old or sluggish seeds have been stimulated to germinate when their vitality was considered very low. Merely place a pinch of hormone dust in a seed packet and shake thoroughly.

A number of experimenters have treated grass seed and obtained a quicker germination and a faster start in root and vegetative growth. This is an advantage in getting a head start on weeds and eliminates the necessity for such careful watering at the start of the lawn.

Effect on Fruit. It has been found that a weak solution of growth promoting substances sprayed upon fruit trees causes the fruit to remain on the trees for a longer period of time. Furthermore, by spraying with hormones scientists have grown seedless Squash, Peppers, Tomatoes, Holly berries, Strawberries, Grapes, Cucumbers, and Watermelons. You may mix 1 ounce of one of the hormone powders in 1 gallon of water and conduct a little experiment on your Apples or Holly in the hopes that the fruits will remain on the tree for a longer period of time. In the case of setting fruits without pollination, the stamens or male parts are removed and a solution of indoleacetic acid, instead of dust, is sprayed upon the flower. Use 100 parts of acid to 200 parts of water. A small atomizer may be used for the purpose.

Bulbs. Even bulbs, corms, and tubers are stimulated by dusting them with hormones placed in a salt shaker, or dipping them in the dust immediately before planting.

Airlayers. John V. Watkins of Florida has conducted experiments in air-layering certain shrubs which are difficult to root. Unlike the layers described on page 79, these are made by selecting a branch about pencil size and making a slanting cut about half way through the stem. A sliver of wood and a small wad of moss is packed into the incision to keep it from growing together again. Moist sphagnum moss is wrapped around the branch until the mass is about the size of a goose egg. Copper wire is used to bind it in place. Such propagation should be done during the rainy season or when the moss can be kept wet at all times. Layers root freely with certain plants, but with others Mr. Watkins painted the bark and cut surfaces with 1 per cent indole-butryic acid in lanolin applied before the moss was wrapped in place. Heavy root systems were more quickly produced on the treated plants.

VITAMINS B_1 AND B_6.

The California Institute of Technology has pointed out that some soils are deficient in Vitamin B_1 which is, however, found in almost all soils to which manure has been added. They tell us that most plants manufacture some Vitamin B_1 or Vitamin B_6 but that some plants do not produce sufficient for the needs of the plant, and for these additional applications are desirable. The vitamins are not expected to initiate the rooting but it assists in stimulating the roots which have started to grow. Many experimenters have reported no results from the use of vitamins, but this is due to the fact that their soils and rooting media are already supplied with sufficient vitamins.

Remember, however, that although the chemicals may be important aids in the propagation of plants, they cannot be substituted for skill, care, experience, and suitable equipment.

Success in Transplanting. Vitamins seem to have a decided advantage in preventing wilting at the time of transplanting, so that it now seems wise to water all newly transplanted shrubs and other tricky plants with root-promoting substances such as Transplantone. The careful gardener uses these substances whenever he transplants.

ROOT CUTTINGS

Many shrubs have a tendency to sucker freely, either naturally or when their roots are injured. Such shrubs as Rose-acacia, Japanese

Quince, Raspberries, Dwarf Horsechestnut, Sumac, Hercules-club, Clerodendron and some Roses are propagated by cutting the roots into 2 to 6 in. lengths and placing them in flats of good soil in early Spring. They may also be planted in the open soil in trenches or in coldframes.

GRAFTING AND BUDDING SHRUBS

It is common for Europeans to graft and bud shrubs of all kinds; the American nurseryman grafts but few sorts. Many unusual shrubs are difficult to root from cuttings; others are not of strong growth unless grafted.

There is a wide range over which one shrub may be grafted upon plants of an entirely different genus. Just how diverse a plant may be has hardly been determined. The members of the Rose family graft rather

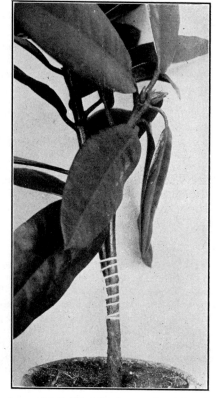

A completed Rhododendron graft, tied and ready to go into the grafting case

freely upon each other. For example, Mountain-ash, European Quince, Japanese Quince, Juneberry, Crab Apple, Pear, Photinia, Medlar and Cotoneaster may be grafted on Crataegus. Cotoneaster may be worked on Quince, Hawthorn or Mountain-ash. The members of the Pea family also graft one with another rather freely. Cytisus and Calophaca may be grafted on Laburnum. Halimodendron is grafted on Caragana and there are many other examples. Most shrub grafting is done in the Winter. Two general methods are common:

1. GRAFTING POTTED PLANTS

Magnolia, Japanese Maple, Corylus, Beech, Viburnum, Crataegus and Rhododendrons are grafted in the greenhouse in late Winter for early Spring.

The stock plants are raised from seed or cuttings and should be about a year old or large enough so that the stems are about ½ in. in diameter. They are potted, stored in frames and brought indoors after freezing weather has given them a short period of rest, generally in January or February.

VENEER GRAFTING. In making the veneer graft which is the sort generally used

1. Make a cut in the stock about 2 in. above the level of the pot

A three-year-old Rhododendron seedling ready for grafting

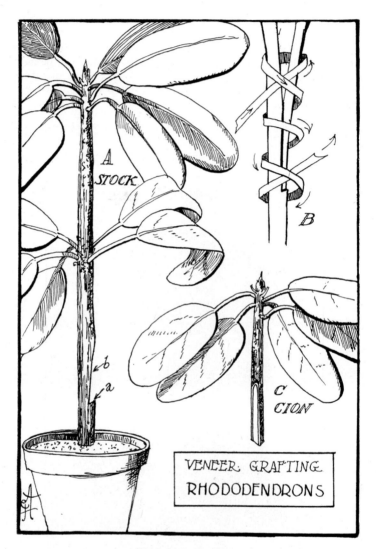

Rhododendron grafting

A, the stock cut for a veneer graft; C, the cion cut to fit into the notch of the stock; B, the cion fitted into place, showing method of tying

This should be somewhat diagonal, but not deep—not over one third of the way through the stem. See "a" in the sketch on opposite page.

2. Start about 1½ in. above and cut downward (b).

3. Select a cion as nearly the same thickness as the stock. Opinions differ as to the length of the cion, but Arthur Grube, of Cleveland, has used Magnolia cions 2 ft. long; other propagators use cions not over 3 in. long. Cions should be gathered in late Fall or only during mild days of Winter. These cions are stored in peat moss, sand or sphagnum moss in a cold place. Growing cions are also used, selected from forced plants.

4. Cut the cion with a long cut which will fit the cut in the stock, and so cut the base that it will fit into the cut of the stock.

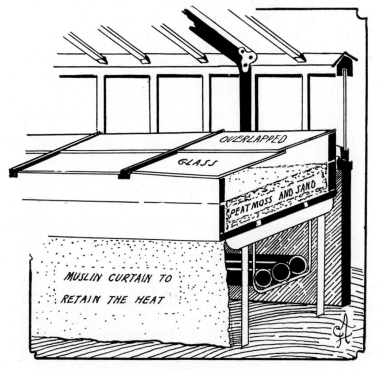

Grafting case

Note that sides of a greenhouse bench are built up. Sash bars are used to hold panes of lapped glass. Curtain hung in front of pipes to retain the heat

5. Fit the cion into the stock so that the cambium ring of both meet. If the stock is larger than the cion, put the cion to one side so that it fits there, at least.

6. When the cion is perfectly fitted, tie with waxed string or merely darning cotton. The string is often cut into 6 to 8 in. lengths for convenience. Hold the cion and stock together with the left hand and wrap as shown in B of the sketch. Make this tight but not tight enough to bruise the stem. Wind rather closely and slip the end of the string through the last turn. In the sketch the string is shown loosely wound because in this way it is easier to see how the tying is done.

GRAFTING CASES. The sides of a greenhouse bench are built up with boards 12 in. to 18 in. high. They are made flat on top and some growers cover them with hotbed sash; others make simple frames covered with muslin. Still others place sash bars across the constructed box far enough apart so that glass fits between the sash bars.

Peat moss is used to a depth of 8 or 10 in. at the bottom of the frame. In this, the pots of the grafts are plunged. The humidity of the case should be high enough so that it will not be necessary to plunge the pots to the extent of covering the grafts. The pots are put in slanting so that one row overlaps the next. This prevents drying of the grafts, gives better drainage to the knitting graft, and allows the use of a lower case than if each stock stood upright.

Grafting houses need shade upon the roof in the form of lath or whitewash.

The grafting cases should be opened each morning to let the excess moisture escape, but during the airing keep the doors and ventilators closed.

Most grafts will unite in about four weeks.* The grafts are moved and part of the stock removed. The grafts are again plunged for three or four weeks. The sashes may be left open a little longer each morning, until about eight weeks after grafting, when they may be left open all day.

CARE OF THE GROWING GRAFTS. The majority of the plants will now be ready to be taken out of the case and placed on a bench in a close house, preferably in the propagating house where they will be under close observation. Examine each plant carefully as it is handled: any that are not perfectly united must be put back in the case and closed down again for a few weeks. Another third of the head of the

---

*Much of this advice is given by J. W. Mallinson in the *Florists' Exchange and Horticultural Trade World* and refers directly to Rhododendrons but may be applied to most grafting.

Grafting case showing hinged sash which can be hooked up to the roof
Grafted stock is laid in on a slant, as shown, with the pots partly plunged in the peat moss
(Photo by courtesy Julius Roehrs Co., Inc., Rutherford, N. J.)

stock can now be cut off on those that are well united. The remaining portion of the stock's growth should be left for about four weeks longer, when it may be cut off entirely, taking great care when doing so not to strain the union in any way. The string may also be cut at the same time by drawing the knife down the back of the stem and the terminal buds of the cions also cut out. By this time the young plants are safely through the operation and all they need is ordinary attention as to watering and shading until such time as the weather will permit of them being planted outside in a sheltered position, preferably in a well-prepared frame under sprinklers, where they can remain undisturbed for at least two years. It is a great mistake to plant young Rhododendrons out in the open field. When they are three years old they can be lifted from the frames and by this time they will have a nice ball of roots and enough vitality to go ahead in the field.

2. WHIP-GRAFTING OR ROOT-GRAFTING

Variegated Weigelas, Hibiscus, Cornus, Tree Peonies, Lilacs, *Hy-*

drangea paniculata grandiflora and many other subjects may be root-grafted. Choose and store the cions in moist moss or sand in a cool place, also get a supply of pieces of root (4 to 5 in. long) of the kind of plant desired. Root graft any time in Winter, wrapping the graft with waxed string. Tie in bunches of 50 and place in boxes of peat moss or sawdust. W. Fletcher Bohlender advises green sawdust from hardwood. This heats enough to cause callousing of the grafts. They are ready to set in nursery rows by Spring and are treated like hardwood cuttings. It is claimed for these grafts that they are far superior in growth to hardwood or softwood cuttings.

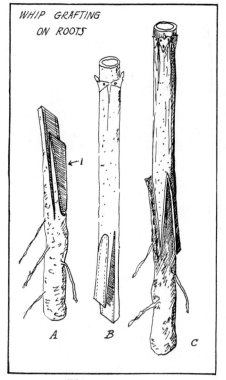

Whip or root grafting

All parts are larger in diameter than necessary, to show characteristics more clearly. A, piece of root used as stock; B, cion of Hydrangea; C, cion fitted into stock
(See text)

MAKING THE ROOT GRAFT. 1. Pieces of roots of the proper diameter (about the size of the cions or a little larger) are cut from dormant plants.

2. Use pieces about 3 in. long. Make a long slanting cut as shown in A of the sketch. Then make one, almost vertical, cut in such a way that both sides of the flap marked "1" are straight and even. The sketch shows stocks and cions of large diameter (larger than usual) but such grafts are good.

3. Choose dormant cions selected in late Fall or on a non-freezing Winter day.

4. The cions may be 3 in. to 6 in. long, with as many eyes as possible, but one is all that is required. Make an oblique cut and a vertical one, the opposite of those made in the stock.

5. Fit the two together and tie with waxed string.

BUDDING

Budding is usually done out of doors during July and August. Stocks are grown from seeds or from cuttings and planted out in the nursery row. Usually one-year-old stocks are about the right diameter. Cultivate the soil, throwing it up toward the base of the stocks so that the wood may be soft. Several weeks previous to budding, or just ahead of the budding, remove the leaves at the base of the shrubs so that a smooth place is made upon the stock for inserting the bud. As soon as the bark peels and large buds are found in the axils of the leaves of the cion, budding may be done. The shield bud shown in illustration on page 80 is used.

Viburnum carlesi is commonly budded upon *V. lantana* in July. The red-flowered Dogwood is budded on the stock of *Cornus florida*. Three-year-old seedlings of *Magnolia glauca* or *M. acuminata* may be budded with *M. soulangeana* or *M. stellata*. Lilacs may be budded on Privet. W. B. Cole reports that Ibota Privet is a good stock. On the Common Privet, *Ligustrum vulgare*, the plants make but a short, stubby growth. He has had little success with *L. amurense*. Koster uses two buds placed in the base of one-year-old California Privet, which is mulched to protect the buds. (See Syringa-Lilacs, page 377.)

Roses are commonly budded in August upon *manetti* or *multiflora japonica* stocks. This is fully described, as is the process of budding in *How To Increase Plants* by the writer.

PROPAGATION BY LAYERS

Layering is a process of propagating plants without severing them from their parent. Shrubs grow readily from layers when some other methods fail; furthermore, the shrub is not destroyed by layering.

SIMPLE LAYERS. If the shrub has branches near the soil they can be bent down so that a portion may be buried. Note illustration which shows that the tip is brought up from the soil. It is usually necessary to hold these layers in the soil by pegging them down, using a rock or a stick with a crotch in it. It is wise to make an oblique cut into the stem at the point where it is buried. This injury causes the production of roots. Persons desiring to layer many shrubs should have a certain section devoted to the purpose. Choose a fertile, sandy spot; incorporate more sand or peat moss into the soil, which will facilitate the work, as well as encourage the growth of the layers. Layering may be put down in Spring or Fall.

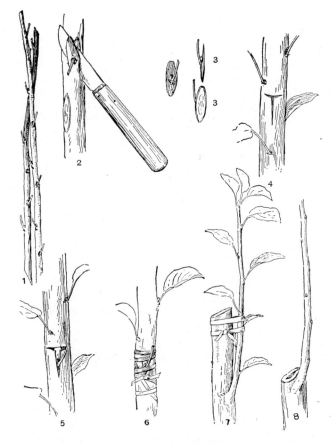

BUDDING OPERATIONS

1, Shoots from which buds are cut (note that leaves have been cut off leaving stubs)·
2, cutting the buds; 3, the buds; 4, T-shaped cuts placed in bark; 5, bud inserted
into T cut; 6, bud tied with raffia; 7, top of stock has been removed and the bud
has grown (note that the new growth is tied to the stock to prevent its being broken
off by the wind); 8, stub cut back to point of budding—Adapted from Cornell Lesson
123, Fruit Growing Series

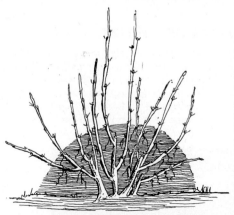

Mound layering of Gooseberries. Observe the roots forming

Mound layer of Gooseberry. Note that the shoots have been cut back previous to mounding the soil about the plants; each shoot is rooting nicely

Japanese Snowball, Oakleaf Hydrangea, Magnolias, Filberts and Purple Hazel, Pearlbush, Snowdroptree, Daphne, Shrubby Cinquefoil, Alnus and many other shrubs are so propagated. See each shrub for definite instructions.

MOUND LAYERS OR STOOLS. If there are few branches near the soil it may be necessary to cut the plants to the soil in early Spring. This results in the growth of many shoots. When these are long enough, bank the soil about the plants to a depth of 6 in. to 12 in. In a short time these shoots will have rooted and may be removed the next Spring, treated as hardwood cuttings. This is the common method of propagating Gooseberries, Quinces and the dwarf Apple Stocks—Paradise and Doucin. It is a good method for propagating *Hydrangea arborescens grandiflora*, Spirea Anthony Waterer, Sweet-shrub, Cercidiphyllum, Hazel, Hollies, Lilacs and others.

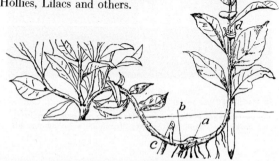

Method of layering a woody or half-woody plant, as for instance, a Rhododendron or a Carnation. a, Slit or tongue cut half way through the stem; b, pebble to keep slit open; c, peg for holding down the layer; d, a stake to keep the shoot firm

DIVISION OF SHRUBS

Such shrubs as *Kerria*, *Philadelphus*, *Hydrangea arborescens*, *Mahonia*, *Symphoricarpos*, *Aesculus parviflora*, *Calycanthus*, *Rubus*, some Roses and many others produce a clumpy growth which may be cut apart in Spring with a hatchet. The larger sections may be 2 to 3 ft. stock; the smaller pieces may be treated as hardwood cuttings and planted deeply in rows, after the tops have been pruned back severely.

Holly and Hollylike Plants

1, Hollyleaf Itea, note the racemes of white flowers; 2, Chinese Holly (*Ilex cornuta*); 3, Holly-olive (*Osmanthus*), note opposite leaves; 4, American Holly (*Ilex opaca*); 5, English Holly (*Ilex aquifolia*); 6, Oregon Hollygrape (*Mahonia*); a compound leaf.

HEDGES

The popularity of hedges is increasing. Persons are more and more desirous of having privacy on their home grounds. There are, necessarily, many sorts of hedges—the excluding, thorny hedge grown for a needed purpose; the low, bordering hedge for parterres of a formal garden; the boundary hedge which merely indicates how far the lot extends; the tall background hedge to shut out unfavorable views; the hedge of formal and pattern clipped lines to serve as a garden feature; the windbreak hedge as a protection for the home or for coldframes—all these hedges to serve a useful purpose or to embellish a garden area.

There is no reason why one should hesitate to plant a hedge about his lot in a city. Too many persons live, as it were, in "glass houses"; they fear that the privacy of a hedge will be considered by the neighbor as a spite fence. Their domains, though small, are open to the traffic of dogs, paper boys and peddlers, to say nothing of neighbors, who tramp on the lawns and intrude, all because we desire to be so democratic. Many gardeners have provided veritable outdoor living rooms by setting aside little areas fenced in with tall hedges or low hedges backed with tall shrubs.

It must be admitted that a formal hedge requires upkeep and labor, but it generally costs less to plant than would the construction of a fence.

VARIOUS HEDGE PLANTS

LOW PLANTS THAT CAN BE KEPT AT A FOOT OR LESS

Berberis thunbergi var. *minor* (Box Barberry) needs careful shearing
Buxus microphylla var. *japonica* (Japanese Box). Very hardy
Cotoneaster apiculata and other low sorts. Rare
Euonymus radicans (Wintercreeper)
    var. *minimus* (Baby Wintercreeper). Tiny leaves
    var. *vegetus* (Bigleaf Wintercreeper). Larger leaves than type
Hedera helix (English Ivy). Good in shade
Ligustrum vulgare var. *lodense* (Lodense Privet). Subject to blight
Ligustrum ovalifolium and others may be kept low if clipped often
Spiraea bumalda (Anthony Waterer Spirea)
Spiraea bumalda (Froebel Spirea). Naturally taller than above
Viburnum opulus var. *nanum* (Dwarf Cranberrybush). Globular plants

FORMAL HEDGES TO BE CLIPPED

Acanthopanax pentaphyllum (Fiveleaf Angelicatree). Thorny; fresh green leaves

Berberis thunbergi (Japanese Barberry). Thorny; well known; often not clipped

Buxus sempervirens (Box). Less hardy. Shade

Cotoneaster acutifolia (Peking C.). Very hardy even in Iowa and Minnesota

Elaeagnus angustifolia (Russian-olive). 10 ft. tall; gray leaves

Ilex crenata (Japanese Holly). Graceful; expensive; slow growth

Ligustrum amurense (Amur Privet). Hardy

Ligustrum ibolium (Ibolium Privet). The best of all; not common as yet

Ligustrum ibota (Ibota Privet). Leaves not as shining as above

Ligustrum ovalifolium (California Privet). Less hardy; worthless in North

Ligustrum vulgare (Common Privet). Very hardy; splendid except subject to blight

Rhamnus cathartica (Buckthorn). Thorny; impenetrable

Rhamnus frangula (Glossy Buckthorn). Good fruit

Rhamnus utilis. Good foliage

FLOWERING HEDGES. INFORMAL OUTLINE

Abelia grandiflora (Glossy Abelia). Less hardy; pink flowers

Caragana arborescens (Siberian Pea-shrub). Yellow flowers

Cornus paniculata (Gray Dogwood). White flowers; blue or white fruit; needs plenty of space

Cotoneaster acutifolia (Peking Cotoneaster). Hardy, N. Dak.; pinkish

Crataegus crusgalli (Cockspur Thorn). Tall; white flowers

Crataegus oxyacantha (English Hawthorn). Lobed leaves; white flowers

Crataegus cordata (Washington H.). Shiny leaves

Cydonia japonica (Flowering Quince). Red flowers; thorny

Deutzia gracilis (Slender Deutzia). Low; white flowers

Deutzia lemoinei (Lemoine Deutzia). Taller; white flowers

Forsythia intermedia (Border Forsythia). Trim often; yellow flowers

Hibiscus syriacus (Shrub-althea). Fall; narrow habit; various colors

Hydrangea paniculata grandiflora (Peegee H.). Massive in time

Lonicera fragrantissima (Winter Honeysuckle). Trim often; almost evergreen; not formal; early white flowers

Lonicera ruprechtiana (Manchurian Honeysuckle). White flowers

Lonicera tatarica (Tatarian Honeysuckle) Pink or white flowers

Malus (Flowering Crab) Pink, white or rose flowers. See page 304

Philadelphus, various (Mockorange). White flowers

FLOWERING HEDGES—*Continued*

Rhodotypos kerrioides (Jetbead). White flowers; black fruit

Rosa rugosa (Japanese R.). Rose, pink or white flowers

Spiraea vanhouttei (Vanhoutte Spirea). Informal but may be clipped; white flowers

Syringa vulgaris and others (Lilac). Tall informal; flowers of various colors

Viburnum dentatum and allies (Arrowwood). White flowers

TALL FOLIAGE HEDGES, 6 TO 10 FEET OR MORE

Acer campestre (Hedge Maple)

Acer ginnala (Amur Maple)

Carpinus betulus (European Hornbeam). Better than American H.

Carpinus caroliniana (American Hornbeam)

Citrus trifoliata (Hardy Orange). Good south of Washington

Crataegus crusgalli (Cockspur Thorn)

Elaeagnus angustifolia (Russian-olive). Hardy; gray leaves.

Fagus sylvatica (European Beech). Better than American Beech

Gleditsia triacanthos (Honeylocust). Thorny

Ligustrum ovalifolium (California Privet). Good south of Washington

Ligustrum vulgare (Common Privet). Hardy; good flowers

Maclura pomifera (Osage-orange). Thorny

Malus (Crab apples). May be clipped formally

Morus alba (White Mulberry)

Philadelphus coronarius (Sweet Mockorange)

Rhamnus frangula (Glossy Buckthorn). Good fruit

Salix pentandra (Laurel Willow). Shiny leaves

Syringa vulgaris and others (Lilacs). Informal

Viburnum lentago (Nannyberry). Splendid flowers

Viburnum prunifolium (Blackhaw). Good foliage

FLORIDA AND CALIFORNIA HEDGES

Acacia armata, *dealbata* and *latifolia* (Wattle)

Buxus sempervirens (Box)

Coprosma baueri (Mirrorplant)

Cotoneaster pannosa, *francheti*, and others

Cytisus andreanus, *racemosus*, and others (Broom)

Diosma ericoides (Breath-of-heaven)

Escallonia montevidensis, *rubra*

Eugenia myrtifolia (Australian Brush-cherry)

Grevillea thelemanniana (Jewelflower-shrub)

FLORIDA AND CALIFORNIA HEDGES—*Continued*

Hibiscus rosa-sinensis (Chinese Hibiscus)
Lantana camara (Lantana).
Laurocerasus caroliniana, lusitanica, officinalis (Laurelcherry)
Ligustrum amurense, lucidum, and *nepalense* (Privets)
Lonicera nitida (Box Honeysuckle)
Myrtus communis (True Myrtle)
Photinia arbutifolia (Christmasberry)
Pittosporum tobira, undulatum
Prunus ilicifolia, lyoni (Cherry)
Pyracantha crenulata and others (Firethorn)
Santolina chamaecyparissus (Lavender-cotton)
Thymus serpyllum (Mother-of-thyme)
Veronica brevifolia, traversi (Evergreen Speedwells)
Viburnum suspensum (Sandankwa Viburnum)
Viburnum tinus (Laurustinus)

PLANTING

It was formerly advised that double hedges are preferable to a single row of plants but such hedges are too difficult to keep clean of weeds. Furthermore, there is no necessity of using so many plants. Of course, if a wide hedge is wanted quickly, a double row of plants may be desirable.

In setting the plants, dig a trench deep enough to receive the roots without wadding them into the furrow and so that the plants may be set down to the lower branches. This insures dense branching at the bottom. Dig the trench so that one side is straight and in perfect alignment; then place the plants against this side to facilitate making the hedge straight.

Privet is usually planted a foot apart, Barberry 18 in. and such shrubs as Spirea and Shrub-althea 2 ft. apart.

As soon as the plants are set, prune them back severely. If the stock is young and unbranched, prune almost to the soil, otherwise cut back one-half. It is essential to induce branching from the base at the start.

It is often wise to stretch a wire over the top of the row to protect young plants from being trodden upon.

If chicken wire is stretched along the row at time of planting, the branches will soon grow up, covering the wire, and will serve to make the hedge dog-proof and chicken-proof from the start.

CARE OF HEDGES

Besides clipping hedges, as will be discussed below, there are several other considerations.

If one desires a perfect hedge upon a private estate, a few plants should be grown and pruned in an out-of-the-way place so that misses in the garden hedges may be supplied. One missing plant spoils a hedge.

When hedges become very old and have spread out so widely that they are taking up too much space, do not prune to the soil but prune one side back one year, the other the next and gradually cut back the top. When so treated the hedge keeps its accustomed appearance from year to year. Do not transplant old hedges; purchase new plants.

If hedges are to retain their vigor, they not only need to be cultivated from time to time, but will benefit by a complete fertilizer and a mulch of decayed manure through the Winter.

CLIPPING HEDGES

Formal hedges are tidy in appearance, but if there is much hedge of this sort in the usual home grounds, it is sorely neglected because it requires clipping almost every two weeks. Therefore, for the average home owner, it is wiser to train his hedges semi-formally and, instead of using Privet and such like plants, he should use Barberry trimmed only so that the longer straggling branches are removed.

The compactness of a hedge results from constant shearing at top and sides. Waiting until the shoots are long causes the cut stubs to become too prominent. The softer the growth, the easier it is to cut to accurate lines. Do not continue to prune California Privet late in the year as new growth freezes in Winter.

Theoretically, a hedge should not be flat topped, nor of equal width at top and bottom. It should be wider at the bottom and pyramidal in end-view. Growth becomes less compact at the base as time passes. Nevertheless, trimming hedges to such tapering forms is difficult for the amateur.

Varying the outline of the hedge adds interest to it, but is a little more difficult to maintain. At the Brooklyn Botanical Garden a tall Privet hedge which is undulating in outline surrounds the school gardens. At the start, this was pruned by suspending a rope between two stakes so that the curves might be judged more accurately than by eye. In the trough of the curve, one shoot was allowed to grow and be come treelike in form.

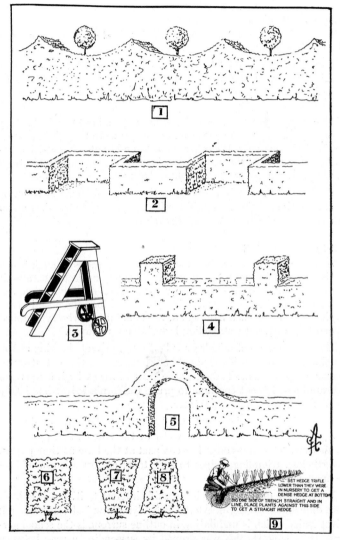

Methods of pruning hedges

1, Tall Privet hedge undulating in outline at Brooklyn Botanical Gardens; 2, this unique method lends itself to long hedges, adding interest to them (see text); 3, convenient ladder for pruning tall hedges; 4, formal pruning; 5, arch started by tying branches to wire frame; 6, 7, 8 show end views, 8, being ideal; 9, planting hedge

In training an arch, it is well to use a wire arch to which the shoots may be tied for the first few years.

In the sketch is seen a hedge so planted that there are recesses in it at intervals. An English hedge along these lines presented the idea. Perennials and annuals may be planted in these recesses. The method lends itself to long hedges that would otherwise be monotonous.

Fuchsias

All are familiar with Fuchsias which in the East are considered to be pot plants 1, The upper truss of bloom is one of the varieties of the characteristic Hybrid Fuchsias; 2, this is *F. fulgens* with soft scarlet flowers; 3, the variety Geerbert which bears petaloids on the stamens; 4, the dainty *F. gracilis*; 5, a fully double sort; 6, the Lilacflowered Fuchsia (*F. arborescens*). (Drawn at the gardens of Alfred Robinson, Pointe Loma, Cal.)

BROAD-LEAVED EVERGREENS

There are two sorts of evergreens—conifers which are characterized by needle or scalelike leaves, and the broad-leaved evergreens which are often flowering sorts.

The broad-leaved evergreens are well suited for the permanent effects desired for foundation plantings in shaded places about the home. They are always attractive, even when not in flower. Most sorts grow slowly and thus preserve the original picture of the planting it was intended to make. Many of the sorts are formal enough without taking the decided shape of the pyramid or the globe. They are considered the most exclusive of all plants, and yet, where they grow well, they are lasting and really simpler to care for than most shrubs and many conifers.

Most of the hardy broad-leaved evergreens belong to the Ericaceae, the Heath family, which indicates that they desire an acid soil or one at least neutral but not limey. This is discussed on pages 20 to 25.

Having broad leaves which are exposed to Winter cold and sun, they readily "burn." The leaves must give off water, even if they are unable to take it from the soil; consequently, Rhododendron leaves curl to reduce the exposed surface. Rapid thawing, due to wind and sun, causes the leaves to uncurl quickly and injures them; either they "burn" or actually die. This necessity of Nature indicates their cultural needs.

CULTURAL REQUIREMENTS*

1. SHADE. Generally some shade is desirable in Winter. Rhododendrons are particularly sensitive to Winter sun, especially *R. maximum*, although *Rhododendron catawbiense*. *R. carolinianum* and *R. minus* are not so easily injured. Most other sorts, such as Pieris, Kalmia and Leucothoe, have smaller leaves and for that reason tolerate sun.

Some gardeners protect each plant in Winter by means of burlap wrapped about four stakes driven into the soil around the plants. Boxes may be built to enclose the plants or windbreaks may be

*Much of the advice here given is derived from LaBar's Rhododendron Nursery whose experience is wide.

planted. Such protection is not in the nature of an overcoat but more like a parasol and windshield. Where evergreen branches are available, they are useful for protection. Discarded Christmas trees will provide a shelter akin to natural protection and are less unsightly than burlap. The trees may be set with a crowbar.

2. Mulch. Many of these plants have very shallow roots which, at the same time, prefer cool soil. Such conditions in Nature are satisfied because there is a continual accumulation of leafmold over the surface of the soil. Hardwood leaves, sawdust, straw, peat moss and marsh hay may be used, but avoid manure. Lawn clippings will heat unless dried first. It is possible that the mulch may become tightly packed so that air does not enter. In that event, stir up the surface, but do not cultivate the soil which is sure to contain roots. Leave the mulch on at all times; do not remove it to make the beds tidy. To tidy the bed, apply more mulch.

3. Moisture. Rhododendrons generally grow in a light soil but inhabit hillsides on which there is a supply of moisture moving to the lower levels. They are not bog plants but must have water. In Highland Park, a constant spray is kept playing upon various sections of the broad-leaved evergreens; but, there must be perfect drainage. Even when such plants are found in swampy places, the feeding roots are above the water level. To grow these plants successfully, provide drainage by tiling, by a layer of rock or plant them in places where natural drainage is possible.

Do not plant so near buildings that rainfall cannot reach them. Planting too close to Soft Maples, Elms, Hemlocks, Spruces and surface rooting trees, which robs them of moisture, should be avoided. Oaks and Beeches are preferable trees to furnish shade but in small plantings Flowering Dogwood, Redbud, and Magnolias are used.

4. Soil. First of all, the soil must be acid or neutral. Sand and gravel containing humus, as well as leafmold, peat moss or muck, are all good. Soils must not be heavy clay nor limey. See discussion of "Acid, Neutral and Alkaline Soils," page 20, also "Building an Acid Soil," page 21.

5. Planting. As soon as soil opens in the Spring these plants may be set. Fall planting is inadvisable in much of the Northern United States. LaBar advises that late August for a period of six or eight weeks is safe, but that late Autumn is unwise.

Set the plants no deeper than they grew in Nature or in the nursery. Pack the soil but avoid tramping vigorously which often breaks the roots. Do not mound the soil about the plants but leave a shallow depression that will retain water.

LISTS OF SHRUBS

When one desires to make any sort of planting it is wise to refer to lists of shrubs even when one is familiar with plants. It is much quicker to refer to lists than to rely on memory. Refer also to the extensive list at end of book, page 415.

*SPECIMEN SHRUBS FOR VARIOUS SECTIONS OF THE COUNTRY

MID-ATLANTIC-STATES
Louise Bush-Brown

Azalea calendulacea (Flame Azalea)

Azalea mucronulatum (Korean Azalea)

Buddleia davidi (Orange-eye Butterflybush)

Carpenteria californica

Chionanthus virginica (Fringetree)

Cydonia japonica (Flowering Quince)

Deutzia lemoinei (Lemoine D.)

Forsythia intermedia spectabilis (Showy Goldenbells)

Kolkwitzia amabilis (Beautybush)

Philadelphus, Virginal

Rosa hugonis (Hugonis Rose)

Spiraea vanhouttei (Vanhoutte Spirea)

Styrax japonica (Japanese Snowbell)

Syringa vulgaris (Common Lilac)

Viburnum carlesi (Fragrant V.)

NORTHERN STATES
Stephen F. Hamblin

Azalea calendulacea (Flame Azalea)

Azalea kaempferi (Torch Azalea)

Azalea vaseyi (Pinkshell Azalea)

Buddleia davidi (Orange-eye Butterflybush)

Cercis canadensis (Redbud)

Cornus kousa (Kousa Dogwood)

Exochorda grandiflora (Pearlbush)

Kalmia latifolia (Mountain-laurel)

Magnolia stellata (Star Magnolia)

Philadelphus lemoinei (Lemoine Mockorange)

Rhododendron carolinianum (Carolina Rhododendron)

Rhododendron catawbiense (Catawba Rhododendron)

Rosa rugosa (Rugosa Rose)

Syringa chinensis (Rouen Lilac)

Syringa vulgaris (Common Lilac)

*List compiled by authorities and published in *House and Garden,* February, 1931.

MIDWEST
Walter D. Popham

Amelanchier alnifolia (Saskatoon Shadblow)

Cydonia japonica (Flowering Quince)

Forsythia intermedia spectabilis (Showy Goldenbells)

Hamamelis mollis (Chinese Witch-hazel)

Hibiscus syriacus (Shrub-althea)

Kolkwitzia amabilis (Beautybush)

Magnolia stellata (Star Magnolia)

Philadelphus, Virginal

Prunus triloba (Flowering Plum)

Rosa ecae (Eca Rose)

Rosa setigera (Prairie Rose)

Spiraea billiardi (Billiard Spirea)

Spiraea vanhouttei (Vanhoutte Spirea)

Syringa vulgaris (Common Lilac)

Viburnum carlesi (Fragrant Viburnum)

CALIFORNIA
Helen Van Pelt

Azalea (around San Francisco) *A. mollis*, *A. kurume* and *A. hinodegiri*

Camellia japonica

Ceanothus cyaneus (Wild-lilac)

Choisya ternata (Mexican-orange)

Cistus ladaniferus (Gum Rockrose)

Cydonia japonica (Flowering Quince)

Daphne odora (Winter Daphne)

Diosma ericoides (Breath-of-heaven)

Erica melanthera (Black-eyed Heath)

Fuchsia

Hibiscus rosa-sinensis (Chinese Hibiscus)

Lagerstroemia indica (Crape-myrtle)

Nerium oleander (Oleander)

Veronica andersoni (Anderson Speedwell)

FLOWERING SHRUBS

WHITE FLOWERING SHRUBS

(The figure before the name represents the month of bloom)

7 *Aesculus parviflora* (Bottlebrush Buckeye)

5 *Amelanchier* various (Shadblow)

6 *Azalea arborescens* (Sweet Azalea)

6   *viscosa* (Swamp Azalea)

7 *Ceanothus americanus* (Jersey-tea)

7–8 *Cephalanthus occidentalis* (Buttonbush)

5 *Chionanthus virginica* (White Fringetree)

7 *Clethra alnifolia* (Summersweet)

5–6 *Cornus* various (Dogwood)

WHITE FLOWERING SHRUBS—*Continued*

5 *Cotoneaster hupehensis* (Hupeh Cotoneaster)
    multiflora var. *calocarpa*
    racemiflora var. *soongarica*
5 *Crataegus* various (Thorn-apple) (Hawthorn)
5 *Cytisus leucanthus* (Pale Broom)
5 *Deutzia* various (Deutzia)
5 *Exochorda grandiflora* (Pearlbush)
6-8 *Helianthemum chamaecistus* (Sunrose)
8 *Hibiscus syriacus* (Shrub-althea)
7 *Holodiscus discolor* (Rockspirea)
7 *Hydrangea arborescens grandiflora* (Snowhill Hydrangea)
7 *Indigofera decora* (Chinese indigo)
7 *Itea virginica* (Sweetspire)
5-6 *Jamesia americana* (Jamesia)
6 *Kalmia latifolia* (Mountain-laurel)
5 *Leiophyllum buxifolium* (Box Sandmyrtle)
5 *Leucothoe catesbaei* (Drooping Leucothoe)
5   *axillaris*
6 *Ligustrum* various (Privets)
4 *Lonicera fragrantissima* (Winter Honeysuckle)
5   *tatarica* (Tatarian H.)
3-4 *Magnolia* various (Magnolia)
5 *Neviusia alabamensis* (Snow-wreath)
6 *Philadelphus* various (Mockorange)
5 *Photinia villosa* (Christmasberry)
6 *Physocarpus opulifolius* (Ninebark)
5 *Pieris floribunda* (Mountain Andromeda)
5   *japonica* (Japanese Andromeda)
5 *Prunus* various (Ornamental Cherries, Plums)
6 *Rhododendron* varieties (Rhododendron)
5 *Rhodotypos kerrioides* (Jetbead)
6 *Robinia hartwigi* (Hartwig Locust)
6 *Rosa multiflora* (Japanese Rose)
6-9   *rugosa* (Rugosa Rose)
6 *Rhus javanica* (Java Sumac)
5 *Sambucus* various (Elder)
7 *Sorbaria assurgens* (False-spirea)
7   *arborea* (Tree-spirea)
7 *Spiraea alba* (Meadow Spirea)

WHITE FLOWERING SHRUBS—*Continued*

5 *Spiraea arguta* (Garland S.)
5 *cantoniensis* (Reeves S.)
6 *henryi* (Henry S.)
5 *prunifolia* (Bridalwreath)
5 *thunbergi* (Thunberg S.)
5 *trichocarpa* (Korean S.)
5 *vanhouttei* (Vanhoutte S.)
6 *veitchi* (Veitch S.)
5-6 *Staphylea colchica* (Colchis Bladdernut)
6 *Styrax japonica* (Japanese Snowbell)
6 *Syringa amurensis* (Manchurian Lilac)
5 *vulgaris* (Lilac) (See varieties pages 380 to 383)
5 *Vaccinium* various (Blueberries)
5-6 *Viburnums* various (Viburnums, Snowballs)
6 *Weigela* varieties (Weigela)
6 *Zenobia pulverulenta* (Dusty Zenobia)

PINK FLOWERING SHRUBS

4-5 *Amygdalus nana* (Russian Almond)
5 *Azalea nudiflora* (Pinxterbloom)
5 *rosea* (Downy Pinxterbloom)
5 *vaseyi* (Pinkshell Azalea)
5 *viscosa* (Swamp Azalea)
4 *Cornus florida* var. *rubra* (Red-flowering Dogwood)
4-10 *Daphne cneorum* (Rose Daphne)
5 *Deutzia gracilis* var. *rosea* (Rose Panicle Deutzia)
5 *Enkianthus campanulatus* (Redvein Enkianthus)
4 *Erica carnea* (Spring Heath)
8 *Hibiscus syriacus* (Shrub-althea)
6 *Kalmia angustifolia* (Lambkill)
6 *latifolia* (Mountain-laurel)
6 *Kolkwitzia amabilis* (Beautybush)
5 *Lonicera* various (Honeysuckles)
5 *Magnolia soulangeana nigra* (Purple Lily Magnolia)
5 *Malus* various (Crabs)
6 *Neillia sinensis* (Tube Neillia)
4-5 *Paeonia suffruticosa* (Tree Peony) (Moutan Peony)
4-5 *Prunus*, various (Plums, Almonds, Cherries)
6 *Robinia hispida* (Rose-acacia)

Pink Flowering Shrubs—*Continued*

4 *Rhododendron* (Rhododendrons)
6–9 *Rosa rugosa* (Rugosa Rose)
7 *Spiraea bumalda* var. Anthony Waterer (Anthony Waterer)
7   *bumalda* var. *froebeli* (Froebel S.)
7   *douglasi* (Douglas S.)
7–8   *superba* (Striped S.)
4–8 *Tamarix* various (Tamarisk)
5   *Viburnum carlesi* (Fragrant Viburnum)
6 *Weigela* various (Weigela)

RED FLOWERING SHRUBS

5 *Azalea hinodegiri* (Hinodegiri Azalea)
5 *Chaenomeles lagenaria* (Flowering Quince)
5 *Crataegus oxyacantha* var. *pauli* (Paul English Hawthorn)
8 *Hibiscus syriacus* (Shrub-althea)

Like lovely silk–clad Japanese ladies, the Tree Peony graces the gardens of early Spring. It is a slow growing shrub and one which often has its buds frozen

4 *Magnolia soulangeana nigra* (Purple Lily Magnolia)
5 *Prunus persica rubra* (Redflowering Peach)
6 *Rosa rugosa* (Rugosa R.)
7 *Spiraea bumalda* var. Anthony Waterer (Anthony Waterer S.)
7   *bumalda* var. *froebeli* (Froebel S.)
6 *Weigela* (Eva Rathke)

MAROON FLOWERING SHRUBS

4 *Asimina triloba* (Papaw)
5-7 *Calycanthus floridus* (Sweetshrub)
6 *Lonicera ledebouri* (Ledebour Honeysuckle)

MAGENTA FLOWERING SHRUBS

6 *Azalea amoena* (Amoena Azalea)
8-9 *Lagerstroemia indica* (Crapemyrtle)
4-5 *Rhododendron* various (Rhododendron)
7 *Rubus odoratus* (Flowering Raspberry)

BLUE OR PURPLE FLOWERING SHRUBS

7 *Amorpha canescens* (Leadplant)
6   *fruticosa* (Indigobush)
7 *Buddleia davidi* (Orange-eye Butterflybush)
8 *Caryopteris incana* (Bluebeard)
7 *Cytisus purpureus* (Purple Broom)
9 *Elsholtzia stauntoni* (Mintshrub)
8 *Hibiscus syriacus* (Shrub-Althea)
7 *Indigofera*, various (Indigo)
9 *Lespedeza bicolor* (Shrub Bushclover)
9   *formosa* (Purple Bushclover)
5 *Lonicera syringantha* (Lilac Honeysuckle)
5-6   *thibetica* (Tibetan H.)
5 *Rhododendron* (Rhododendrons)
7 *Rhus cotinus* (Smoketree)
6 *Robinia hartwigi* (Hartwig Locust)
5 *Syringa vulgaris* (Lilac)
8 *Vitex agnus-castus* (Lilac Chaste-tree)

LILAC FLOWERING SHRUBS

8-10 *Perowskia atriplicifolia*
5 *Syringa vulgaris* (Lilac)

YELLOW FLOWERING SHRUBS

3–4 *Alnus* various (Alder)
 6 *Azalea mollis* (Chinese Azalea)
 4 *Benzoin aestivale* (Spicebush)
 5 *Berberis* various (Barberry)
 5 *Caragana arborescens* (Siberian Pea-tree)
 6 *Colutea arborescens* (Bladder-senna)
 3 *Cornus mas* (Cornelian-cherry)
 4 *Corylopsis pauciflora* (Buttercup Winterhazel)
 7 *Cytisus hirsutus* (Hairy Broom)
 7 *nigricans* (Spike Broom)
 6 *scoparius* (Scotch Broom)
 7 *supinus* (Bigflower Broom)
 6 *Diervilla sessilifolia* (Southern Bush Honeysuckle)
 4 *Forsythia* various (Goldenbells)
 2 *Hamamelis japonica* (Japanese Witch-hazel)
10 *Hamamelis virginiana* (Witch-hazel)
 6 *Helianthemum chamaecistus* (Sunrose)
 7 *Hypericum* various (St. Johnswort)
 5 *Kerria japonica* (Kerria)
 5 *Laburnum alpinum* (Scotch Laburnum)
 5 *anagyroides* (Goldenchain)
 5 *Mahonia aquifolium* (Oregon Hollygrape)
 7 *Potentilla fruticosa* (Shrubby Cinquefoil)
 5 *Ribes aureum* (Slender Golden Currant)
 5 *Rosa ecae* (Eca Rose)
 6 *harrisoni* (Harrison's Yellow)
 5 *persiana* (Persian Yellow R.)

ORANGE FLOWERING SHRUBS

 6 *Azalea calendulacea* (Flame Azalea)
 5 *kaempferi* (Torch Azalea)
 6 *schlippenbachi* (Royal A.)
 6 *Colutea orientalis* (Oriental Bladder-senna)

ATTRACTIVE FRUITS

RED FRUITS

Acer tataricum (Tatarian Maple)
Arctostaphylos uva-ursi (Bearberry)
Aronia arbutifolia (Red Chokeberry)

Red Fruits—*Continued*

Benzoin aestivale (Spicebush)
Berberis various (Barberry)
Cornus florida (Flowering Dogwood)
Cornus mas (Cornelian-cherry)
Cotoneaster acuminata
   dielsiana (Diels Cotoneaster)
   divaricata (Spreading C.)
   francheti
   horizontalis (Rock C.)
   hupehensis (Hupeh C.)
   microphylla (Rockspray)
   multiflora var. *calocarpa*
   pannosa
   racemiflora var. *soongarica*
   simonsi (Simons C.)
Crataegus various (Hawthorn)

Elaeagnus pungens (Thorny Elaeagnus)
Euonymus americanus (Brook Euonymus)
   atropurpureus (Wahoo)
   latifolius (Broadleaf Burningbush)

Ilex cornuta (Chinese Holly)
   geniculata
   laevigata (Smooth Winterberry)
   serrata (Finetooth Holly)
   verticillata (Winterberry)

Leycesteria formosa (Himalaya-honeysuckle)
Lonicera maacki (Amur H.)
   spinosa var. *alberti* (Albert H.)
   standishi (Standish H.)
   syringantha (Lilac H.)
Lonicera tatarica (Tartarian H.)
   thibetica (Tibetan H.)
   xylosteum (European Fly H.)
Lycium halmifolium (Matrimony-vine)

Malus various (Crab, Apple)

Nandina domestica (Nandina)
Nemopanthus mucronatus (Mountain-holly)

Photinia serrulata (Low Photinia)
   villosa (Hairy P.)

RED FRUITS—*Continued*

Prunus tomentosa (Nanking Cherry)
Pyracantha angustifolia, coccinea, crenulata (Firethorn)
Rhus various (Sumac)
Rosa multiflora (Japanese Rose)
   rugosa (Rugosa R.)
Rubus odoratus (Flowering Raspberry)
Sambucus racemosa (European Red Elder)
Shepherdia argentea (Silver Buffaloberry)
Symphoricarpos vulgaris (Coralberry)
Viburnum dilatatum (Linden Viburnum)
   opulus (European Cranberrybush)
   sargenti (Sargent C.)
   theiferum (Tea Viburnum)
   wrighti (Wright V.)

PINK FRUITS

Euonymus bungeanus (Winterberry Euonymus)
   europaeus (European Burningbush)
   patens (Spreading Euonymus)
   yedoensis (Yeddo E.)

WHITE FRUITS

Cornus alba sibirica (Coral Dogwood)
Cornus baileyi (Bailey D.)
Cornus stolonifera (Red-osier D.)
Ligustrum vulgare (European Privet)
   var. *leucocarpa* (Whiteberry Privet)
Symphoricarpos racemosus (Snowberry)

BLACK FRUITS

Amelanchier various (Shadblow)
Aralia spinosa (Devils-walkingstick)
Aronia melanocarpa (Black Chokeberry)
Cotoneaster acutifolia (Peking Cotoneaster)
   foveolata
Ilex crenata (Japanese Holly)
   glabra (Inkberry)
Ligustrum ibota (Ibota Privet)
   ibota var. *regelianum* (Regal P.)
   vulgare (Common Privet)

BLACK FRUITS—*Continued*

Lonicera ledebouri
Mahonia bealei (Leatherleaf Hollygrape)
   repens (Creeping Hollygrape)
Rhamnus various (Buckthorn)
Rhodotypos kerrioides (Jetbead)
Sambucus canadensis (American Elder)
Viburnum acerifolium (Mapleleaf Viburnum)
   cassinoides (Withe-rod)
   dentatum (Arrowwood)
   lentago (Nannyberry)
   prunifolium (Blackhaw)

BLUE FRUITS

Chionanthus virginica (White Fringetree)
Cornus alternifolia (Pagoda Dogwood)
   amomum (Silky D.)
   paniculata (Gray D.)
   rugosa (Roundleaf D.)
Lonicera caerulea (Sweetberry Honeysuckle)
Mahonia aquifolium (Oregon Hollygrape)
Symplocos paniculata (Asiatic Sweetleaf)
Osmanthus aquifolium (Holly Osmanthus)
Vaccinium corymbosum (Highbush Blueberry)

PURPLE FRUITS

Callicarpa purpurea (Chinese Beautyberry)
Ligustrum quihoui (Quihou Privet)
Lonicera nitida (Box Honeysuckle)
   pileata (Privet Honeysuckle)
Robinia kelseyi (Kelsey Locust)
Viburnum lantana (Wayfaring-tree)

BRONZE FRUITS

Colutea arborescens (Bladder-senna)

ORANGE FRUITS

Celastrus (Bittersweet)
Citrus trifoliata (Hardy Orange)
Cotoneaster francheti (Franchet Cotoneaster)

ORANGE FRUITS—*Continued*

Euonymus various (Euonymus)
Magnolias various (Magnolia)
Pyracantha coccinea (Scarlet Firethorn)

YELLOW FRUITS

Hippophae rhamnoides (Common Sea-buckthorn)
Elaeagnus angustifolia (Russian-olive)
Lonicera ruprechtiana var. *zanthocarpa* (Manchurian Honeysuckle)
    tatarica var. *zanthocarpa* (Tatarian Honeysuckle)
Shepherdia various (Buffaloberry)
Viburnum opulus var. *lutea* (Yellow Cranberrybush)
    theiferum (Tea Viburnum)

GRAY FRUITS

Elaeagnus argentea (Silverberry)
Myrica carolinensis (Northern Bayberry)

FOLIAGE COLORS

WHITE VARIEGATIONS

Cornus alba var. *argenteo-marginata* (Silveredge Dogwood)
Euonymus radicans var. *argenteo-marginatus* (Silveredge Wintercreeper)
Hibiscus syriacus var. *variegata* (Variegated Shrub-althea)
Kerria japonica var. *argenteo-variegata* (Silver Kerria)
Weigela sieboldi var. *argenteo-marginata* (Silveredge Weigela)

GRAY

Amorpha canescens (Leadplant)
Elaeagnus angustifolia (Russian-olive)
    argentea (Silverberry)
    multiflora (Cherry Elaeagnus)
    umbellata (Autumn Elaeagnus)
Hippophae rhamnoides (Sea-buckthorn)
Salix incana (Rosemary Willow)
Shepherdia argentea (Buffaloberry)
Tamarix hispida (Kashgar Tamarix)
    pentandra (Fivestamen Tamarix)
Zenobia pulverulenta (Dusty Zenobia)

Foliage Colors—*Continued*

BLUE-GREEN

Berberis dictyophylla var. *albicaulis* (Chalkleaf Barberry)
Lonicera korolkowi (Blueleaf Honeysuckle)
   morrowi (Morrow H.)
Zenobia pulverulenta (Dusty Zenobia)

YELLOW

Acer palmatum var. *aureum* (Golden Japanese Maple)
Cornus alba var. *gouchaulti* (Gouchault Dogwood)
   alba spaethi (Spaeth D.)
Ligustrum ovalifolium var. *aureum* (Golden California Privet)
Philadelphus coronarius var. *aureus* (Golden Mockorange)
Physocarpus opulifolius var. *aureus* (Golden Ninebark)
Ptelea trifoliata var. *aurea* (Golden Hoptree)
Sambucus canadensis var. *aureus* (Golden American Elder)

RED

Acer palmatum rubrum (Red Japanese Maple)
Berberis thunbergi var. *purpurea* (Purple Japanese Barberry)
Euonymus radicans var. *colorata*

PURPLE

Acer palmatum var. *atropurpureum* (Bloodleaf Japanese Maple)
Corylus avellana var. *atropurpurea* (Purple Filbert)
   maxima var. *purpurea* (Purple Giant F.)
Leucothoe catesbaei (Leucothoe)
Mahonia repens (Creeping Hollygrape)
Prunus cerasifera var. *pissardi* (Purpleleaf Plum)
Rosa rubrifolia (Redleaf Rose)

GREENS OF VARIOUS TINTS

   (This list is derived from the notes of Ralph W. Curtis)

Abelia (Bush-arbutus). Glossy, dark, evergreen.
Baccharis (Groundselbush). Dull, light gray green.
Buxus (Box). Dark, glossy green leaves.
Chaenomeles (Flowering Quince). Medium to glossy, dark green.
Cornus rugosa (Roundleaf Dogwood). Medium dark green.
Cotoneaster horizontalis (Rockspray). Evergreen in some sections; glossy
   dark green.
Deutzia gracilis (Slender Deutzia). Dull, light green.
Dirca (Leatherwood). Medium light green.

Euonymus radicans (Wintercreeper). Dark, glossy, evergreen.

Exochorda (Pearlbush). Dull, light, gray green.

Gaylussacia baccata (Black Huckleberry). Dull, light yellow green.

Ilex crenata (Japanese Holly). Evergreen, dark, glossy.

Ilex glabra (Inkberry). Evergreen, dark, glossy.

Kalmia latifolia (Mountain-laurel). Evergreen, dark green, medium glossy.

Kerria. Medium light green.

Leucothoe catesbaei (Leucothoe). Evergreen, medium glossy, dark green.

Ligustrum ovalifolium (California Privet). Medium to glossy, dark green.

Lycium halimifolium (Matrimony-vine). Grayish dull green.

Magnolia glauca (Sweetbay). Medium to glossy, light green; under surface gray.

Pieris japonica (Japanese Andromeda). Evergreen, dark glossy green.

Rhamnus alpina (Alpine Buckthorn). Glossy, dark green.

Rosa rugosa (Rugosa Rose). Wrinkled, medium to glossy, dark green.

Viburnum dentatum (Arrowwood). Glossy dark green.

AUTUMN COLOR

Glorious are the tints of Autumn! Where the planter envies the effects found in Nature, he can copy them to a limited extent.

The intensity of Fall coloration is dependent upon several factors:

1. The poorer soils produce the richer colors.

2. Sunlight increases color.

3. Great individual differences in plants.

4. Lack of freezes.

5. Humidity at time of color change.

COLOR CHANGES IN PLANTS IN FALL

R—red. Y—yellow. O—orange. B—bronze. P—purple. G—shrubs which retain green foliage long after freezing even though not evergreen.

Acanthopanax penta-phyllum	Y	Berberis	R.	
Acer ginnala	R. or O.	Callicarpa	P.	
palmatum	R.	Cercidiphyllum	R., O., Y.	
tataricum	R.	Chionanthus	Y.	
Amelanchier	R. or Y.	Cornus florida	R.	
ronia arbutifolia	R.	Cornus paniculata	P.	
		Cotoneaster	R.	

COLOR CHANGES IN PLANTS—*Continued*

Enkianthus.......... R., Y.
Euonymus alatus..... R.
   latifolius.......... O., R.
   radicans var. colorata R.
Euptelea............. R., Y.
Forsythia viridissima.. P.
Fothergilla.......... Y.
Hamamelis.......... Y.
Hypericum.......... G.
Leucothoe.......... R., B.
Ligustrum ibota var.
   regalianum........ P.
   vulgare........... G.
Lonicera fragrantissima G.
Mahonia............ R., B.

Nandina............ R.
Oxydendrum......... O., R.
Parrotia............ R., Y.
Photinia............ R., Y.
Rhus................ R., O., Y.
Ribes alpinum........ R.
   aureum........... R.
Spiraea froebeli...... R., O.
Syringa oblata....... R.
Vaccinium corymbo-
   sum.............. R.
Viburnum acerifolium. P.
   cassinoides........ P., O., R.
   dentatum.......... R.
   lantana .... R.
   opulus............ R.

LOW GROWING SHRUBS

Useful for foundation planting at the base of the house where taller shrubs will hide the windows.

T.—Taller but may be kept low easily. E.—Evergreen. R.—Less common or rare. hh—Half hardy.

Amorpha canescens (Leadplant)
   microphylla (Dwarf-indigo)
Andromeda glaucophylla (Downy Bog-rosemary) E.
   polifolia (Bog-rosemary) E.
Arctostaphylos uva-ursi (Bearberry) E.
Azalea amoena (Amoena Azalea) E.
   kaempferi (Torch A.)
   kurume (Kurume A.)
   mollis (Chinese A.)
Baccharis halimifolia (Groundselbush) T.
Berberis sargentiana (Sargent Barberry) E.R.
   thunbergi (Japanese B.) T.
   verruculosa (Warty B.) E.R.
   wilsonae (Wilson B.)
Bruckenthalia spiculifolia (Spikeheath) E.
Buxus microphylla var. *japonica* (Japanese Box) E.
   sempervirens varieties (Common B.) E. hh.
Callicarpa purpurea (Chinese Beautyberry)

Low Growing Shrubs—*Continued*

Calluna vulgaris (Heather) E.
Caragana chamlagu (Mongolian Pea-shrub) R. hh.
　microphylla (Littleleaf P.) R.
Ceanothus americanus (Jersey-tea)
Chaenomeles japonica (Lesser Flowering Quince)
　sargenti (Sargent Flowering Quince)
Chamaedaphne calyculata (Leatherleaf)
Comptonia asplenifolia (Sweetfern)
Corylopsis pauciflora (Buttercup Winterhazel)
Cotoneaster apiculata (Cotoneaster)
　adpressa (Creeping C.)
　horizontalis (Rock C.)
　microphylla (Rockspray)
　rotundifolia (Roundleaf C.)
Cytisus hirsutus (Hairy Broom)
　purgans (Provence B.)
　purpureus (Purple B.)
Daphne cneorum (Rose D.) E.
　mezereum (February D.) R.
Deutzia rosea (Rose Panicle D.)
　gracilis (Slender D.)
Diervilla lonicera (Bush-honey-
　suckle)
　trifida (Dwarf Bush-honey-
　suckle)
Dirca palustris (Leatherwood)
Erica carnea (Spring Heath) E.
　cinerea (Twisted H.) E.
　tetralix (Crossleaf H.) E.
　vagans (Cornish H.) E.
Euonymus radicans (Winter-
　creeper) E.
Fothergilla gardeni (Dwarf
　Fothergilla)
Genista tinctoria (Woodwaxen)
Hypericums (St. Johnswort)
Ilex, various (Holly) E.
Indigofera decora (Chinese In-
　digo)
　kirilowi (Kirilow I.)
Itea virginica (Sweetspire)

The larger flower is Hypericum moserianum; the smaller one, H. densiflorum

Low Growing Shrubs—*Continued*

Kalmia angustifolia (Lambkill) E.
  polifolia (Bog Kalmia) E.

Kerria japonica var. *argenteovariegata* (Silver Kerria)

Ledum groenlandicum (True Labrador-tea) E.

Leiophyllum buxifolium (Box Sandmyrtle) E.

Lespedeza formosa (Purple Bushclover)

Leucothoe catesbaei (Drooping Leucothoe) E.

Ligustrum ibota nanum (Pygmy Privet)
  ibota var. *regelianum* (Regal P.) T.
  vulgaris var. *lodense* (Lodense P.)
  ovalifolium (California P.) T.

Lonicera nitida (Box Honeysuckle) E. hh.
  pileata (Privet H.) E. hh.
  spinosa alberti (Albert H.) E. R.
  syringantha var. *wolfi* (Wolf H.) T.

Mahoberberis bealei (Holly-leaf Barberry) E.

Mahonia aquifolium (Oregon Hollygrape) E.
  neuberti (Neubert H.)
  repens (Creeping H.) E.

Myrica carolinensis (Northern Bayberry) T.

Pachistima canbyi (Canby Pachistima) E.

Pachysandra terminalis (Japanese Pachysandra) E.

Philadelphus lemoinei (Lemoine Mockorange)
  microphyllus (Littleleaf M.) R.

Pieris floribunda (Mountain Andromeda) E.
  japonica (Japanese A.) E.

Potentilla fruticosa and varieties (Shrubby Cinquefoil)

Rhododendron smirnovi (Smirnow Rhododendron) E.

Rhus canadensis (Fragrant Sumac)
  cotinoides (American Smoketree)

Ribes alpinum (Mountain Currant) T.

Rosa spinosissima (Scotch Rose)
  multiflora (Japanese R.)

Salix adenophylla (Glandleaf Willow)
  gracilistyla (Longstyle W.)
  irrorata (Bluestem W.)

Spiraea arguta (Garland Spirea)
  bumalda var. Anthony Waterer (Anthony Waterer S.)
  bumalda var. *froebeli* (Froebel S.)
  thunbergi (Thunberg S.)
  tomentosa (Hardhack)

Stephanandra incisa (Cutleaf Stephanandra)

Symphoricarpos vulgaris (Coralberry)

Viburnum acerifolium (Mapleleaf Viburnum)
  opulus var. *nanum* (Dwarf Cranberrybush)

Zanthorhiza apiifolia (Yellowroot)

Zenobia pulverulenta (Dusty Zenobia) E.

TALL SHRUBS, OFTEN TREE-LIKE

Aralia spinosa (Devils-walkingstick)

Cercidiphyllum japonicum (Katsuratree)

Chionanthus virginica (White Fringetree)

Colutea arborescens (Bladder-senna)

Cornus alternifolia (Pagoda Dogwood)
  brachypoda (Shortstem D.)
  florida (Flowering D.)
  kousa (Kousa D.)
  mas (Cornelian-cherry)
  paniculata (Gray D.)

Elaeagnus angustifolia (Russian-olive)

Halesia tetraptera (Great Silverbell)

Malus various (Crabs)

Physocarpus opulifolius (Ninebark)

Rhus cotinus (Smoketree)

Tamarix various (Tamarisk)

Viburnum lentago (Nannyberry)
  prunifolium (Blackhaw)

LOW GROWING SHRUBS FOR ROCKERIES

Arctostaphylos uva-ursi (Bearberry)

Azalea canadensis (Rhodora)

Berberis thunbergi var. *minor* (Box Barberry)

Low Growing Shrubs for Rockeries—*Continued*

Berberis verruculosa (Warty B.)
   wilsonae (Wilson B.)
Buxus japonica (Japanese Box)
Chaenomeles japonica and var. (Flowering Quince)
Caragana chamlagu (Mongolian Pea-shrub)
Cotoneaster adpressa (Creeping C.)
   apiculata
   horizontalis (Rock C.)
Cytisus leucanthus (Pale Broom)
   glabrescens (Smooth B.)
   hirsutus (Hairy B.)
   nigricans (Spike B.)
   purpureus (Purple B.)
   supinus (Bigflower B.)
Daboecia cantabrica (Irish Heath)
Daphne cneorum (Rose Daphne)
   mezereum (February D.)
Erica, various (Heath)
Euonymus radicans (Wintercreeper)
Genista tinctoria (Woodwaxen)
Helianthemum chamaecistus (Sunrose)
Hypericum aureum (Golden St. Johnswort)
   calycinum (Aaronsbeard)
   patulum (Japanese H.)
Indigofera decora (Chinese I.)
   gerardiana (Himalayan Indigo)
Kalmia angustifolia (Lambkill)
Leiophyllum buxifolium (Box Sandmyrtle)
Leucothoe catesbaei (Drooping Leucothoe)
Lonicera nitida (Box Honeysuckle)
   pileata (Privet Honeysuckle)
   spinosa var. *alberti* (Albert H.)
   syringantha var. *wolfi* (Lilac H.)

Mahonia repens (Creeping Hollygrape)
Ononis frutescens (Restharrow)
Pachistima canbyi (Canby Pachistima)
Potentilla fruticosa (Shrubby Cinquefoil)
   tridentata (Wineleaf C.)
Zenobia pulverulenta (Dusty Zenobia)

The purple and white bells of the Irish Heath (Daboecia cantabrica) are especially at home in the acid spots of the rock garden.

HARDY SHRUBS FOR THE SHADE

Abelia grandiflora (Glossy Abelia)
Acanthopanax pentaphyllum (Fiveleaf Aralia)
Amelanchier various (Shadblow)
Aronia various (Chokeberry)
Azalea various (Azalea)
Benzoin aestivale (Spicebush)
Berberis thunbergi (Japanese Barberry)
Buxus japonica (Japanese Box)
  sempervirens (Common B.)
Calycanthus floridus (Sweetshrub)
Ceanothus americanus (Jersey-tea)
Cephalanthus occidentalis (Buttonbush)
Chionanthus virginica (White Fringetree)
Clethra alnifolia (Summersweet)
Cornus alba var. *sibirica* (Coral Dogwood)
  alternifolia (Pagoda D.)
  florida (Flowering D.)
  mas (Cornelian-cherry)
  paniculata (Gray Dogwood)
Corylopsis spicata (Spike Winterhazel)

Dirca palustris (Leatherwood)
Euonymus radicans varieties (Wintercreeper)

Forsythia various (Goldenbells)

Hamamelis virginiana (Witch-hazel)
Hydrangea arborescens grandiflora (Snowhill Hydrangea)
  paniculata (Peegee Hydrangea)
  quercifolia (Oakleaf H.)
Hypericum various (St. Johnswort)

Ilex crenata (Japanese Holly)
  glabra (Inkberry)
  verticillata (Winterberry)
Kalmia latifolia (Mountain-laurel)

Leucothoe catesbaei (Drooping Leucothoe)
Ligustrum various (Privets)
Lonicera morrowi (Morrow Honeysuckle)
  tatarica (Tatarian H.)
Mahonia aquifolium (Oregon Hollygrape)
Myrica carolinensis (Northern Bayberry)
  cerifera (Southern Waxmyrtle)
  gale (Sweetgale)

Pieris floribunda (Mountain Andromeda)
  japonica (Japanese A.)
Rhododendron various (Rhododendrons)
Rhodotypos kerrioides (Jetbead)
Rhus canadensis (Fragrant Sumac)
Ribes alpinum (Mountain Currant)
Rubus odoratus (Flowering Raspberry)
Sambucus racemosa (Red Elder)
Sorbaria sorbifolia (Ural False-spirea)
Stephanandra flexuosa (Cutleaf Stephanandra)
Symphoricarpos racemosus (Snowberry)
  vulgaris (Coralberry)
Viburnum acerifolium (Mapleleaf Viburnum)
  dentatum (Arrowwood)
  lentago (Nannyberry)
  prunifolium (Blackhaw)
  sieboldi (Siebold V.)

SHRUBS USED IN FLORIDA FOR SEMI-SHADE

Ardisia crenulata
Azalea indica (Indica Azalea)
Callicarpa americana (Beautyberry)
Camellia japonica (Camellia)
Ilex vomitoria (Yaupon)
Ligustrum lucidum and others (Wax Privet)
Malvaviscus conzetti (Turkscap)
Michelia fuscata (Banana-shrub)
Pittosporum tobira (Pittosporum)
Raphiolepis indica (India-hawthorn)

HARDY SEASHORE SHRUBS

Baccharis halimifolia (Groundselbush)
Cytisus scoparius (Scotch Broom)
Hippophae rhamnoides (Sea-buckthorn)
Hydrangea various (Hydrangea)
Itea virginica (Sweetspire)

Ligustrum ovalifolium (California Privet)
Myrica carolinensis (Northern Bayberry)
Prunus maritima (Beach Plum)
Rhus typhina (Staghorn Sumac)
Salix pentandra (Laurel Willow)
Tamarix various (Tamarisk)

SEASHORE SHRUBS FOR FLORIDA

Acacia, various (Wattle)
Baccharis halimifolia (Groundselshrub)
Callistemon, various (Bottlebrush)
Elaeagnus pungens (Thorny Elaeagnus)
Lagerstroemia indica (Crapemyrtle)
Ligustrum lucidum (Wax Privet)
Nerium oleander (Oleander)
Pittosporum tobira (Pittosporum)

HARDY SHRUBS FOR DRY PLACES

Acanthopanax pentaphylla (Fiveleaf Aralia)
Baccharis halimifolia (Groundselbush)
Berberis thunbergi (Japanese Barberry)
Caragana arborescens (Siberian Pea-tree)
Colutea arborescens (Bladder-senna)
Cornus paniculata (Panicle Dogwood)
Elaeagnus angustifolia (Russian-olive)
    longipes (Cherry Elaeagnus)
Helianthemum chamaecistus (Sunrose)
Lespedeza formosa (Purple Bushclover)
Ligustrum various (Privet)
Lonicera morrowi (Morrow Honeysuckle)
Potentilla fruticosa (Shrubby Cinquefoil)
Prunus pumila (Sand Cherry)
Rhamnus frangula (Glossy Buckthorn)

Rhodotypos kerrioides (Jetbead)
Rhus canadensis (Fragrant Sumac)
Symphoricarpos vulgaris (Coralberry)
Viburnum lantana (Wayfaring-tree)

SHRUBS FOR ADVERSE CITY CONDITIONS

Tolerating smoke and dust.

Acanthopanax pentaphyllum (Fiveleaf Aralia)
Amorpha fruticosa (Indigobush)
Aralia spinosa (Devils-walkingstick)
Berberis thunbergi (Japanese Barberry)
Colutea arborescens (Bladder-senna)
Cornus alba var. *sibirica* (Coral Dogwood)
Crataegus cordata (Washington Hawthorn)
Deutzia scabra (Fuzzy Deutzia)
Elaeagnus angustifolia (Russian-olive)
Exochorda grandiflora (Pearlbush)
Forsythia various (Goldenbells)
Hibiscus syriacus (Shrub-althea)
Ligustrum ibota (Ibota Privet)
  ovalifolium (California Privet)
Lonicera fragrantissima (Winter Honeysuckle)
Philadelphus various (Mockorange)
Physocarpus opulifolius (Ninebark)
Rhamnus frangula (Glossy Buckthorn)
Rhodotypos kerrioides (Jetbead)
Rhus cotinus (Smoketree)
Sambucus nigra (European Elder)
Spiraea vanhouttei (Vanhoutte Spirea)
Symphoricarpos various (Snowberry)
Syringa vulgaris (Lilac)
Tamarix various (Tamarisk)
Viburnum various (Viburnum)
Vitex agnus-castus (Lilac Chaste-tree)
Weigela hybrids (Weigela)

SHRUBS HARDY AT OTTAWA, CANADA

(This list is suggested by W. T. Macoun)

Those marked with a star (*) will give a selection of twelve shrubs which cover the season of bloom.

Amelanchier laevis (Shadblow)

Amorpha canescens (Leadplant)

Atraphaxis frutescens. Buckwheatlike pinkish flowers with persistent calyxes; flowering in Summer, but remaining attractive until Fall; low growth

Azalea viscosa

Berberis thunbergi (Japanese Barberry)

Caragana arborescens (Siberian Pea-tree)
  *frutex var. *grandiflora* (Russian Pea-shrub)
  pygmaea (Dwarf Pea-shrub)

Chaenomeles japonica (Flowering Quince)

Chionanthus virginica (White Fringetree)

Clethra alnifolia (Summersweet)

Cornus alba var. *sibirica* (Coral Dogwood).
  stolonifera var. *flaviramea* (Goldentwig D.)

Cytisus elongatus (Broom). Hardiest.
  hirsutus (Hairy B.)
  nigricans (Spike B.) Not quite as hardy as others.
  purgans (Provence B.)
  purpureus
  ratisbonensis
  versicolor

Daphne cneorum (Rose Daphne)
  mezereum (February D.)

Deutzia gracilis (Slender Deutzia). Not quite as hardy as next.
  lemoinei (Lemoine D.)

Forsythia intermedia (Border F.) Hardy when planted where they are out of the sweep of the wind.
  suspensa (Weeping F.)

Genista tinctoria (Woadwaxen)

Halesia carolina (Silverbell).

Halimodendron halodendron (Salt-tree)

*Hydrangea arborescens var. *grandiflora* (Snowhill H.)
* *paniculata* var. *grandiflora* (Peegee H.)

Lespedeza formosa (Purple Bushclover).

*Lonicera tatarica (Tatarian Honeysuckle).

Mahonia aquifolium (Oregon Hollygrape)

Philadelphus coronarius (Sweet Mockorange)
Physocarpus opulifolius (Ninebark)
Potentilla fruticosa (Shrubby Cinquefoil)
Prunus nana (Russian Almond)
  tomentosa (Nanking Cherry)
  triloba (Flowering Plum)
Rhododendrons not successful.
Ribes aureum (Slender Golden Currant)
Robinia hispida (Rose-acacia)
Rosa centifolia (Cabbage and Moss Roses)
  damascena (Damask Rose)
  foetida (Persian Yellow and Austrian Brier R.)
  harisoni (Harison Yellow R.)
  rubrifolia (Redleaf R.)
  rugosa (Rugosa R.)
  spinosissima (Scotch R.)
Sambucus canadensis (American Elder)
  nigra (European E.)
Sambucus racemosa (European Red E.)
Sorbaria sorbifolia (Ural False-spirea)
Spiraea alba (Meadow Spirea)
  arguta (Garland S.)
  billiardi (Billiard S.)
  latifolia (Pink Meadow S.)
  salicifolia (Willowleaf S.)
  vanhouttei (Vanhoutte S.)
Syringa chinensis (Chinese Lilac)
  japonica (Japanese Tree L.)
  pubescens (Hairy L.)
  villosa (Late L.)
  vulgaris (Common L.)
Tamarix pentandra (Fivestamen Tamarisk)
Viburnum cassinoides (Withe-rod)
  dentatum (Arrowwood)
  lantana (Wayfaring-tree)
  lentago (Nannyberry)
  opulus (European Cranberrybush)
  prunifolium (Blackhaw)
Weigela Eva Rathke

HARDY SHRUBS FOR WET PLACES

Alnus various (Alder)
Amelanchier canadensis (Downy Shadblow)
Aronia arbutifolia (Red Chokeberry)
Azalea viscosa (Swamp Azalea)
Benzoin aestivale (Spicebush)
Calycanthus floridus (Sweetshrub)
Cephalanthus occidentalis (Buttonbush)
Chamaedaphne calyculata (Leatherleaf)
Clethra alnifolia (Summersweet)
Cornus stolonifera (Red-osier Dogwood)
Hypericum densiflorum (Bushy St. Johnswort)
Ilex glabra (Inkberry)
    verticillata (Winterberry)
Itea virginica (Sweetspire)
Rosa palustris (Swamp Rose)
Salix various (Willow)
Sambucus canadensis (American Elder)
Spiraea tomentosa (Hardhack)
Vaccinium corymbosum (Highbush Blueberry)
Viburnum cassinoides (Withe-rod)
  dentatum (Arrowwood)
  lentago (Nannyberry)

FLORIDA SHRUBS FOR WET PLACES

Azalea austrina (Florida Flame Azalea)
Baccharis halimifolia (Groundselshrub)
Cephalanthus occidentalis (Buttonbush)
Ilex cassine (Dahoon)
Ilex glabra (Inkberry)
Ilex vomitoria (Yaupon)
Myrica cerifera (Southern Waxmyrtle)
Vaccinium virgatum (Rabbiteye Blueberry)

SHRUBS FOR STEEP BANKS

Acanthopanax pentaphyllum (Fiveleaf Aralia)
Berberis thunbergi (Japanese Barberry)

Comptonia asplenifolia (Sweetfern)
Lonicera japonica var. *halliana* (Hall Japanese Honeysuckle)
Rhus canadensis (Fragrant Sumac)
   copallina (Shining S.)
   glabra (Smooth S.)
   typhina (Staghorn S.)
Rosa, trailing sorts (Roses)
Spiraea tomentosa (Hardhack)
Symphoricarpos vulgaris (Coralberry)

THE BEST OF THE COLORED TWIG SHRUBS

GREEN

Acer pennsylvanicum (Striped Maple)
Cornus sanguinea var. *viridissima* (Green-twig Dogwood)
Cytisus scoparius (Scotch Broom)
Euonymus europaeus (European Burningbush)
Forsythia viridissima (Greenstem Goldenbells)
Itea virginica (Sweetspire)
Kerria japonica (Kerria)

RED

Cornus alba var. *sibirica* (Coral Dogwood)
   baileyi (Bailey D.)
   sanguinea (Bloodtwig D.)
   stolonifera (Red-osier D.)
Rosa rubrifolia (Redleaf Rose)
Salix vitellina var. *britzensis* (Bronze Golden Willow)
Tamarix parviflora (Tamarisk)

YELLOW

Cornus stolonifera var. *flaviramea* (Goldentwig Dogwood)
Forsythia suspensa var. *fortunei* (Fortune Goldenbells)
Salix vitellina (Golden Willow)

GRAY

Lonicera tatarica (Tatarian Honeysuckle)
Salix gracilistyla (Longstyle Willow)
   irrorata (Bluestem Willow)
Zenobia pulverulenta (Dusty Zenobia)

HARDY BROAD-LEAVED EVERGREENS

GROUND COVER

Arctostaphylos uva-ursi (Bearberry)
Calluna vulgaris (Heather)
Chimaphila maculata (Striped Pipsissewa)
   umbellata (Pipsissewa)
Cotoneaster microphylla (Rockspray)
Empetrum nigrum (Crowberry)
Erica carnea (Spring Heath)
Euonymus radicans (Wintercreeper)
   var. *acutus* (Sharpleaf W.), var. *colorata*, var. *minimus* (Baby W.),
   var. *vegetus* (Bigleaf W.)
Galax aphylla (Galax)
Gaultheria procumbens (Wintergreen)
Hedera helix (English Ivy)
Helianthemum chamaecistus (Sunrose)
Iberis gibraltarica (Gibraltar Candytuft)
   sempervirens (Evergreen C.)
Leiophyllum buxifolium (Box Sandmyrtle)
Lonicera pileata (Privet Honeysuckle)
   spinosa var. *alberti* (Albert H.)
Mahonia repens (Creeping Hollygrape)
Mitchella repens (Partridgeberry)
Pachysandra terminalis (Pachysandra)
Potentilla tridentata (Wineleaf Cinquefoil)
Thymus serpyllum (Mother-of-thyme)
Vinca minor (Periwinkle)

GROWING 1 FOOT TO 3 FEET TALL

Andromeda polifolia (Bog-rosemary)
Berberis julianae (Wintergreen Barberry)
   sargentiana (Sargent B.)
   wilsonae (Wilson B.)
Buxus sempervirens var. *suffruticosa* (Truedwarf Box)
Chamaedaphne calyculata (Leatherleaf)
Cotoneaster horizontalis (Rock Cotoneaster)
   apiculata
   rotundifolia (Roundleaf C.)
Daphne cneorum (Rose Daphne)
Ledum groenlandicum (True Labrador-tea)
Leucothoe catesbaei (Drooping Leucothoe)
Mahonia aquifolium (Oregon Hollygrape)

Growing 1 Foot to 3 Feet Tall—*Continued*

Mahonia bealei (*japonica*) (Leatherleaf H.)
Pieris floribunda (Mountain Andromeda)
   japonica (Japanese A.)

GROWING 3 FEET TO 6 FEET TALL

Abelia grandiflora (Glossy Abelia)
Buxus sempervirens and vars. (Box)
Elaeagnus pungens and vars. (Thorny Elaeagnus)
Euonymus patens (Spreading Enonymus)
   japonicus (Evergreen Burningbush)
   radicans var. *carrierei* (Glossy Wintercreeper)
Ilex crenata and vars. (Japanese Holly)
   glabra (Inkberry)
   opaca (American Holly)
Kalmia latifolia (Mountain-laurel)
Ligustrum japonicum (Japanese Privet)
   lucidum (Glossy P.)
Mahonia aquifolium (Oregon Hollygrape)
Pyracantha coccinea (Scarlet Firethorn)
Rhododendron various
Viburnum rhytidophyllum (Leatherleaf Viburnum)
Yucca filamentosa (Yucca)

The Mexican Flamebush (variously catalogued as Inga or Calliandra pulcherrima) is one of the rare shrubs for California. The flowers are brilliant pomponlike masses of scarlet stamens

SHRUBS TO ATTRACT THE BIRDS

*Attractive to birds as nesting sites. †Having fruit in Winter, furnishing food ‡Are both nesting sites and have fruit in Winter.

An excellent list of such shrubs and trees has been prepared by R. E. Horsey and W. L. G. Edson, of the Park System of Rochester, N. Y., and is published in Cornell Bulletin 361.   The list follows:

*Virginia Creeper (*Ampelopsis quinquefolia*).

Japanese Creeper (*Ampelopsis tricuspidata*).

Black Chokeberry (*Aronia melanocarpa*).

Red Chokeberry (*A. arbutifolia*).

Spicebush (*Benzoin aestivale*).

‡Japanese Barberry (*Berberis thunbergi*). The berries are not often eaten when other fruits are available, but the shrubs furnish good nesting sites.

‡European Barberry (*B. vulgaris*).

†Sweet Birch (*Betula lenta*).

†Yellow Birch (*B. lutea*).

River Birch (*B. nigra*). All the birches furnish food during Fall and Winter, except the river, or red, birch, the fruit of which ripens from June to September.

†European Weeping Birch (*B. alba* var. *pendula*).

†Canoe Birch (*B. papyrifera*).

Hackberry (*Celtis occidentalis*).

*Dogwood (*Cornus alba*, *C. alternifolia* and *C. rugosa*)

‡Flowering Dogwood (*Cornus florida*).

*Cornelian-cherry (*C. mas*).

‡American Hawthorn (*Crataegus coccinea* and others).

‡English Hawthorn (*C. oxyacantha*)

†Russian-olive (*Elaeagnus angustifolia*).

Cherry Elaeagnus (*E. longipes*).

Japanese Oleaster (*E. longipes* var. *ovata*). As soon as the fruit ripens in July it is attacked by robins, catbirds, and cedar waxwings, and the tree is soon stripped.

*Euonymus (*E. bungeana*, *E. europaea*). Fruits are eaten by the myrtle warbler.

Wintergreen (*Gaultheria procumbens*).

Black Huckleberry (*Gaylussacia baccata*).

†Shrubby St. Johnswort (*Hypericum prolificum*). In Winter, slate-colored juncos, tree sparrows, and redpolls are always found feeding on the minute seeds of this plant.

‡Common Juniper (*Juniperus communis*).

‡Irish Juniper (*J. communis* var. *hibernica*).

‡Redcedar (*J. virginiana*). A favorite food of cedar waxwings and myrtle warblers.

†American Larch (*Larix laricina*). European Larch (*L. europaea*).

‡European Privet (*Ligustrum vulgare*).

Belle Honeysuckles (*Lonicera bella*, hybrids between *L. morrowi* and *L. tatarica*).

Japanese Honeysuckle (*L. japonica*).

Morrow Honeysuckle (*L. morrowi*). Very attractive to birds.

Manchurian Honeysuckle (*L. ruprechtiana*).

*Tatarian Honeysuckle (*L. tatarica*).

*Matrimony-vine (*Lycium halimifolium*).

‡Flowering Crab (*Malus floribunda*). The best Winter food for cedar waxwings, robins, northern flickers, pheasants, and pine and evening grosbeaks.

Partridgeberry (*Mitchella repens*).

Mulberries (*Morus alba* and *M. rubra*). One of the best bird foods.

†Bayberry (*Myrica carolinensis*). The best food to attract and hold the myrtle warblers.

*Tupelo (*Nyssa sylvatica*).

*White Spruce (*Picea canadensis*), Black Spruce (*P. mariana*), Tigertail Spruce (*P. polita*).

‡Austrian Pine (*Pinus nigra*). White Pine (*P. strobus*), Red Pine (*P. resinosa*). All the Pines attract crossbills and grosbeaks.

Mahaleb Cherry (*Prunus mahaleb*). One of best wild-cherry bird foods.

European Bird Cherry (*P. padus*), Pin Cherry (*P. pennsylvanica*), Sand Cherry (*P. pumila*), Black Cherry (*P. serotina*).

‡Buckthorn (*Rhamnus cathartica*) Fragment Sumac (*Rhus canadensis*).

*Shining Sumac (*R. copallina*).

†Smooth Sumac (*R. glabra*).

†Staghorn Sumac (*R. typhina*).

Mountain Currant (*Ribes alpinum*). The most desirable of the currants.

Slender Golden Currant (*R. aureum*).

Allegheny Blackberry (*Rubus allegheniensis*), Blackcap (*R. occidentalis*). Flowering Raspberry (*R. odoratus*).

*American Elder (*Sambucus canadensis*).

European Red Elder (*S. racemosa*.) Best for bird food.

Sassafras (*Sassafras variifolium*).

Silver Buffaloberry (*Shepherdia argentea*).

Russet Buffaloberry (*S. canadensis*).

Greenbriar (*Smilax rotundifolia*).

Bitter Nightshade (*Solanum dulcamara*).

†Mountain-ash (*Sorbus americana* and *S. aucuparia*).

*Snowberry (*Symphoricarpos racemosus*).

*Coralberry (*S. vulgaris*).

Hemlock (*Tsuga canadensis*).

*American, English and Scotch Elms (*Ulmus americana*, *U. campestre*, and *U. glabra*). These trees furnish food for goldfinches and nesting sites for Baltimore orioles.

Blueberries (*Vaccinium corymbosum*).

*Viburnums (*Viburnum acerifolium*, *V. dentatum*, *V. lantana*, *V. lentago*, *V. prunifolium*, *V. pubescens*, *V. tomentosum*, and *V. venosum*).

European Cranberry (*Viburnum opulus*).

Grapes (*Vitis*).

†Weigela (*Weigela* or *Diervilla*). The seeds are freely eaten in Winter by slate-colored juncos, tree sparrows, redpolls, and pine siskins.

SHRUB BRANCHES FOR FORCING

The Missouri Botanical Garden Bulletin, vol. 14, 1926, discusses this subject rather fully:

"It is unfortunate that more people do not know the ease with which branches of Springflowering shrubs may be brought to bloom indoors during the Winter. During February and March, when anything green and growing is appreciated, they make interesting, and in some cases, very beautiful, decorations for the home.

"If the best results are to be obtained, certain simple precautions need to be followed. In the first place, the branches selected should be well supplied with flower buds. In most shrubs the flowers are produced only from certain specialized buds, and there is no general rule by which these may be told from the leaf buds. In some species the leaf buds are set between flower buds, while in others the reverse is the rule. Generally, the flower buds are larger and less closely appressed to the twigs. Sometimes, as in the Pear and Apple, they are borne on short, crooked side branches, called spurs by nurserymen. The form of the branches should be considered when selecting sprays for forcing. They will be bare, or practically so, for at least the first week, and the flowers, when they do appear, are usually smaller than those which open naturally out of doors. The branches may be of any size, however, from small twigs to six foot sprays.

"All that is needed to force the sprays is a jar of water, ordinary room temperature, and a little sunlight. Quicker results may usually be obtained if the entire branch is soaked in warm water for ten to fifteen minutes when first brought into the house.

"There are a large number of plants which can be brought to bloom indoors. Almost any of the Springflowering shrubs will produce a few leaves and a flower or two, and some bloom almost as well as they do out of doors. The Cornelian-cherry, *Cornus mas*, is one of the very best, as the flowers begin to appear almost at once and are fully open inside of a week. The Goldenbell, or Forsythia, is almost as desirable. The flowers are larger than those of the Cornelian-cherry, but they take longer to appear and wilt sooner. Other promising subjects are Pear, Crab Apple, Sycamore (with flowers like small fuzzy, green Lemons), Barberry, Silverbell and Japanese Quince. Strangely enough, there seems to be no absolute relation between the flowering time of the shrub and the ease with which it may be forced. The Fragrant Sumac (*Rhus canadensis*) and the Spicebush (*Benzoin aestivale*) are both among the very earliest of our flowering shrubs, but the Sumac blooms almost as soon outdoors as when forced inside, and the Spicebush is very slow to open its flowers.

"The branches may be brought into the house almost any time after the turn of the year, although it goes without saying that much better results are obtained by waiting until late February or early March." The following table summarizes the results of an experiment conducted by one of the pupils in the School for gardening. The branches were all cut during the third week in February and kept in a warm, light place:

Common name	Botanical name	Number of days required to force into flower	Number of days flowers remained in bloom
Goldenbells.............	*Forsythia* species......	9	7
Cornelian-cherry........	*Cornus mas*...........	8	10
Japanese Barberry.......	*Berberis thunbergi*......	12	12
Silverbell..............	*Halesia* species........	14	7
Japanese Quince.........	*Cydonia japonica*......	14	6
Bladder Nut............	*Staphylea trifolia*......	10	7
Winter Honeysuckle.....	*Lonicera fragrantissima*	3	3
Wild Plum.............	*Prunus americana*.....	14	3
Chionanthus...........	*Chionanthus virginica*..	16	7

SHRUBS FOR CUT FLOWERS

Buddleia (Butterflybush) July—September
Chaenomeles (Flowering Quince) April
Cornus mas (Cornelian-cherry) March
Deutzia (Deutzia) June
Forsythia (Goldenbells) April
Philadelphus (Mockorange) June
Physocarpus (Ninebark) June
Prunus (Peach, Plum) April, May
Salix caprea (Pussy Willow) March
Sorbaria (False-spirea) June—September
Spiraea (Spirea) May—September
Syringa (Lilac) June
Tamarix (Tamarisk) June, Summer
Weigela June

FOR FOLIAGE TO USE WITH CUT FLOWERS

Kerria japonica (Kerria)
Ligustrum various (Privets)
Physocarpus opulifolius (Ninebark)
Prunus pissardi (Purple-leaf Plum)
Spiraea thunbergi (Thunberg Spirea)
Tamarix various (Tamarisk)

IMPORTANT SHRUBS

In the following pages will be found notes on the species of shrubs and how they differ from one another. Each shrub here described has some merit.

*—The preferred method of propagation is marked with an asterisk (*).

N. M.—When facts are derived from L. H. Bailey's *Nursery Manual* they are so marked.

pH.—This expression under the discussion of soil indicates the preference for soil alkalinity or acidity as found in *Soil Reaction in Relation to Horticulture*, by Edgar T. Wherry, American Horticultural Society Bulletin 4, 1926. An explanation of these terms is found on page 20.

pH 4.0–5.0 mediacid
pH 5.0–6.0 subacid
pH 6.0–7.0 minimacid
pH 6.0–8.0 circumneutral
pH 7.0–8.0 minimalkaline

ABELIA—(Bush-arbutus)
(Named for Dr. Clark Abel, Physician and Author, resident in China)

The shining, evergreen foliage of the various Abelias is attractive and serves to endear this shrub to gardeners who live in regions with mild enough Winters.

Abelia grandiflora (rupestris) (A. chinensis x A. uniflora). This is the commonest species cultivated and comes from the hills of China and Japan and the uplands of India and Mexico. The plant grows to a height of 3 to 6 ft., is of graceful habit and bears blooms all Summer. It is hardy as far north as New York and in protected places, even farther north. The flowers are white, flushed pink, bell-shaped, borne in pairs in terminal clusters on small side branches. The season may be said to extend from June to November, inasmuch as the plants are in bloom all Summer until nipped by the frost. The leaves are quite evergreen, shining, 1¼ in. long, opposite, and finely toothed; they turn a bronzy tint in the Fall and Winter. The slender branches are hollow and more or less square.

Comparisons. *Abelia chinensis* is not evergreen, is not as hardy and has smaller leaves than the other sorts. In *A. floribunda,* the Mexican Abelia, the flowers are in the axils of the leaves and are rosy purple. It is not as hardy as *A. grandiflora* and may be used as a pot plant for greenhouse use.

Uses. Abelias are attractively used in combination with evergreens, both the conifers and the broad-leaved sorts, such as Androm-

The large flowered tender Abelia at the left is A. schumanni, a rosy pink adapted to California gardens. The smaller flowered sort, A. grandiflora, is a lovely horizontal branched shrub, excellent with evergreens, even in the North

edas. For the refined plantings at the foundations of a house, they may be mixed with the Japanese Holly, *Ilex crenata*. In mild climates they may be used as hedge plants. Samuel N. Baxter advises their use in front of Arborvitae as a foil for dogs.

SOIL. The Abelia prefers a light, peaty soil and delights in Summer heat which will mature the wood and result in greater hardiness. (Circumneutral. pH 6.0–8.0.)

PRUNING. In colder climates the pruning necessary each Spring will be quite a task, inasmuch as the younger twigs will all be frozen back. Vigorous pruning is advised to keep the bush shapely. This may be done in the Spring because the blooms are produced on new wood.

OBJECTIONS. The painstaking pruning necessary in cold climates is the only objection.

PROPAGATION. 1. *Softwood cuttings rooted under glass in October are advised by Oliver. Jos. Meehan propagated in the Summer. Cuttings about 4 in. long seem best. They must be kept in a greenhouse for the first Winter.

2. Hardwood cuttings may also be used, taken in October. No doubt, this is more satisfactory in the south, where wood is not likely to freeze.

3. Seedlings bloom when three years old. Sow in Spring.

4. Layers in Spring (N.M.), or planted in greenhouse benches and layered there. This takes great space.

ACANTHOPANAX (ARALIA)—(Fiveleaf Aralia) (Angelica-shrub)

This upright, graceful shrub has arching branches clothed with leaves even at the base. It is well used in the most adverse situations. The common species, *Acanthopanax pentaphyllum* (*sieboldianus*) is a native of Japan and is hardy throughout the greater part of the United States. The upright plants grow 4 to 6 ft. tall. The small heads of tiny white flowers seldom produce fruit. The branches are spiny; there are one to three straight prickles beneath each leaf. The leaves are dark and glossy and are compound into five to seven finger-like leaflets.

USES. The Fiveleaf Aralia tolerates dust and smoke and is very drought resistant. It is therefore a good shrub for large, smoky cities, and in shrub beds in Chicago and New York it may be noted in fresh, green appearance at a time when other sorts are shabby and half-dead looking. It will even tolerate shade. Insect pests do not attack it. It is advised for rocky slopes and for railroad embankments. Aralia hedges may be kept very upright.

Acanthopanax
pentaphylla

Soil.   Not particular; but rich, heavy soil results in better growth·

Pruning.   It may be pruned to the soil in Spring to renew the up-right branches when the position in which it is planted demands such a type of plant. With age some of the branches become rather zig-zag or curling, so that these may be pruned if desired.

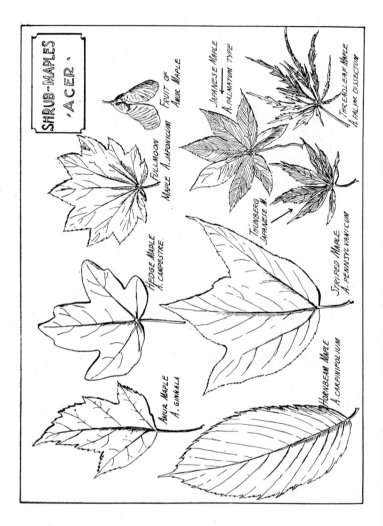

SHRUB-MAPLES 'ACER'

Fruit of Amur Maple

Japanese Maple A. Palmatum type

Threadleaf Maple A. Palm. Dissectum

Fullmoon Maple A. Japonicum

Thunberg Japanese M.

Hedge Maple A. Campestre.

Striped Maple A. Pennsylvanicum

Amur Maple A. Ginnala

Hornbeam Maple A. Carpinifolium

OBJECTIONS. Aralias are too stiffly upright for some uses; but when a shrub is as useful as this one, we must not make too many objections to it.

PROPAGATION. 1. *Root cuttings will be the simplest method of propagation. Take them 2 to 4 in. long and bury in flats of sandy soil in late Winter. Hardwood cuttings are made in September or October. The usual plants seen are female, there being few male plants in cultivation; hence no seed is produced.

2. *Softwood cuttings taken from forced plants in late Winter early Spring, or Summer.

3. The plants sucker freely.

ACER—Maple

Many Maples remain small and are considered to be shrubs. Among these are the Japanese Maples of all forms and colors. An interesting story explains why some leaves are green and others red. There grew in Japan a tree of marvelous beauty having red leaves. A poet passed and wrote so ecstatically of the tree that it never changed color again; it knows that the poet will not be there to admire it. All green-leaved sorts descended from that tree; the red sorts are constantly arraying themselves in the hope that a passing poet will do them justice in the poems of the future. The Maple is the Autumn welcoming tree and in Japanese gardens is planted to the west from which Autumn comes.

The Japanese Maples are derived from *Acer palmatum* (cataloged as *polymorphum*). The leaves are deeply five- to nine-lobed and in the varieties often deeply dissected and skeletonized. The colors vary from green to yellow and crimson and scarlet and variety names are given to them. The winged seeds are produced on rather mature trees.

Acer pennsylvanicum (*striatum*), the Striped Maple or Moosewood is also shrubby. It is a native with gray-striped, green bark on the young twigs. It will attain a height of 25 ft. The foliage is large and clean. The fruits are produced in pendulous racemes.

Acer ginnala, the Amur M., grows in bush form frequently. The leaves are three-lobed, rather small, with a longer central lobe. The flowers and winged fruits are produced in long-stemmed panicles. The wings of the fruit are quite parallel. It is valued for its neat, bushy habit, and because the leaves turn red. It is a substitute for Japanese Maples. It is frequently cataloged as a variety of *A. tataricum* and is then called the Siberian Maple. "On dry soils it is short lived, as it is susceptible to blight," says M. V. Horvath. This Maple produces seed so freely as to exhaust the tree.

Acer tataricum, the Tatarian M., is bushy, often 25 ft. tall, less lobed than the Amur M., and of greater beauty, because after the seeds are mature they have a salmon-pink color following which the leaves turn brilliant scarlet—so red in dry soils as to appear painted.

Acer campestre, Hedge or English Cork M., has corky bark and small, handsome, thick appearing leaves, the branches extending down to the soil. It makes a round headed tree and the leaves are distinctly blunt lobed. The foliage is brilliant yellow in Autumn.

USES. Japanese Maples are used as specimens in the sun although enduring considerable shade, and vary greatly in height and habit. The deeply cut-leaved sorts are apt to be very horizontal in their branching. In certain cities they are common but of late years the nurseries have not been able to supply material of any great size. The green-leaved sorts are fully as good as the red and purple varieties, inasmuch as they change color in the Fall and are not so gaudy in landscape combinations where they often prove a discordant note. They are not susceptible to injury from drought.

The Striped Maple is good for woods planting, although as a specimen it is attractive in leaf, also when in bloom and fruit, and through the Winter its green twigs are showy. When the Red- and Yellowtwig Dogwoods or Kerrias are planted with this they give a pleasing contrast in Winter.

The Amur Maple is excellent for specimens, as also for bold clumps, or it can be confined to a lower growth for hedge purposes.

The Hedge Maple, as its name implies, is excellent for hedges, as it stands pruning, grows slowly and is by nature compact. It is used for pleached allees in England. This Maple produces seed so freely as to exhaust the tree.

SOIL. Most species circumneutral pH 6.0–8.0, except *A. spicatum* and *A. pennsylvanicum*, both of which prefer a subacid (pH 5.0–6.0) soil.

HANDLING JAPANESE MAPLES. Young plants are very sensitive to cold. Sometimes they will go through the Winter uninjured but will be badly damaged by late frosts. They start growing early and complete growth early; consequently, a freeze often sets the plants back a year or it actually kills them.

They should be moved with ball-and-burlap, or, better yet, grown in pots as the nurseries are doing. They are potted in early Fall and stored in a coldhouse or coldframe until after late Spring freezes.

Plant them in sheltered places near trees at all times, inasmuch as a cold blast will freeze the young growth of old plants as well as the tiny plants. They are at home among evergreens or near the foundations of a house.

PROPAGATION. 1. *Seed*. Japanese Maples may be easily propagated from seed which must be soaked in hot water if it has been allowed to dry out. There is much difference in the speed of germination and the vigor and color of the seedlings. They require a three months' period of cool temperatures (32 to 50 deg.) after sowing; some will not germinate under six months.

Other Maples require immediate sowing after they ripen; others again may be stored. See discussion of after-ripening, page 50. *A. ginnala, A. campestre* and *A. pennsylvanicum* are also raised from seed.

2. *Grafting Japanese Maples*. J. W. Mallinson describes the method of grafting as follows:

"Actually the choice varieties are not difficult to propagate by grafting, while they can also be increased by layering. They are grafted on seedlings of *Acer polymorphum*. Two or three year old seedlings are used and should be well established in 2¼ in. Rose pots. These seedlings are easily raised or they can be bought. Occasionally seedlings can be collected under a large, old specimen in some old garden.

"There are two seasons for grafting: (1) In Spring grafting, the polymorphum seedlings are started into growth previous to grafting, in a moderate temperature. The cions are taken from outdoor plants, of course, when quite dormant. The grafting is usually done in February and March. The side graft is used and the cions are tied with unwaxed string. They are then laid in the grafting case and handled afterward exactly the same as grafted conifers.

"The grafts will unite in three to four weeks, after which they can then gradually have air for a few weeks. The seedling stock is gradually cut back as recommended for conifers. The young plants must be kept in the house or a frame until the middle of May and when planted out, should have good soil, preferably in a frame or a prepared bed under the sprinklers, and where it will be easy to protect them in Winter.

"(2) In August grafting, the side graft is also used, but at this date the cion has foliage. The cions need to be carefully selected at this time, more so than in Spring. They should be firm and well ripened, but not too hard and of the present season's growth. Considerable care is needed to see that the cions do not wilt in the least, or they will drop their foliage after they have been in the case a few days. They need careful shading when in the grafting case, but do not require bottom heat.

"The only really safe way to handle these August grafted Maples is to keep them in a cool house over Winter. They can be carried over in a concrete frame with sash and mats, but there will be some loss. Mice seem to be very fond of Maples in Winter and can do a lot of damage in a frame, so be on the safe side and find a place for the young plants in a cool house."

3. *Inarching*. Another method is advised by Marinus van Cleef who in Summer grafting chooses cions 8 to 10 in. long. The tops are

Inarching Japanese Maples

A, stock; B, stock with oblique cut and with bark cut from the flap; C, cion, prepared similar
to the stock; D, the inarch complete, the flaps fitted together so that the cambiums of
both stock and cion are in contact (note that lower end of cion is placed in bottle of water);
E, another view of the inarch

shortened a little. The cions should be quite mature. Then proceed as
follows:

(1). Make two downward cuts in the stock to form an inverted V.
Choose the smoothest spot about 6 in. above the soil.

(2). Cut the cions on two sides, 3 in. from the lower end. The cut
on cion is to be same length as that on stock.

(3) Fit the flaps together, and place the cion obliquely in order
that cambiums cross. The cions will be smaller in diameter so that this
is necessary.

(4) Tie with wool or cotton thread.

(5) Fasten a bottle to the stock or place it on the soil and fill with
water in which the lower end of the cion is placed. The water helps to
keep the cion from drying.

(6) When united, cut off end of cion that was in the bottle and the next Spring cut off the top of the stock just above the point of union, tying the plant to a short stake.

4. *Layering.* The branches near the soil can be layered. It takes two years to root.

AESCULUS (PAVIA)—Buckeye, Horsechestnut

The perfect hemispheres of growth made by this majestic shrub should commend it to wider usefulness but, except in certain sections, this shrub is rare.

Aesculus parviflora (*macrostachya*) (*Pavia alba*) Bottlebrush Buckeye. This large shrub attains a height of from 3 to 10 ft. but spreads

The Bottlebush Buckeye, Aesculus parviflora, makes a low, wide clump

by prostrate branches to form huge clumps, often 20 ft. across. It produces tiny white flowers in long candlelike clusters. The stamens are over twice as long as the petals and give the flowers a feathery appearance. The flowers blooming in July and August come at a season when they are most welcome. The leaves are grayish beneath and not unlike the Horsechestnut, being five- to seven-parted. The seeds are chestnut brown, borne in capsules several inches long. *Le Bon Jardinier* says the seeds are edible. Späth, the German nurseryman, lists a variety, *folius variegatus* or *neglecta erythrobiastos*, which has carmine-red young leaves.

Aesculus pavia (*Pavia rubra*) is the Red Buckeye which is often treelike, growing 4 to 20 ft. tall. The flowers are dark red or purplish, produced in loose clusters (panicles) 5 to 8 in. long.

Uses. The huge clump-forming character of this shrub suggests its use for specimen groups. It will not be useful for the ordinary shrub border. The late flowers give it special charm and merit, coming when other shrubs have finished blooming. It is desirable to have an evergreen background.

Soil. Rich, damp loam suits these plants best. *A. pavia* minimacid pH 6.0–7.0; others circumneutral pH 6.0–8.0.

Pruning. Little pruning will be necessary except to keep the plants in shape. They are sometimes inclined to make an unsymmetrical growth.

Objections. In certain locations the suckering habit might be a disadvantage; but they should be planted where they are allowed to spread at will.

Propagation. 1. *The branches naturally layer; this is the usual method of propagation, done either in Spring or Fall. When large clumps have been produced due to natural layers, they may be divided, the tops pruned back and planted in nursery rows.

2. *Root cuttings may be used.

3. Seeds are produced sparsely, but may be sown as soon as ripe or stratified until Spring.

ALNUS —Alder

A familar shrub of watersides and low places, the Alders are also useful and beautiful for cultivation.

The Hazel Alder, *Alnus rugosa*, is a tall shrub of coarse growth, growing 25 ft. tall. The leaves are smooth and green, often a little hairy on veins beneath. The flower of an Alder is a catkin which opens in late Winter, draping every branch with brown pendulous sprays. Because the leaves are quite serrulate margined, this species is often cataloged as *A. serrulata*.

The Speckled Alder, *Alnus incana*, has leaves which are doubly serrate, grayish and hairy beneath. The leaves are very variable in shape, some varieties being deeply lobed or even pinnatifid; there is a golden form and a pendulous one.

COMPARISONS. In Winter the Alder is distinguished by the catkins ready to open, the cones and the buds which are produced on short stalks. Witch-hazel is the only other common shrub with stalked buds.

USE. The Alders, as stated, are useful for wet places. The catkins and cones are ornamental in the Winter and early Spring.

SOIL. Circumneutral pH 6.0–8.0. It thrives in places that are flooded part of the year but tolerates ordinary soil.

PROPAGATION. 1. The dry seeds may be sown in Spring. 2. A number of horticultural varieties are on the market which are sometimes grafted upon seedlings of *A. glutinosa*.

AMELANCHIER—Shadblow—(Juneberry) (Shadbush) (Serviceberry) (Canadian Medlar) (Bilberry) (Sugarpear) (Maycherry) (Showy Mespilus)

With the first flowers of Spring in bloom, the Shadbush (*Amelanchier canadensis*) casts its sprays of whiteness above the surrounding shrubs and evergreens of the woods. The flowers are numerous, but the petals are narrow and the bloom appears rather wilted and nondescript. The flowers open before the leaves are fully expanded and are borne in nodding, dense, woolly racemes. The leaves are obovate, pointed at tip and heart-shaped at base. When young they are densely hairy beneath, less so above. The fruit is maroon-purple and quite tasteless.

A. laevis, the Allegheny Shadblow, is similar but the leaves are smooth, not hairy, the young ones being quite purple.

A. oblongifolia (*botryapium*) the Thicket S., as the name indicates, has quite oblong leaves, blunt at tip often. The racemes are erect, short, dense, silky, hairy. It differs from other species by its erect sepals upon the fruit, which is black and sweet. The plants are quite clumpy and often grow 20 ft. tall. These plants had good foliage and a greater profusion of fruit than other sorts during 1927 at the Arnold Arboretum.

A. alnifolia, called the Saskatoon, from which a city in Saskatchewan was named. This sort is low and shrubby and is reported to be a most excellent shrub for extreme northern regions. For its foliage, flowers and fruits and for hedge purposes, it is highly recommended by the Experiment Station at Alberta, Canada.

A. stolonifera, the Running S., grows upright, 3 to 8 ft. tall, very clumpy and suckering over a large area. It blooms a few days later than *A. laevis* and bears a tremendous crop of sweet, purplish black fruit.

Uses. The typical form of *A. canadensis* is horizontal branching, a form rare among plants. It is splendid for semi-wild places or in large plantings where it is conspicuous among the leafless trees.

The name Shadblow is given these shrubs because they are supposed to bloom when the shads leave the sea and come up the rivers.

A. stolonifera will bind loose, shifting sand.

The berries are delicious to eat, resembling Blueberries but inferior because of seeds and persistent calyx; they are good for jam. The wood is called "lancewood" and used for fish poles and umbrella handles. *The National Geographic Magazine* says:

"The Indians often made bows and arrows from it and it was in considerable demand for tool handles. The pemmican of the Indians was composed of deer or buffalo meat dried and pounded to a powder, to which was added dried Juneberries or Blueberries, the mixture being then stirred into boiling fat. When cooled, the mass was molded into cakes. When the Lewis and Clark expeditions made the first overland journey to the Pacific Ocean, their provisions ran short while in the region of the upper Missouri River, and it was one of the Amelanchier species, *alnifolia*, that came to their rescue with a bountiful supply of luscious berries."

Soil. They like limestone and grow wild in loamy leaf soil. Hicks advises *A. stolonifera* as a sand binder for shifting soils. Minimacid pH 6.0–7.0.

Transplanting. Remarking upon the transplanting of *A. alnifolia*, a writer from Canada says that pruning must be very severe; in fact, pieces of root strewn along a row grew better than shrubs having top growth.

Propagation. 1. *John Dunbar wrote, "Gather the fruit when ripe, in July, remove the pulp, and sow the seeds which are always kept moist. They germinate the following year. In three or four years they are ready for permanent planting."

2. *Root cuttings may be made in Fall and stored in sand for the Winter. See "Transplanting" above.

3. Layers are successful.

4. Most sorts may be divided.

5. Softwood cuttings, for some reason, root poorly.

AMORPHA—Indigobush (Bastard-indigo), False-indigo, Leadplant

(Name derived from *a*—without, *morphe*—form, refers to lack of form of flowers)

Amorpha fruticosa, the Indigobush, is wild along streams in the Mississippi Valley from Wisconsin to Florida. It is of a loose, upright habit and varies in height from 6 ft. to 18 ft. The flowers are very tiny, produced in July, in compact spikes 2 to 7 in. long. A dull purple in color, the numerous long, orange stamens set off the flower attractively. Surely, they are not showy flowers, but are interesting when seen close at hand. The foliage is Locust-like, pinnately compound, as the botanist would call it, and a trifle grayish-green. The twigs are slender and slightly angled beneath the nodes. The Winter buds are placed one above the other. The pods on first sight are not pealike, but such is truly the case, inasmuch as they open like pea pods. They are very tiny, hardly over $\frac{1}{4}$ in. long, and covered with resinous glands which cause them to give off a pleasant odor.

Amorpha canescens, the Leadplant, is of smaller growth than the former species, reaching a height of but 2 to 4 ft. It is a native of sandy knolls and gravel ridges and dry, sunny places in prairies, and sometimes does not take to cultivation except in favorable soils and situations. Like the girl in the nursery rhyme, when the plant is good "it is very, very good." The flowers are borne from June to July in long clusters (panicles) of bluish-purple and are densely produced at the tips of the branches. The foliage is very attractive, having a gray down; there are 14 to 24 pairs of leaflets which are so crowded they overlap.

Amorpha microphylla (*nana*), Dwarf Indigo, grows 18 in. tall and has rosier flowers and tinier, more graceful foliage than *A. fruticosa*.

Uses. A border shrub of considerable beauty, *Amorpha fruticosa*, is also useful for holding the soil of steep banks according to Mr. Jas. B. Allan, of the Cincinnati Park System. It should be used where other shrubs are planted in front of it. Late flowering is one of its merits.

The Leadplant may be used in the perennial border or rockery.

Soil. It would seem that the Indigobush is adaptable for many sorts of soils. Some report that it does well when its roots are in water; others have seen it succeeding equally well in sandy or chalky soil. Circumneutral pH 6.0–8.0.

Pruning. When grown in backgrounds, frequent pruning should not be necessary. Vigorous pruning results in a rather clubby growth and gives the plant a less natural looking character.

Objections. As indicated above, the plants are often bare at the base, ragged and stringy. They sucker somewhat. The flowers are not of sufficient attractiveness. The foliage is often affected by a leaf-tyer, against which spraying with arsenate of lead is necessary before the leaves are bound together. The leaves also tip burn.

PROPAGATION. 1. Suckers and layers may be utilized in a small way.

2. *Greenwood cuttings in Summer will root. Generally rooted under glass.

3. **Seeds grow readily and should be sown as soon as ripe.

4. Hardwood cuttings may be planted in the open, in a protected place, in Autumn and allowed to remain for a year (N.M.)

ANDRACHNE

A shrub seldom seen outside the botanical garden is *Andrachne phyllanthoides*. It is related to the popular Christmas Poinsettia and is found wild from Missouri to Arkansas and Texas. It is low growing, seldom over 3 ft. tall, and of an upright habit. It is hardy at the Arnold

Left, **Andromeda polifolia, the true Andromeda;** *right,* **Andrachne phyllanthoides, a dainty yellow-green leaved shrub**

Arboretum. The flowers are green, tiny and inconspicuous, borne in the axils of each leaf in late June. The light green oval leaves are seldom over ¾ in. long and are produced at various angles.

Uses. The plants serve as low growing shrubs which freeze to the soil during the colder Winters, but the light pea-green foliage would be attractive in the front line of the shrubbery border.

Pruning. No doubt, there will be dead tips to remove each Spring.

Propagation. Because of the great numbers of shoots coming from the soil, it would seem that division would be an ideal method of propagation.

ANDROMEDA—Bog-rosemary (Marsh-holyrose)

(Named for Andromeda, the daughter of Cepheus and Cassiope.)

These low growing filler shrubs for Rhododendron beds, are not in themselves showy, but they are very useful for the definite purpose of providing a natural appearance to a broad-leaved evergreen planting.

Growing over much of Northern Europe and Asia, as well as America, is a low spreading evergreen shrub, the Bog-rosemary (*Andromeda polifolia*), which produces many stems 6 in. to 18 in. tall and often few branched. The bell- or urn-shaped flowers are pale pink or white, and are produced from May until July. The leaves are narrow, 1 to 3 in. long, less than ¼ in. wide, dark green above and whitish beneath; though they are not truly white.

Andromeda glaucophylla (*canescens*) is similar to the above; the leaves are white beneath and rolled at the edges.

Among the acid soil plants many sorts are cataloged as Andromedas which are now called *Pieris* (See page 323), *Zenobia* (See page 407), *Lyonia* (See page 294), *Chamaedaphne* (See page 183), and *Leucothoe* (See page 283).

Uses. In the "*Tour of Lapland*" Linnæus, who named this plant Andromeda, writes, "This plant is always fixed in some turfy hillock in the midst of swamps, as Andromeda herself was chained to a rock in the sea which bathed her feet as the fresh water does the roots of this plant." From this it may be seen that the plants prefer shaded, wet conditions in a bog garden or peat bed. They may be used for beds of acid soil plants. The first species is more graceful; the second more interesting because of its whitish underside of leaves.

Soil.   Acid soils are necessary for their growth.   pH 4.0–5.0.   See page 20.

Propagation.   1. Seed may be sown as advised for Azalea, see page 150.   2. *Layers may be made in September but they are slow to root and must remain for a year. Peg the branches to the soil.

ARALIA—Devils-walkingstick (Hercules-club) (Angelica-tree) (Tearblanket) (Monkeytree)

The Devils-walkingstick (*Aralia spinosa*) is a treelike shrub bearing an umbrella-shaped crown of leaves and has stout prickly stems. In favored places it attains a height of 30 ft. It is found wild over a wide area of S. Pennsylvania, S. Indiana, E. Iowa to Florida and E. Texas. The flowers are white and very tiny, but are produced in large carrot-like heads (compound umbels forming a large, terminal panicle) often 2 ft. long and a foot across; these appear in August, and are very showy.   The leaves are often 20 to 40 in. long, cut into oval divisions 2 to 3 in. long.   The stout branches are spiny, especially at the nodes. The fruit is very showy, consisting of black berries produced on red stems. These berries ripen in September and for one month are eaten by the birds.

Comparisons.   The *A. chinensis* (Chinese Angelica-tree) has leaves which are made up of leaflets with very short or no stalks and the veins of the leaves end in the teeth. It is less prickly. *A. elata* (*mandshurica*) (*Dimorphanthus*) (*A. japonica*) has coarsely toothed leaves which are whitish beneath. The teeth of the leaves are far apart; in *A. chinensis* they are close together. The flower cluster has a short main axis, whereas in the other two species, the main axis is much elongated.

Uses.   Aralias will grow in the shade under trees which are not too dense. In too open situations, the heavy crown of leaves may cause the plants to break. The large mass of foliage, flowers or fruits makes this a most interesting background shrub which would be effective against a dark foliage background. Specimens are attractive but should be used only in larger plantings. Useful for Spanish architecture.

The juice of the fruit is said to be used as a black hair dye.

The large leaves, attractive flowers and fruit commend this shrub for limited use in large areas.

Soil.   They are not particular as to soil but are found wild in the moister places.   A rich, heavy soil adds to their luxuriant leafage. Minimacid pH 6.0–7.0.

OBJECTIONS. For many locations the spines would be objectionable, especially where children would play about them. Some gardeners rub off the spines. Do not give them too conspicuous a situation as they appear like dead stumps in Winter. They sucker very freely and soon produce large clumps. Suckers are encouraged by every injury to the roots. They are top-heavy.

PROPAGATION. 1. *By suckers is the natural method; therefore, root cuttings are most used. Pieces of the root 3 in. long are started in the Spring in sand or moss. 2. Seeds may be used for quantity production but usually it is too much trouble when roots are available. Sow seeds as soon as ripe or in Spring.

ARCTOSTAPHYLOS—Bearberry
(Name from *arktos*—bear, *staphyle*—berry. Bears eat the fruit)

A superb ground cover in sandy regions, the Bearberry (*Arctostaphylos uva-ursi*) has evergreen leaves 1 in. long which are thick and glossy and become bronzed in the Autumn. The plants are very hardy. The flowers are tiny, white or pinkish, and are produced sparingly. The red fruits are lustrous, ¼ in. in diameter. They persist through the Winter and are food for game birds.

COMPARISONS. Several other species are found, sometimes cultivated. *A. manzanita* is an upright shrub growing to 12 ft. in California and Oregon where it is native. It is evergreen and has white or light pink flowers in Spring. Also tall and shrubby is *A. tomentosa* which resembles the latter sort, but because of its hairy underside of the leaves is known as the Woolly Manzanita.

USES. For rocky slopes, the moraine areas of a rock garden, as undergrowth for Rhododendrons and as a general ground cover, the Bearberry is almost unexcelled. In the Northwest, the natives frequently used the leaves for kidney and bladder troubles and smoked them as a substitute for tobacco. The plants are at home along the seashore.

SOIL AND CULTURE. A sandy, very well drained soil seems almost a requisite for growth. At the Brooklyn Botanical Garden they were quite unable to grow Bearberries until Mr. Free excavated the beds and incorporated almost pure sand with the soil. It is generally thought that they resent lime in the soil.

They will require planting in the shade, unless covered with snow throughout the entire Winter, in which case they will grow nicely in the sun.

In transplanting, cut back the plants severely. Purchase pot grown plants from nurseries.

OBJECTIONS. Difficult to transplant. Particular as to soil.

PROPAGATION. 1. Cuttings may be taken in late Summer from rather mature wood. Bailey says to take cuttings in January. Insert them shallowly in sand in the greenhouse. Remove as few leaves as possible. 2. Layers take more than a year to root. 3. Seeds are rarely successful. 4. *Division of collected plants is the commonest method.

ARDISIA

(From the Greek *ardis*, a point, referring to the pointed anthers)

The Coral Ardisia, *Ardisia crenulata (crispa)* is a low shrub grown in Florida for its red berries. The flowers are white, not very showy. The leaves are thick, glossy, wavy margined. The red berries remain for a long time upon the plants.

PROPAGATION. 1. The propagation of Ardisia is usually by seed when grown in the South, but when Ardisias are grown as pot plants for florists' use they must be handled with extreme care in the Northern States. I quote from H. D. D. in the *Florists Exchange and Horticultural Trade World:*

"Select at Christmas as many plants as you think will produce the amount of seed you wish to sow; pick out the plants with the best berries, and allow the latter to get fully ripe; this will be in January. Wash the seed to get it free of pulp and sow in flats, using a good light soil; put the flats in a house at 60 degrees to 65 degrees. By May or early June they should have two or three leaves; put them in 1¾- or 2 in. pots and carry in a partially shaded house during Summer; by a partly shaded house I mean one with a strip of shading drawn down the glass, which allows plenty of light but breaks the force of the sun. They will probably need a shift to 3 in. pots by September. Keep during the Winter at 50 degrees to 60 degrees and by Spring you will have excellent stock in 3 in. pots. In May prepare a hotbed of manure in a deep frame. Try to have the manure turned once or twice so the heat will last as long as possible. Put 4 to 5 in. of good soil on top of the manure, as soon as the heat has subsided. When the thermometer drops to 80 degrees plant out the stock, cover with shaded sash, syringe often, to prevent them from getting dry, and watch the ventilation. Allow plenty of room in planting out, for they will grow fast and form the tiers that will produce the berries. By August or early September they will be fine stock, large enough to fill 5½ or 6 in. pots, and 12 to 18 in. tall, that is, of fruiting size.

"Now comes the critical time. Have prepared another lot of manure, for another hotbed, in a deep frame, with shaded sash. See that you have plenty of headroom above the manure. Put in 5 or 6 in. of saw dust, shavings or spent hops in which to plunge the stock. Lift and pot the plants and put back in the new hotbed, plunging the pots. Look after the syringing with care. They will root and be safe in about two weeks. Get them inside by October 1; any light house kept at 50° to 60° will do now. They will flower in March or early April. During the flowering period cut down on the syringing. Give what air you can to keep the atmosphere dry; it is a great assistance in setting the fruit. During the Summer keep in a partly shaded house with plenty of air. By September or October give full

The Ardisia, as grown by the florist, is a superior pot plant for Christmas

sun, but do not raise the temperature—50° to 55° will do. All fruiting plants, as Oranges, Ardisias, and Solanums, mature their fruit far better in a moderate temperature than in a high one, since heat induces growth. You will have no trouble about the fruit coloring; they will be right for Christmas and stock will sell well.

"You may feel that a second hotbed is not necessary, but it is; it is the making of the plant. If after potting you put the plants in a close, warm house they root slowly and drop many leaves, but the heat of the second hotbed starts root action quickly and establishes your plant. It is worth far more than it costs. If you wish smaller stock, plant out the smaller plants from the 1¾ in. or 2 in. pots and treat the same. In the Fall you will have nice stock with one tier of berries."

2. Cuttings. The cuttings taken in late Winter will root at 65° to 70° without trouble in about four weeks. Some growers prefer cuttings because the plants branch near the soil. Of course, only a limited stock could be grown by this method.

3. Air Layers. The tops of plants which have become leggy as a result of dropping their lower leaves, can be rooted by air layering. An incision is made in the stem at the point where the roots are wanted. A ball of moss is tied around the stem and if placed in a propagating case the new plants will root in about six weeks. The stub of the old plant will send out shoots which can be used as cuttings.

ARONIA—Chokeberry

Several of the Chokeberries are very valuable because of their attractive fruits which hang upon the plants for a long time.

Aronia arbutifolia. Red Chokeberry. (This shrub is often cataloged as *Pyrus* or *Sorbus*.) The plants are upright, generally not over 6 ft. tall. The flowers are white, pinkish tinted, produced in May in rather dense 9–24 flowered clusters (corymbs). The leaves are elliptical or oval, woolly beneath. They turn red in the Autumn. The twigs are brown, somewhat hairy. The fruits are red, ¼ in. across, and ripen in September. This is the most showy fruited sort.

Aronia melanocarpa (nigra) Black Chokeberry. The fruits of this sort are black and the leaves are smooth, not hairy beneath. The fruits do not remain on the plants as long as the red sort. Persons who mistake these fruits for Juneberries (Amelanchier) soon discover their error as Black Chokeberries are very astringent. The type of this species is low growing and suckers freely so as to serve as a filler shrub among others with bare stems. The variety *elata* is the sort usually sold as *A. melanocarpa.* It is taller and less suckering.

Left, **Aronia arbutifolia, beautiful in the Fall with brilliant red leaves and fruit;** *right,* **Amorpha canescens, with blue-gray foliage and bearing long spikes of purple flowers**

COMPARISONS. The variety Brilliantissima is an improved form of the Red Chokeberry with shinier red fruits. *A. atropurpurea (floribunda)*, the Purple C., has black fruits but hairy leaves. In this way it is intermediate between the two above named but it is not a hybrid.

USES. The foliage turns yellow and red so that the Aronias serve as attractive shrubs because of flower, fruit and foliage. The dense clean foliage is, furthermore, attractive all season through. Kelsey suggests their use in Rhododendron beds. As suggested above, *A. melanocarpa* in its low form is of value for an undershrub. The Chokeberries have a treelike form, even though they do not attain great heights. Good with berried shrubs, such as *Rosa setigera*, the Prairie Rose.

SOIL. Chokeberries prefer a moist soil, even wet, but succeed in ordinary soils as well. *A. melanocarpa* grows on rocky slopes. Subacid pH 5.0–6.0.

PROPAGATION.   1. *Stratify seeds in the Fall, removing the pulp first.

2. *Suckers.

3.   Layers

4. *Softwood cuttings under glass.

ASIMINA—Papaw

Conspicuous clumps of Papaws are seen when one travels the roads of Ohio, Indiana and in fact, most of the states south of New York. The leaves of *Asimina triloba* are 8 to 10 in. long. The twigs and, especially the buds, are red, hairy. The pith of the twigs is found to be made up of partitions close together. The large dull purple, six-petaled flowers nod from the branches in March and April and accompany the unfolding of the leaves. The fruits are 3 in. long, egg-shaped and are sweet and edible after the frost turns them black in October. This Papaw is the only hardy representative of a large tropical family of plants, the Custard-apple Family (Annonaceae).

USES.   Seldom cultivated but when so used it may be trained as a tree and grown for its curious early flowers and its fruit of unusual flavor. It thrives only by itself. Old plants are not attractive. The fruit may collect flies. Its only proper use is in natural landscapes.

SOIL.   The Papaws generally grow in rich, moist soil. They are difficult to transplant.

PROPAGATION.   1. *As the plants sucker freely, this would be a means of propagation. 2. Seeds grow freely in nature, but if raised from seed at home or in the nursery, one would infer that they should be stratified immediately and not allowed to dry out. 3. Root cuttings could also be resorted to. 4. Most plants are collected.

AUCUBA (Also spelled Aukuba) (Golddust-tree)
(Name latinized from its Japanese name *Aokiba*)

The Aucubas are evergreen shrubs grown in the Gulf States for foundation planting around homes. North of Washington, D. C. they are grown as tub plants and are frequently used for window boxes. In the Gulf States the plants grow from 4 to 14 ft. tall. The foliage is evergreen, opposite, coarsely toothed, and glossy. The leaves are blotched yellow; hence, the name Golddust-tree. The flowers are not showy, only one sex produced on a plant, so that the fruit is rarely set unless the female flowers are artificially pollinated.

CULTURE. *Aucuba japonica* prefers half shade either when used as a window box plant or when grown in the South. The soil should preferably be clay, moist but well drained. In the Northern States the plants are kept in cool greenhouses in the Winter. The fruits are scarlet.

PROPAGATION. 1. Seeds.

2. Varieties with the largest yellow spots are sometimes grafted.

AZALEA

A spectacular group of woody plants, the Azaleas are coming into more and more prominence as people learn how to grow them. The breathtaking color effects produced in gardens of the South has attracted great attention and whole communities, where the climate is favorable, are using Azaleas for color display in streets and parks. Such effects as those in the South are possible where temperatures do not go lower than zero, using Oriental species. Elsewhere, deciduous hardy Azaleas, mostly of American origin, and slightly less floriferous, must be used. These, however, can be highly effective, as has been demonstrated in several locations in the North, such as at Highland Park in Rochester, N. Y.*

Azaleas do best in the acid-soil regions of the East, South and West Coast, but are also quite adaptable for use in some of the Midwest states such as Ohio and in the Mississippi basin. Arid regions, or places with hot, dry winds are generally unfavorable unless highly artificial conditions are created. Generally, the conditions described as favorable for Rhododendrons are indicated also for Azaleas, although most Azaleas will tolerate a slightly less acid soil than true Rhododendrons. All are quite specific in their adaptation to definite climates, so it is important to choose those kinds that are adapted to the region in which you live. Also, periodic soil testing for acidity is desirable.

For the latest information on all phases of Azaleas, one should refer to *The Azalea Handbook*, published, 1952, by the American Horticultural Society, Washington, D. C.

---

*Clement Gray Bowers supplied this information on Azaleas. See also Rhododendrons, page 336.

Kinds. All Azaleas bear the generic name of *Rhododendron*, and constitute a subdivision of that genus now known as the Azalea Series. This, in turn, is divided into five sub-series, of which, however, only two (Obtusum and Luteum subseries) contain many species of horticultural significance. These sub-groups will be discussed separately:

1. The Obtusum Subseries (Asiatic). These are all of oriental origin and comprise the florists' Azaleas and their allies, including the so-called Indian Azaleas of Southern gardens, the dwarf, compact Kurume Azaleas (seen growing outdoors around Eastern cities) and the Torch (*kaempferi*) Azaleas which are hardy as far North as Boston and Rochester. There are innumerable other forms, including many from Japan, which hybridize so freely and are variable. The members of the Obtusum Subseries are unique in their ability to root easily from cuttings and hence are more readily available in the trade under individual names than are other members of the genus. This partially explains their popularity as compared with some other Azaleas which are meritorious but lesser-known because they are not so readily propagated. The racial and hybrid groups within the Obtusum Subseries may be classified and described with reference to their temperature-range and usefulness as follows:

(a) Obtusum Group (*R. obtusum*). This includes *R. obtusum* and its clone, *Amoenum*; also *R. kiusianum* and its clone Hinodegiri, which are hardy to slightly below zero; the Kurume Azaleas and their derivatives, which are variable but generally not hardy below zero; the Sander hybrids, which will endure 5 degs.; the Arnold hybrids, will withstand 10 degs.; and the forms and some hybrids of *R. kaempferi* (the Torch Azalea) which are deciduous in cold climates and will endure 15 degs. Hybrids of *R. kaempferi* are known by various racial names such as Chisholm, Sherwood, Deerfield, DeWilde, Mayo and Yerkes, representing groups produced by certain breeders. In general, *R. kaempferi* is the more useful species of this section for outdoor culture.

(b) Ryukyu Group. This includes *R. scabrum*, *R. macrosepalum* and *R. mucronatum* (*Azalea indica alba*), the latter being a very useful white species for climates about zero.

(c) Indian Azalea Group. Includes *R. simsi*, *R. indicum* and *R. phoeniceum* and hybrid races under the following names: Indian Hybrids, old-time and modern groups for the South; Belgian Hybrids, mostly greenhouse types; Rutherford Hybrids, greenhouse; Dawson Hybrids, to zero only; Pericat Hybrids, to –5 degs.; Gable Hybrids, to –10 degs., recommended for colder climates than others in this section; and other hybrid races generally not hardy below –5 degs., under names of Exbury, Bobbink & Atkins, Chugai, Wada, and Vuyk races; most recently a large and fine series of hybrids, probably variously hardy from zero to –10 degs., depending upon the individual clone, produced by B. Y. Morrison of the U. S. Department of Agriculture, and known as the Glenn Dale hybrids. There are over 100 named clones of the latter, some with excellent and very large flowers. Although bred for Washington, D. C., it is expected that certain variants will have a much wider range of adaptability when tested elsewhere. To date, the Glenn Dale Hybrids are probably the largest and best garden Azaleas of the whole Obtusum Subseries for the Middle Atlantic region. The Gable Azaleas are recommended for colder places, not exceeding –10 degs., and the Indian Azaleas are still good for the lower South.

(d) Korean Azalea Group. These comprise *R. poukhanense*. These are the hardiest of the section and will endure –20 degs. Their principal drawback is their lilac-purple color which looks dull beside the brighter hues. Yodagawa is a double form.

(e) Macrantha Azalea Group. These are hardy only to zero. They include *R. indicum* and the clones J. T. Lovett and Balsaminaeflorum. *R. eriocarpum* clone Gumpo is also included.

2. THE LUTUEM SUBSERIES (MOSTLY AMERICAN). These are all deciduous Azaleas, in a wide color range including yellows and reds, and many are adapted to sub-zero climates. Two species, comprising the Mollis Group, are from Asia, and one, *R. flavum* (*luteum*), the Pontic Azalea, is from the Black Sea region; otherwise, the members of this subseries are all of American origin. They are less easily propagated from cuttings than are the Obtusums, but grow readily from seeds and superior clones may be increased by layering. Grafted plants appear less hardy than own-root plants. Certain species native to the Lower South are adapted to that region, but the species and hybrids generally in this group prefer Northern or Mountain climates. Certain species and hybrids are delightfully fragrant, especially *R. roseum*, *R. viscosum* and *R. arborescens*. These plants offer opportunities, yet largely unrealized, for highly colorful effects outdoors in the North, although it cannot be said that they are quite so floriferous as the best Obtusums. Their color range goes from white, through pink, rose and purplish red, to vermilion, scarlet, orange, salmon, bright yellow and cream, with all intermediate shades. Some have two-color effects, with a bright yellow blotch on the upper lobe. Although they shed their leaves in Autumn, their branching habit is

interesting in Winter. They can be combined with evergreen species, including true Rhododendrons, in mixed plantings. In size they vary from the dwarfish *R. atlanticum* to shrubs of 10 or 15 feet. Their principal hybrid and racial groups are as follows:

(a) Austrinum-Prunifolium Group. Mostly yellow, orange or vermilion flowers. Includes *R. austrinum* and *R. prunifolium*, both Southern species, the latter blooming in July. *R. flavum* (the Pontic Azalea) is hardy on Long Island, but has no special advantage over *R. calendulaceum* in its yellow form. *R. cumberlandense* and some of its variants, have tight, Rhododendron-like trusses of orange to red flowers which at high altitudes may be blood-red and bloom later in the season than most (June 20th). *R. calendulaceum* is unexcelled as a hardy yellow and orange Azalea. It is quite variable in nature. Collected plants, in selected shades and patterns, are very satisfactory, and seedlings are good. It will endure temperatures to –20 degs., but does not do well at low altitudes in the South.

(b) Alabamense-Atlanticum Group. Low-growing Azaleas with spreading, underground stems and mildly fragrant flowers. *R. alabamense* is from Northern Alabama hills. *R. atlanticum* is an excellent dwarfish species from Southern Pennsylvania to the Carolinas along the Coastal Plain, hardy to sub-zero (–20 degs.) in its northern range. Both species come in light pink to white, sometimes yellow-blotched. The white form of *R. atlanticum* is highly recommended.

(c) Roseum-Nudiflorum Group. These are the common Pinxters of the North, plus others, including a form from Florida (*R. canescens*). *R. nudiflorum* is inferior as a garden plant to *R. roseum* which has a clearer rose-colored flower and a delightful spicy scent. The inland plants, from the highlands of New England, New York, Pennsylvania and the Blue Ridge are the best and are reliably hardy. This species is more tolerant of alkalinity than is *R. calendulaceum* and will endure very severe Winter weather. Plants growing in the woods are sometimes scrawny, but when cut back and given good light and soil they will bloom better. Superior individuals will become very floriferous and quite showy, but tend to be biennial bloomers unless flowers are removed immediately after blooming. *R. roseum* ranks at the top of rose-colored deciduous species. Plants usually grow to less than 6 feet. *R. canescens* is of little value in the North, and is recommended only for the Lower South. Included also is *R. occidentale*, a very superior species from the West Coast, yellow-blotched on a creamy white or bronzed pink flower, is not hardy in the Northeast, but is valuable elsewhere and is a parent of fine hybrids. Another species is *R. oblongifolium*, a white form from Eastern Texas.

(d) Arborescens-Serrulatum Group. These are late-blooming whites. *R. arborescens*, from the mid-Atlantic States, is a tallish shrub, white or pinkish, with red styles; is variable but in superior individuals is our best deciduous hardy white. Its flowers are delightfully heliotrope-scented, blooming in mid-June. Hardy to –20 degs. or colder. *R. viscosum* is smaller, pure white and blooming July 1 or later. It is entirely hardy in coldest gardens and has a lovely clove-like scent. Its Southern counterpart is *R. serrulatum*, from Georgia and Florida, recommended only for the Lower South.

(e) Molle-Japonicum Group. It is almost impossible to distinguish *R. molle* from *R. japonicum*, and the two are perhaps geographical forms of the same basic kind. Their flowers are broader and more open than those of the other groups, sometimes nearly 3 inches in diameter, and are quite distinct. They are quite variable in color, but *R. molle*, from China, is typically yellowish and less hardy, while *R. japonicum*, from Japan, is considered more hardy and is frequently a coral-rose in color. Neither is fragrant. They resent dryness in Spring and Summer, and, unless maintained in vigorous growth, are apt to be short-lived, although the hardier forms, when growing well on their own roots, will endure severe Winter temperatures of –20 degs. or so.

(f) The Ghent Hybrid Group. This is a complex mixture of many of the American species, plus more or less of the European *R. luteum*, and is highly variable. The color range is tremendous and the best forms are magnificent, but are not always available on the market because of propagation limitations. Flowers may be either single or double. It is advisable to buy own-root plants rather than those grafted. The Knaphill strain and Slocock's Goldsworth strain of Knaphill Ghent hybrids are gorgeous English forms whose hardiness is not entirely determined. There are many named kinds, and they vary considerably in hardiness. In the Northeast, Ghent Hybrids are more durable than Mollis hybrids.

(g) The Mollis Hybrid Group. These are hybrids of the Molle-Japonicum group, crossed with Ghent Hybrids, both single and double. The flowers and plants tend to be larger in size but are less enduring and do not quite possess the wide color range of the Ghents.

3. THE SCHLIPPENBACHI SUBSERIES. These are Asiatic deciduous Azaleas, with their leaves generally in whorls. The principal species is *R. schlippenbachi* (the Royal Azalea) from Korea; a large, light pink flower on a tall, good-sized plant which is hardy, but sometimes fastidious when young. It is rated high where it grows well. Less important are *R. weyrichi* and *R. reticulatum*.

**Azalea Hinodegiri
is in the Obtusum group**

4. THE CANADENSE SUBSERIES. This section contains three very excellent species: *R. canadense*, the Rhodora, is a low-growing plant with grayish foliage and lilac-colored flowers, blooming early. It is hardy to –30 degs. or colder and is excellent for the Northeast. *R. vaseyi* is a large shrub and rapid-growing. It comes from below the Blue Ridge but will endure almost any amount of Winter cold. It gets to be a tall shrub, blooming before midseason and has distinctive flowers of Apple-blossom pink. Because of its vigor and general appearance, this is one of the best Azaleas for cold regions. A pure white form is very fine. The above are American species. A Japanese relative is *R. pentaphyllum*, a large, early-blooming plant with flowers of bright magenta, but which is not hardy North of Long Island, or in sub-zero weather.

The fifth Subseries is omitted here. Mention should be made, however, of *R. mucronulatum*, a deciduous Rhododendron which resembles an Azalea and is used as such. This is a medium shrub, reliably hardy at sub-zero temperatures and blooming very early in Spring with dull magenta-lilac flowers. Where late Spring frosts prevail, the flowers are in danger of injury because of their early development.

PROPAGATION. This is mainly for the commercial growers with greenhouse facilities. Only the members of the Obtusum Subseries root readily from cuttings, and layerage, rather than grafting, is recommended for the deciduous sorts. Seeds of the Ghent hybrids and *R. calendulaceum* will produce offspring of great variability but great beauty, so this method is feasible where clonal varieties are not required.

SOIL AND CULTURE. Azaleas require acid soil and the peaty mixtures recommended for Rhododendrons are equally applicable here. They respond to fertilizers and are less subject to Winter injury if kept in robust Summer growth until late July. Fertilizers should be applied before June and not repeated. Water during the growing season is a critical factor, but do not use "hard" water; mulches are definitely advised. Total shade results is spindly growth and sparse bloom. Azaleas are useful for many kinds of formal effects in addition to naturalistic planting. When buying plants, be sure that the varieties advertised as "hardy" are hardy in *your* locality. Site and exposure makes considerable difference. South of Philadelphia, Azaleas do best when planted in "high shade," such as in an Oak grove. In the North, however, they will endure more sunlight and often require it in order to bloom abundantly. Generally, the directions for growing Rhododendrons apply equally to Azaleas. (See page 340.)

BACCHARIS—Groundselbush (Saltbush) (Sea-purslane) (Ploughmans-spikenard)

(Name derived from Bacchus—wine, referring to the spicy odor of the roots)

From Massachusetts to Georgia, near the sea, there grows the only hardy shrubby member of the Daisy Family, *Baccharis halimifolia*, the Groundselbush, generally but 4 ft. tall but sometimes attaining twice that height. The leaves are notched and somewhat covered with a resinous white powder. The branches are angular. The flowers are insignificant, white, and are produced in clusters (panicles) during August and September. They are followed by fluffy, often ornamental, white seed heads which last until October. Rehder points out that these shrubs are either male or female plants, so that for good seed display both sorts of plants are necessary.

USES. They serve as ideal seaside shrubs and even tolerate salt spray. Low hedges may be made. The Fall display of plumy seed heads gives contrast to the shrub border.

SOIL. *Le Bon Jardinier* says a warm, sheltered situation suits the Baccharis best. It is generally believed that although they are seashore shrubs, they desire good drainage and the light soil characteristic of such places. Minimalkaline pH 7.0–8.0.

PRUNING. Cut back the plants severely each Spring as the strong shoots from the base are more attractive in foliage and flower.

OBJECTIONS. The fact that male plants produce no seed head display is regrettable. The flowers themselves are never showy. The foliage does not harmonize with other shrubs and is only good in clumps by itself.

PROPAGATION. 1. Layers may be made in Spring. 2. Softwood cuttings root under glass taken from forced plants. 3. Seeds are also sown after the soil is warm in the Spring.

BENZOIN (LINDERA)—Spicebush (Wild-allspice) (Benjaminbush) (Feverbush)

When the nature lover believes that Spring is approaching, he goes to his favorite haunt in the woods and there finds the Spicebush covered, generally in March, with greenish yellow tiny blooms produced three to six in a cluster, upon the leafless shrubs.

Spicebush, *Benzoin aestivale* (*odoriferum*) has alternate, oval or almost round leaves which are spicy when crushed. The branches are green, even in Winter, and are pleasant in flavor. The Winter buds are produced one above the other. The fruits ripen in October and are about ½ in. long, red in color and very strong in flavor. The plants often attain a height of 15 ft. although more commonly they are only as tall as a man.

Uses. It is thus seen that the Spicebush practically opens and closes the season of shrub attractiveness. Added to the flower and fruit display, the leaves turn a golden yellow in early Fall. The shrubs are usually considered when swamp material is needed for large plantings.

Benzoin or Spicebush
The foliage and twigs are aromatic. Good for damp, shaded places

When the cut branches of bloom are used indoors, they give a spicy fragrance to the air. Dried and powdered berries are said to have been used as a substitute for Allspice during the Revolutionary War and the leaves for tea during the Civil War. Dr. Showalter says that an Asiatic species is prized for making toothpicks because of its aromatic fragrance, also that a new perfume, *Kuromoji*, is made from the oil.

Soil. As indicated above, the Benzoin is a native of wet places, but it will thrive in ordinary garden soil and in the shade. It grows well in peaty or sandy soil. Subacid pH 5.0–6.0.

PROPAGATION. 1. *Sow seeds as soon as ripe as they soon deteriorate in quality. Use peaty soil. Remove the pulp.

2. Suckers.

3. Cuttings are considered difficult.

4. Collected plants are usually sold.

BERBERIS—Barberry

There is an extremely large number of handsome Barberries which are gradually becoming known to gardens. Some of them, being evergreen, should be better known, although they are not of the hardiest.

Perhaps no shrub is as universally useful as the Japanese Barberry, *Berberis thunbergi (sinensis) (japonica)*. It is generally considered a low shrub but will attain a height of 6 ft. in many gardens. The flowers are

The natural growth of Berberis thunbergi makes this shrub a desirable lawn specimen

yellow, a trifle tinged with red on the outside, produced solitary or two to five flowers together. The foliage is without teeth and oval, but quite variable in form. It turns a glorious red in the Autumn. The twigs are reddish, brownish or purplish and have spines which are simple; that is, they are not branched. The bright red oval fruit is attractive, even until Spring, persisting as it does upon the plants all through the Autumn and Winter. Numerous varieties are being cultivated, among which are:

Var. *minor*. Box Barberry. Smaller in growth and leaf. Because of its slow growth it may be kept to a low height, but for very small hedges, 5 to 6 in. tall, it is not as useful as was at first thought because it requires too frequent and painstaking pruning. It does, however, fill a long felt need for a low hedge. Many purchasers of this shrub have been disappointed in it for the name Box Barberry suggested in their minds that the hedge would be evergreen which, of course, is not the case.

Var. *atropurpurea*. Purple-leaf Japanese B. This plant resembles the typical Japanese Barberry, but the leaves are deep red or purple and seem to be more lustrous. When grown in the shade, this plant does not retain its desirable red color but becomes green. As the color is not too intense, it is a desirable addition to the shrub border.

Var. *maximowiczi*. Coral B. Has small leaves and the same desirable growth as the type. It is rare in nursery catalogs but would be a worth while addition to the list of foundation planting shrubs.

Var. *plurifolia erecta*. Upright Japanese B. M. V. Horvath has produced a type of Japanese Barberry with perfectly erect branches. It should serve as an ideal hedge which would never require much clipping at the sides. It was selected through five generations of seed production from an especially upright plant of var. *plurifolia*, which has clustered leaves. It is now sold as the Truehedge Columnberry.

The Common Barberry, *B. vulgaris*, has had a bad name at present in the wheat growing sections of the country, inasmuch as it is supposed to carry wheat rust. It is a European shrub which has escaped from cultivation and is frequently naturalized in the Eastern States. It is a handsome shrub in foliage, flower and fruit. The flowers and fruits are borne in long pendulous clusters. It is distinguished from the Japanese B. in that way as well as by the fact that the spines are three-parted and the leaves finely toothed.

Var. *atropurpurea*. Purple B. Has purple leaves which are enhanced in depth of color by vigorous pruning of the bush. There are also yellow, white and violet fruited sorts, as well as those with white and yellow variegated leaves.

Berberis thunbergi—Japanese Barberry
One of the best shrubs for informal hedges. Beautiful in Fall with red foliage and berries.
At the back is seen the Vanhoutte Spirea

Berberis canadensis, the Allegheny B., is more profuse fruiting and superior to *B. vulgaris*, but not as well known.

Berberis sargentiana, the Sargent Barberry, is one of the handsome evergreen sorts from Western China. It grows to a height of 6 ft. and although it is not perfectly hardy, it will thrive in protected places at Highland Park, Rochester. The leaves are rather oblong, closely spiny toothed, leathery, dark green above and lighter green beneath. The branches are covered with extremely long, three-parted light colored spines.

Berberis vernae has small leaves and salmon-red fruit

Berberis julianae, the Wintergreen B., is named for Queen Juliana of the Netherlands and is another evergreen sort differing from *B. sargentiana* in that the branchlets are slightly angled and yellowish brown when young, whereas the branchlets of *B. sargentiana* are quite round and reddish when young and the leaves are veiny beneath and generally larger and lighter green.

A third evergreen Barberry which is quite hardy is *B. verruculosa*, the Warty B., a very dense, low spreading sort with very shining leaves, seldom over ½ in. to 1 in. long, dark green above but quite whitish beneath. The teeth are far apart and the margins of the leaf are rolled. The new growth is red. At Highland Park the plants are 2 ft. tall and will apparently grow but little taller.

Smith, superintendent of the Arnold Arboretum, recommends *Berberis vernae*, a Barberry with small, narrow leaves very unequal in size, some being only ½ in. long, others as much as 2 in., very veiny in appearance. The slender branches of this shrub give it a most graceful appearance and when it is in fruit, it is truly one of the best of the Barberries. The fruits are salmon-red.

For rockeries or where a very slow growing plant is desired the Wilson Barberry (*B. wilsonae*) is very beautiful. It is often of prostrate growth; at least the shrub is very spreading. The leaves are small, pale green and dull above but white beneath. The leaves become brilliant in the Fall. The branches are angled, very spiny, with three-parted slender prickles. The fruits are salmon-red and Waterer suggests that the numerous spines protect the fruit from the birds. The tips are often winterkilled at Rochester, but this is not a serious matter. At Mentor, Ohio, it freezes out completely.

Resembling this is *B. aggregata*, the Salmon Barberry, which has angled twigs with grayish-brown, old bark. The leaves are obovate, sharp, often spiny toothed, grayish beneath. The fruits are coral colored in dense clusters. It is inclined to flower on new wood. It is hardier than *B. wilsonae*.

TENDER BARBERRIES

Berberis darwini, the Darwin Barberry, is an evergreen which grows 10 ft. tall. The branches are beset with long, 3-7 pointed spines. The hollylike leaves are usually 1 in. long and spiny toothed, paler beneath. The long drooping racemes of flowers which appear in June are 4 in. long. The fruit is dark purple.

Berberis buxifolia (*dulcis*), the Magellan Barberry, is an evergreen with leaves less than an inch long. They are not spiny toothed. The flowers are orange yellow, solitary and open in May. The fruits are dark purple, globular. Var. *nana compacta* is dwarfer and more compact.

HYBRIDS. The prevalence of wheat rust upon the Common Barberry having prohibited its use in wheat producing states, hybridists have turned to produce a substitute for these glorious tall plants. M. V. Horvath has now produced hybrids between *B.thunbergi* and *B.julianae B. sieboldi, B. sargentiana* and *B. macracantha*. It is hoped that they are immune to wheat rust and will add variety to our plantings. Some are found to be perfectly hardy in private estates near Cleveland, O.

USES. It is my contention that the Japanese Barberry is the most useful of all the shrubs.

1. It has a graceful, rounded form.

2. It has attractive, small leaves which merge into the grass.

3. In Autumn the leaves turn to tints of red and yellow.

4. The fruits are abundant, beautiful and hang for a longer time than most others.

5. It makes a formidable hedge but not cruel.

6. Not seriously affected by any insects.

7. Grows indifferent to soil or exposure, being even decent in some shade.

8. Excellent single specimen.

9. Can be kept as low as desired or it can be allowed to become tall.

10. Can be trained to resemble a formal Boxwood where the latter is not hardy or allowed to produce its graceful and informal branches.

11. Samuel N. Baxter suggests its use as a foil for dogs to be planted in front of conifers. Take care that it does not encroach upon the slower growing evergreens.

12. Rarely looses its lower branches.

13. Useful for cut branches of leaves, flowers or fruits.

14. As cheap as California Privet when it is considered that it can be planted as far apart as 24 in.

15. Does not demand the constant shearing that most hedges do.

As a contrast in beds of conifers the evergreen Barberries, such as *B. sargentiana, B. julianae*, and *B. verruculosa*, are most attractive. For contrast in foliage color, the newer sort, the Purple-leaf Japanese Barberry, will be found useful for sunny places.

SOIL. Circumneutral 6.0–8.0.

PRUNING. Barberries may be sheared to formal shapes, or by merely pruning off the most forward branches, they can be trained to most graceful form. With age it is often necessary to remove some of the old branches by reaching into the clump with a pruning shears.

OBJECTIONS. The Common Barberry, as before mentioned, should not be planted in wheat-growing sections because it harbors aecidium stage of the wheat rust.

PROPAGATION. 1. *Seeds should be cleaned of the pulp and sown in rows out of doors in the Fall or else sown in flats and allowed to remain cool, or even freeze, during the Winter. It prefers a fluctuating temperature for germination. Mulch with leaves through the Winter. The rarer sorts may be sown in the greenhouse. Seedlings prefer partial shade.

2. Cuttings of desirable types of Japanese Barberry will inherit their habit of growth, color of foliage and often the profusion of fruiting. Parker Leonard inserts cuttings in a frame in September and leaves them over Winter. Cuttings are, of course, very thorny and difficult to handle and are not used for quantity production. Box Barberry may be raised from either hard or softwood cuttings. It is not necessary to strip the leaves.

3. Some of the unusual species are grafted upon *B. vulgaris* or *B. thunbergi*. This is done in the greenhouse in August or under glass in the Spring. Such plants frequently sucker badly.

BUDDLEIA—Butterflybush

(Named for A. Buddle, an English botanist)

Among the beautiful Chinese shrubs now growing in our gardens, Buddleias are perhaps as widely used as any others, especially the Orange-eye Butterflybush, *Buddleia davidi (variabilis)*. The plants are compact in growth, often as tall as 8 ft. The wood is not very hardy so that in most northern gardens the plants almost die to the soil each year. The flowers are lilac and have an orange-yellow throat; they are produced in terminal clusters (panicles) 6 to 12 in. long. Such a profusion of these fragrant flowers is produced that it is doubtful whether any other shrub blooms so abundantly and over so long a period, the season of bloom extending as it does from July until late Autumn. The leaves are long and rather narrow, closely toothed and gray beneath. The twigs are apt to be four-ridged and somewhat hairy.

There are a number of varieties of *B. davidi* which are quite similar.

Var. *magnifica* is generally considered the best of all. The panicles are dense, the flowers are large, violet-purple with a deep orange eye and the margins of the petals are somewhat rolled.

Var. *superba* is similar to the first but with larger panicles and the margins of the petals are not rolled.

Var. *veitchiana* is more robust than the type, erect at first, later with gracefully arching branches and denser and larger panicles of mauve colored flowers with an orange eye; the first to bloom.

Var. *wilsoni* is tall and arching with longer, narrower leaves and looser, drooping spikes, bearing smaller flowers of rosy-lilac, the petals being rolled.

Buddleia lindleyana has purplish-red flowers in small upright spikes and although not as profuse flowering as the varieties of *B. davidi*, it is distinct.

Varieties of unusual colors are of garden interest and include: Charming, lavender-pink; Dubonnet, quite red; Elstead Hybrid, apricot—a new color mentioned in England; Ile de France, rose-purple tinted violet; Nanhoensis, almost prostrate but will grow to 4 feet tall; Peace, white; Pink Charming, lavender-purple contrasts with yellow of the tube; Purple Prince, imperial purple with golden orange eye; Pink Pearl, perhaps best pink much like Ile de France except color is pinkish lavender; Fortune, pale lilac, abundant bloom, about 4 feet tall and wide.

USES. Buddleias are splendid for specimens and are often much at home in small yards where few other shrubs are planted. They are often used at the back of a large perennial border. Good plants will be wider than high so that they take up 6 to 8 ft. in diameter. As a source of cut flowers the Butterflybush is unexcelled. Webster writes that they are good for smoky places.

SOIL. They must be planted in well drained soil, for it must be remembered that in the colder regions they are not perfectly hardy. Circumneutral pH 6.0–8.0.

PRUNING. Rarely does the top remain alive until Spring at Columbus, O., and when such is the case, the flowering is greatly impaired by allowing the tops to remain. Cut the plants to the soil each Spring. If the plants lack symmetry throughout the early Summer, it may be useful to pinch the ends of the branches to make the plants bushier.

PROPAGATION. 1. *The easiest way to propagate Buddleias is from softwood cuttings made in Summer. Winter them in a coolhouse or in protected frames.

2. Hardwood cuttings taken in Fall and stored out of danger of frost. Usually not raised in northern states by this method.

3. *Seed sown under glass in February grows a foot a month after it gets started. It may be sown in open soil in April. Of course, the varieties are not absolutely true from seed.

BUXUS—Box

"The Living Antique"*

Casting about in my mind for adequate words to express the spirit of Box, this apostrophe by Edwin Matthews was found:

"When we think of Boxwood, we instinctively place it among ancient things and associate it with works of antiquity. Yet like an immortal poem, song or saying, it lives today; it, too, is 'of the ages.' Fashion and fads in gardening have brought about many and varied kinds of gardens. Plants have come, reigned—and finally abdicated in favor of others. But Box has survived fashions, changes, and the hand of time for centuries. It is as popular today as it was when 'knighthood was in flower.'

"Old English gardens are world-famous for their hedges of Box, their Box trees and their Box arbors and mazes, which in that favored climate do so wonderfully well. It is natural that the love and desire for Box gardens should have found its way to these shores along with those who migrated. Without a doubt it has been the scions of ancestral gardens that have formed the nuclei of the wonderful old Box plantings now found in this country, such as those in the States of Virginia and Maryland especially.

"Considering the popularity of Box we may ask: What is it that makes it so well liked? Viewing a beautiful Box-bush, it looks to us like a fusion of the finer and better qualities of many other plants. It has the tenacity of a rugged Oak, with all the beauty of the finest and most aristocratic evergreen. Its tenacity is such that it is often the only survivor in a garden where care and culture have been withheld for years and years.

"Summer and Winter it metes out its delightful lights and shadows in green; it thrives in shade as well as in sunlight. Here we see it, a column of green, in memory of some loved one; there as an edging to a flower or Rose garden; elsewhere as a billowy mass, softening masonry or making an inviting entry to the home doorway. As green walls for a formal garden, as clipped globes, as trained pyramids and in tree form it is used, while for the city window garden in Winter it is away ahead of all other evergreens."

In spite of the fact that many sorts of Box are seen, only two species are commonly grown and from these many forms have been derived.

The Common Box, *Buxus sempervirens*, is a native of S. Europe, N. Africa and W. Asia. It is a branchy, dense, evergreen with opposite, lustrous leaves which are characteristically oval, a trifle broader below the middle. The flowers and fruits are generally quite inconspicuous.

---

*So Linda Clement Hines calls it.

A plant of Buxus sempervirens,

VARIETIES.

angustifolia. Willow Box. Leaves lance-oblong, sometimes called *salicifolia.* More rapid growth than type. Loose in habit.

arborescens. Truetree Box. Leaves elliptical; type form, becoming a small tree, and commonest for use in training to tree, pyramid, globe, standard, or bush form or for topiary work.

argenteo-variegata. Leaves variegated white.

aureo-variegata. Leaves variegated yellow or entirely yellow.

bullata. Leaves large, blistered or puckered.

glauca. Leaves oval and grayish. Called *macrophylla glauca.*

handsworthi. Upright habit. Large, dark green leaves regularly arranged to form a cross when viewed from above. A little hardier than some other sorts.

marginata. Leaves edged yellow.

myrtifolia. Leaves small, elliptic oblong, that is, narrow, pointed. Low growth.

pendula. Branches pendulous.

pyramidata. Upright, pyramidal habit.

rosmarinifolia. Low growth. Leaves small, linear-oblong, curled over at edge.

rotundifolia (latifolia). Leaves broad, oval.

suffruticosa (nana). Truedwarf Box. Edging Box. Low growth and very slow. Leaves small, oval. Commonly used for the lowest sorts of hedges.

The *Buxus microphylla*, the Korean B., differs from *B. sempervirens* in having leaves which are broadest above the middle. The leaves are ⅛ to 1 in. long, light green in color. The branches are more conspicuously angled than the *sempervirens*. The young shoots are smooth, not hairy. The habit varies from a prostrate to a compact shrub, seldom over 3 ft. tall.

Var. *japonica* has more wedge-shaped leaves, a trifle larger, sometimes over an inch long, rounded or notched at the tip. Quite prostrate in habit.

Var. *koreana*. Very similar but rather hairy on branchlets and petioles. E. H. Wilson says of it:

"It was discovered some years ago by Japanese botanists and was brought to the Arnold Arboretum in 1919 by the writer. Never exceeding 2 ft. in height this Box grows freely, is easily increased by cuttings, and so far has not suffered Winter injury here. Like the Japanese Box (*B. microphylla japonica*) the Korean variety takes on a golden-brown hue throughout the Winter and so lacks the cheerful greenness of its European relative. However, since it possesses the supreme quality of hardiness, it is assured of a hearty welcome."

USES. From Box are made caskets and rulers and the wood is used for inlaying with ivory and for carving. It is the typical formal plant for gardens where pyramids, globes, and pillars are desired. As a low or high hedge it has been employed for centuries. It is tenacious of life and tolerates the gases and dust of cities. As a tub plant it flourishes for years. It thrives from Florida to New England.

In colder regions it must be sheltered from Winter winds. It prefers a moist atmosphere and plenty of water. The Japanese Box, *B. microphylla* and its varieties, *japonica* and *koreana*, are hardier than *B. sempervirens* varieties, but are not so well known.

SOIL. Tolerant though it is to adversity, Box likes plenty of good and a friable soil. Tubbed plants should be enriched from time to time. Marinus van Kleef mentions that in Holland where Box is grown by the millions, the plants are placed in the most fertile spot in the nursery and, no matter how fertile the soil, cow manure is applied abundantly and dug in before the plants are set out. Circumneutral pH 6.0–8.0.

TRANSPLANTING. Readers desiring to know how a century-old Boxwood hedge was moved in Philadelphia may be interested in an article in *Country Life in America*, Aug. 1909, by Claude H. Miller. It was found that the Box roots, which in former years had penetrated the soil beneath the plants, had died because the soil was exhausted. Since then, the roots had spread to a diameter of over 8 ft. and only 4 to 6 in. below the surface of the soil. The roots were planked in on two sides and knife blades were forced through the soil beneath the plants with such force that ordinary sandstone "was cut as easily as if it were cheese." Twelve hundred feet of hedge was moved. The work started in March and finished in November, with twenty to thirty men and from one to seven horses employed, at a cost of $9 per foot. Moving these plants "was like a huge game of chess in which the moves of the Box and the workmen could be planned about two weeks ahead because it was impossible to move bushes across from one part of the garden to another, owing to the mass of intervening Box." I never knew that reading about moving plants could be so exciting!

WINTERING BOX. *Horticulture* remarks:

"In New England a Boxwood hedge has been growing thriftily for some years in a garden. The gardener makes a point of having the Box go into the Winter thoroughly moist at the roots. If the weather has been dry, the plants are liberally watered about the last half of October.

"Before the ground freezes a mulch of leaves or some rough material is added to keep the frost out of the ground, and care is taken not to bank it up too close to the Box or the latter will lose its leaves. The mulch extends a foot from the base of the plants.

"About the end of December the plants are covered with evergreen boughs as a protection from frosty winds. Burlap is good, if not tied too close to the plants."

PESTS. *Box Leaf Miner.* C. C. Hamilton who has studied the pest gives us the following facts:

1. Pupates mid to end of April, lasts three weeks, at end of which legs and wing pads turn black.

2. Mating occurs shortly after emergence.

3. Female deposits eggs shortly.

4. Eggs hatch in about three weeks.

5. To control use cheap molasses diluted four times with water. Of this syrup then use 100–500 parts to one part nicotine sulphate. The molasses helps to retain the nicotine upon the bodies of the pupae for five or six days. Best time to spray is when legs and wing pads of pupae become black. Keep sprayed while adults emerge; that is three weeks.

Red spider. A common pest when the Box is planted in sunny, dry places. Syringe with water, spray with Volck or dust with sulphur.

FAULTS. It is not hardy enough; slow growing; peculiar odor of foliage; branches die out; snow splits open a plant easily. In spite of these faults, it is valued for its adaptability to various formal uses.

TRIMMING. Shear Box just as it comes into growth, perhaps in May. If necessary to cut back to hard wood in shaping up the plants, this is safe as they branch easily from old wood.

PROPAGATION.   1. *The commonest method is to take ripe or half-ripe cuttings in Fall, inserted in sand in a cool greenhouse. In Spring they may be placed in shaded frames. Young wood can be rooted in Summer. Marinus van Kleef advises rather hard wood in Summer, choosing large wood. Strip the foliage from the lower end for $2\frac{1}{2}$ in. Do not cut off the foliage but strip it, because in that way a small piece of bark is torn off, which hastens root development from the nodes. Press the cutting into the soil, using the forefinger to do this. Roots start readily from the strained, bent portion.

2. Seedlings develop slowly. But if seeds are obtainable soak them before sowing in the Spring or sow in greenhouse as soon as ripe.

3. The Edging Box is generally propagated by division. Tear up the plants and use each section as a cutting.

CALLICARPA—Beautyberry

(Name from *kalos*—beautiful, *carpos*—fruit)

This attractive berried shrub is rarely planted considering its charm. *Callicarpa purpurea (dichotoma) (gracilis)* is a native of China and Korea and belongs to the Verbena family. The pinkish flowers are not very conspicuous, but are followed by clusters of lilac-violet berries in the axils of the leaves. The berries ripen in September and October. The leaves are opposite, 1 to 3 in. long, elliptical and with tiny rounded teeth, except toward the base and apex. The twigs are rather rough and scurfy.

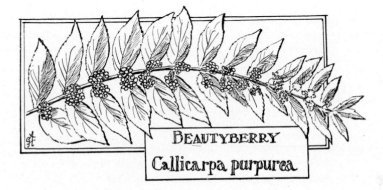

BEAUTYBERRY
Callicarpa purpurea

Callicarpa japonica, the Japanese Beautyberry, has larger berries and leaves (2½ to 5 in. long). The leaves are toothed even at the base. There are fewer berries than the previous mentioned sort.

C. americana, the American B. or French Mulberry, is found wild from Virginia to Texas. The leaves are densely rusty, downy beneath. A stronger grower, it attains a height of 6 ft. The flowers are bluish; the fruits reddish violet.

C. giraldiana grows 9 ft. tall and has the flowers and fruit borne on short stems (peduncles), shorter than the leaf stems (petioles). The leaves are sparsely hairy beneath. Leaves turn purple in the Fall.

Uses. The Beautyberries produce attractive leaves and the shrubs are quite graceful though upright. In planting them give a rather protected place. Although the fruits are tiny, they are attractive upon the plants for garden effect. When the fruit is cut and placed in vases, it displays its true charm.

Soil. Circumneutral pH 6.0–8.0.

Pruning. Prune back the plants severely each Spring as the flowers and fruits are borne on new wood.

Objections. The winterkilling of much of the top growth necessitates annual pruning. The berries are covered by the leaves so that they are not as showy as they should be.

Propagation. 1. *Cuttings of half-ripe wood are generally used. Give a little bottom heat and humid conditions. Some cover cuttings with a belljar. Protect in frames for Winter or bring into greenhouse.

2. Layers.

3. *Seed sown indoors in Fall.

4. Hardwood cuttings would only be successful where they do not freeze.

CALLUNA—Scotch Heather

(From the Greek "to sweep." The branches are used for brooms)

The Scotch Heather, *Calluna vulgaris*, grows from 6 in. to 3 ft. tall. The flowers are normally pink but there are many varieties which are carmine and white. It differs botanically from Erica in that the flowers have a deeply four-parted, rose-colored calyx, longer and concealing the corolla, and with four bracts at the base which resembles a calyx.

For culture and propagation see Erica, page 224.

CALLISTEMON (Metrosideros)—Bottlebrush

(From the Greek *beauty* and *stamen*)

The Bottlebrushes are Australian shrubs and trees with long spikes of bloom which consist principally of stamens, and appear quite like a bottle brush. They are grown in greenhouses in the Northern States but are splendid specimen shrubs in Southern California and Southern Florida. There are 25 species which resemble each other very closely. Callistemon differs from Melaleuca in that the stamens are not united in bundles.

Callistemon lanceolatus (floribundus) (citrinus), the Lemon Bottlebrush, grows from 12 to 30 ft. tall in the wild, but is frequently seen as a low shrub. The flowers are produced from January to June. The stamens in this case are bright red, the bottlebrushlike heads

Callistemon lanceolatus has the typical bright red, bottlebrush-like flowers

being from 2 to 4 in. long. The leaves are fragrant when crushed because of resin filled dots. The leaves are alternate, long narrow, 1 to 3 in. long and ¼ in. wide, stiff with a prominent midrib.

Callistemon rigidis (linearifolius). The long branches are very rigid. The leaves are quite narrow, ⅛ in. wide, stiff, sharp pointed, from

2 to 5 in. long; leaves with resinous dots. Flowers are deep red, spike very dense.

Callistemon speciosus, the Showy Bottlebrush. This graceful, large shrub often becomes treelike, 40 ft. tall. The branches are quite drooping. The leaves are narrow, lance shaped, 1½ to 4 in. long and ¼ in. wide. This is one of the richest red sorts.

CULTURE. These plants make slow growth in clay soil but prefer the sandier loams. Prune them in the Autumn to keep them bushy.

OBJECTIONS. The Callistemons bear woody seed capsules quite close to the twigs. These remain from year to year and are considered unsightly by some people.

PROPAGATION. 1. *Seeds. The twigs are cut bearing the seed capsules as they are about to open and are placed in a paper bag to dry. Otherwise the seeds are lost. Sow the seeds in early Spring, in sand, leafmold, and loam.

2. They can be grown from immature wood cuttings.

CALYCANTHUS (BUTNERIA)—Sweetshrub (Sweet betsy) (Carolina-allspice) (Strawberryshrub)

(Name derived from *Kalyx*—calyx, *anthos*—flower, refers to colored calyx)

The common Sweetshrub, *Calycanthus floridus*, is found from Virginia to Florida and is quite hardy northward. The normal habit of the shrub is somewhat straggling and open. The flowers are purplish-brown or reddish-brown, the petals and stamens grading into each other and also into the sepals so that, botanically, the flower is a very primitive type. The flowers bloom from June to July and exhale a fragrance which changes with the age of the flower until it is not unlike that of over-ripe apples. The leaves are ovate, pale green, shining, hairy beneath and opposite. The branchlets are hairy or woolly, compressed at the nodes and exhale a camphorlike odor.

Another species, variously called *Calycanthus fertilis* (*glaucus*), (*laevigatus*), has leaves which are not so shining above and not hairy beneath as is *C. floridus*. This sort produces seed freely, whereas the former species does not. But much more important, the flowers are not as fragrant.

For *Calycanthus praecox*, see *Meratia*, page 305.

USE. The true *C. floridus*, being the most fragrant in flower and with the glossier leaves, is much desired for the old-fashioned garden. The pungent flowers and leaves have been associated with American gardens from the time that America was colonized.

Left, **Calycanthus floridus or Sweetshrub;** *right,* **Buddleia magnifica, or Butterfly-bush, with its long sprays of light purple flowers**

The Sweetshrub is excellent even in partial shade.

The bark is said to have been used as a substitute for cinnamon in former years.

Soil. Calycanthus is adapted to a fairly moist loam, and in heavy clay soils some believe the plants are too open and not compact. Circumneutral pH 6.0–8.0.

Objections. C. P. Halligan writes: "Its general lack of hardiness and thriftiness, unless planted in a rich, moist soil in a partially shaded and sheltered situation, and its lack of such character in flower, fruit, or foliage as to make it especially effective or distinctive in a landscape planting, combine to make it less desirable for general planting than many other kinds now available."

Culture. Johnson says that if the terminal buds are pinched out, two flower buds result, thus the flowering season is lengthened.

Propagation. 1. *Softwood cuttings root rather easily when taken early. They are rather tender for the first Winter and must be in a good frame or greenhouse.

2. *Root cuttings may be taken in early Winter. Cut the roots in 3 in. lengths and store till Spring, after which they start nicely.

3. They are also propagated by suckers and division.

4. Seeds of *C. fertilis* are freely produced and grow easily when sown in early Spring. Hence their abundance in nurseries where they replace the more fragrant species. Sow thinly as the seed leaves are large.

5. Mound layers are successful.

CAMELLIA (Thea)—Camellia (Japonica)
(Named for George Joseph Kamellus, Moravian Jesuit who lived in Asia
in the Seventeenth Century)

Few travelers to the Southern States, especially to Louisiana and Mississippi, have not marveled at the beauty of the Southern Camellias. No shrub has such waxy flowers and leaves. They have been cultivated since 1742. Camellias grow well along the Gulf Coast and in the Northwest, but the sun is too strong for them in Southern Florida. In the Northern States they were formerly grown as conservatory plants. Because they lack fragrance, they have not been used extensively by florists, and the Gardenia, which resembles the Camellia, has surpassed it in interest. Some of the first Camellias to be imported to the United States are now 45 ft. tall, producing trees of great beauty. During the last few years there has been a great revival of interest in these plants in the South, so that large estates have been collecting the many old specimen plants, in which case they are often able to move specimens of great size and age. The writer saw one plant being move in New Orleans, in the middle of January, which was fully 30 ft. in diameter.

The common species, *Camellia japonica*, produces red, white, rose, pink, and variegated flowers. According to temperatures, the Camellia will bloom either in the Winter or Spring. The leaves are oval, pointed, and lustrous. The plants usually make a slow growth, and should be set in half shaded, moist places. They are usually mulched with manure and given a supplementary feed of commercial plant food.

GREENHOUSE CULTURE. In repotting Camellias, this is best done after the flowers fall. The proper soil is: Two parts loam, one part peatmoss or leafmold—and a little sand. They thrive best with limited root room. They need frequent syringing in order to keep them free from pests. They should be given heavy shade in Summer, but abundant light in the Winter. High temperatures will cause the buds to drop, so they should be grown cool, from 45° to 50°. Be sure to water them plentifully when they are growing and blooming. One good drying-out also causes the buds to drop. But when the plants are resting they should be given little water and kept as cool as possible.

The double Camellia japonica is popular in the South for its waxy flowers and glossy leaves

PESTS. Two pests are serious—mealy bug and scale. But since the advent of the splendid insecticides, such as the miscible oils, Volck, and the glue spray, the plants can be kept very clean.

PROPAGATION. The varieties are perpetuated by: 1. *Cuttings of the ripe growths placed in a sandy peat, cool at first, then given bottom heat, in late Summer.

2. By grafting before the growth starts, using stocks of strong growing kinds, raised from cuttings.

3. Also seeds soaked in warm water, sown in sandy peat, germinate in four to six weeks.

4. Budded as Roses are.

5. Air layering.

6. Inarching, just after flowering.

CARAGANA—Pea-shrub, Pea-tree
(From Caragan, the Tartar name)

The upright, almost treelike growth of *Caragana arborescens*, the Siberian Pea-shrub, commends itself for various uses. It attains a height of 20 ft. The tiny pealike flowers are yellow and are borne singly during June. The foliage is made up of four to six pairs of oval leaflets, rounded at the apex. The branches are somewhat spiny; the bark is almost winged on the young branchlets. There is a weeping variety which is grafted on the type, seen more frequently in European gardens than here.

Caragana maximowicziana only grows about 3 ft. tall and is very dense in habit. The leaves are small and the golden yellow flowers open in May.

The Mongolian Pea-tree, *C. chamlagu*, has shiny green leaves of a papery texture. The rather large flowers are bright yellow at first but change to red-brown. They open in May and June. The plants grow 4 ft. tall. The leaves have two pairs of unequal leaflets, the rachis is spiny tipped. The bruised bark has the odor of licorice.

Left, **Carpenteria californica, a rather tender but wonderful shrub:** *right*, **Caragana arborescens or Pea–shrub, a treelike shrub with yellow, pealike flowers in June**

The Russian Pea-shrub (*C. frutex (frutescens)*), bears long, erect yellowish branches. The leaves consist of two pairs of leaflets, close together, as compared with *C. chamlagu*, in which they are far apart. The flowers are borne in 1–3 upon stems almost as long as the flowers.

USES. The Siberian Pea-shrub is an accent plant for shrub combinations. It may be used for a tall hedge, and Rehder notes that it is used for shelter plantations in the Northwest. It is interesting in Winter, upright, and with green twigs. *C. maximowicziana* is a really excellent, low growing shrub.

SOIL AND CULTURE. Although rather indifferent as to soil, they seem more truly adapted to soils of a sandy nature. The plants prefer sun. Young shrubs produce blooms regardless of age.

OBJECTIONS. With age most sorts become bare at the base and seem sparsely furnished with foliage. For many uses the Siberian Pea-shrub is too upright and stiff.

PRUNING. To avoid awkward appearance of plants, vigorous pruning should be resorted to every few years. Cut out old wood and shorten in the straggling branches.

PROPAGATION. 1. *Seed may be sown as soon as ripe or kept till Spring. Soak for 48 hours before sowing.

2. Root cuttings may be made in Winter or Spring.

3. The Weeping Pea-shrub is grafted on seedlings of *C. arborescens* after they have grown 6 ft. tall.

4. They layer readily.

CARPENTERIA
(Named for Wm. Carpenter, 1811-1848)

This evergreen shrub is confined to use from Philadelphia southward. Even in Philadelphia it requires a sheltered situation. It is a charming plant related to the Philadelphus. The only species is *Carpenteria californica* and is found wild in the Sierra Nevadas and California. The plants attain a height of from 6 to 10 ft. The flowers are white with yellow stamens, and are anemone-like, produced from June to August, in terminal loose clusters (cymes) of three to seven flowers. They are almost 3 in. across and fragrant. The leaves are grayish beneath, long, and narrowed at the ends.

USES. They are useful for a general shrub collection.

Soil and Culture. The Carpenteria is happy in dry sandy places, protected from sun and high winds. Water in Winter is more injurious to them than cold.

Propagation. 1. Seeds may be sown in Spring.

2. Greenwood cuttings may be inserted in Summer under glass.

3. The plants show some tendency to sucker.

CARYOPTERIS—Bluebeard (Blue-spirea) (Verbena-shrub) (Chinese Beardwort)

(Name derived from *Karyon*—nut, *pteron*—wing; the fruits are winged)

The late flowers of this shrub commend it to garden culture. It has been most generally cataloged as the Blue-spirea, but as it is related to the Verbena and is not spirealike, this latter name is not appropriate. *Caryopteris incana* (*mastacanthus*) (*sinensis*) is the species most generally cultivated. It is a native of E. China and Japan. The plants are usually low, but in mild climates it attains a height of 6 ft. The flowers are violet-blue, rarely white, borne in axillary or terminal clusters (cymes) and produced in September. The leaves, which are

Left, Caryopteris incana or Bluebeard, a low shrub bearing violet-blue flowers in September; *right*, Ceanothus americanus, or Jersey-tea, the leaves of which shrub were used to make tea during the Revolutionary War

coarsely toothed, opposite and oval lanceolate, have the odor of varnish and are gray beneath.

Uses. Few shrubs bloom as late as the Bluebeard which in the North is often planted in the perennial border. The plants are a thing of great beauty in that the color is rare for a shrub. In Australia it is said that they are used as bee plants. They may be used as pot plants for greenhouse flowering.

Soil and Culture. They like sunshine and a well-drained soil and only in such situations is the Bluebeard hardy in the North. Protecting the plants with a light mulch is also advisable.

Pruning. The shrubs should be pruned to the soil each Spring. This will not impair the blooming quality as each new shoot will be crowned with bloom.

Propagation. 1. *Stock plants may be potted and taken to the greenhouse for the Winter. From these plants cuttings may be taken all Spring. Each of the young plants will bloom the same year.

2. Seed may be sown in Spring. Gather in early Fall. Keep seedlings in pots. They bloom the same year.

3. Division.

4. Softwood cuttings rooted outdoors must be carried over Winter in a greenhouse or protected frame.

CEANOTHUS—Jersey-tea (Redroot) (Mountainsweet)

Rarely cultivated, but commonly found in the woods from Canada to South Carolina and Texas, is the Jersey-tea, *Ceanothus americanus*. It forms a low, compact shrub, generally 2 ft. tall, but sometimes attaining 4 ft. The flowers are very tiny, white, and borne in dense clusters (corymbose panicles) at the end of the branches. Some flowers are being produced from June to October. The foliage is oval, pointed, and irregularly toothed. There are three prominent veins in the leaf. A three-celled capsule ripens in September and is shed to leave a cup with silver lining.

At the Arnold Arboretum is a pale rose sort, known as *hybridus roseus*, which produces flowers in such great profusion as to almost hide the leaves.

Ceanothus delilianus (*arnauldi*), (*azureus*), (*hybridus*). This Ceanothus is a hybrid between *C. americanus* × *C. caeruleus*. The plants are upright, grow 3 ft. tall, and are hardy south of Washington, D. C., but they are at their best in California. All of the following sorts are given various names, such as Wild-lilac, Summer-lilac, or Mountain-lilac. The flowers are pale to deep blue. The leaves are oval, 2 to 3 in. long, pointed, finely toothed, dark green. Unlike the Jersey-tea, they prefer full sun. To this group belong the following varieties: Gloire de Versailles, bright blue, one of the best, good foliage; Gloire de Plantieres, deep blue; Ciel de Provence, deep blue.

Ceanothus prostratus, Mahala-mats or Squaw-carpet, is useful for the rock garden. It is a creeping shrub found only on the Pacific coast. The leaves are evergreen, dark, glossy, ½ to 1 in. long, wedge shaped with a few teeth at the apex, hairy when young. The *National Horticultural Magazine* describes the plant in these words:

"If there were no flowers at all, the evergreen leafage and rugged habit of the plant itself were enough to recommend it strongly to rock gardeners. The blossoming comes on in the Spring and effects a powder-blue cloud of finest lace above the plant. The flowers are in small, umbel-like clusters, forming panicles on the short branches. The individual flower is small and five-parted. The sepals have blue, petal-like borders and are incurved. The petals are of the same color but longer and are arched to form a tiny hood. *Ceanothus prostratus* does not delight in being transplanted but it may be transported if the journey be not too long, and this is done with the least loss when it is dormant. It does, however, come readily from seed and pot grown plants are tractable though the slow growth demands patience. Cuttings of the mature wood in Fall, placed in coldframes, are said to give a fair percentage of plants. Friability of soil and good drainage are most important. In its natural habitat, when once it is covered by the snow, it is well guarded against too cold and drying winds. In gardens, also, protection from evaporating blasts must be afforded, although at its lower elevations it endures a temperature of six degrees below zero."

Ceanothus thyrsiflorus, Blueblossom. These tall shrubs grow commonly from Oregon to California and the visitor to the West in June and July is thrilled by the sight of these plants which he believes to be blueflowered Lilacs. This is the hardiest of the evergreen species, but is confined to the warmer regions. The branches are slightly hairy when young, and strongly angled. The foliage is evergreen, oblong, shining above, often hairy beneath.

Uses. Such low shrubs are always attractive, for in small gardens of persons who like variety, they do not take up so much room. They may be naturalized in a woods.

During the Revolutionary War, the leaves were used as a substitute for tea.

Soil. Dry, though rich soils, suit the Jersey-tea. Subacid pH 5.0–6.0. In nature they are frequently found on hillsides. They will thrive best when the situation is at least partially sunny.

Pruning. The plants are rather half shrubby by nature so that they will need an annual Spring pruning. As they bloom upon wood of the current season's growth, they can be cut almost to the soil.

Transplanting. The root system is large and rambling which causes the plants to be a little difficult to transplant. For this reason nurserymen have not listed them. Young plants are more successfully moved. They are generally unsatisfactory in cultivation.

Propagation. 1. *Cuttings may be rooted in September. The less hardy sorts are propagated from forced plants in the greenhouse.

2. Seeds may be sown in Spring; perhaps best stratified for Winter.

3. Root cuttings may be made in Autumn and placed in flats of sandy soil.

CEPHALANTHUS—Buttonbush (Honeyballs)
(Name derived from *kephale*—head, *anthos*—flower; globular heads)

Wandering through the swamps from New Brunswick to Cuba one comes upon a shrub with globular heads of bloom, white in color, with pinkish pistils, which look like pins stuck into a cushion. The flowers

Cephalanthus occidentalis or Buttonbush
A shrub which is admirably adapted to wet, swampy places, and which bears globular headed flowers

are fragrant and open from July to August. The leaves are opposite or in whorls of three or four. They are lustrous, bright green above, and lighter, somewhat hairy, beneath. The branches are four-sided, reddish at the tips.

The common species is *Cephalanthus occidentalis*, but there is a variety *angustifolia* which has narrower leaves which are quite reddish.

USES. For masses in swampy, wet soil of meadows and along streams the Buttonbush is admirably adapted. The sweet flowers are generally visited by numerous insects. It is reputed that a tea was made from the bark of the roots as a cure for diabetes.

SOIL. Circumneutral pH 6.0–8.0.

OBJECTIONS. Foliage is usually riddled by insects. The foliage is too coarse to be a really refined shrub.

PROPAGATION. 1. Sow seed in Fall or Spring.
2. Root cuttings may be used.
3. Softwood cuttings from forced plants in Spring.
4. *Hardwood roots readily.

CERCIDIPHYLLUM—Katsura-tree

Although the Cercidiphyllum in Japan grows to be a tree 100 ft. tall and some at the Arnold Arboretum are 30 ft. tall, the nature of the plants is to be shrubby for some years. The leaves of *Cercidiphyllum japonicum* are heart-shaped and not unlike the leaves of the Redbud (*Cercis*); hence, the name. Unlike those of *Cercis*, these are opposite, dark green above, silvery green beneath with red veins and leaf stalks. A curious feature of the leaf production is that leaves are produced not only on new current growing wood but along the branches for several years back. The leaves are at all times attractive, coppery when unfolding and purplish red or yellow in the Autumn. Various trees differ greatly in their beauty of coloration. The plants are either male or female but not both. Francis Canning writes, "I think the female form of this tree much handsomer of the two forms; it is more spreading. The male tree is quite columnar." The flowers are not showy and appear before the leaves unfold. The variety *sinense* has leaves a trifle hairy beneath and is not as hardy as the Japanese type; furthermore, it is more often found growing to a single trunk.

USES. The Katsura-tree is ideally used as a small lawn specimen or it may be planted in the background. Its coppery foliage commends it for wider planting.

SOIL. It likes a deep, rich soil and one that is damp rather than dry. "It will not tolerate manure as a mulch or for enriching the soil," says M. V. Horvath.

PRUNING. Some gardeners have believed that root pruning increases the coloration of the leaves and keeps the plants low and bushy.

OBJECTIONS. It is difficult to transplant and, therefore, shunned by some nurseries. It must be transplanted only when perfectly dormant in November or early April. The plants are very regular in outline and appear as though sheared.

PROPAGATION. 1. Seeds may be obtained from Japan and sown in Spring, but kept moist until sown.

2. Plants may be cut down and the new shoots layered in sandy soil.

3. Meehan suggests that softwood cuttings when rooted in Summer should be allowed to dry a bit. Best obtained from forced plants.

CHAENOMELES — (CYDONIA) — Flowering Quince (Japanese Quince) (Japonica) (Firebush)

(From Greek *chainein*—to split, and *meles*—apple, because Thunberg supposed that the fruit split into five valves)

The Flowering Quince has been popular as a garden shrub for many years because of its dazzling, early, scarlet flowers.

Chaenomeles lagenaria (Cydonia japonica). The plants vary in height from 4 ft. upward; some are upright, others very spreading. The flowers are usually a brilliant scarlet, although varieties are white, pink, rose and various orange tints of red. The flowers are produced in April and hug the leafless branches, especially back from the tips. The leaves are glossy green, clustered, the tips of the branches and leaves being red. Attractive stipules are found at the base of the leaves. The branches are often irregular and thorny. The fruit is yellowish green, a trifle pear-shaped, over 2 in. in diameter. Even as late as July 1 one sort was in full bloom in the Arnold Arboretum, known as var. *Kermesina semiplena*. It was a plant 5 ft. tall with a spread of 10 ft. The very shiny foliage was gloriously glistening and the bronze tips of the young branches added to its attractiveness. The flowers were scarlet and extremely large.

Chaenomeles japonica (Cydonia maulei). The Lesser Flowering Quince, unlike the above, is a low shrub seldom over 3 ft. tall, with roughened branchlets, quite round, rather than long leaves, and with

teeth rounded at their tips. The flowers are brick-red. Var. *alpina*
(*sargenti*) Sargent Q. is dwarf with creeping stems, small leaves and
flowers.

Chaenomeles sinensis, the Chinese Quince has light pink flowers.
The fruit is often 6 in. long and golden yellow. The autumnal foliage
is most attractive, turning first to orange then to scarlet, the older
leaves changing first and following up the branches. It becomes almost
a small tree. It is hardy in Philadelphia.

Uses. The Flowering Quinces should be freely used about our
homes, because the red flowers are most welcome in earliest Spring.
The branches may be cut any time after Christmas and brought indoors to force.

As a hedge this shrub is admirable and forbidding but it must be
allowed to grow wide as well as high.

The fruits are fragrant and are sometimes placed in clothes closets.
Some persons have used them for jelly.

The Sargent Quince will be useful for rockeries and for the front line
border of shrub beds.

The lustrous foliage and brilliant blossoms of the Flowering Quince,
Chaenomeles, is a welcome early Spring shrub

Soil.   Circumneutral pH 6.0–8.0.

Pruning.   *Gardening Illustrated* (England) suggests training the Flowering Quince to tree form in which case the branches droop in a graceful manner and appear to advantage at the center of a bed of low shrubs.

In the general pruning of shrubs or hedges, be sure that no pruning is done in Spring before these shrubs bloom; otherwise, much bloom is cut off.

Objections.   San José scale once prohibited the culture and killed most of these shrubs but now we spray with lime and sulphur or other insecticide (See page 43).

Suckering may be objectionable sometimes.

Pests.   See above.   San José scale.

Propagation.   1. *Root cuttings furnish the easiest method of propagation. Take them 2 in. long in the Fall, storing in sand in cool places over Winter and plant them horizontal in rows in the Spring.

2. The plants sucker freely so that it is possible to divide the plants of choice varieties. Cut the new plants back severely as many of these suckers are poorly rooted.

3. *Hardwood cuttings will root.

4. Grafting the varieties upon the type is often done in the green-house in the early Spring.

5. Seeds may be stratified and sown in the Spring.

CHAMAEDAPHNE (CASSANDRA) Leatherleaf
(Name derived from *chamai*—on the ground, and *daphne*—laurel, referring to its being a low evergreen)

Another of the relatives of the Rhododendron is *Chamaedaphne calyculata*, the Leatherleaf. It generally grows but 1 ft. tall but will attain 3 ft. It is very hardy. The flowers are white, solitary cylindrical bells in the axils of the upper small leaves and are produced in April and May. The leaves are oval, generally about 1 in. or less long, rusty beneath and nearly evergreen. The branches are upright and the branchlets are zigzag.

Uses.   It may be used for semi-aquatic places in combination with the Huckleberries, Blueberries, Swamp Azaleas and other refined wet soil plants.

SOIL. Likes wet places, at least peaty or acid, sandy soil. Subacid pH 5.0–6.0.

PROPAGATION. 1. Seeds may be sown in sandy peat and kept quite shaded.

2. Mature cuttings may be rooted under glass in the Summer.

3. The plants may be divided.

4. Layers.

5. Suckers.

CHILOPSIS—Desertwillow (Flowering-willow) (Willow-shrub) (Mimbres)

(Name derived from *cheilos*—lip, *opsis*—like; refers to irregular flower)

The Desertwillow, *Chilopsis linearis* (*saligna*) is related to the Trumpetcreeper and is found throughout Southwestern United States. It is good for planting in the Gulf States but not even hardy in Washington, D.C. The plants are of a straggling, willowy appearance and often attain a height of 30 ft. The flowers are not unlike a Trumpetcreeper or a Catalpa, lilac in color, borne in terminal clusters (racemes) blooming throughout the whole Summer. The leaves are opposite or in whorls and are narrow lanceolate.

USES. Good as specimens because of the long season of bloom.

PROPAGATION. 1. *Cuttings may be rooted under glass in Summer.

2. Seeds.

CHIONANTHUS—Fringetree (Oldmans-beard)

(Name derived from *chion*—snow, *anthos*—flower)

Chionanthus virginica is a large shrub which is rather treelike, usually 10 ft. tall, but sometimes attaining a height of 30 ft. They are native from Pennsylvania to Texas. The flowers are greenish-white with narrow drooping petals and are arranged in dropping clusters (panicles) of from 5 to 10 in. long. Often the flowers are of one sex only; the male flowers are the showier. So profuse blooming are these plants that they are completely covered with flowers. The leaves are opposite, coarse, 3 to 8 in. long, variable in width on certain plants. The plants come into leaf late in the Spring. The Winter twigs resemble the Ash, to which the Fringetree is related, except for the fact that Ash buds have no scales visible, whereas Chionanthus buds are scaly. The fruit is blue, a one-seeded drupe, and produced in clusters like grapes. It ripens in September.

The Chinese Fringetree, *C. retusa*, has smaller and more oval leaves, is even more profuse flowering and blooms a week later. Rehder does not consider this as handsome as our native sort.

Chionanthus virginica or Fringetree
A treelike shrub bearing drooping, showy clusters of white flowers early in Spring

Uses. The Fringetree is best used as a lawn specimen. At Spring Grove Cemetery, Cincinnati, they present a very showy appearance, being at their height of bloom when Iris is at its best. Plant them in the sun. "They will endure a more smoky and generally bad atmosphere than most plants."—M. V. Horvath.

Soil. A deep, moist, sandy loam is its natural habitat. Subacid pH 5.0–6.0.

Objections. They make a slow growth but bloom when 3 ft. tall. Somewhat tender.

Propagation. 1. Mix seed with damp soil and sow in boxes. It takes one year to germinate.

2. They are frequently grafted on roots of Ash, *Fraxinus ornus*, because of their slow development from seed. Set the plants rather deeply so that they will grow on their own roots or growth will be delayed in Spring. The grafting is done under glass but they may be budded in the open.

3. Softwood cuttings may be taken from forced plants in early Spring.

CHOISYA—Mexican-orange
(Named for Mons. J. D. Choisy, a Geneva botanist)

As the common name would indicate, the Mexican-orange is related to the Orange and is native to Mexico. There is only one species, *Choisya ternata*. It forms a round bush and bears fragrant white flowers in Spring. The flowers are produced in large terminal and axillary clusters (slender stalked 3-6 flowered cymes). The leaves are evergreen, opposite, lustrous, leathery and consist of three, rarely two or four leaflets. Both the petals and the leaves are transparent dotted.

The Choisya will endure but several degrees of frost and is adapted to the Southern States only. Bailey writes:

"It blossoms in southern California at different seasons and can be made to bloom, it is said, every two months by withholding water and then watering liberally, as is done with Roses in southern France. It is hardy against the walls in southern England."

Uses. In the North it can be used as a pot plant, in which case it blooms in 6 to 8 weeks after bringing into heat.

Soil. A loose, gravelly, lime soil is advised.

Propagation. 1. It layers easily.
2. Half-ripe wood roots with bottom heat.

CISTUS—Rockrose
(From *Kistos*, its ancient Greek name)

There are many species of lovely Rockroses which have been grown for many years in European gardens, so that the European traveler usually sees these lovely flowers in the Mediterranean regions. The various species are quite similar, so we shall describe but one.

Cistus ladaniferus, Gum Rockrose. This shrub is a native of the western Mediterranean region. It is not hardy north of the Middle Atlantic States, although it will stand a little frost. The twigs are gummy. The leaves are opposite, narrow, a little over 1 in. long, gummy above, hairy beneath, and evergreen. The flowers are large, roselike, and last only part of a day, but they are produced in abundance. They bloom from June to July and in this species are white with blotched petals, with a large purple spot at the base of each petal. Some species are purple.

Culture. The Rockroses prefer a sandy, limestone, well-drained soil and should be planted in the sun. English books advise that they are best for seaside planting, inasmuch as they will tolerate the salt air. They are difficult to transplant except from pots.

Propagation. 1. Sow the seeds in shallow pots when obtainable.
2. Softwood cuttings may be taken in Summer.
3. *Layers are unusually successful.

CITRUS (PONCIRUS)—Hardy Orange (Trifoliate Orange)

The Hardy Orange was introduced from Japan in 1869 and has been used as an understock for adapting commercial Oranges for colder regions.

Citrus trifoliata, as the name indicates, has three-parted leaves, glossy and bright green, even in Winter. The branches are smooth, angled and very thorny. The flowers are white, opening in April, the first coming into bloom before the leaves. Unlike other Orange blossoms they are not fragrant. The fruit is orange in color, mostly seeds and rind, and too bitter to eat. It ripens in September. It will endure 10 deg. below zero when in protected places.

Uses. In the South it makes an impenetrable hedge, due to the large, forbidding thorns. In the North it is valuable for its foliage, flowers and fruit. Hybridized with the Orange, the Citrange was produced.

Soil. Circumneutral pH 6.0–8.0.

PROPAGATION. *Store seeds in moist sand through the Winter and sow in the Spring, or else sow them in the greenhouse shortly after ripening. If the seeds have dried, soak them until they swell.

CLERODENDRON (VOLKAMERIA)—Glorybower

A large-leaved shrub for specimen planting is the *Clerodendron trichotomum* (*serotinum*) the Harlequin Glorybower. It grows 10 ft. tall and bears white flowers with a reddish brown calyx which turns red. The flower stalks are reddish and the flowers are produced in loose clusters (cymes) in threes during September for three weeks. The leaves are opposite, slightly curled, remotely toothed, ovate, 5 in. long, and exhale a strong odor when bruised. The branchlets and petioles are rather white woolly. The fruit is blue with a crimson calyx and ripens in September. The variety *fargesi* is said to be hardier. It has smaller leaves and smooth, not hairy, leaves and branchlets.

C. foetidum (*bungei*), the Rose Glorybower, is not as hardy as the above. The flowers are lilac-rose, produced in August. The leaves are metallic-green, deeply toothed. It grows 3 to 6 ft. tall. The branches are spiny. If killed to soil, it blooms in Fall instead of August.

USES. Large specimen plants are seen at the Brooklyn Botanical Garden that are 10 ft. or more in diameter.

PRUNING. The density of large specimens would necessitate pruning to thin out the branches. In cold climates even *C. trichotonum* may freeze at the tips. The method of pruning in this case is to shear the shoots in to live wood.

OBJECTIONS. The plants sucker freely if the roots are injured by cultivation. There is a coarseness of growth and leaf which is not completely satisfactory.

PROPAGATION. 1. *Root cuttings may be made in Winter and planted out of doors in the Spring. Use pieces 2 in. long. The cuttings may be obtained by digging around the plants without actually transplanting the shrub.

2. Sow seeds when ripe.

3. Nearly ripe wood may be rooted under glass in Summer.

CLETHRA—Summersweet (Sweet Pepperbush)
(*Klethra*—Greek name for Alder)

In marshy places from Canada to Georgia the Summersweet (*Clethra alnifolia*) gives off its spicy fragrance and delights the nature lover with its white racemes of bloom.

Clethra alnifolia or Summersweet

A native of moist, acid soil where the spicy, fragrant spikes of bloom are borne in great profusion during July. An unusually fine specimen such as grows only in situations well adapted to it

The plants grow 3 to 8 ft. tall. The flowers are generally white, but often with a pinkish tinge, and are produced in great profusion at the ends of each of the branches. They start to bloom in July and continue until September. The leaves are shining, 2 to 3 in. long, toothed, and resemble those of the Alder with their seven to nine pairs of prominent veins.

A more mountainous species, the Cinnamon Summersweet, *C. acuminata*, is taller, growing to 18 ft. Its leaves scarcely widen upward, (are not wider above the middle), and are prominently embossed with 10 to 15 pairs of veins. The white flowers have purple anthers. The stems are golden brown.

The Woolly Summersweet, *C. tomentosa*, is less hardy, being reliable only south of Washington. The flowers open two to three weeks later than *C. alnifolia*. The distinction from other sorts is that the leaves are hairy beneath.

USES. In wild places the Summersweet is associated with *Magnolia virginiana*, the Sweetbay, and Alder. These shrubs seem to prefer a little shade. Bees like the flowers. Blooming through the Summer, it is a welcome shrub for waterside planting.

SOIL. Only in peaty or acid sandy soil does the Clethra do its best. Low, wet places are its native habitat but it will thrive in soil of a medium degree of moisture if other soil factors are favorable. Subacid pH 5.0–6.0.

OBJECTIONS. Inclined to be straggling rather than compact unless in favorable environment and soil. Rather difficult to transplant. Subject to attacks of red spider in dry or limy soil.

PROPAGATION. 1. The plants seed freely. Seeds should be sown in pans of peat in early Spring.

2. Layers root slowly. *Most nursery stock is collected, divided, and grown for a year or two under cultivation.

3. Softwood cuttings may be obtained from forced plants and rooted in Spring.

4. Natural division of collected clumps.

COLUTEA—Bladder-senna

(Name derived from *Koloutea*, a name used by Theophrastus)

A native of Southern and Southeastern Europe, the Bladder-senna (*Colutea arborescens*) has been in cultivation for three centuries. Meehan mentions that it grows on the crater of Mt. Vesuvius. The shrubs are 10 to 12 ft. tall, bear yellow pea-shaped flowers in six to eight flowered clusters (racemes). The standard of the flower is marked with reddish-brown lines and blotches. The flowers open over a long period from Summer to Autumn so that the plants have both flowers and fruits at the same time. The fruit is an inflated, bladderlike pod, 2 to 3 in. long, bronze red in color. Youngsters and the author like to pop

The Bladder-senna, Colutea, produces yellow, pealike flowers and large, inflated, bronze-green pods

them. The compound leaves are nine to seventeen parted, dull green, notched or rounded at the tips, grayish beneath. The young branches are hairy.

The Oriental Bladder-senna, *Colutea orientalis (cruenta)* has a burnt-orange standard with an orange blotch and quite purple pods. The leaves are gray on both sides. The flowers open later, the leaves are smaller and the plants seldom attain a height of 6 ft. It is a little less hardy, inasmuch as the plants at Highland Park freeze back each year.

Uses. The Bladder-senna is a most ornamental shrub. Its leaves are graceful and the attractive display of bloom and fruit serves to make it a good background shrub or specimen for the lawn. They will stand shade. These plants were pioneers in balloon construction, for the pods are blown some distance.

The leaves are used as an adulterant for the druggists' Senna.

Soil. These shrubs thrive in adversity and are more at home in dry than in wet soils. *Le Bon Jardinier* notes that they prefer limestone soils.

Insects. They are quite subject to aphides so that they may require spraying with a nicotine compound.

PRUNING. Vigorous pruning in Spring is advisable to make the shrubs more compact; otherwise they open, become loose and straggling.

PROPAGATION. 1. Softwood cuttings are often used, taken in Summer.

2. *Seeds are borne profusely and may be sown in Spring after soaking to swell the seeds.

3. Rarer sorts are grafted upon *C. arborescens*.

COMPTONIA—Sweetfern
(Named for Bishop Henry Compton)

The tourist who travels through the Alleghenies of Pennsylvania or the Berkshires of Massachusetts notes the masses of Sweetfern along the roadsides. The plants of *Comptonia* (*Myrica*) *asplenifolia* are exceedingly hardy, generally attaining a height of 2 ft. but sometimes 4 ft. The leaves are quite fernlike and give off a pungent odor when crushed. The flowers are inconspicuous.

USES. Sweetfern makes a splendid game cover or a ground cover for sterile banks. It is used by landscape architects for covering steep banks. Sweetfern leaves serve as a behind-the-garage smoke for the youngsters of regions where it grows.

The Sweetfern, Comptonia, prefers peaty soil

SOIL. A peaty or sandy black soil is their natural one, but it is generally considered that soil which is so sterile that nothing else will grow suits the Sweetfern. Subacid pH 5.0–6.0. Nevertheless, it will not tolerate a rich, limy soil.

TRANSPLANTING. Move the plants only when dormant and prune them to the soil so that the roots only are planted.

PROPAGATION. Most nurseries furnish collected plants and do not propagate them.

They may be divided or layered in Autumn.

COPROSMA—(Mirrorplant)
(From *kopros*—dung, *osme*—odor, referring to the fetid odor of the plant)

The commonest species, *Coprosma baueri*, the Coral Coprosma, is a native of New Zealand and is grown for its evergreen leaves. The plant is of a rather climbing nature, attaining a height of from 20 to 25 ft. They are often used as hedges. The flowers are inconspicuous. The leaves are opposite, thick, obtuse, and of such glossiness that they appear to be freshly varnished. The fruits are showy, bright yellow.

PROPAGATION. Cuttings of ripe wood should be rooted in sand.

CORNUS—Dogwood
(The name Cornus comes from *cornu*—horn, alluding to the toughness of the wood. The derivation of the common name Dogwood is much in question. Bailey says that a decoction of the bark of *Cornus sanguinea* was used in England to wash mangy dogs. Some authors have mentioned that the word is derived from the same root as our word "dagger" because the hardwood was used for making spears and daggers. Another story is current that the term "dogwood" is one of derision, and carries the idea that the wood is too small to be useful.)

Among the garden Dogwoods are many sorts of unusual merit for ornamental flowers, fruits and twigs. It is a large group, but, as in some large families, a few members are too gaudy, too wild and some are apt to be sickly, why should the entire family be despised for the poor relations?

We shall arrange the various Dogwoods first according to the color of the twigs:

Twigs red. *Cornus alba* var. *sibirica*, Coral Dogwood (White fruit D.) This shrub is one of the commonest sorts used for its brilliant twigs. The plants are of a broad, spreading habit and grow 5 to 10 ft.

tall. The flowers are creamy-white, appear in May or June, and are arranged in dense small clusters (cymes). The fruit is bluish-white, a little larger than a pea, produced in July; the stone is longer than wide and flattened, narrowed at the ends. The leaves are opposite, oval, acute, rounded at the base, dark green above, grayish beneath. The branches are rather stout, bright coral red, bloomy when young, with white pith. By bloom, we mean the same as a grape or plum has a frosty appearance.

Var. *spaethi*, Spaeth D, is a variegated sort in which the leaves have a mixture of gold and green through the surface of leaf and with an irregular margin of gold green surrounding the leaf. It has a better color when shaded part of the day by a tree or the house. The foliage does not scorch in bright sun as much as some variegated sorts.

Var. *argenteo-marginata*, Silveredge D., has leaves edged with creamy white. Often cataloged as *C. alba elegantissima* or *variegata*.

Var. *gouchaulti*, Gouchault D.,has leaves variegated with yellowish white and pink.

Cornus stolonifera, the Red-osier D., differs from above by its spreading habit, some branches being prostrate and producing suckers freely. The branches are blood-red. The flowers are dull white in clusters (cymes) larger than *C. alba*; the disk of the flower is red (in *C. alba* the disk is yellow). The fruit is white; the stone is as broad as high and rounded at the base. The leaves are dark green above, whitish beneath, more gradually pointed than *C. alba*.

Var. *coloradensis* has deeper red branches (a brownish red) and smaller leaves than the type.

Cornus baileyi, the Bailey D., has leaves, branchlets and flower stems more or less hairy.

Cornus sanguinea, the Bloodtwig D., is more upright than the Coral D. The leaves are hairy on both sides; the hairs beneath are woolly whereas most Dogwoods have straight hairs. The fruit is black. The bark is a darker, duller red than the Coral D.

Twigs yellow.   *Cornus stolonifera* var. *flaviramea*, Goldentwig D. (cataloged as *lutea*) resembles the species but has yellow twigs.

Twigs green in Winter.   *Cornus sanguinea* var. *viridissima*, the Greentwig D. has green branches and fruits and like the type, hairy leaves.

Cornus stolonifera var. *nitida*, is another green bark sort but the leaves are lustrous and quite smooth, not hairy.

Twigs yellowish- or reddish - brown. *Cornus brachypoda* (*macrophylla*) is a more treelike Dogwood which at the Brooklyn (N. Y.) Botanical Garden and Highland Park, Rochester (N. Y.), grows to a height of 15 ft. The branches are quite horizontal and produce a rather open head. The large flat clusters (cymes), 3 to 6 in., of yellowish-white flowers have a slightly disagreeable odor and are produced in great profusion in July and August, later than most sorts. The leaves are large, often 6 in. long, slightly grayish beneath, with long tapering points. They have splendid Autumnal tints. The black fruits are produced in October. It is considered somewhat tender unless planted in a well-drained soil.

Twigs gray, sometimes turning reddish-purple in Winter. Pith brown.

Cornus paniculata (*racemosa*) (*candidissima*), the Gray D. (Panicle D.) A common wild species, showy along the roadsides from Maine to North Carolina and west to Minnesota. This Dogwood is variable in height, sometimes but 3 ft. tall; in other places becoming 15 ft. high. Its outstanding characteristic is its narrow, long leaves, tapering into a sharp point, grayish beneath and either smooth or a trifle hairy on upper surface. Another notable feature is the red stems which bear the creamy-white flowers and the white or pale blue fruits. This offers a strong contrast. The plants are of a good form, regular branching and splendid foliage. Birds are fond of the fruits which are stripped from the plants soon after ripening. It likes moist soil and partial shade.

Twigs purple. Pith brown. *Cornus amomum* (*sericea*), the Silky D., (Blueberried D.) (Redbrush) (Kinnikinnik) (Squawbush) (Swamp D.) The purple branches have a brown pith. The plants are more treelike than the other Dogwoods which have a reddish bark. The oval leaves are brownish woolly on the veins. The fruit is blue, sometimes almost white. The flowers are later than the other colored twig Dogwoods, opening in June. It is good in moist or wet soils and needs room to range.

(See *C. paniculata* above which may have purple branches.)

Twigs green or purple. Pith white. *Cornus rugosa* (*circinata*) Roundleaf D. The leaves are more circular than most species, abruptly pointed at the tip, densely white, woolly beneath. The branches are green in Summer and blotched purple when young; the older are purplish, although sometimes somewhat yellow. The shrub is upright and treelike, as in *C. amomum*, but branches are greener. The fruits are light blue or greenish-white, hollowed at base and borne on reddish stems. Horvath says it is hard to transplant.

Twigs brown, but greenish-yellow or even red in Summer. Flowers yellow and not surrounded by showy bracts. Early flowering.

Cornus mas (mascula), Cornelian-cherry. This treelike Dogwood has been in cultivation for 300 years. It is found through Europe to Western Siberia. One of the earliest flowering woody plants for the hardy garden; the flowers are not like those of the other Dogwoods, being bright golden yellow, tiny, and borne in clusters in the axils of the unfolded leaves. The effect of these flowers in March, as the branches are wreathed with bloom, is a sight always charming and yet the Cornelian-cherry is not seen as frequently in gardens as it should be. The leaves are oval, often hairy beneath but very lustrous above. The young branchlets are quadrangular, greenish-yellow when young and turn reddish-brown toward Winter. The fruits, unlike the other Dogwoods, are like small plums, scarlet, produced in August, hidden by the leaves and borne profusely on old plants. A sort with creamy

Largeflowering Dogwoods

1, The common Flowering Dogwood (*Cornus florida*) is shown in the large spray; 2, the tender Evergreen Dogwood (*C. capitata*) often has five bracts and is a native of the Pacific Coast; 3, the Kousa Dogwood, a hardy sort, has pointed bracts instead of the notched bracts of the Flowering Dogwood

white and pinkish variegations is known as *elegantissima*. It should not be confused with *C. alba gouchaulti* which is a different type of plant.

Cornus officinalis, the Japanese Cornelian-cherry, closely resembles *C. mas* but the flowers are a week earlier. There are tufts of brown hairs in the axils of the leaves and the flowers have long stems (pedicels).

Twigs brown, but reddish or yellowish green when young. Flowers yellow and surrounded by large white, sometimes rosy, petal-like bracts.

Cornus florida. Flowering D. This lovely treelike shrub perhaps belongs only in a book on trees, but it is so useful that it could not be omitted. The flowers bear four large white bracts which are really the bud scales, serving as a protection in Winter. Because the frost injures these scales, the exposed part does not grow, or turn white, consequently, these white bracts each have a notch at the apex when they are fully expanded. The woods from Maine to Florida are glorious with these flowers in May. The leaves are elliptical, and abruptly pointed and unfold after the flowers are well open. The fruits are red and so numerous in certain trees as to be very showy in September.

Var. *rubra* is a choice sort having bracts which vary from blush-pink to deep rose. As seen in the distance, this form is lovely, but the color is not clear, so that close inspection is never desirable. Var. *plena*, the Doubleflowering D., has an extra row of white bracts. It is more showy than the type.

Cornus kousa, the Kousa D., is a very compact bushy tree. It differs from the Flowering Dogwood in that the flowers do not open until about June 10, at which time the leaves are fully expanded; also the four large white bracts are pointed, not notched at the edge. The leaves are rather ruffled along the margins, prominently and often red-veined. The fruits are pinkish, almost an inch across. Var. *chinensis* has larger, overlapping bracts, larger leaves. It is considered superior to the type.

Alternate Leaves. All of the above sorts have opposite leaves but there is another sort which has alternate leaves, *Cornus alternifolia*, Pagoda D. (Alternate-leaf D.) The branches are in irregular tiers, forming a somewhat flat horizontal shrub or small tree, often 20 ft. tall. The flowers open in May, and are pale yellow, produced in slender stalked clusters (cymes). The fruit is bluish-black on red stems. The branches are smooth, green when young. The leaves are usually crowded at the ends of short branchlets and are grayish and hairy beneath. The berries are eaten, even before ripening, by birds.

Uses. There are a multitude of uses for Dogwoods—trees and shrubs, with showy flowers, fruits, branches, and leaves. They are adapted to all sorts of soil conditions; most of them stand a little shade. In fact, *C. florida, C. mas* and *C. alternifolia* are often planted in naturalistic, woodsy places.

For wet places we have *C. stolonifera, C. paniculata, C. amomum, C. sanguinea.*

For dry places we use *C. baileyi* and *C. brachypoda.*

Those of the most attractive habit are: *C. florida, C. kousa, C. alternifolia, C. mas, C. brachypoda,* and *C. paniculata.*

For Autumnal tints of foliage there are *C. florida, C. brachypoda, C. kousa, C. sanguinea,* and *C. baileyi.*

For foliage variegated throughout the year we may choose *C. alba spaethi, C. alba argenteo-marginata, C. alba gouchaulti, C. mas elegantissima.*

For red twig Winter effects we have: *C. stolonifera, C. sanguinea, C. alba sibirica, C. stolonifera coloradensis, C. baileyi,* and for yellow *C. stolonifera flaviramea;* green twigs are found in *C. sanguinea viridissima* and *C. stolonifera nitida.*

For fruits most sorts are showy, some being not only showy but useful for birds and therefore planted in zoological gardens. It is said that monkeys are fond of the fruits of *C. alba sibirica.* The profuse white or bluish fruits of *C. paniculata* with their red stems are much to be admired. The Flowering Dogwoods would be worth planting for their red fruits alone. The large plumlike fruits of *C. mas,* the Cornelian-cherry, are most attractive, even though somewhat hidden by the leaves. Bailey notes that the green fruits have been substituted for olives. Some others have recommended the fruits for acid beverages and tarts.

Few flowering trees are as popular as the Flowering Dogwood, *Cornus florida,* with its snowy mass of loveliness. Especially effective against evergreens, the Cornelian-cherry rivals the Goldenbells in beauty, but coming earlier than the latter, these two are not rivals but actors in a different scene. The Kousa Dogwood comes later than *C. florida* but does not need a background as its leaves are expanded when the flowers open. Later than most sorts, the horizontal branches of *C. brachypoda* are loaded with the feathery masses of bloom so characteristic of the greater part of the commoner Dogwoods, all of which are profuse in flower production.

Besides these uses, Bailey mentions that our native *C. florida* is a substitute for quinine, the bark containing the same substance as found in cinchona. It is believed that chewing the twigs will ward off fever. The powdered bark makes a good tooth powder. The bark mixed with sulphate of iron makes a black ink. The bark of the roots yields a scarlet dye. The wood is useful for tool handles, being tough and hard.

The bark of the Silky D. was dried and smoked by the Indians.

It is a source of pride to note that *The Garden* (London) some time ago contained an article on Dogwoods by E. H. Wilson, of the Arnold Arboretum:

"Dogwoods cannot be successfully grown in the British Isles, due to the lack of Summer heat and steady cold, as prevail, particularly in New England, where the finest Dogwoods are found. In passing, Mr. Wilson mentions that in the Spring of 1913, he had the privilege of showing Sir Herbert Maxwell, one of the most famous amateur plantsmen in the world, around the Arboretum at Jamaica Plains, Mass. Sir Herbert, after seeing everything, sighed: 'Give me your Dogwoods, the rest you may keep.' And yet there are people who will desecrate the woods by breaking down and mutilating the Dogwoods just because they are wild. I can imagine that if Sir H. Maxwell had the Dogwood flourishing in his woods, he would surround them with mantraps and spring guns."

INSECTS. The low, bushy sorts are often troubled with scale, especially oyster-shell scale. It is necessary to spray with miscible oils. (See page 43.) Shrubs badly affected should be cut to the soil. For some reason, *Cornus baileyi* is reputed to be less subject to scale than *C. alba sibirica*.

Newly transplanted Flowering Dogwoods are especially subject to a borer, *Sesia scitula*, a whitish caterpillar which works under the bark until the small trees are girdled. These insects must be searched for and dug out before they destroy the plant. The adult of this insect is a clear wing moth, not unlike a bee or wasp in appearance.

SOIL. Most sorts circumneutral pH 6.0–8.0, but *Cornus florida* minimacid pH 6.0–7.0 and *C. canadensis* mediacid pH 4.0–5.0.

PRUNING. The Dogwoods grown for colored bark must be pruned yearly and rigorously to renew the young twigs which are the only ones with a highly ornamental color.

C. mas is best pruned when young so that it may be trained into tree form. Remove all shoots from soil, except one, and prune the top accordingly.

PROPAGATION. 1. *Most species may be raised from seed which is stratified for the Winter. Generally the seeds germinate the second year. See page 50, after-ripening necessary. Seeds of *C. kousa* are often infertile. Further facts about *C. florida* seed are found on page 48.

2. Hardwood cuttings of osierlike sorts, such as *C. alba, C. amomum, C. paniculata, C. sanguinea* and *C. stolonifera*.

3. Softwood will root in Summer, selecting that which is quite matured. *Cornus kousa* roots readily.

4. Suckers and division of such sorts as *C. stolonifera*.

5. Grafting. *Cornus alba sibirica* and *C. mas* may be whip grafted on piece roots in Winter, stored in a cool place in sand or green sawdust. Plant in rows in Spring.

6. Budding. *C. florida rubra* is budded on type in August. *C. alba spaethi, C. alba gouchaulti* and variegated sorts budded on *C. stolonifera* and *C. alba* var. *sibirica*.

CORONILLA—Scorpion-senna
(Name derived from *corona*—a crown, refers to method in which the flowers are borne)

A dense shrub, seldom over 3 or 4 ft. tall, but possibly 9 ft. high, *Coronilla emerus* produces clusters (umbels) of yellow pealike flowers upon slender stems in the axils of the leaves. The blooming season is May to September. The leaves are dark glossy green, seven to nine parted. The branches are green. The pods are long and slender, 2 in. long.

Uses. Although growing in Highland Park, Rochester, N. Y., the Coronilla is at home farther south where it is almost evergreen. There is nothing extremely desirable about this shrub; it is another yellow leguminous plant, but has a long season of bloom, even though few flowers are open at one time.

Soil. Due to its sensitivity to cold, a well-drained soil should be chosen.

Pests. Subject to aphides.

Propagation. 1. *Softwood cuttings should be taken in Summer.

2. Seeds should be soaked before sowing.

CORYLOPSIS—Winterhazel
(Named from *Korulos*—hazel, *opsis*—like)

A much-branched relative of the Witch-hazel is *Corylopsis pauciflora*, the Buttercup Winterhazel. It grows from 4 to 6 ft. tall and is hardy from New York southward. The primrose-yellow flowers are produced in two to four flowered spikes (less than 1 in. long) with large bracts at their base. The flowers open before the leaves are expanded. The leaves resemble the true Hazel, being obliquely heart-shaped, prominently veined, coarsely toothed, sharp pointed. The young leaves and the tips of the branchlets are purplish-red. The capsules are furnished with two horns, and contain two black seeds.

C. spicata, the Spike W., is not quite as hardy, although it is reported as growing nicely in New York State. It has larger leaves 2 to 4 in. long. The young branches are hairy. The yellow, fragrant flowers are produced in 8 to 12 flowered racemes 1 to 2 in. long.

USES. The symmetrical and compact, flat-topped shrubs would serve as interesting specimens because of the attractive leaves and early

Corylopsis or Winterhazel
Distinctive, symmetrical and compact growth

flowers. *C. spicata* will flower in the shade of trees, according to S. N. Baxter. "Where they are hardy they are among the most graceful of shrubs. They are not vulgar like Forsythias, but lovely. Unfortunately, however, they are too tender."—M. V. Horvath.

SOIL.   Peaty and sandy soil preferable.

PRUNING.   Summer pruning is advisable as it causes the plants to be more bushy.

PROPAGATION.   1. *Half-ripe wood may be rooted under glass in Summer.

2. *Layers may be made in Spring and left two years to root. Root best in peaty soil.

3. Seeds may be sown in Spring with bottom heat.

4. Witch-hazel may be used as a stock for grafting.

CORYLUS—Hazel · Filbert

(Name from *Korus*—a helmet, calyx covers fruit)

The Hazels and Filberts have been cultivated for many years for their delicious nuts. The fruits have long involucres, or husks, in Filberts. and shorter ones hardly longer than the nut itself in the Hazels. The cat-kins, which bear the male flowers, hang upon the plants all Winter awaiting the first warmth of Spring, when they open. In gardens we are concerned mostly with *Corylus avellana fusco-rubra*, the Purple Hazele which is often cataloged as *C. atropurpurea*. The leaves are dull purple or brownish-red; almost round, hairy beneath. As the season advances the leaves become greener and less purple. The nuts are surrounded by a husk which is rarely longer than the nut. Another variety *aurea*, the Golden Filbert, has yellow leaves and yellowish branchlets. Var. *heter-ophylla*, also called var. *laciniata* and *pinnatifida*, has the leaves cut deeply into pinnate lobes.

A taller growing species, *C. maxima*, produces nuts with a very long husk which is quite tubular, purplish. This species also has a purple leaf variety, *purpurea*, which is deeper in color. The nuts are produced in clusters of three or four mature nuts with several others which are aborted.

The Beaked Hazelnut, *C. rostrata* (*cornuta*), has a very long beaked husk. The nuts in this sort are quite small but the ornamental husks are of interest.

Uses. Persons who desire a contrast in foliage in their plantings enjoy the Purple and Golden Filberts, either as specimens or for massing back of other shrubs. In the shade the purple sorts are greener. The squirrels get most of the wild nuts.

Soils. *C. rostrata* minimacid pH 6.0–7.0.

Pruning. To produce large, ornamental leaves these plants may be pruned back severely each year.

Propagation. 1. Fresh nuts could be kept damp during the Winter and sown in the Spring.

2. Purple and Golden sorts are grafted on roots of the green species.

3. *Plants may be cut to the soil and layered in Summer or early Spring but left a year to root properly. The shoots will need to be pegged down to the soil in layering.

4. Suckers are often obtainable.

COTONEASTER—Rockspray (Quinceberry)
(*Cotonea*, Pliny's name for the Quince—*ad instar*, usually used to express likeness)

Few shrubs have come to the front in recent years comparable to the group of Cotoneasters. The beautiful red and black fruits, the showy but small flowers and the evergreen leaves of some of the sorts invite us to widen our acquaintance with these shrubs.

Among the Cotoneasters there are 30 principal species and many varieties mentioned by Rehder. One grades into the other so imperceptibly that only a specialist can distinguish closely related sorts; even then, one needs a descriptive manual to be sure of his determinations. The amateur will be interested in a few outstanding species which are useful for their fruits, unusual habit of growth or wealth of bloom.

Small leaf sorts which are low in growth. *Cotoneaster horizontalis* (*davidiana*), the Rock Cotoneaster (Quinceberry) (Plumed C.), is one of the commonest sorts from Western China. The horizontal, quite prostrate branches form flat sprays with branchlets arranged in fishbone fashion (regularly distichously branched). They seldom grow 2 ft. tall unless placed against a wall. The leaves are quite evergreen in Southern regions but in the North they turn red in the Autumn and drop. The leaves are ½ in. long, rounded or broad elliptical, sharp pointed, glossy dark green above and hairy beneath. The flowers are pinkish-white, not

Left, Cotoneaster horizontalis, a horizontal, branching, low-growing shrub covered in the Fall with interesting small red fruit; *right,* Cotoneaster acutifolia, a valuable subject for poor, dry soil producing clusters of black fruits in the Fall

very showy, produced one or two together. The bright red fruit is produced very abundantly during September and is one of the chief charms of this sort, although the fruits are only ¼ in. in diameter.

Var. *perpusilla* is a smaller growing sort for the rockery and with larger fruit.

Cotoneaster dammeri (humifusa). This trailing species has evergreen leaves which are slightly hairy when young. The branches are so prostrate that they usually root as they trail over the soil. Unlike *C. horizontalis,* the leaves are not hairy beneath. This sort is not hardy in most of the Northern states.

Cotoneaster adpressa, Creeping C., resembles above but the branches are less regularly branched in one plane. The leaves are slightly undulate and not so hairy beneath. The plants are more prostrate and will root as they grow, being adpressed to the soil; hence the name.

Cotoneaster apiculata. Another handsome sort resembling the above. The branches are not fishbonelike; the leaves are a little curled and quite hairless. This is a most desirable type at the Arnold Arboretum. It forms a little mound of growth for the branches are more upright.

Cotoneaster microphylla, the Rockspray (Wall C.), grows flat on the soil but has spreading branchlets. The leaves are shining dark green and more evergreen than *C. horizontalis*, obovate to cuneate-oblong, ⅓ in. or less long, with wedge-shaped base, and almost never pointed at tip, hairy beneath. Unlike *C. horizontalis*, the flowers are white, usually solitary and the petals are more spreading and round. The scarlet fruits are about ½ in. in diameter.

Var. *thymifolia* is very dwarf with minute, roundish leaves.

Small leaf sorts which are more upright. *Cotoneaster rotundifolia*, Roundleaf C., is a more upright sort with branches quite fishbonelike in arrangement. The semi-evergreen leaves are quite round, the tips being rounded or abruptly pointed (mucronate); the base broad, wedge-shaped, dark green above and hairy on both sides, especially when young, but less so than *C. horizontalis*. Flowers white, pink tinted, usually solitary. Fruit red, ½ in. long, globose.

Upright sorts, at least taller and with usually larger leaves. Red fruited. *Cotoneaster divaricata*, Spreading C., is upright in growth, though the branches are spreading and the growth is intricate. The plants are frequently 6 ft. tall. The leaves are 1 in. long, elliptical, generally pointed, glossy green above, lighter and sometimes a little hairy on midrib below. They turn red in Autumn and covering the branches are very attractive. The flowers are pink, in three flowered clusters produced in June. The fruit is less than ½ in. long, oblong, ripening in August or September; it stays red for a long period. One of the hardiest and most reliable sorts with branches completely loaded with fruit.

Cotoneaster simonsi, Simons C., is a vigorous, compact sort with erect but spreading branches. The leaves are half evergreen, ¾ in. long, deep dull green, paler beneath, hairy when young, roundish, pointed. Young growth woolly. Flowers white in 2–4 flowered clusters, followed by bright red, obovoid fruit in October. Resembles *C. acutifolia* but with scarlet rather than black fruit. The leaves and branchlets are so similar that only a botanist can tell the difference.

Cotoneaster dielsiana (*applanata*), Diels C., grows 6 ft. tall and has arching branches with a spread of 7 or 8 ft. This is an excellent sort at Highland Park, Rochester. The leaves are small, ¾ in. to 1¼ in. long, somewhat pointed, rounded at base, yellowish or grayish hairy beneath. The veins are prominently depressed in the leaves. The flowers are pinkish, opening in June, and are followed by scarlet fruits on short stalks produced in September. The fruits and brilliant color of the orange-red leaves in Fall makes this a desirable shrub. It differs from *C. simonsi* and *C. divaricata* in having densely hairy leaves and branchlets.

Cotoneaster francheti, Franchet C., has gracefully arching branches. It differs from the preceding in that the fruit is more orange and the flowers are borne in larger clusters. The leaves and branchlets are hairy when young, the leaves becoming lustrous above, but are densely yellow or white, woolly beneath. They are often green until December in Rochester. The fruits persist the greater part of the Winter.

Cotoneaster acuminata grows 8 to 12 ft. tall. The leaves are 1½ to 2 in. long, sharp pointed, dark dull green above and hairy beneath when young but paler and smooth at maturity. The young shoots are densely hairy. The fruits are large, bright red, hairy at apex. Resembles *C. simonsi* but with larger leaves.

Cotoneaster multiflora var. *calocarpa* is a slender arching sort, attractive on account of its white flowers and its large scarlet fruits. The branches are smooth at maturity and purplish. The leaves are broad, bluish-green and glossy. The flowers are produced erect in 6 to 20 flowered clusters along the whole length of the branches. The fruits drop rather early, although they are beautiful.

Cotoneaster racemiflora var. *soongarica*. A wide spreading shrub with rarely upright branches—"one of the most attractive shrubs in the Arnold Arboretum judged from bloom abundance, and the size, quantity and quality of the fruit." The leaves are oval and blunt, nearly round, although often with an abrupt sharp point, quite densely hairy. The young branches are gray, hairy. The flowers are produced in 3 to 12 flowered upright clusters. The fruits are large, ⅓ in. long.

Cotoneaster hupehensis, the Hupeh C., resembles the two preceding species but has more of a yellow-green cast to the leaves. The branches are hairy at first, becoming smooth and purple. The leaves, unlike *C. multiflora*, are hairy beneath, and unlike *C. racemiflora*, are usually sharp pointed, more oval, and grayish, hairy beneath. Rehder says of this that it is one of the handsomest species with long arching branchlets studded with clusters of white flowers in May, followed by bright red fruits in August; the leaves turn yellow in Autumn.

Cotoneaster frigida, the Himalayan C., is a tall shrub or small tree which is less hardy than the others mentioned. The leaves are narrow, elliptical, pointed, often 5 in. long, and hairy when young. The white flowers are borne in dense clusters. The fruits are very showy in Fall. It is a common shrub for foundation planting in the warmer regions of our country.

Cotoneaster pannosa, the Silverleaf C., has quite evergreen leaves which are white woolly beneath and gray green above. The white flowers are followed by masses of deep red berries which remain all Winter. Resembles *C. francheti* but the leaves are not hairy above. It is not a hardy sort.

Black fruited sorts. One of the hardiest of all Cotoneasters is *Cotoneaster acutifolia* (*pekinensis*) Peking C., which is useful for hedges in Minnesota. The shrub is erect, slightly spreading and makes a beautiful appearance. The leaves are dark, shiny, 2 in. long, rather smooth, pointed (acute but rarely acuminate), lighter green beneath, sparingly hairy, but generally not so at maturity. The two to five flowered clusters of bloom develop conspicuous black fruits. Thrives in poor, rather dry soil.

C. foveolata resembles the above but is less compact and has larger and duller leaves. It is not as good in habit at the Arnold Arboretum. The black fruits are very large. The leaves turn to brilliant scarlet and orange in the Autumn.

Uses. The general usefulness of the Cotoneasters is shown in lists which follow:

QUITE EVERGREEN
C. horizontalis
C. microphylla
C. rotundifolia
C. simonsi

ROCKERY SPECIES
C. adpressa
C. apiculata
C. horizontalis
C. microphylla

RED FRUITS
C. acuminata
C. adpressa
C. dielsiana
C. divaricata
C. francheti
C. horizontalis

C. hupehensis
C. microphylla
C. multiflora var. *colocarpa*
C. racemiflora var. *soongarica*
C. simonsi

LEAVES TURN RED
C. divaricata
C. horizontalis

LEAVES TURN ORANGE
C. dielsiana

BLACK FRUITS
C. acutifolia
C. foveolata

VALUED FOR FLOWERS
C. multiflora var. *calocarpa*
C. racemiflora var. *soongarica*

USEFUL FOR SOUTHERN PLANTING

1. UPRIGHT	2. PROSTRATE
C. acuminata	*C. dammeri*
C. francheti	*C. horizontalis*
C. frigida	*C. microphylla*
C. pannosa	*C. microphylla thymifolia*

SOIL. Circumneutral pH 6.0–8.0.

PROPAGATION. 1. *The Cotoneasters, being profuse seed bearers, are often propagated by this method. An after-ripening period is necessary (see page 50). Do not sow or store the seeds in peat moss as they resent the acid.

2. Softwood cuttings are taken rather long, rooted in August or September and carried through the Winter in the greenhouse. Propagated from stock planted in Winter.

3. Layers may be put down in the Autumn.

4. The sorts may be grafted upon Quince, Hawthorn, or Mountain-ash.

CYDONIA—(See Chaenomeles, page 181)

The names for the sorts of Cydonia are now somewhat changed, so that the author feels it necessary to follow the names given by Bailey, Rehder, and *Standardized Plant Names*.

CYRILLA (Leatherwood) (Black Ji-ti)

(Named for Dominico Cyrillo, professor at Naples)

Native to the warmer parts of America, *Cyrilla racemiflora* grows to almost 30 ft. tall. It is not unlike the *Oxydendrum*, or Sorreltree. The flowers are produced in slender racemes, are lily-of-the-valley-like, white, opening in June and July. The handsome, nearly evergreen leaves are oblanceolate, glossy and bright green, turning orange and crimson in the Autumn. This sort is hardy at the Arnold Arboretum.

USES. A border shrub or small specimen tree for semi-shaded places.

SOIL. Sandy loam or peaty soils suit best. Moister soils are desired.

PROPAGATION. Root softwood cuttings under glass.

CYTISUS—Broom

(Some authors say the name is derived from Cythrus—one of the Cyclades where one species is found; other writers believe the name is from the Greek *Kytisos*—a kind of Clover)

In this group of shrubs we have several excellent yellow-flowered plants which are so profuse blooming and hardy that they should be more generally planted.

Two large groups of pealike flowers resemble each other so closely that the gardener finds difficulty in knowing the differences between *Cytisus* and *Genista*.

Cytisus. Spineless. Seeds with callous appendage. Leaves often three-parted but seldom simple and alternate. Petals free at base. Flowers yellow or white, rarely purple.

Genista. Branches often spiny. Seeds without callous appendage. Leaves simple but often three-parted and alternate or opposite. Lower petals attached to stamen tube. Flowers usually yellow.

Quite leafless plants. The best known sort is the Scotch Broom, *Cytisus (Spartium) scoparius*, a shrub which is extremely common throughout Central and Southern Europe. It is occasionally naturalized in the Eastern States and on Vancouver Island. It is an upright shrub with slender, erect, angular green branches, pubescent when young. In favored locations it attains a height of 10 ft. It is a trifle tender and in the North must be planted in protected places. The yellow flowers are large, pealike and produced solitary along the almost leafless branches during May or June. Leaves are one- to three-parted and sparingly hairy. The pods are nearly black, with a hairy edge and are 1 to 2 in. long. Var. *andreanus*, the Paradise Broom, has red and yellow flowers.

The Provence Broom, *C. purgans*, resembles the Scotch Broom, but it is not quite as tall. Botanically it differs by having a shorter pistil. It is hardy at the Arnold Arboretum.

Flowers crowded together in heads. The Bigflower Broom, *C. supinus (capitatus)* bears a crown of yellow flowers crowded together at the top of the stem. At the Hunnewell Estate, Wellesley, Mass., the plants were of exceptional beauty. It blooms in July.

Like the preceding, but with yellowish-white flowers is *C. leucanthus (albus)*, the Pale Broom. It grows 18 in. tall and the flowers crown the stems with a whorl of bloom.

Flowers in short, dense clusters. The Canary Broom, *C. canariensis*, is an extremely floriferous species grown in greenhouses as a pot plant in the Northern States, and as a flowering subject for Southern gardens. The flowers are bright yellow, fragrant, in short clusters.

In the greenhouse they bloom in March and April, but in the Southern States they continue to bloom during Spring and Summer. This is the so-called Genista of the florist.

Flowers arranged in elongated clusters. The Spike (or Black root) Broom, *C. nigricans*, is a beautiful sort growing 3 ft. tall at the Brooklyn Botanical Garden. In June and July it bears terminal clusters (racemes) of fragrant yellow flowers. Leaves are three-parted and branches slightly hairy. The plants are apt to freeze to the soil each year.

C. hirsutus, the Hairy Broom, also freezes back and resembles a herbaceous perennial. The branches and leaves are very hairy. This plant is very leafy. There is a profusion of yellow flowers upon plants which are often over 3 ft. in diameter so that it would be an excellent addition to the low growing (2 ft.) garden subjects.

Two more or less prostrate sorts which are hardy at the Arnold Arboretum are: *C. purpureus*, with purple flowers, and *C. glabrescens*, with yellow flowers.

Uses. The low growing sorts, such as *C. supinus*, *C. leucanthus*, *C. nigricans* and *C. hirsutus* are valuable additions to our short list of low growing shrubs for bordering the taller ones. Nowhere in the East has the writer seen such effective use made of these small species of Brooms as at the Arnold Arboretum, where they make a glorious mass of bloom at the base of the taller shrubs bordering the roadsides. These, together with *C. purpureus* and *C. glabrescens*, are good for large rockeries or they would be at home in the herbaceous perennial border, inasmuch as many of them freeze to the soil each year, although the roots are hardy.

C. scoparius and *C. purgans* are taller sorts and generally a little more tender. Their unusual, almost leafless, character makes them rather unique in appearance and, therefore, valuable additions to protected shrub borders. They are advised for seashore planting and in their native haunts grow in waste places.

Soil. The Scotch and Provence Brooms prefer sandy soil but the other sorts apparently succeed as well in clay as in sand. They appear to be indifferent to acidity in the soil. Subacid pH 5.0–6.0.

Objections. In regions not adapted to the Scotch Broom, there is a great deal of dead wood in the plants and it appears leggy at the base.

Propagation. 1. Seeds are advertised by a number of European growers. Seed should be soaked and sown in May. Generally bloom second year.

2. Cuttings of half-ripe wood may be rooted in a close frame of the greenhouse.

DAPHNE—(Garlandflower)

(Named after the Nymph, Daphne)

An exquisite shrub bearing clusters of the most fragrant pink flowers, the Rose Daphne or Garlandflower, *Daphne cneorum* grows in the mountains of Europe. It is often considered a perennial but is really shrubby, 12 to 18 in. tall, inclined to be trailing. The pink flowers, borne in dense heads at the ends of the branches, are four- or rarely five-parted. They bloom in April and again in September. The leaves are evergreen, dark green, lustrous above and grayish beneath. The yellowish-brown berries are rarely seen. This is the most desirable species. There are possibly two forms in cultivation, one of which does not bloom but propagates more easily and for that reason is often seen. In pronouncing the name "cneorum," the "c" is silent.

The February D. (*D. mezereum*) is an upright shrub with stout, smooth, olive-colored branches bearing three-flowered clusters of pink, rose or purple flowers before Winter is hardly over and before the leaves develop. The leaves are alternate, long, oval, green above but grayish beneath. The fruits are scarlet, and being stemless, are produced close to the branches in August and September. It is quite hardy but a slow grower. It is an extremely showy bush. Best planted in a cool, sheltered, humid place, otherwise troubled with red spider.

Daphne blagayana, the Balkan D., is a trailing sort resembling the *D. mezereum* in foliage but with creamy-white flowers and with evergreen leaves. It is hardy at the Arnold Arboretum.

Daphne genkwa, the Lilac D., has opposite leaves, $1\frac{1}{4}$ to 2 in. long, and silky, hairy beneath. The flowers are violet, thickly set upon the leafless branches in early April, borne on short stalks, and without fragrance. M. V. Horvath considers this one of the loveliest of early flowering shrubs, but it often freezes to the soil, in which case it is cut down to the soil and not left unpruned; otherwise it may not renew itself.

Uses. Most of the Daphnes are admirably adapted to the rock garden. *Daphne cneorum* is frequently used as an edging shrub in beds of evergreens which have been used in foundation plantings.

Soils. All sorts of Daphnes prefer conditions such as are found in rockeries with perfect drainage and a cool root run. They are thought to like lime but, nevertheless, grow well in soil undoubtedly acid. Robinson says that peaty or very sandy soil is best. They are short

Daphne mezereum or Garlandflower
Extremely attractive, upright shrub producing its pink, fragrant flowers close to the stem, followed by scarlet fruits in August

lived in clay. *Daphne mezereum* prefers minimalkaline soil pH 7.0-8.0.

It is believed that some shade is not detrimental, although they thrive best in full sun.

Remarking upon *Daphne blagayana*, an article in Gardener's Chronicle of America suggests that the secret of success is the continuous layering of the growths by covering the woody parts with leafmold, sand and a few stones as the development proceeds. Thus the plants will be growing in a mound of rocks and humus.

OBJECTIONS. Most sorts make a slow growth. They are susceptible to the same sort of injury as are all broadleaved evergreens which suffer from Winter sun which activates the leaves, even though these are frozen and cannot supply the water for transpiration. There is a tendency for whole branches to die out.

In some regions the flower buds are frozen in early Spring.

For cut flowers *Daphne cneorum* has an almost nauseating sweet fragrance.

PROPAGATION. 1. Miss Nettie Nieman of Cincinnati has been successful in propagating *D. cneorum* by taking the blooming shoots in Spring or Fall just before the flowers open. Pinch out the flowers and the shoots will root nicely.

2. Another nurseryman suggests taking cuttings the first week in

August. Insert in a frame in sand over which a layer of peat is spread. Give no air for ten days but keep the sash upon the frame. Gradually give air until at the end of six weeks the cuttings are rooted.

The best method of propagation, according to G. W. Oliver, is to layer the trailing branches in Spring, making an incision, or tongue, in the under part of the stem. Have the cut part at least 2 in. under the soil; secure with wooden pegs; press the soil firmly over it, and cover with sphagnum to insure moisture. Leave until the following Spring before separating from the parent plant.

3. Another method described by Bailey (N. M.) is to remove the soil about the plants in the Spring to a depth of 2 or 3 in. and fill with good compost to within 2 in. of the tops of the shoots. The next Spring wash away the compost, and plant the small white buds in pots of fine soil. Place in frames.

4. *Daphne mezereum* is often propagated by hardwood cuttings in the greenhouse in Fall and wintered indoors.

5. Seeds should be stratified in sand. It takes two years to germinate and then the germination is irregular.

DEUTZIA

Among the shrubs called Deutzia are many lovely flowers although many of the choicer sorts are not hardy enough for open situations in the more Northern States. Except for several species, it is the named hybrids produced by V. Lemoine that are the worthiest to grow.

Among the species none is more attractive than *Deutzia gracilis*, the Slender Deutzia, a sort from Japan. It is one of our best low growing, flowering shrubs, generally attaining a height of 3 ft., although sometimes growing to 6 ft. The white flowers are produced in graceful, upright clusters (panicles or racemes) about the time that Tulips are in bloom, generally May. The leaves are opposite, smooth, long-pointed, unequally toothed. The branchlets have yellowish-gray, smooth bark.

Of this lower growing type we may enumerate certain varieties found in catalogs:

Var. *campanulata*, Bellflower D. Larger flowers than type, more bell-shaped.

Var *carminea*, Carmine D. Buds carmine, flowers pink or reverse darker, sepals purplish.

Var. *carnea*. Pink flowers in loose upright panicles, sepals purplish.

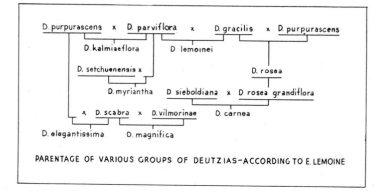

PARENTAGE OF VARIOUS GROUPS OF DEUTZIAS—ACCORDING TO E. LEMOINE

Var. *eximia*, Pink Choice D. Buds carmine-pink, flowers white, sepals purplish.

Var. *floribunda*. Dense upright panicles, slightly pink outside, stamens toothed.

Var. *grandiflora*. Similar to var. *floribunda* but panicles less dense.

Var. *multiflora*. Flowers white, profuse; plants compact and bushy.

Var. *rosea*. Rose Panicle D. Light pink outside; brown flaking bark; taller than type.

Var. *venusta*, White Panicle D. White, late May. Improvement upon *D. gracilis*.

Another hybrid form is *D. lemoinei*, the Lemoine Deutzia, which is taller than *D. gracilis*, one of its parents, and lower than *D. parviflora*, its other early flowered, tender parent. This is one of the hardiest types, hardier than either parent. The branches bend gracefully with their masses of white flowers, borne in broad 20 to 30 flowered clusters (panicles). It should be used in all extensive shrub combinations because of its profusion of bloom.

This group crossed with *D. setchuenensis* has given rise to a group known as the Cherry Blossom, or Myriantha, Deutzias, which have pink on the outside of the flower. They include Boule Rose, an erect plant with white flowers bordered rose, and Fleur de Pommier (Apple-blossom), a dwarf compact plant with rose-tinted white flowers.

The third principal group is derived from *Deutzia scabra crenata*. The taller growing sorts belong here. The foliage is dull green, rough and sandpaperlike. The twigs are hollow, red-brown or gray-brown with bark which peels when twigs are old. This group is not as hardy as the others. There are many named varieties, and among the best are:

1. Plena. Double white flowers suffused with pale rosy purple outside.

2. Pride of Rochester. Double; earlier than Plena but with rose-purple on outside also.

3. Snowflake (*candidissima*) (*wellsi*). Double, with erect clusters of purest white flowers. Handsome; profuse flowering. Good in shade.

4. Waterer D. Single pink flowers which open quite flat. Grows 7 to 8 ft. tall. One of the hardiest.

5. Magnifica varieties. Flowers in denser, shorter clusters. (*D. scabra* x *D. vilmorinae*.)

(1) Eburnea. Deep rose; bell-shaped flowers in loose clusters.

(2) Erecta. One of the best singles; white.

(3) Formosa. One of the best double whites; very profuse flowering.

(4) Latifolia. Single white. 1 in. in diameter, spreading petals; 18 to 20 blooms on the stems.

(5) Superba. Bell-shaped single flowers; little larger flowers and spikes than the similar variety Erecta.

Left, a spray of bloom typical of the Deutzia scabra varieties; *right,* an effective planting of the Slender Deutzia along a garden walk

PRUNING. The very soft wood of the younger branches is often tender in the colder climates so that early Spring pruning is necessary.

In general, however, prune as little as possible, except to take out the old wood. The wood of Deutzias is not long lived and must be renewed by taking out entire branches from the base of the plants. Shearing the plants results in too vigorous wood at top of plant which destroys the grace of the shrub.

The Deutzia, however, produces its flower trusses at the ends of short leafy stems, but other leafy shoots which do not flower appear below the flowering ones, waiting to continue the growth of the shoot. It is to these shoots the branches should be cut in pruning after bloom.

SOIL AND CULTURE. The lighter soils are preferable for Deutzias because the plants mature better and are hardier. Circumneutral pH. 6.0–8.0. Most sorts will enjoy a little shade.

PROPAGATION. 1. *Softwood cuttings in Summer root 100 per cent in 7 to 14 days, easier than most shrubs. Some are taken just before flowering.

2. *Hardwood cuttings should be gathered before the twigs are frozen hard, *Deutzia scabra* and its hybrids especially.

3. Plants of *Deutzia gracilis* may be divided.

4. Layers.

DIERVILLA—Bush-honeysuckle
(Named for M. Dierville, a French surgeon)

Several species of Diervillas are wild throughout the Northern States, also as far north as Newfoundland and Saskatchewan; and as far South as North Carolina. They have yellow flowers and seldom grow over 3 ft. tall.

The Standardized Plant Name, Bush-honeysuckle, is unfortunate, inasmuch as the various shrubby Loniceras have always been called Bush-honeysuckles.

Certain of the plants called by some botanists *Diervilla* must be sought under *Weigela*, page 405, these being Asiatic sorts.

D. trifida (*lonicera*) (*canadensis*) Dwarf Bush-honeysuckle. A very hardy sort as its native range would indicate. The yellow flowers are funnel-shaped in three- to five-flowered clusters borne in June and July. The flowers turn red with age. The leaves are opposite and distinctly petioled. The branchlets are reddish and the tip leaves are quite metallic green.

D. sessilifolia, the Southern B., has leaves without petioles; otherwise the two species are similar. The twigs are also rather four-angled.

USES. These native shrubs are excellent for clothing steep slopes and are useful for the foreground of a naturalistic planting. They are good in shaded places but often grow in the full sun in nature.

PROPAGATION. 1. *They sucker freely so that the common method of propagation is to divide the plants as perennials are divided.

2. Softwood cuttings may be made in Summer and wintered in a frame or greenhouse.

DIOSMA—Breath-of-heaven
(From *Dios*—divine, and *osme*—odor)

The Diosma includes a small group of South African shrubs, most of which are Heathlike.

Diosma ericoides, the Breath-of-heaven (Buchu) grows but 2 ft. tall. The flowers are white, star-shaped, and very tiny. The twigs and the flowers are fragrant. These tiny shrubs are grown in the South as they are not hardy except in the semi-tropics. They prefer a peaty or acid soil and should be planted in a mixture of loam, leafmold, and peatmoss.

PROPAGATION. Cuttings of short young shoots root in Spring. Confine the air with a bell jar.

DIRCA—Leatherwood (Moosewood) (Wicopy)
(From Dirke—a Greek mythological name)

This rounded shrub grows from 2 to 4 ft. tall but its habit is rather treelike. The flowers are yellow, produced in clusters, and have pendant yellow stamens. The blooms appear in March and April upon the leafless shoots. The leaves spread out in one plane, are alternate, simple and oval. A yellowish hue prevades the whole plant. The branches are curiously socket-jointed; in other words, the nodes are swollen. The twigs are flexible, olive-brown in color, glossy and are furnished with small, white dots. The bark is tough. The fruit is a red fleshy one, ½ in. long. The species is *Dirca palustris*.

USES. This native shrub is rarely cultivated although it might be attractive for moist places to serve as a companion to the Spicebush and the Summersweet.

The bark when eaten causes vomiting, and its toughness has served to make it useful for cordage.

Soil. Circumneutral pH 6.0–8.0.

Propagation. Seeds are abundantly produced. Layers are possible

DOMBEYA (Assonia) (Astrapaea)—Pinkball, Cape-weddingflower

(Named for Joseph Dombey, French botanist, 1742-1795)

The Dombeyas are treelike shrubs from Africa. The casual observer would call this a Snowball-tree, and his delight would be increased should he see the pinkflowered one.

The most attractive species is *Dombeya wallichi*, the Pinkball. This shrub often grows 30 ft. tall. The flowers are pink, in showy, snowball-like clusters, 5 in. in diameter, which hang down on long stems, 8 to 10 in. long. The flowers are slightly fragrant. The leaves are evergreen, velvety palmately veined, angled and lobed. The season of bloom extends throughout most of the Winter in southern California.

Dombeya natalensis, the Cape-weddingflower, has white flowers, but because they turn brown, it is less often grown. The leaves are poplar-like and coarsely toothed. These shrubs, or small trees, make rapid growth.

Soil. Francis Lazenby recommends a sandy loam and turfy peat mixture.

Objections. These splendid shrubs do not shed their old flowers. which become brown and must be cut off. They are not particularly good as cut flowers as they do not last.

Propagation. 1. Cuttings of nearly firm, young wood placed in sand with bottom heat, should be rooted in a frame in April.

DURANTA—Skyflower (Pigeonberry) (Golden-dewdrop)

(Named for Castor Durantes, Roman physician and botanist, about 1590)

Duranta plumieri (*repens*), the Skyflower, is so called because its flowers are blue, and Golden-dewdrop for its showy yellow berries. It is a native of Key West, Mexico to Brazil. It is a rampant grower, attaining a height of 18 ft. The branches are often rather pendant and vinelike, sometimes with spines. The blue flowers, like large Forget-me-nots, are produced in August. The leaves are opposite, light green varying to brownish, and are usually coarsely toothed. When this shrub is planted in the garden it has a threefold appeal—the blue flowers, the orange fruit, and the fact that it attracts numerous gay colored butterflies.

Duranta stenostachya is superior, being less thorny and more compact, also with larger leaves.

PROPAGATION. 1. It sows itself, in Florida.

2. Cuttings may be taken in Spring.

ELAEAGNUS—(Includes Russian-olive, Silverberry, Gumi) (Silverthorns)

(Dioscorides named the Wild Olive, Elaeagnos)

Most sorts of Elaeagnus have silvery leaves and often silvery branches. The flowers are generally very tiny but possess an exquisite fragrance. The berries are attractive, salmon or red in color, and produced from June to October.

The Russian-olive (Oleaster), *Elaeagnus angustifolia* (*hortensis*) is really treelike, attaining a height of 20 ft. It is hardy in the coldest regions. The fragrant yellowish flowers are silvery on the outside, produced in axillary clusters of two or three in June. The leaves are alternate, long, narrow, 2 to 3 in. long, light green above and silvery beneath. The branches are silvery, without brown scales and sometimes spiny. The fruit is yellowish, covered with silvery scales, sweet, mealy, ½ in. long and ripens in August.

Silverberry (Wolfwillow) (Missouri Silvertree) or *Elaeagnus argentea*. A native of Eastern Canada to the West and South to Minnesota, this is one of the most silvery shrubs in cultivation. The growth is erect, 6 to 12 ft. tall. The flowers are silver outside and yellow within; although fragrant, they are not showy. The leaves are silvery on both sides, oval-oblong, undulating margins, rusty dotted beneath. The branches are not spiny and, unlike *E. angustifolia*, they are brown, although the Winter buds are silvery. The fruit is globular, dry, mealy, silvery, not yellow, ripening in September. One of the hardiest of shrubs but suffering from heat, according to C. P. Halligan.

A common sort is the Cherry E. (Gumi) *Elaeagnus longipes* (*multiflora*) (*edulis*). This is a broad, spreading bush, often to 9 ft. The greenish-white flowers are solitary generally and are not showy, although the plants are often so full of bloom as to make a display. The leaves have silvery hairs sparsely scattered over their upper surface and are silvery beneath, obovate and undulate margined. The branches have reddish-brown scales. The fruits are brick-red, oval, brown spotted and have an astringent, acid flavor.

The Autumn E., *Elaeagnus umbellata*, is a native of the Himalayas and Japan. The growth is spreading and attains a height of 12 ft. The dull yellow flowers are not showy. The leaves are crisped at the margins, smooth and deep green above, silvery beneath. The branches are often spiny, yellow-brown, a bit silvery. The Winter terminal bud is long. The fruit is salmony-scarlet, brown scaly when young. It ripens in October and is showy. The fruits are produced at the base of the twigs.

The Thorny E., *Elaeagnus pungens*, is a handsome evergreen species, often variegated, hardy only south of Philadelphia. A spiny plant with long, flexible branches, variable in habit, it grows from 6 to 12 ft. tall. The slightly fragrant flowers are silvery white. The leaves are leathery, the margins a little undulate and crisped, at first scaly above but at maturity becoming lustrous, the lower side covered with silvery and brown scales. The branches are green, spotted brown. The fruit is light red (brown at first), ripening during the Winter in Philadelphia. Many varieties are in trade, among them:

Var. *frederici*, leaves small and narrow, variegated pale yellow center and dark green narrow margin.

Elaeagnus longipes or Cherry Elaeagnus
Note the silvery leaves and the cherrylike dotted fruits

Var. *simoni*, commoner than type, leaves rather large with few brown scales beneath; plants are more compact and not spiny.

Var. *variegata*, leaves margined yellowish-white.

USES. The gray foliage of the Russian-olive and the Silverthorn often offer interesting contrasts in foliage. The gray foliage produces distance in the landscape. The attractive fruit display of *E. umbellata* late in the Fall, and the profusion of edible fruit in *E. longipes* commend both to the garden.

In milder climates *E. pungens* is a shrub with attractive green and variegated foliage which is evergreen.

Many of the sorts, namely *E. argentea*, *E. angustifolia*, *E. longipes* and *E. umbellata* are good seaside plants.

For tall hedges *E. angustifolia* and *E. argentea* give an unusual type of background.

SOIL. Grows well in sandy as well as clayey soil. They are all drought-resisting shrubs. Circumneutral pH 6.0–8.0.

PRUNING. Most of the shrubby sorts do not need pruning for many years. Owing to their neat habit, they are no trouble to maintain.

PROPAGATION. 1. *Seeds require two years to germinate, so they may be stratified for one year and sown the next. *E. umbellata* and *E. angustifolia*.

2. Half-ripe wood of *E. longipes* under glass (N.M.) in June or July.

3. Hardwood, especially *E. angustifolia* and *E. umbellata*, easy.

4. Layers in May.

ELSHOLTZIA—(Mintshrub)

(Named for J. S. Elsholtz, a Berlin botanist)

Elsholtzia stauntoni is a half woody plant of the Mint family. It grows 3 to 5 ft. tall and in severe Winters freezes to the soil in the Arnold Arboretum. The flowers remind one of Veronica, the spikes being 4 to 8 in. long, cylindrical, one-sided. The lipped flowers are reddish purple, becoming rose, with prominent stamens. The lateness of the season commends them for the garden as they do not bloom until September and remain attractive for two or three weeks. The leaves are sharply toothed and have a minty odor. The branches are hairy.

USES. They are valuable for late flowers in the herbaceous border or may be planted in beds in front of taller and earlier flowering subjects. Sunshine is wanted for good flowers. Protect plants a little for the Winter by a mulch of straw.

Elsholtzia or Mintshrub

A late blooming, half woody plant. The spikes of reddish-purple lipped flowers appear in September

SOIL. The soil must be well drained.

PRUNING. It is wise to cut the plants to the soil each Spring as they either freeze to the soil or else are badly injured at the tops.

PROPAGATION. 1. *Softwood cuttings may be taken from stock plants kept in the greenhouse or coldframes for the Winter, or Summer cuttings may be taken from outdoor plants.

2. Seeds may be sown in Spring.

EMPETRUM—Crowberry

The Crowberry, *Empetrum nigrum*, is a creeping shrub native to Arcticlike conditions or the mountain tops of Northern Europe, Asia and California.

The leaves are evergreen, short and narrow, $\frac{1}{4}$ in. long; they are inrolled to form a narrow groove. The flowers are purplish, axillary on the branches, and opening in April and May. The small black fruits ripening in August are edible.

USES. It may be used for ground cover or for a rockery.

SOIL. The Crowberry is adapted to damp, peaty places and is therefore difficult to establish in the illy adapted soils of most gardens. Mediacid pH 4.0–5.0.

PROPAGATION. Cuttings of rather ripened wood in August. Seeds.

ENKIANTHUS—(Bellflowertree)
(Name derived from *enkuos*—enlarged, *anthos*—flower, refers to the flower being enlarged in the middle.)

The Redvein Enkianthus, *Enkianthus campanulatus* (*Andromeda campanulata*) is an interesting shrub, generally seen at a height of 6 ft., but in nature attaining a height of 30 ft. It is hardy in Boston. The bell-shaped flowers are in pendulous clusters and are pale yellow, veined rosy red. The flowers open in May and hasten into fruit, small, oblong capsules produced on hairy stems which bend downward. The leaves are crowded on the ends of the branches, elliptical, 1 to $3\frac{1}{2}$ in., sharp-pointed, with bristle-tipped teeth. The leaves turn scarlet in Autumn.

Enkianthus campanulatus or Redvein Enkianthus
Pale yellow, bell-shaped flowers borne in May, with upright branches carrying leaves in tufts, characterize this acid loving plant

The Nikko Enkianthus, *E. subsessilis*, is of compact growth and has clean, glossy foliage, smaller than *E. campanulatus*, ¾ to 1½ in., and the great masses of drooping capsules serve to make this a handsome sort. The leaves are bronzy all Summer and become red in Fall.

Uses. The Enkianthus is much at home in the Rhododendron bed, associated with Azaleas, Leucothoe and Kalmia. Because of the bronze-tipped foliage of *E. subsessilis*, it is superior to *E. campanulatus* for the all-season effect.

Soil. Requires acid soil for proper beauty and prefers a plentiful supply of moisture. Grows in New York State in non-acid soil.

Objections. Because of the tufted character of the leaves, arranged so that the branches are not covered with bloom, *E. campanulatus* often has a leggy appearance. Possibly pruning would serve to make for greater compactness. The slow growth of these plants is the main complaint made by nurserymen.

Propagation. 1. Half-ripe wood may be used for cuttings inserted in sand or mixture of sand and peat moss, in the Summer.

2. Hardwood cuttings may be taken under glass in the Fall.

3. Layers may be made in Spring.

4. Seeds may be sown in early Spring. (See Azalea page 150.)

ERICA—Heath
(Name of doubtful origin)

Heather is associated with the history and life of many of the inhabitants of the moorlands of Europe. It was used to thatch roofs. They mixed it with a sort of cement made of black earth and straw. It is a Highland practice to sleep on beds of Heather as it was supposed to be conducive to health. Bunches of the sprays of branches are tied together to make brooms. Yarn was dyed a yellowish orange by steeping the plants in a decoction of the tops. The old herbals attribute many cures to the use of Heather. Eating the Heather by the Highland flocks is supposed to supply a fine flavor to mutton. The Heather flower imparts an extra flavor to honey gathered from it. Heather as a source of peat to use as fuel is well known. It may still be seen along the roads, cut and piled to dry.

But the appeal of the Heather is not purely utilitarian. Alexander Wallace in *The Heather in Lore, Lyric and Lay* writes:

"What potent charm have the gods bequeathed this mountain blossom, so that the heart of a Scotsman clings to this moorland flower with a pathos of tender, reverent emotion? Is it that within his heart the bonnie native bloom brightens anew those cherished scenes and friendships and severed ties of 'auld lang syne'—and brings back, like quivering echo-strains from a far-away distance, the music of those sweet hame-fireside hours 'that will never come again' ? "

In Scotland the White Heather is considered even more lucky than is the fourleaved Clover with us. King Edward VII was exceedingly superstitious on this point and was constantly on the lookout for White Heather when shooting grouse on the mountains of Scotland where a plant of the white variety in the midst of thousands of acres of the purple sort is a rare find. Might it not be possible for the florists in this country to similarly work up an appreciation of and demand for the "lucky" White Heather? It is in great demand in fashionable circles in Britain for brides' bouquets, for which purpose several nurserymen in the Matlock district grow immense quantities of it.

SPECIES. This introduction has not pertained to any one species of Heath, but now we must get "down to cases." There are many sorts of plants known as Heath. The true Scotch Heather is *Calluna vulgaris* (see page 168). The Irish Heather or St. Dabeoc Heath is *Daboecia cantabrica* with its oval flowers ranging in color from dark purple to pure white. The Spikeheath is *Bruckenthalia spiculifolia*, a pinkflowered plant less than a foot tall, a native of Southeastern Europe and Asia Minor. The Mountain-heath, *Phyllodoce empetriformis*, is found from British Columbia to California. The Menziesia, *M. ferruginea*, which grows from Alaska to Oregon together with *M. pilosa*, native to the Southern mountains, are heathlike plants which when found in our mountains give rise to stories that Heather can be found wild in America. The Scots insist that Calluna only should be called Heather; all other sorts are properly called Heaths.

Of the true species of Erica the following are found:

Erica carnea (herbacea), the Spring Heath, is of prostrate growth, attaining a height of only 6 in. The flowers are deep red, with red anthers, open from February to April. They are bell-shaped, solitary or in pairs, and form a raceme 1 to 2 in. long. The leaves are glossy and in whorls of four.

Erica mediterranea, the Biscay Heath, is a tall shrub 4 to 10 ft. tall. The flowers are dark red or white produced in short racemes, appearing in April or May. The leaves are in whorls of four or five.

Erica melanthera, the Black-eyed Heath, is a South African species which is extremely prolific of bloom. It grows 2 ft. tall. The flowers are rosy with black anthers. It blooms in Winter and is grown extensively on the Pacific Coast. It is shipped to florists for cut flower work. The leaves are in whorls of three.

Erica President Carnot is one of the varieties grown in greenhouses for pot plants

Erica persoluta (*subdivaricata*), the Garland Heath, grows 1 to 2 ft. tall. The flowers are white or rosy in whorls of four at the ends of the twigs to appear as a raceme. The leaves are in whorls of four.

Erica stricta, the Corsican Heath, is found in Southwest Europe. It grows 9 ft. tall. The flowers are rose purple, produced from June to September in terminal umbels. The leaves are in whorls of four, or rarely five and six.

Erica vagans, the Cornish Heath, inhabits Southwest Europe. It grows 1 ft. tall. The flowers are purple, pink, or white, produced in pairs in the axils of the leaves forming a leafy raceme. They flower from July to October. The leaves are in whorls of four or five.

GREENHOUSE CULTURE. H. D. Darlington in the *Florists' Exchange and Horticultural Trade World*, has written fully of the forcing of various greenhouse Heaths:

"Ericas were among the first flowering plants grown in glass houses. They have had periods of great popularity and it is now up to the progressive grower to take advantage of the many beautiful Heaths that are just suited to the best plant trade. Also, if the grower is of an inquisitive turn of mind the opportunities for introducing varieties new to our trade are numerous. The once popular idea that the Heaths are difficult to grow in the United States is now thoroughly dispelled and there is every reason why they should be more extensively grown than they are.

"Many popular sorts are not at all difficult to propagate and grow; in fact, give them proper conditions and you are almost certain of an 80 per cent strike. The notes given in an earlier article on propagation methods for hardwooded plants explain a system used here for many years, so we may at this time omit the details.

"Assuming that your young stock is in small pots (1¾ in.) in February or March, the plants may be carried on in any light bench at 50° to 55° and by May 1 to 20 they should be large enough to shift. For most of the free growing sorts a shift to 3½ in. pots will be about right. See that you provide ample drainage. For soil, two parts peat or leafmold, three parts good loam and one part sand will make a good mixture. In potting set the plants firmly; make a special point of this, and fill the pots full of soil. If you see a block of Ericas a sickly yellow, look to the drainage; Ericas want plenty of water, but in small quantities and often. In the case of a plant supplied with good drainage, potted hard and with the pot filled full or nearly so, it is almost impossible to overwater it.

"During Summer the young stock should be plunged outside and, for most varieties, in full sunshine. If you intend growing the plants into larger stock, pinch them during the Summer in order to induce bushy growth, but if you expect to have them bloom the first season it is best not to pinch them. If the plants are for growing on, plunge them in a shallow heated frame; that is not only about the nicest place you can put them, but also it saves work. If during Summer they are not in a heated frame, they should be moved inside before frost. During Winter 40° to 45° will be right. If you intend to flower the small plants, the early flowering varieties should have a little warmer position, say 50° to 55°, but that will depend on the varieties selected and just when you want them in bloom. But don't try this temperature until the buds are well formed and the plants are approaching the proper blooming season. During the second season you may use either of two methods with your young stock: Shift on into larger pots and in Summer plunge outside in full sunshine, or plant out during Summer. If you are not accustomed to growing Ericas try a few each way.

"A number of kinds do splendidly planted out in good loam in full sunshine, but all should be mulched during the Summer; *Erica melanthera*, *E. persoluta* vars. *alba* and *rosea*, and the French hybrids all do well if handled in this manner, and make splendid stock. If planted out during Summer all the attention they will need is watering and the keeping down of weeds. You should start lifting and potting about September 1, taking the French hybrids first. These should have made tall, spikelike growths, and show the buds forming. By lifting them between September 1 and 15 you run very little danger of blighting the buds, but if you allow them to stand until October—and they do grow wonderfully during September— the buds get so far advanced they are apt to blight in lifting. Therefore, I prefer to get them potted first and to stand them in a shaded house.

being careful with the ventilation and water for the first ten days; then reduce the shade and give more air. *E. melanthera* and *E. persoluta alba* and *E. p. rosea* should be potted and treated likewise. In a block of *melanthera* treated in this way oftentimes a portion of the plants will not set buds and those that do set will not show buds right up to the tips of the growths. Flower the best plants, and those that are not well enough set with buds carry in a cool house at from 40° to 45°. Don't crowd the plants; this will make them lose the lower foliage. The following May plunge the pots outside again in full sunshine. This season, being grown in pots, they will set buds right up to the tips and make the finest Christmas stock you can have. As the *persolutas* are Springflowering you run little risk of their planted out stock going blind, if you carry them cool during Winter (40° to 45°) and give them plenty of air whenever possible. But don't raise the temperature or they will start a new growth and go blind.

"*Erica cupressina (bergeriana)* is a beautiful little Heath that does well and sells easily in 3½ in. or 4 in. pots. I prefer keeping it in pots, but excellent stock is often grown planted out. However, it should have a little shade during hot weather. A good plan is to plunge the plants in beds 5 ft. wide, build 2½ ft. or 3 ft. above them a skeleton frame of shingle, lath or any light material, and lay sash (3 ft. by 6 ft.) on top, without any other shading, the sash being enough to break the glare of the sun. Or you may cover the plants with lath racks. In any case the shade should be removed about September 1 to 10 and the plants got into the house before frost. Hold them at 40° to 45° until March 1, when (depending on the date of Easter or the time you wish them in bloom) you can then raise the temperature to 55° to 60°.

"*Erica regerminans* var. *ovata*, is a beautiful sort that flowers just right for Thanksgiving Day, when two year old plants in 5 in. pots are a mass of bloom. If plunged during Summer in 5 ft. beds, as Autumn approaches a temporary frame can be built around them and covered with sash; often they may thus be used without being taken into the house.

"Don't let anyone tell you: 'Yes they do finely near the coast, but they won't do well inland.' Now, I have seen, 300 miles from the coast, some of the finest blocks of Ericas that could be grown, so don't let that old idea annoy you. If you are interested get a few *melanthera*, watch them this Summer and make some cuttings this Fall; soon you'll try others."

PROPAGATION. 1. Seed. William Anderson, superintendent of the Thayer estate, probably knows more about growing Heather from seed than any other man in this country.

In *Horticulture*, Mr. Anderson says that seed can be sown in flats in the Spring, and if protected and shaded in a frame it germinates very quickly. Then if the plants are pricked off as soon as large enough to be handled, they will make good plants for planting out the following Spring. It is true that the plants will still be small, but they are the easier to handle on that account. Mr. Anderson reports that he has raised thousands of plants of Heather in this way. He has also sown seed in the greenhouse in February, pricked the plants off as soon as large enough, and had them in flower in September. Sometimes plant-

Heather Cuttings and others ready for the sand

Reading from left to right, they are: Arctostaphylos uva-ursi (Bearberry), Daphne cneorum (Rose Daphne or Garland Flower), Calluna vulgaris (Common Heather), Menziesia polifolia (Irish Heath), Bruckenthalia spiculifolia (Spike Heath), Erica mediterranea hybrida (Mediterranean Heath), Erica mackayi fl. pl. (Mackay's Heath), Erica stricta (Corsican Heath)

ing the seed out of doors where the plants are to go is recommended, but this method has not been found a success with Mr. Anderson.

Some nurserymen are now selling potted plants of Heather, which can be transferred to any garden, where they will probably grow well if they are given full sun and a sandy soil. In some gardens they are used very nicely as edging for beds of Rhododendrons and Laurel, and also are to be seen in rock gardens. One firm lists nearly 20 varieties of *Calluna vulgaris*, including early and late blooming varieties and one with golden foliage.

2. Cuttings. The notes on propagation quoted below were made by J. W. Mallinson in the *Florists Exchange and Horticultural Trade World:*

"Cuttings of Heather can be put in at any time during Winter as occasion offers and when the weather permits. They should be taken preferably with a heel; the young side shoots can be stripped off the main branches without injury to the plant.

"Do not make the cuttings too large; 1 in. to 1½ in. is large enough.

"They prefer a cool, shady house free from drafts. They can do with about the same treatment as cuttings of such conifers as *Retinospora*; if space in the benches is scarce, they can be rooted in flats of sand. A night temperature of 40° to 45° is best, but the cuttings will stand 10° more if necessary. It is essential, however, that they have a close, moist atmosphere with plenty of moisture in the sand until they have rooted.

"Under such conditions Heather will root in from four to five weeks— and with very slight loss. The cuttings can be set quite close together in the sand; ½ in. apart each way is enough room.

"Heather cuttings can be left in the sand for quite a while after they have rooted without suffering any injury. About the middle of March pot them up using a soil containing some leafmold or other humus and quite free from any trace of lime. In potting up use nothing larger than a 2 in. pot—rather a smaller size if you have it. This will carry the plant until the end of May when it can be shifted into a 2½ or 3 and plunged in a frame outdoors where, however, care should be taken to protect it from wind and sunlight until root action commences. Or, better still, keep the potted stock in the house for two or three weeks after it is potted."

ESCALLONIA

(Named for Escallon, Spanish traveler in the United States)

The Escallonias are South American evergreen shrubs, grown principally in the Gulf States and on the Pacific Coast. They are by nature of compact habit, with good foliage and Winter flowers.

The various Escallonia garden hybrids are profuse blooming tender plants with white, red or pink trusses of flowers

Escallonia montevidensis (alba) grows to a height of 9 ft. The flowers are white, produced in terminal panicles in Fall and Winter. The leaves are simple, elliptical, 2 to 4 in. long.

Escallonia rubra is usually seen growing about 3 to 6 ft. tall, although its ultimate height is 15 ft. The shrub is erect and compact. The branches are very twiggy and the younger parts are more or less sticky to the touch. The leaves are broader toward the tip. The flowers are bright red in short clusters.

PROPAGATION. 1. Cuttings are made in the Autumn and root during the Winter.

2. Layers furnish a successful amateur method of increase.

3. Suckers are not a rapid, but a sure method of propagation.

EUGENIA—Australian Brush-cherry
(Named for Prince Eugene of Savoy)

Eugenias are very commonly seen all through Florida and California where they are used for formal foundation planting and for hedges. There are many species which resemble each other quite closely, and quite a number of them are treelike, among them the Clovetree and the Rose-apple.

The commonest ornamental shrub, however, is *Eugenia myrtifolia (australis) (hookeri)*, Australian Brush-cherry. This tall, erect shrub is a native of Queensland and New South Wales. It grows to a height of 12 ft. The flowers are white or creamy. The foliage is evergreen, opposite, dark, glossy, and green but the new growth has a beautiful bronze cast. The leaves are aromatic and are 2 to 3 in. long. The fruits are cherrylike, edible, red or violet.

PROPAGATION. 1. Seeds.

2. Rather easily raised from cuttings.

EUONYMUS (Spindletree) (Includes the Wintercreeper, Burningbush and Wahoo)
(Name means a plant of good repute.)

The various types of Euonymus (evergreen, climbing, low ground covers, veritable trees, gorgeous fruiting sorts) serve to make this a useful group of shrubs for garden planting.

Evergreen Bittersweet, Euonymus fortunei
var. vegetus

Evergreen, or nearly so. The forms of *Euonymus fortunei* (*radicans*) make this species one of the most useful of all shrubs. Known as the Wintercreeper, the typical form is a climber or ground cover with opposite, thick evergreen leaves, oval, hardly an inch long, with rounded teeth, dull green above and lighter colored veins. A number of varieties have been selected which are distinct in appearance but there are many gradations between the typical form and the well-marked varieties. These are not worthy of names but constantly confuse the plantsman who wonders what to name them because they are attractive, although not distinct enough for definite names. From youth to old age, *E. fortunei* has varied to the following good varieties.

Var. *vegetus*. Bigleaf Wintercreeper, also called the Japanese Evergreen Bittersweet. This is an ornamental fruiting sort with quite rounded elliptical leaves. It clings to stone or brick but not to stucco. It is low and spreading and can be cut back to become bushy but any height which it attains is due to a piling up of its branches. It is not upright.

Var. *carrierei*. Glossy W. This is the mature form of *E. radicans*, which is not used for climbing but which produces quite erect branches, as well as others which are spreading and take root in the soil. The leaves are a little thinner, more pointed and a lighter green than var. *vegetus*. (See also *E. patens* which is confused with this in nurseries.) This is a profuse fruiting sort.

Var. *acutus*. The Sharpleaf W. has sharp, pointed, narrower leaves than var. *vegetus*, 1 to 2 in. long, and is perfectly prostrate upon the soil or else climbing.

Var. *colorata*. This handsome variety resembles var. *acutus*, but has larger, thinner leaves which are green in Summer but changing to blood-red, rarely bronze, in the Winter. It is hardy in the Northeast, withstanding 14 deg. F., retaining the foliage until Spring. Even when not covered with snow in a sunny place, it is hardy. Its color is not as attractive in the shade.

Var. *kewensis* (*minimus*). Baby W. The tiny leaves are only ½ to ¾ in. long and have lighter veins. It is a climber or prostrate plant.

Var. *picta* (*reticulatus*). Whitevein W. Like type with small leaves but marked white on veins.

Var. *argenteo-marginatus*. Silveredge W. Like type with small leaves bordered white.

Var. *roseo-marginatus*. Pinkedge W. Like type with small leaves bordered pink.

Similar to *Euonymus fortunei* var. *carrierei*, one often cataloged as *E. sieboldianus*, or *E. kiautschovicus* and called the Spreading E. It is half evergreen and more upright than var. *carrierei*, with thinner leaves. It is profuse in flower and fruit. The fruits are pink, ovoid, four-ribbed but not lobed. It is not quite as hardy as *E. fortunei* varieties. Good in dense shade. The flowers produce much nectar and attract flies which serve to make this shrub objectionable in some places.

E. japonicus, Evergreen Burningbush. These shrubs are perfectly upright, and have extremely thick, shining, broadly oval leaves, 1 to 3 in. long, with dull-pointed teeth. They rarely fruit in the North and are not hardy north of Philadelphia without being in a very favorable place. Young plants in Columbus, Ohio, survived each Winter for five years, but they never attained height due to freezing back severely.

As a florist's plant it is used extensively, the following varieties being in the trade:

Giltedge var. *aureo-marginatus*. Leaves margined gold.

Pearledge var. *albo-marginatus*. Leaves margined white.

Boxleaf var. *microphylla*. Small leaf, ½ to 1 in. long, dwarf and compact.

Largeleaf var. *macrophylla*. Large leaf, 2 to 3 in. long.

Column var. *fastigiatus*. Erect, pyramidal habit.

Var. Pres. Gauthier. Upright, leaves silvery variegated, margined pink.

Treelike sorts. European Burningbush (Spindletree), *Euonymus europaeus*. This upright growing small tree or large shrub grows

Euonymus europaeus

The Fall coloring of this species is distinguished by the purple leaves and pink capsules splitting and revealing the orange berries

20 ft. tall. The leaves are ovate, 1 to 3 in. long, round-toothed. The branches are green, polished and quadrangular. The flowers are yellow-green, appear in May and have an unpleasant odor. The fruit is pink-orange inside, larger than that of *E. americanus* and not warty. It is a better grower than *E. americanus*. Var. *fructo-coccineus* with red fruits and var. *fructo-alba* with white fruits are the best forms.

Brook E. (Strawberrybush) (American Spindletree) (Burstingheart) (American Burningbush), *E. americanus*. Upright, like above, but only 5 to 8 ft. tall and unlike it the flowers are greenish purple, the fruits are rough, warty, light scarlet with orange pulp. Both sorts ripen in September and October. Likes partial shade and rather moist soil. This species is not as desirable as *E. europaeus*.

Wahoo (Burningbush), *E. atropurpureus*. Leaves larger than *E. europaeus*, hairy beneath, anthers and flowers purple, four petals (preceding two species have five petals). Fruit crimson (pomegranate purple), pulp scarlet, darker than above, not warty but smooth.

Winterberry E. *E. bungeanus.* Treelike but not stiff as in first three treelike sorts; a freer growth of careless grace. Often 15 ft. tall. This is one of the most profuse flowering sorts. The fruits are deeply four-lobed, yellowish or pinkish, inside pale yellow, $\frac{1}{2}$ in. across; remain after leaves have fallen. The leaves are droopy in appearance and yellowish-green and have long pointed tips. Var. *semipersistens* has semi-evergreen leaves and produces fruit sparingly. The young branches are green (the older ones gray) in this species and its variety.

Yeddo E. *E. yedoensis.* The round top and the stiff, upright branches are characteristic. Unlike the foregoing the leaves are more oval, abruptly pointed, round-toothed, and wider above the middle. The young branches are green, the older reddish brown and the old bark gray. The flowers are greenish, produced profusely on stalks at base of new growth. The rose-colored fruits are dull and remain long after the leaves fall. The Winter buds are round to oval and dry margined.

Broadleaf Burningbush. *E. latifolius.* The stems are erect but the branching is loose and complicated. The leaves are broad and change to orange and crimson in the Autumn. The flowers are produced in 7 to 15 flowered clusters. The petioles are grooved above. The fruit is bright red, four-winged, the pulp being orange and the seeds white.

E. planipes is similar but the capsules are smooth, without wings. The leaves are narrower and the petioles are without grooves. Handsome in fruit

Shrubby sort with corky wings. Winged E., *E. alatus (stricta) (armurensis).* This sort makes a shrub 6 to 8 ft. high and is usually broader than high. The outstanding characteristic is its winged branches. When growing properly, it is most regular in outline, the branches coming from the plant in horizontal planes. The leaves are smaller than most shrubby sorts, finely toothed, tapering at both ends; they change in Autumn to deep rose, a color unusual among shrubs. The fruits are small, purple in color with orange pulp and not as conspicuous as in other species. This is best used as a specimen as its horizontal grace is lost in mass plantings. Not of the hardiest. Good in Japanese gardens, but M. V. Horvath believes it too regular in form.

Uses. An ingenious gardener finds hundreds of uses for the vast range of good forms of Euonymus.

The Wintercreeper and its many varieties may be used for graves

Euonymus alatus or Winged Euonymus
This plant is characterized by the corky wings on the branches and the flaming color it assumes in the Fall when the leaves turn a brilliant red along with the small scarlet fruits it bears

as a ground cover, for steep banks, for low hedges, for foundation plantings beneath evergreens, for climbing on stone walls, for the shade under trees and for porch boxes. They tolerate shade on steep banks. Var. *minimus* is useful for the rockery, for draping large boulders and for small spots where a most refined and evergreen ground cover is needed.

E. f. carrieri, E. f. vegetus, E. sieboldianus, E. europaeus, E. atropurpureus, E. bungeanus, E. yedoensis and *E. latifolius* are all splendid late Fall and early Winter display shrubs because of their fruits which resemble the wild Bittersweet.

For Fall leaf coloration few shrubs compare with *E. alatus*, which turns deep rose, *E. europaeus* which is purple, and *E. atropurpureus* which is scarlet.

Attractive low hedges may be made of *E. f. radicans* if the young plants are tied to a wire to hold them upright and then trimmed frequently.

Le Bon Jardinier remarks that the leaves of *Euonymus atropurpureus* and *E. americanus* are poisonous and the fruits act as a violent purgative. The wood burned in closed urns gives the charcoal used for sketching.

SOIL. Except for *E. japonicus*, the evergreen sort, these shrubs are not particular about the soil. This species is hardier in either dry soil or sandy places, because rich soil causes too vigorous, sappy, easily frozen growth. Meehan says that it does not kill out at the seaside as much as inland. The same remarks apply in a lesser degree to *E. kiautschovicus*, which is hardier, but often injured about Boston and other Northern places.

E. americanus is a native of damp places and will tolerate shade. Circumneutral pH 6.0–8.0.

PESTS. Euonymus of various sorts is troubled by a scale insect, known as *Chionapis euonymi*, somewhat like the oyster shell scale. They are often so abundant as to stop the growth of the plants. The eggs hatch the 15th to 30th of May, which is the ideal time for control, but the leaves are so soft then that it would injure them to spray with anything strong. Use one of the miscible oils weakly, or if the infestation is upon an individual plant, merely apply with a brush.

PROPAGATION. 1. Seeds should be stratified until Spring. Be sure to remove the pulp.

2. Cuttings of *E. f. radicans* root easily in Summer from July to August 15 in shaded frames. Softwood of most sorts. Half-ripe wood of *E. japonicus* roots readily after February in the greenhouse.

3. Layers. *E. f. radicans, E. f. carrierei, E. f. acutus, E. f. minimus, E. r. vegetus* and *E. kiautschovicus* root naturally when branches touch the soil.

4. *The deciduous sorts root from hardwood cuttings.

5. Meehan says that grafting *E. americanus* on *E. europaeus* increases the profusion of fruit.

EXOCHORDA—Pearlbush

The white buds of the Pearlbush, *Exochorda grandiflora* (*racemosa*) (*Spiraea grandiflora*), are globular and pearl-like, thus accounting for its common name. It is almost treelike with age, upright when young but becoming spreading and often 10 ft. tall. The white flowers are produced in six to ten flowered racemes. The green calyx is visible between the five petals. The flowers open in April and May. The leaves are pale green, oval and smooth. On leafy shoots the leaves have a few teeth near the tip, but on the flowering shoots the leaves are without teeth. The fruit is a dry, three-winged capsule which hangs upon the plants from one year to another.

Exochorda giraldi, the Redbud P., is larger, and more vigorous, with narrower petals, giving the blooms a star-shaped appearance rather than circular. The calyx is often reddish inside. Rehder writes, "This species is even handsomer than the preceding one; particularly var.

Note the pearllike buds which give the name to the Pearlbush or Exochorda

wilsoni which is of more upright and vigorous habit and more floriferous than the type."

Exochorda korolkowi (alberti), Turkestan P., is more compact and upright and less profuse flowering than the other species. The petals are cut a little, the flowers being produced in five to eight flowered racemes. The branchlets are glabrous, redder brown than other sorts. The leaves are large, acute, abruptly tipped with a sharp point, teeth above the middle on the strong shoots and with a tendency toward lobing. The leaves are darker green and thicker than *E. grandiflora*.

E. macrantha (E. grandiflora × E. korolkowi). A vigorous hybrid form, more profuse flowering with larger flowers and earlier.

Uses. Pearlbushes make better specimens than shrubs for combination because they are somewhat treelike; nevertheless, a few shrubs planted at the base would help to hide their leggy character which develops with age.

Soil. Sandy or loamy best. *Le Bon Jardinier* notes that they decline at a young age when planted in limestone soils.

Pruning. Prune the plants after flowering to make them more compact.

TRANSPLANTING. They are considered a little difficult to transplant so that careful gardeners order them balled and burlapped.

OBJECTIONS. The season of bloom is short. With age and when not pruned often enough, they become leggy and irregular in shape. The horny seed vessels are rather unsightly.

PROPAGATION. Propagation by any method is rather slow; therefore, they are not planted as widely as they deserve.

1. Cuttings may be inserted in February under glass, taken from forced plants.

2. Layers root slowly. Put down lower branches in Summer.

3. Splice grafting on own piece roots may be done.

4. *Seed sown in Spring after stratifying through the Winter.

FATSIA (Tetrapanax)—(Rice-paperplant)
(Fatsia is derived from the Japanese name)

Fatsia papyrifera (the Ricepaper-plant) produces a straight stem with an umbrellalike head. The plants are hardy south of Washington and grow from 5 to 15 ft. tall. The leaves are from five to seven lobed. They are heart-shaped at the base, shining above, dense, white-woolly beneath, and 12 in. across. The stems have a large pith and are covered with dense, white down. The flowers are inconspicuous. This species is grown especially for sub-tropical foliage in California and Florida and its native country is Formosa. The large, white pith of the stem is used for making ricepaper in the Orient. A little shade is necessary for the plants, which should be placed in a position protected from heavy winds in order to keep the large leaves from being torn.

PROPAGATION. 1. Seeds.

2. Cuttings.

3. Suckers.

FONTANESIA—Syrian-privet
(Named for a French botanist, Des Fontaines)

The growth of the Syrian-privet, *Fontanesia phillyreoides*, is not unlike Privet. It is slender and willowy, holding the leaves until late in the Fall. The flowers are creamy-yellow, produced in August, and inconspicuous. The leaves are opposite, long-oval. The twigs are slender, four-angled, with rough bark and green pith. Fruit is a flat nutlet, winged all around.

A related species, *F. fortunei*, grows 15 ft. tall, has white flowers blooming in June and July. Upright in habit and with willowlike leaves. This is generally considered hardier than the above.

USES. Robinson says that this species is of slight garden value. Rehder notes that it is used for hedges in China. It is extremely drought resistant.

PRUNING. Compactness results from heading the plants in.

PROPAGATION. 1. Summer cuttings.
2. Layers.
3. Seed.
4. Hardwood cuttings taken in early Winter.

FORSYTHIA—(Goldenbells)
(Named for Wm. Forsythe, Royal Gardener of Kensington)

What city in the United States is not more beautiful because of the masses of Forsythias? Blooming in April before their leaves unfold, they scatter gold about our homes, upon steep banks and in the public parks. Spring is surely here when the countryside is golden with these flowers.

Drooping or Weeping Goldenbells, *Forsythia suspensa*. The flowers are four-petaled, produced in clusters of one to three, sometimes more. The leaves are opposite, oblong-oval, coarsely toothed, sometimes three-parted. The branches are hollow. In habit the plants are furnished with pendulous shoots, although some branches are a little upright.

Var. *fortunei*, Fortune Goldenbells, is stiffer, more upright, often with three-parted leaves.

Var. *sieboldi*, Siebold G., resembles *F. suspensa*, but blooms eight days later than *F. fortunei*, is more profuse blooming and a darker yellow. Leaves generally simple. Flowers usually solitary. Rehder says, "This is the type of the species."

Greenstem Goldenbells, *F. viridissima*, is of upright growth, less showy than *F. suspensa*, and less hardy than the others. The branchlets are olive green and the pith is partitioned. The flowers are darker yellow than the above and with a greenish tinge. They bloom a little later. One to three flowers are found at a node produced on pendant stems. The leaves are simple and turn olive in the Fall. The buds are very susceptible to Spring frost injury.

The Border Goldenbells, *F. intermedia*, is a cross between *F. suspensa* and *F. viridissima*. The branches have partitioned pith, as in *F. viridissima*, but are solid at the nodes and some branches are arching; the leaves are often three-parted as in *F. suspensa*. This sort is hardier than *F. viridissima* and blooms five to six days after *F. suspensa*. The habit thus is similar to *F. suspensa* var. *fortunei* with some erect and some pendulous branches.

Var. *spectabilis*, Showy Border G., is more profuse blooming and flowers are larger, crowded, sometimes five or six petals. Short pistil. One of the showiest of all Goldenbells and with buds opening late enough so that there is no likelihood of injury by frost.

Var. *densiflora* is very profuse flowering. Flowers are much crowded, paler in color, long pistils, growth pendulous, spreading. Petals rather flat, but slightly rolling.

Var. *primulinum*, Primrose G., has large flowers much crowded, pale primrose, short pistils. The four petals roll back.

Forsythia europaea has leaves without teeth which stand very erect, overlapping each other. The branches are perfectly upright and hold the leaves until late Winter. It is difficult to propagate.

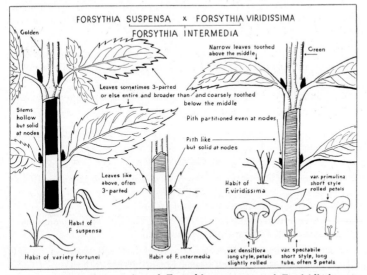

Scheme showing the crossing of Forsythia suspensa and F. viridissima to produce F. intermedia and its varieties. Note how truly intermediate this type really is

Forsythia ovata, introduced by Wilson in 1917 from seed collected in Northern Korea, has ascending branches which arch gracefully. It is said to be hardier than the others, standing a temperature much below zero. The flowers are pale primrose-yellow, solitary, short stalked and produced ten days before the other sorts. The leaves are ovate, blunt at base or almost heart-shaped, pointed at tip, coarsely toothed. The bark is grayish-yellow or yellow-gray when old.

USES. The Greenstem Goldenbells may be trained to tree form. The Weeping G. may be used for holding steep banks; it may be trained upon a trellis or wall like a climber, or by staking up a single branch to the desired height, it will serve as a weeping tree.

SOIL AND CULTURE. The soil is unimportant. Circumneutral pH 6.0–8.0. Note that the Greenstem G. is less hardy than the others and that the newly introduced *F. ovata* although the earliest to bloom, is extremely hardy. These shrubs are notable in withstanding drought.

PRUNING. In refined plantings Goldenbells require pruning directly following their period of bloom; otherwise, they become a wilderness of growth.

OBJECTIONS. Forsythias become very involved in their branching and are not refined for plantings which are closely inspected. Much can be done by pruning, however.

PROPAGATION. 1. *This is one of the easiest sorts to root from hardwood cuttings. However, *F. suspensa* and *F. fortunei* are not as easy as the other species.

2. *Summer cuttings may be used, which is the commonest method.

3. *F. suspensa* roots naturally from its procumbent branches.

FOTHERGILLA
(Named for Dr. John Fothergill, English physician who introduced many new plants)

Fothergillas are natives of Southeastern United States and are related to the Witch-hazels. They grow slowly but are conspicuous in Spring because of their white flowers.

Fothergilla gardeni (*alnifolia*) (*carolina*) is a low shrub, 4 ft. tall, with rounded, zigzag, slender twigs. The leaves are Alderlike, 1 to 2 in. long, oval, irregularly notched and turn red in the Fall. The flowers are white, with pink stamens, and are produced in short, dense spikes to

Rarely seen in cultivation, the Fothergilla is unique in flower

give a bottlebrush appearance. They appear just as the leaves unfold in April. The seed capsule resembles that of the Witch-hazel.

Fothergilla major is a more vigorous, erect species, often over 6 ft. tall. The leaves are 2 to 5 in. long. The flower buds set in the Fall and flower in April or May. Leaves turn bright yellow before they fall.

USES. Fothergillas are interesting shrubs because of their white flowers so early in Spring and their Autumn coloration.

SOIL. *Gardening Illustrated* notes that light soils are best. They are natives of the shady margins of swamps. Rehder notes that peat soils are desired. Subacid pH 5.0–6.0.

OBJECTIONS. There is a coarseness of the foliage which is not attractive. They sucker freely. Difficult to grow.

PROPAGATION. 1. Seeds remain a year before germination. Sow in Spring.

2. Difficult to root from cuttings and it takes two years for layers.

3. *F. gardeni* suckers and may be propagated by this method or root cuttings.

FREMONTIA—(Flannelbush)
(Named for John Charles Fremont, eminent Western explorer)

The Flannelbush (*Fremontia californica*) is a yellowflowered shrub growing in California to a height of 10 ft. It is sure to arrest the attention of any visitor to that state during the early Summer. The flowers are solitary, with five petals and many gold stamens. The stiff, straight branches, when young, are coated with a felty covering. The leaves are three to five lobed, felty beneath, shaped like a Fig leaf (in other words, they are palmately lobed). See sketch, page 9.

CULTURE. Fremontias like a sunny, sheltered position and require a dry soil. They are typical of California and cannot be grown in the colder regions of our country.

PROPAGATION. 1. Seed is freely set.

2. Softwood cuttings may be used in coldframes.

FUCHSIA—(Ladys-eardrops)
(Named for Leonard Fuchs, German botanical author and physician, 1501-1565)

The scores of beautiful Fuchsias which we now grow have been derived from a group of Peruvian and Chilean plants. We shall always consider the Fuchsia as an old-fashioned flower, for it has been greatly admired for many years. If there is any place in the world where Fuchsias do well it is in Scotland. No one who has seen the Fuchsia clambering over arches, loaded with the pendant flowers can soon forget the beauty of these Fuchsias.

SPECIES. There are about one hundred species of Fuchsias. The reader who wishes to know them should refer to Philip A. Munz, *A Revision of the Genus Fuchsia*, California Academy of Sciences. About a dozen are grown in the gardens of California and hundreds of named varieties have been derived from a few of them. These named varieties generally come under the name *Fuchsia hybrida*.

Of the species, the commonest is the Magellan Fuchsia, *F. magellanica* with its small, pendant flowers of deep red sepals and purple purple petals. A number of varieties are known, but Scarlet Beauty must be mentioned because it is hardy in Painesville, Ohio. It freezes to the soil but comes up from the roots and blooms freely. Unlike the typical Magellan Fuchsia in warmer regions which grows 6 to 8 feet tall, this grows a few feet tall.

The Lilac Fuchsia, *F. arborescens*, is treelike with great, erect masses of lilac flowers, quite unlike other Fuchsias.

VARIETIES. The reader is referred to *A to Z on Fuchsias*, published by the California Fuchsia Society, for an extensive list of varieties but here may be listed a selection for the beginner:

(S—single. SD—semidouble. D—double)

Anna. S. Huge, showy magenta and scarlet flowers. Trailing, good for baskets.

Aurora Superba (Salmon Queen). S. Apricot and orange. Bush.

Cascade. S. Easily grown hanging basket. Carmine red flowers.

Commander in Chief. D. Very large flower. Red and purple. Upright growth, can be espaliered.

Erecta. S. Light pink and red. Flowers erect. Heavy flowering.

Fascination. D. White, veined rose. Good pot plant.

Gartenmeister Bonstedt. S. A reddish leaved sort derived from *F. triphylla.* Coral-red. Makes big plants.

Joan of Arc. S. All white. Weak grower.

Jupiter. S. Heavy flowering. Violet and red. Upright but a weak bush.

Melody. S. Neyron rose. Easy to grow. Can be treated as a basket plant.

Mrs. John D. Fredericks. S. Salmon-pink, small flowers in great clusters. Upright growth.

Mrs. Victor Reiter. S. Large flowers, long tubes. Crimson. Basket variety.

Muriel. S. Cherry red. Petals long, twisted. Profuse flowering. Basket variety.

Nonpariel. SD. Pale rose and lavender. Excellent. Can be grown as a bush or a basket.

Patty Evans. SD. Pale rose and white, a near white. Can be grown as a bush or basket.

Storm King. D. Red and white. Upright growth, vigorous, an old variety.

Sunset. S. Orange-salmon. Good in garden.

Whitemost. S to SD. White with pale pink sepals. Upright growth.

CULTURE. They prefer an acid, rich garden loam, sand, leafmold, and peatmoss. In the Middle West the Fuchsias are not valuable garden subjects because of the extremely hot, dry Summers, but when purchased from florists it usually succeeds well along the seacoast. Fuchsias need moisture in the atmosphere as well as in their roots. When planted in the open soil one should cultivate cautiously as the roots are near the surface.

PRUNING. Prune the plants heavily during the dormant season, cutting out the old wood and trimming back the new.

PESTS. Scale and mealy bug are serious pests on Fuchsias so that one must spray with a miscible oil or some scale destroying insecticide. Should leafspot appear, the plants should be sprayed with Bordeaux mixture.

PROPAGATION. 1. When grown as greenhouse plants the Fuchsia propagates from cuttings most easily when shoots are taken from plants which have been severely cut back.

2. In California medium mature wood is best to use. Insert the cuttings in a misture of leafmold, peat, and sand.

GARDENIA (Warneria) Cape-jasmine
(Named for Alexander Garden, physician of Charleston, South Carolina, and a correspondent of Linnaeus)

The Cape-jasmine, *Gardenia florida* (*jasminoides*) (*augusta*), is a native of China and is grown in Florida except in the extreme South where it is too hot, and in the extreme North where frosts sometimes spoil the flowers. It is also used as a florists' plant in the Northern States and is grown in greenhouse benches or pots. The plants grow 2 to 6 ft. tall and produce pure white or yellowish white flowers. The leaves are opposite, or in threes. They are thick and glossy green. The twigs are sometimes slightly hairy and are often smooth. The variety *fortuniana*, or *veitchi* has larger flowers and is without doubt more commonly grafted than the type.

GREENHOUSE CULTURE. Gardenias are grown by Northern florists for their sweet-scented, boutonniere flowers. The culture resembles that given to Roses. It is decidedly a group for a specialist. Gardenias like a loose, open soil, free from lime; otherwise the leaves turn yellow. The temperature should range around 60° to 65° at night. They need full sunlight at all times and should be fed with weak nitrogen liquid. Mulch when they are in active growth and bloom, but there is danger in overfeeding when the plants are not in active growth. Flowering starts in October and continues to April, with the heaviest crop in December. The average plant yields ten blossoms per year. Syringe the plants frequently, but be sure to have them dry before nightfall. Suckers will appear at the sides of the buds. These need instant removal to throw the strength into the flowers.

PROPAGATION. Propagate plants to be grown in greenhouse every year as old plants throw short stemmed flowers. Take the cuttings in

The Cape-jasmine, or Gardenia, is one of the most fragrant of flowers

February and March. Give them a temperature from 65° to 70° with the bottom heat at 75°. Wood for cuttings should be selected which is moderately firm. From the terminal bud to the base the cutting should be about 2½ in. long; the sand should be sharp and free from impurities. In from two to three weeks the cuttings will have formed a sufficient quantity of roots; they are then potted in 2½ in. pots and subsequently placed in 4 in. from which size they are planted out in the benches in June. It is essential that the plants be kept growing right along from the rooted cutting to the flowering period.

GREVILLEA (Jewelflower-shrub)
(Named for Charles F. Greville, vice-president of The Royal Society of England, and patron of botany)

The Grevillea most commonly grown is the tree known as the Silk-oak, *Grevillea robusta*, and there are many other species of trees and shrubs native to Australia and New Caledonia.

Grevillea thelemanniana (the Jewelflower-shrub) is found in South and West Australia. It grows 5 ft. tall. It bears red flowers with green tips. They are borne in dense racemes 1½ in. long. The young growth is hairy. The foliage is pale green, divided into numerous slender sections. It is a popular shrub in Florida and on the Pacific Coast, but tolerates no frost and is considered extremely drought resistent.

PROPAGATION. It is easily raised from seed.

HAKEA
(Named for Baron Von Hake, friend of botany)

The Hakeas are strange Australian shrubs. *Hakea pugioniformis,* the Dagger Hakea, forms a dense, rounded shrub 8 to 10 ft. tall. It produces fragrant white flowers in globular clusters. The foliage is cylindrical, spiny tipped, 2 to 4 in. long, alternate, and evergreen. The Hakea is used in extremely dry situations, for it is drought resistant. It likes a light soil.

PROPAGATION. 1. Cuttings may be used.

2. The seeds are produced in bony capsules which should be collected and stored until they crack open.

HALIMODENDRON—Salt-tree
(Name derived from *halimos*—sea coast, *dendron*—tree)

The Salt-tree, *Halimodendron halodendron (argenteum)*, is a pea-like plant, native of Siberia. The branches are very divergent, whitish when young. It grows 6 ft. tall and has pale purple, fragrant flowers borne in short clusters (racemes) in May. The leaves are silvery, two to four parted, compound, the leaflets rounded or with abrupt point at the tip. The pod is short, bladderlike with two swellings, brownish.

USES. Good for salty or limestone soil. Graceful when in bloom. It is drought and heat resistant.

OBJECTIONS. Irregular growth. Looses foliage in Midsummer.

PROPAGATION. 1. Meehan advises grafting on Caragana and Wm. Robinson advises Laburnum because it is difficult from cuttings.

2. Hardwood cuttings may be rooted with bottom heat in the greenhouse.

3. Meehan suggests that seeds left on the plants through the Winter germinate readily.

4. Layers root slowly.

HAMAMELIS—Witch-hazel

(Name derived from *hema*—together, *mela*—fruit, refers to fact that the flowers and fruits are produced together on the plants at the same time)

Their unusual time of flowering makes these shrubs particularly desirable in large plantings.

Virginia Witch-hazel, *Hamamelis virginiana*, is found native to slopes along streams from Canada to Georgia and westward to Nebraska and Arkansas. It is a shrub or small tree, 10 to 25 ft. tall. Of straggling habit and large leaves. The yellow flowers open later than those of any northern shrub, in October or November. The twisted petals are narrow and four in number. The leaves have coarse, round

Curiously the Witch-hazel (Hamamelis virginiana) has flowers and unripe fruits at the same time, inasmuch as it takes a year to ripen the fruits

teeth and are 6 to 8 in. long. They are hairy on the veins beneath but otherwise smooth. The plant fruits the Autumn after blooming. The capsule is woody and opens suddenly by ripening and drying so that the black seeds are shot several feet. In Fall the foliage turns gold and orange.

The Japanese Witch-hazel, *H. japonica*, unlike the native one, blooms in late Winter, often February and March, according to the severity of the weather. The leaves are only 2 to 4 in. long. The flowers are lemon-yellow, often purplish within and not as fragrant.

The Chinese Witch-hazel, *H. mollis*, is the handsomest of the Winter blooming sorts. The flowers are golden and the calyx is reddish-brown, and, as in the foregoing, opens in February or March. The petals are less wavy than the others. The foliage is densely soft, hairy above and gray woolly beneath. The branches also are hairy. The leaves are from 3 to 6 in. long, heart-shaped at base and pointed at the tips.

The Vernal Witch-hazel, *H. vernalis*, native to Missouri, Arkansas and Louisiana is of low growth, rarely 6 ft. tall. The flowers are not as showy as the Japanese or Chinese sorts, but are fragrant and Winter flowering. The plants sucker freely.

USES. Most of the sorts are at home in woodsy places but, strangely enough, endure city conditions with their accompanying dust and smoke.

In a large planting of shrubbery, the Virginia Witch-hazel is an excellent background shrub planted in clumps to show off the bloom. Specimens of the Chinese species would be an object of wonder to all your friends, blooming when the snow is flying. Cut branches may be brought into the home to produce their fragrant, yellow flowers.

The branches of *H. virginiana* are distilled and, mixed with 15 per cent of alcohol, this liquid is sold as extract of witch-hazel, the common remedy for children's bumps. Old settlers used branches as divining rods.

SOIL AND CULTURE. They are not particular as to soil, but it is advisable to have the oriental sorts in the sun so that the branches may ripen properly. Virginia Witch-hazel will grow nicely in the shade. Minimacid pH 6.0–7.0.

TRANSPLANTING. The wild plants are difficult to transplant.

OBJECTIONS. Young plants do not bloom for some time.

PROPAGATION. 1. Collect seed capsules just before they burst and put a fine sieve over them to prevent loss of seeds. It takes two years for seed to germinate and five years to produce salable plants.

2. The oriental sorts may be grafted upon *H. virginiana* roots in the greenhouse.

3. Layers may be made.

HELIANTHEMUM—Sunrose

The Helianthemum is one of the evergreen, rather low, almost prostrate shrubs which many persons consider a herbaceous perennial, but which is truly shrubby.

Helianthemum chamaecistus (*nummularium*) (*vulgare*) is the commonest species which varies greatly and is cataloged in many varieties, some with green, others with gray leaves, and with flowers ranging from yellow to rose, crimson and white. The colors are cheery, the flowers being about 1 in. across, borne in loose, many-flowered racemes, produced from June to August. They open in the morning and close later in the day.

Uses. They are ideal rockery plants or good for steep banks. Mons. Henri Correvon on his recent visit to America was surprised that Americans had not used this tiny gem upon the steep terraces so prominently barren in our cities. The plants are frequently used in the front line of perennial borders, making a mat of foliage and a smattering of bloom through the season. They thrive in full sun. In England they grow so rampantly that it is advised to cut them back severely, but here they usually do not spread rapidly enough.

Soil. They prefer limestone soil. Dry conditions suit them and they do not thrive when kept moist in Winter. Minimacid, pH 6.0–7.0.

Protection. A light protection of straw is advised where they are not covered by snow through the Winter.

Transplanting. Transplant in Spring. Nurserymen carry them in pots.

Faults. Rather tender. Not profuse blooming sometimes.

Propagation. 1. Cuttings may be taken in early Spring or in Summer. Root in a coldframe. Some advise rooting them in pots of sandy soil plunged in frames.

2. Division is possible.

HIBISCUS—Shrub-althea

When the Shrub-althea or Rose-of-sharon, *Hibiscus syriacus*, blooms in August, we feel that Summer is fast waning and that the days are becoming shorter. Erect, sometimes treelike, this shrub has very vertical branches. The flowers are hollyhocklike, ranging from white to rose or purple, according to variety. The foliage starts growth very late in Spring; newly transplanted shrubs often wait until early July to leaf out. The leaves are three-lobed and coarsely toothed. The seed capsules hang upon the plants for a long time and are unsightly unless cut off.

A list of varieties follows:

S—single; SD—semi-double; D—double.

Admiral Dewey. D. Pure white.

Ardens. D. Bluish-purple, carmine center fades blue. Medium size.

Alba plena. D. White, carmine on outer petals. Small; very double.

Banner. D. Variegated pink and white.

Boule de Feu. D. Deep violet-pink.

Coelestis. S. Violet-blue; medium size.

Hibiscus Crested Beauty

Comte de Haimont. D. Delicate pink.

Crested Beauty. S. White, crimson eye.

Double Rouge. D. Bluish-pink.

Duc de Bretagne. D. Pale pink, marked carmine; large.

Duchesse de Brabant. D. Reddish-lilac; large.

Fleur de Panache. D. Variegated white and pink.

Glenwood's Favorite. S. White, crimson center.

Grandiflorus superbus. S. Rosy.

Hamabo. S. Blush, carmine blotched.

Jeanne d'Arc. D. White; free flowering.

Lady Stanley. S. D. Pale pink, splashed carmine.

Leopardleaf (*Variegatus*). D. Purple; leaves variegated.

Lucy. D. Rose, crimson center; broad petals.

Monstrosa. S. White, center dark purple.

Paeoniflora. S. D. White, center carmine.

Pulcherrimus. D. Pink and white.

Puniceus. D. Red.

Purity. S. Pure white.

Ranunculaeflora. D. Blush, center crimson; petals notched.

Rubis. Dark violet-pink.

R. W. Downer. D. Brilliant red; small.

Speciosus. D. Pink, blotched rose.

Snowstorm (Totus albus). S. White; large.

Van Houtte. D. White, center red, splashed carmine.

Violaceus. Reddish-violet.

Wm. R. Smith. S. White.

Hibiscus rosa-sinensis, the Chinese Hibiscus (Shoe-black-plant). *In Ornamental Gardens in Florida*, Charles Simpson writes: "There is hardly a home, either white or black, in Southern Florida that does not have one or more of these Hibiscus, as they are simply called."

Everyone is familiar with the large, showy flowers of the Chinese Hibiscus, for they are grown in conservatories throughout the country and are frequently grown as tub plants in private homes. The lovely flowers of Hibiscus are single, semi-double, or fully double, and range through all the tints and shades of crimson to soft salmon pink and pure white. The leaves are broad, abruptly pointed, and the margins are toothed and notched. In the semi-tropics they grow in sun or semi-shade.

Uses. Shrub-althea make specimens and are good for city conditions. They may be trained to tree form by removing all shoots from

Hibiscus chinensis is the semi-tropical species which rivals the other Southern flowers for popularity

the soil except one. As a narrow, pyramidal hedge for places where a natural spreading one would be out of place, the Bush-althea serves nicely; furthermore, it is a showy flowering hedge. It makes a good background for the sparse leafage of Tamarix. Hibiscus tolerates shade.

SOIL. The Hibiscus tolerates adverse soils, except those that are too sandy, in which case the leaves turn yellow and drop. In such conditions plenty of water should be applied. Circumneutral pH 6.0–8.0.

PRUNING. The flowers are produced on new wood so that the plants may be pruned in late Winter or early Spring before sap rises. Promote shapely plants by thinning out old growth. To confine growth, wood of last year's growth can be cut back to two eyes. Severe pruning does not interfere with its ability to flower freely.

OBJECTIONS. Capsules appear shabby in Winter unless removed. Double flowered sorts often do not open their flowers, and the variegated sorts almost never. There is often difficulty in transplanting them. They fit into combinations poorly. In some cold sections of the United States they often freeze back at the tips.

PROPAGATION. 1. The varieties do not come true from seed, although they self-sow freely.

2. Hardwood cuttings may be made in late Fall before they have frozen too often.

3. *Greenwood cuttings rooted in Summer must be stored carefully or they freeze out the first Winter.

4. Seedlings may be grafted with good varieties or piece roots may be used. This is usually done in Winter indoors.

5. Mound layering may be done.

HIPPOPHAE—Sea-buckthorn

These small treelike shrubs resembles the Elaeagnus with their silvery leaves.

Hippophae rhamnoides grows 30 ft. tall but as usually seen is only 8 to 12 ft. high. The yellowish flowers appear in Spring before the leaves and are not showy. The branches are gray, spiny tipped; the young growth is covered with silvery scales. The leaves are alternate, ½ to 2½ in. long, narrow linear, covered by silvery white scales on both sides. The ovoid fruits are ¼ to ⅓ in. long, bright orange, ripening in September. They hang all Winter and are ornamental.

The flowers are of one sex only; the male plants are more upright whereas the female plants are spreading, twiggy and with smaller leaves. It is wise to plant one male plant for each three pistillate plants to guarantee fruit production.

DISTINCTIONS. Elaeagnus has four sepals, alternate leaves lanceolate to ovate. Shepherdia has opposite leaves, lanceolate and four sepals. Hippophae has alternate leaves, linear to lanceolate and two sepals. Both Hippophae and Elaeagnus have four stamens, Shepherdia has eight stamens.

USES. When trained to tree form the fruits show to better advantage. At the seashore the Hippophae will hold sand from drifting. As a silver-leaved hedge it is very interesting. The berries are reputed to be slightly poisonous. Good combined with Elaeagnus.

SOIL. The best position is one that is damp, near running water, so that the subsoil is always moist. Sandy soils are the natural ones for Hippophae, although Edwin Mathews reports that the Sea-buckthorn will grow in the moister clays. In sandy soil it suckers freely and becomes clumpy.

PROPAGATION. 1. Seed may be stratified and sown in Spring. Seedlings may be grafted with both sexes.

2. Layers root slowly.

3. Suckers may be divided from parent plant.

4. Root cuttings may be used.

The Spirea-like Holodiscus discolor is little known but worthy of planting

HOLODISCUS (SERICOTHECA) (SCHIZONOTUS) —
Rockspirea

This Spirealike shrub is found from British Columbia to California. *Holodiscus discolor* (*Sericotheca dumosa*) (*Spiraea discolor*) is the species which is characterized by its large, drooping clusters of creamy-white flowers, so large (8 in. long) as to arch the slender branches. The blooms appear in July. The leaves are broad ovate, doubly toothed and somewhat lobed. In the variety *ariaefolius*, which is the one commonly seen, the leaves are hairy, grayish-green beneath, whereas those of the type are whitish, hairy beneath. The veins are very prominent.

USES. The graceful arching branches and the profusion of bloom would make this a welcome shrub for more shrub borders. It is hardy except in the extreme North. It prefers sun.

PRUNING. It may be necessary in such latitudes as Boston to trim off the twigs which have been winterkilled.

PROPAGATION. 1. *Softwood cuttings may be rooted under glass in Summer, but this method is reputed to be difficult.

2. Seeds, when available, will grow. Sow in Fall.

3. Layers should be successful.

4. Hardwood cuttings are used. Meehan advises those taken in Spring.

HYDRANGEA

(Named from *hydor*—water, *aggeion*—vessel, referring to the cup-shaped seed vessels)

The likes and dislikes for various Hydrangeas are great. Some like the Peegee Hydrangea with its large heads of bloom so much that any other one less colossal is puerile; others dislike this sort so much that they are prejudiced against all Hydrangeas. The fact remains that the nurseryman has both sorts and the gardener can take his choice.

The Panicle Hydrangea (*Hydrangea paniculata*) in its typical form is not so often seen, although cataloged by some nurseries. The branches are quite upright and cause the shrub to appear decidedly different from its variety *grandiflora*. Hydrangea flower heads often bear showy florets which are sterile, or sexless, and inconspicuous florets which bear sta-

The Hydrangeas in bloom are known as Hydrangea paniculata type
The usual form of this species has larger heads of bloom, but the plants are not so upright

mens and pistils. Naturally, the sterile forms are the showier, but in this case the typical form is able to stand up well and becomes a most attractive background shrub. The nurserymen have abbreviated the long name of the sterile form, *paniculata grandiflora*, to *p. g.* which has now come to be written Peegee. The sterile flowers are white, changing to pink and then to bronze green. These plants when trained to tree form often attain a height of 25 ft. The large, coarsely toothed leaves are hairy beneath on the midribs. Var. *praecox* blooms in early July six weeks before var. *grandiflora*, and is said to have larger florets than the later type. It is desirable for the more formal plantings but is discredited for use because it is grown so extensively in poorly adapted places. Tall hedges are very effective.

Equally popular among Hydrangeas is *H. arborescens grandiflora*, the Snowhill H., which was first found in a gorge near Yellow Springs, Ohio. The large clusters of snow-white flowers are rather flatter than those of Peegee; they bloom in June. The fertile form of this is not attractive for cultivation as there are very few sterile flowers. The leaves are smooth below, rounded or heart-shaped at base, ovate to elliptical.

Closely resembling the above is the Ashy H. (*H. cinerea*), wild from North Carolina to Tennessee and Alabama. It is more upright than *H. arborescens*, and hairy beneath. It has broader, thinner, more obtuse leaves than *H. radiata* which it resembles, and is gray rather than white beneath. The form *sterile* is known as Teas Snowball Hydrangea.

The Silverleaf H., *H. radiata* (*nivea*) is erect and produces smaller clusters of bloom from the upper buds. The leaves are white, hairy beneath. This species has no sterile form in commerce.

An outstanding sort with lobed leaves is known as the Oakleaf H. (*Hydrangea quercifolia*). It is native from Georgia to Mississippi, but hardy in the North. The flowers are pinkish-white, turning purplish, borne in narrow upright clusters (panicles), appearing in June. The

The Snowhill Hydrangea at its best

A curious Hydrangea, known as Hydrangea quercifolia, with leaves somewhat like those of the Oak

leaves are three- to five-lobed, whitish, woolly beneath. The twigs are brown-woolly when young.

Two other Hydrangeas are of interest although they are seldom cataloged by nurserymen; namely *H. xanthoneura*, the Yellowvein H., and *H. bretschneideri*, the Shaggy H. The Yellowvein H., as the name implies, has yellow veins in the leaves as seen from below and hairy only on the veins. The Shaggy H. is so called because the bark of last year's branches flakes off. Both have panicles of white flowers. A specimen of the Yellowvein H. growing at the Hunnewell estate is 12 to 15 ft. tall and completely covered with bloom in July.

Hydrangea opuloides (*hortensia*) (*macrophylla*), the House H., is the type often grown by florists. The plants are dense and round. They should grow 8 ft. tall but in cold regions they freeze to 2½ ft. The flowers are blue or pink, sometimes white, and are produced in immense clusters. The leaves are large and broad with triangular dull teeth. Var. *coerulea* is considered one of the hardier forms. Naturally, where they are hardy, they are the most desirable of Hydrangeas because of their colors and their often fringed petals.

Uses. In the Panicle, the Oakleaf, the Yellowvein and the Shaggy Hydrangeas the pyramid clusters of bloom add a vertical, aspiring accent to the shrub border.

The Peegee Hydrangea flowers may be cut when still pink and dried, in which case they will be decorative for vases all Winter.

The contrasting foliage of the Oakleaf sort is especially beautiful in Louisville, Ky., in which city it grows 8 ft. tall and is loaded with quite clear pink blooms.

Almost any one of the various sorts may be used as specimens.

The House or Hortensia type is exquisite wherever it is hardy and for other localities it is used as a tub plant to serve as a porch decoration or in formal gardens. In acid soils the pink sorts become blue, but in neutral or limey soils they remain pink, which explains the differences in color in different localities.

CULTURE. Most Hydrangeas do best in a moist soil, or at least they thrive when given lots of water. They like a little shade. The more fertility in the soil and the more severely the Peegee Hydrangea is pruned, the larger become the flowering heads.

PRUNING. The *H. arborescens* and *H. paniculata* types are best when pruned very severely each Spring. Let the plants of these types be big because they are old, not big because they are not pruned severely. In other words, prune severely so that few stems are produced, in which case each head of bloom will be larger and will be borne splendidly erect instead of drooping. It is not injurious to prune the *H. arborescens* type to the soil each year.

The Oakleaf, the Yellowvein and the Shaggy Hydrangea types should not be pruned so vigorously.

The pruning of the *H. opuloides* types is different from the others. In this type, the terminal buds of the previous season produce the flowers, so that any injury to these tip buds by cold or pruning results in loss of flowers. Plants are pruned after flowering but not in Spring.

SOIL. Circumneutral pH 6.0–8.0. The House H. has blue flowers in acid soils and pink in circumneutral.

PROTECTION OF THE OPULOIDES TYPE. The opuloides type is hardy along the seacoast and South of Philadelphia. They may live in other regions but the buds when injured by cold seldom bloom. In Cleveland, Ohio, and Rochester, N. Y., the plants make a luxuriant growth each Summer owing to their proximity to the Great Lakes, but they freeze almost every Winter; consequently, there is no bloom. Even in favorable locations it is well to protect the plants by bending the branches to the ground and covering with soil, or the plants may be covered with a barrel filled with soil, peat moss, ashes or dry sawdust. In still, cold regions the plants can be dug and stored in a root cellar.

OBJECTIONS. If faults must be found, each sort of shrub has some, but the Peegee is the subject of many attacks because of its too gigantic head of bloom which turns to an unpleasant red. Some have gone so far as to say, "no other shrub has done so much to disfigure the surroundings of the homes of the people of the Northern United States."

The arborescens type is not particularly attractive after flowering, the white flowers becoming green and then brown, after which they must be removed; this causes a shabby appearance of the shrubs. This type is rather less upright than we would desire so that many home-owners employ a proverbial mop stick to support it. As noted above, the sterile form of *H. cinerea* is more upright but its flowers are not as snowy white.

At the Arnold Arboretum the writer is not impressed with the *H. bretschneideri* because of its untidy bark on the plants which are not clothed with leaves to the soil.

PROPAGATION. 1. Hydrangea Peegee, Snowhill and others may be propagated early before they show signs of flowering, using softer wood than usual. They root in two to three weeks. They are particular about water requirements and either dry up or damp-off.

2. Hydrangea Peegee is commonly propagated from hardwood cuttings about 2 in. long, inserted in greenhouse benches of sand, deep enough to be almost covered. The wood is gathered in early Winter and the cuttings made in late February.

3. Mound layers are successful, the plants being cut to the soil in Spring and mounded when they have made sufficient growth.

4. Large plants of *H. arborescens* may be divided in the Spring.

5. Commenting on the propagation of *H. quercifolia* G. W. Oliver advises as follows:

"The smallest of the ripened shoots should be taken with the leaves attached, placing the stems deep in the sand bed of the cool propagating house. If put in about the middle of October, most of them will root by the end of February. Suckers, with small roots attached, may be lifted and potted in Spring. The most certain method is to layer the lower branches allowing them to remain at least a year before removing. Seeds are now always obtainable, but they germinate readily in sandy soil covered with finely screened sphagnum moss."

6. Grafted stock of Peegee and some of the unusual sorts is said to be stronger and healthier. From the plants remove some large roots in Winter and use them as stocks. Use the wedge or cleft graft, storing grafts in sand or sawdust until Spring.

HYPERICUM—St. Johnswort

(Name from *hyper*—among, *ereike*—heather)

The St. Johnswort is dedicated to Balder, the Sun God, because of its gold flowers. Balder's Day of pagan times became St. John's Day in the Christian era. These plants were held in high repute because of their supposed ability to ward off evil spirits and were always planted about the home.

The lovely shrubs in this group have golden-yellow flowers, at the center of which are found hundreds of golden stamens.

Each sort grades into the next so imperceptibly that they are difficult to remember apart. A number of the outstanding sorts will be mentioned but there are many others equally valuable.

KEY TO HYPERICUMS MENTIONED HERE

1. Flowers large, 2 to 3 in. diameter, leaves oval, styles five.........2
1. Flowers smaller, 1 to 2 in. diameter, sepals leaflike, styles three.
   H. aureum
1. Flowers tiny, ½ to 1 in. diameter...........................4
2. Low, prostrate plants, stoloniferous growth.........*H. calycinum*
   includes *henryi*
2. Plants 18 in. or taller.....................................3
3. Branches round...............................*H. moserianum*
3. Branches two-edged..............................*H. patulum*
4. Styles five, leaves linear ....*H. kalmianum*
4. Styles three..5
5. Flowers axillary................................*H. prolificum*
5. Flowers terminal...............................*H. densiflorum*

Large flowered sorts (2 in. in diameter) *Hypericum calycinum* (Aaronsbeard) (Rose-of-sharon of England). Low, spreading shrub about a foot tall of tufted stoloniferous growth. The flowers appear in July and August and are large (3 in.) in terminal clusters of one, two or three; the sepals are large, spreading and have uneven points; the stamens are numerous in five bunches; the styles five-spreading, shorter than the stamens. The leaves are evergreen in the South, turning brown in the North; they are ovate-oblong, 2 to 3 in. long, blunt, without stems (sessile), grayish beneath. The stems are reddish, four-angled.

Typical blooms of the lovely Golden St. Johnswort, Hypericum calycinum

Hypericum patulum, Japanese H. Arching, spreading shrub to 2 ft. tall. The flowers are about 2 in. in diameter, solitary or in small clusters; the calyx has a few teeth and is about half as long as the petals; styles five, upright, about as long as the stamens. The leaves are half evergreen, ovate-lanceolate, 1 to 2½ in. long, rather narrow pointed, gray beneath and nearly sessile. The stems are purplish, two-edged. Var. *henryi*, more vigorous, leaves obtuse (blunt), 2 to 2¾ in. long, clusters larger, individual flowers ½ in. larger.

Hypericum moserianum (Goldflower). This is a hybrid, raised by M. Moser at Versailles in 1887, between *H. patulum* and *H. calycinum*. It grows 18 in. tall and has arching stems. The flowers are about the same size as var. *henryi*. Unlike *H. patulum*, the stems are round and reddish and, like *H. calycinum*, the leaves are blunt but with a very abrupt fine point. In other words, for practical purposes the three above mentioned sorts are almost identical, except that *H. patulum* is a little less hardy.

Flowers less than 2 in. in diameter. *Hypericum aureum*, the Golden S., is a stiff, dense, upright shrub, 3 ft. tall, perfectly hardy, often with a single stem. The flowers bloom in July and August and are 1 to 2 in. across, produced solitary or few together, sessile; the sepals are leaflike, unequal, the three styles grown together. The leaves are bluish-green, pale beneath, ovate-oblong to oblong, 1 to 2½ in. long, blunt but abruptly bristle pointed. The twigs are two-angled; the bark reddish brown and peeling.

In July, 1776, the younger Bartram discovered this plant upon the banks of Patse-Lega Creek in Georgia. In nature it associated itself with *Rosa humilis*, the Hoptree, and the Fragrant Sumac, growing in rocky situations on bluffs and cliffs.

Hypericum densiflorum, the Bushy S., grows from New Jersey to Florida and from Missouri to Texas. This shrub, which will attain a height of 6 ft., is so profuse flowering as to almost hide the leaves. It blooms from July to September, has small flowers ½ to ¾ in. in diameter, densely crowded in many flowered clusters (corymbs), styles three, more or less united. The leaves are ½ to 2 in. long, linear, narrow, sharp pointed with rolled edges. The twigs are two-angled and densely leafy.

Hypericum prolificum, the Shrubby S., grows from Ontario to Iowa and Georgia, often to 4 ft. tall. It has rather stout, upright branches with light brown bark which peels. The flowers are less than 1 in. in diameter in few flowered clusters. The leaves are thin, narrow, oblong, blunt, 1 to 3 in. long, lustrous green, transparent, dotted. Twigs reddish two-edged, the angles disappearing with age.

Hypericum kalmianum, the Kalm S., is a free branching, straggling shrub 2 to 3 ft. tall. The flowers are ½ to 1 in. in diameter, produced in three to seven flowered clusters; the sepals are leaflike. The leaves are linear, obtuse, 1 to 2 in. long, bluish above, grayish beneath; smaller leaves are often tufted in axils. Branches are somewhat four-angled, two of which are winged.

Uses. The St. Johnsworts are useful garden and shrubbery plants. For foundation planting about a house, *H. prolificum* is handsome; its leaves are fresh green and remain for a long time.

Hypericum moserianum and *H. patulum* var. *henryi* are useful for the perennial border or in front of other low shrubs.

For the large rock garden all sorts are of value but for the small rockery *H. calycinum* is especially charming. It also makes a good ground cover.

Soil and Culture. Most sorts are more at home in sandy soil and will be hardier than in heavy water-holding clays. Circumneutral pH. 6.0–8.0.

The St. Johnsworts like a little shade.

H. patulum and var. *henryi*, *H. calycinum* and *H. moserianum* will profit by a slight protection in Winter, using for the purpose evergreen boughs or coarse litter. They generally freeze to the soil each Winter but spring up from the roots. The first named sort is the hardiest of the three.

Propagation. 1. Seeds may be used for the propagation of most sorts. It takes three to four weeks for germination.

2. Softwood cuttings under glass in September.

3. *H. calycinum* and several others may be divided.

4. Root cuttings may be used for those sorts having fleshy roots.

ILEX—Holly

When Holly is mentioned most persons think of the American Holly, a tree which is used so much for Christmas decoration. There are many other sorts of Holly which do not resemble the American Holly but which are very handsome shrubs for the most refined plantings. See page 82 for a plate showing the tree Hollies and several Hollylike plants. The tree Hollies one discussed in *The Book of Trees*.

Evergreen Hollies—Shrubs with leaves less than 2 in. long.
Ilex glabra (Prinos glaber) Inkberry,(Gallberry in South) (Winterberry). In describing this shrub, superlatives must be used. It is one of the best lesser known native shrubs, with handsome, shiny, evergreen leaves, 1¾ in. long, with a few teeth, usually near the tip of the leaf. The leaves are so dark green in Winter that they are called black. Holly flowers in themselves are never showy, but when these shrubs are in bloom with the tiny white flowers wreathing the stems and peeping from the axils of the leaves, they give a distinct flower effect. The fruits in this case are shining black, ripening in September and remaining until late Spring. The branchlets have greenish-brown bark.

Ilex crenata (fortunei), Japanese Holly. This shrubby sort is about 5 ft. tall but will attain 12 ft. The branches are intricately arranged. The leaves are small, ½ to 1¼ in. long, shiny, with round teeth. Like the above species, the flowers are small individually but are massed among the foliage. Fruit black. Var. *microphylla* has smaller leaves, ⅜ to ⅝ in. long, hardier than the type.

Ilex vomitoria, Yaupon. This much branched native from Virginia to Florida, West to Arkansas and Texas, is a small tree or large shrub with evergreen leaves, smaller than the Dahoon, although the range of the two species is much the same. In this case the leaves are rarely an inch long, elliptical, short stemmed, and with round teeth. The fruit also is red. The Northern gardener can well envy the resident of the South for the abundance of the Yaupon along the streams and road-sides. Few native shrubs give such a long seasonal effect. The species is splendid for hedges, specimens, formal clipping, and grows in semi-shade or full sun. Few shrubs are as meritorious as this, which, un-fortunately, is not hardy in the Northern States.

Evergreens with leaves over 2 in. long. *Ilex cornuta*, Chinese H. This is a broad shrub, 9 to 15 ft. tall. It is hardy south of Washington. The leaves are 1½ to 4 in. long, almost rectangular, with three strong, almost equal spines at the broad apex and one or two spines each side of the base. The fruit is shining, red, produced in large clusters at base of last year's wood.

Ilex cassine (*dahoon*). The name "Dahoon" is used as a common name as well as the species name by many gardeners. This splendid evergreen Holly is found wild from North Carolina to Florida and West to Louisiana. It is a large shrub, or sometimes grows as a tree 30 ft. tall. The leaves are obovate generally, either blunt or pointed, and are usually shallow toothed, 2 to 3 in. long. The berries are dull red, so that this shrub is a prominent feature of the southern landscape.

Leaves not evergreen, deciduous Hollies. *Ilex verticillata*, Common Winterberry (Black-alder). This shrub is a native of Eastern North America and grows to a height of 8 ft. The leaves are a light green, dull above, usually slightly hairy beneath on the veins, obovate to oblanceolate, 1½ to 3 in. long, turning black or brown after a frost.

Ilex verticillata
Attractive because of its bright red berries which make such a charming display in Winter

The foliage is not attractive when the shrubs are not succeeding perfectly, for the leaves have a yellowish cast. The bark is grayish-black. The bright red fruits, $\frac{1}{4}$ in. in diameter, are often produced in pairs. This shrub is grown primarily for its display of berries which last from September to January.

Ilex laevigata, the Smooth Winterberry, which is wild from Maine to Pennsylvania and Virginia, is so nearly like the above that by most persons they are considered identical. The leaves in this sort are lustrous above and usually lack the hair on the veins beneath. The fruits are on short stalks, flatter, more orange-red. The leaves turn yellow in Autumn.

Ilex serrata (*sieboldi*), Japanese Winterberry. This sort also resembles *I. verticillata* but is smaller in every way with a more graceful habit. The flowers have their parts in multiples of four or five, whereas the latter has parts in multiples of six or nine. Leaves appear to be more embossed between the veins. The fruit is smaller, more abundant and shiny and drops in early Winter.

Ilex geniculata has thin, ascending branches and resembles the three preceding sorts, but the fruits are red and borne on long stalks, 1 to 2 in. long, with a knee, or joint, at the center, hence the name *geniculata*. The leaves are dull green, ovate to elliptical. Commended for its fruits by Arnold Arboretum.

SOIL AND CULTURE. *Ilex verticillata* is a denizen of low, marshy places but does not absolutely require these conditions. This shrub does not like lime but thrives in a light or heavy soil and partial shade.

Ilex glabra is also a low, swampy, sandy soil plant but it thrives on high ground as well. Mediacid pH 4.0–5.0.

Ilex glabra and *opaca*, subacid pH 5.0–6.0.

OBJECTIONS. The only faults with *I. crenata* is its slow growth and the fact that in open, exposed places in the North, the tips freeze, although it is reported to stand 30 degrees below zero.

Large plants of *I. verticillata* are difficult to transplant and should be cut back severely when moved. They appear horrible for first year.

ORDERING HOLLIES. All Hollies are difficult to transplant and should be ordered from nurseries who practice root pruning or frequent transplanting. Insist upon having them balled and burlapped.

USE. Few shrubs of small dense foliage are as truly beautiful as *Ilex crenata* var. *microphylla*, the plants being of unusual attraction for foundation plantings where the rather formal horizontal branching fits into a scheme as few other shrubs do. Also good for low hedges.

We are constantly attempting to use medium large Boxwoods in the North in sunny places, situations not adapted to Boxwood, but perfectly satisfactory to the Inkberry. It is true that the shrubs are not quite as green in Winter or as formal in growth but, all in all, they are more satisfactory. *Ilex glabra* is not so good for hedges because of its stoloniferous habit and its lack of density at the base.

As noted before, *Ilex verticillata, I. geniculata, I. laevigata* and *I. serrata* produce wonderful displays of red fruit. Birds eat these fruits. The bark of the first species was used as a substitute for Peruvian bark.

PROPAGATION. The Hollies usually bear flowers of one sex only. For this reason, they fruit better when planted in clumps, and one should be sure that berry producers are purchased. Some plants can produce fruit without others being near, but it is safer to have a number of plants.

1. Holly seed has an immature embryo and waits a year before germinating. (See page 48 for discussion.) Store the seed then in boxes of moist sand for a year.

2. *Ilex crenata* and *I. glabra* may be raised from cuttings under glass in Summer.

3. Cut down the plant to force shoots, injure the branches and layer. Use a sandy soil heaped about the plants. They root in Fall when layered in Spring, but should be left two Summers for best rooting.

4. To get both sexes on the same plant, they are veneer grafted in the greenhouse during the late Winter.

INDIGOFERA—Indigo

(From Indigo and *fero*—to bear, one species produces the blue Indigo dye)

Leguminous plants, the species of Indigo bear pealike flowers and have locustlike leaves.

Indigofera potanini, the Potanin I., is a native of China. It grows 3 to 6 ft. tall. The young branches are hairy at first. The flowers are rosy purple in axillary clusters (racemes), 6 in. long, and are produced in June. The leaves are grayish and hairy beneath, nine to eleven parted. Smaller flowers than other sorts.

I. kirilowi, Kirilow I., grows 3 ft. tall or taller. The leaves are seven to eleven parted; the oval leaflets are rounded at the tip but with an abrupt bristlelike point. A few hairs, not evident, are scattered over both surfaces of the leaves. The flowers are rosy-purple produced in June through the season on long stems.

I. gerardiana (*dosua*), the Himalayan I., is not unlike a Lespedeza. It freezes to the soil at Rochester, N. Y. The leaves are 13 to 21 parted.

Left, **Indigofera kirilowi, one of the hardy Indigoes;** *right,* **Itea virginica, a shrub for moist spots**

the leaflets oval, rounded or notched at the tip, hardly ½ in. long, gray-green. The flowers are purplish-rose, borne in dense racemes 3 to 6 in. long.

I. decora, the Chinese I., has been growing at Arnold Arboretum since 1885. It kills to the soil and appears like a herbaceous perennial 8 to 20 in. tall. It has leaves smooth above, seven to thirteen parted. The flowers are pink or white on slender stems, 4 to 8 in. long. Spreads by underground stems. Flowering period for two months, July and August.

Uses. Undoubtedly there are many pealike flowers more attractive, but the writer was interested in Indigoferas when he first saw them because he had heard that certain species were the true Indigos from which dye is obtained. He read that the blue cloths that enwrap Egyptian mummies were dyed with Indigo and that in 1897 a million acres in India were devoted to the growing of Indigo valued at twenty millions of dollars. Since then the dye has been derived from coal tar products. *I. decora* and *I. gerardiana* would be useful in the rock garden.

OBJECTIONS. Quite hardy and really shrubby, *I. potanini*, due to its luxuriant foliage, almost hides the flowers. Furthermore, the branches are too stiffly upright.

SOIL. All sorts are said to prefer light sandy or peaty soil and perfect drainage.

PROPAGATION. 1. Cuttings of half-ripened wood should root during the Summer. 2. *I. decora* and *I. gerardiana* may be divided in early Spring.

ITEA—Sweetspire (Virginia-willow)

(Itea is the Greek name for Willow)

The *Itea virginica*, or Sweetspire, is a very upright shrub, generally 3 ft. tall but seldom 8 ft. It is hardy at Arnold Arboretum. The flowers are white, fragrant, produced in July in dense, hairy, drooping clusters (racemes), 2 to 6 in. long. The leaves are alternate, long oval, 2 to 4 in. long, finely toothed, gray-green, turning red in late Summer. The twigs are slender, green, and have a partitioned pith. The Winter buds are small, one above the other.

See page 82 for the tender sort, *I. ilicifolia* which resembles the Holly.

USES. Where low growing unusual shrubs are needed in a partly shaded place, try the Sweetspire. It might be good in semi-aquatic garden spots and lends fragrance to a wild garden.

SOIL. Likes the water's edge in damp soil. Minimacid pH 6.0–7.0 or indifferent.

PRUNING. Prune vigorously each Spring to renew the growth to keep it vigorous and provide good wood for flowering. The tips of the plants at Ohio State University winterkill which makes pruning necessary.

OBJECTIONS. Too upright in growth; the attractive flowers are not displayed to good advantage at the Arnold Arboretum.

PROPAGATION. 1. Seed should be sown in early Spring.

2. Hardwood cuttings.

3. *Division of the plants is possible as they produce a sort of suckering crown.

4. Root cuttings.

JAMESIA (EDWINIA)

(Named for Dr. Edwin James, American botanist, its discoverer)

This shrub is a native of the Rockies, related to the Deutzia. *Jame·sia americana* is erect, rigid branched, 3 ft. tall. It is hardy in Massachusetts. The young branches are brownish, woolly; the older with flaking bark. The leaves are opposite, oval, coarsely toothed, gray, woolly beneath, rough above. The white flowers are pinkish outside, five petaled, produced in large terminal clusters (cymes) in May and June. In the Autumn the foliage turns orange and scarlet.

USE. An unusual shrub but not particularly outstanding in its merits, it may be used where variety is wanted among low shrubs. It prefers cool, shady conditions.

SOIL. Peaty or sandy soil, well drained.

PROPAGATION. 1. Seeds.

2. Cuttings of ripe wood.

KALMIA—Mountain-laurel

(Named for Peter Kalmia, Swedish botanist)

Few lovelier shrubs exist than the Mountain-laurel, *Kalmia latifolia*, yet it is found by the million in the Eastern hills and mountains from New Brunswick to Florida and West to Ohio and Tennessee. The plants attain a height of 8 ft. The flowers range in color from deep rose to pure white; the deeper colors are the choicer ones but most nurserymen have not selected them for color so that it is almost impossible to get a desired color. The buds are unusually attractive, with ten little pouches into which the stamens fit. As the flower opens the stamens are pulled from the pouches and scatter the pollen as though thrown by a catapult. They are in bloom from May to late June. The clusters (corymbs) of bloom are large and the stems of the flowers (pedicels) are glandular hairy. The leaves are evergreen, glossy, yellowish-green below, sharp-pointed.

Common in the same habitat of North America but confined to fields, roadsides and open places is the less showy Lambkill (Sheep-laurel), *K. angustifolia*. The flowers are small, less than ½ in. across, and produced in axillary clusters so that new growth is always found above the flowers. The leaves are smaller, narrower, grayer beneath than the first species. It grows 6 to 24 in. tall.

The Bog Kalmia or Pale-laurel (*K. polifolia*) (*glauca*) grows but 1 ft. tall. The flowers are in terminal umbels, varying from white to lilac purple. The leaves are narrow, shining, about 1 in. long, white beneath, almost stemless (sessile).

Left, **Jamesia americana, related to Deutzia;** *right,* **one of the loveliest of all flowers, Kalmia latifolia or Mountain-laurel**

Uses. Mountain-laurel is admirably suited to clothing banks in acid soil regions. Foundation plantings of this shrub are attractive throughout the whole year. It makes a good undergrowth for woodland planting.

The hard wood is used for chisel handles, for spoons and for pipes. It has been proposed as our National flower.

Kalmia angustifolia and *K. polifolia* are both splendid for massing with the taller *K. latifolia* or for beds of Rhododendrons and for semiwild places, planted with *Azalea viscosa.*

Soil. The Mountain-laurel is at home in sandy acid soils, but dislikes clay and lime. Where these soils are not natural they must be treated. (See page 21.) Subacid pH 5.0–6.0.

The latter two species are denizens of marshy places.

Pruning. Little pruning is done except at planting time. When not moved with ball and burlap, it is wise to cut the plants to the soil, in which case they recuperate by making compact and handsome plants.

Objections. Difficult to transplant without pruning.

The Lambkill is reputed poisonous to sheep. However, several authorities dispute this, claiming that the leaves are indigestible to lambs which causes their death.

PROPAGATION. 1. Seed grows readily but it takes some time to produce good salable plants. Sow in Spring as advised for Azalea (see page 150).

2. Most plants are collected from the wild, pruned and grown for a couple of years in the nursery.

3. Layers are slow.

4. Cuttings are usually very slow to root unless very soft wood is chosen. Peat and sand is the best medium for rooting.

KERRIA—(Kerrybush) (Jews-mallow)
(Corchorus)
(Named for M. Kerr, superintendent of botanical garden in Ceylon)

A slender branched shrub of great beauty, *Kerria japonica* is ever popular. The plants may be kept low, 4 ft. usually, with 6 ft. as the maximum height. The flowers are orange-yellow, five-petaled, with numerous stamens. The alternate leaves are coarsely and doubly toothed and prominently veined. The branches are green in Winter and, therefore, showy. Var. *pleniflora* is known as the Globeflower Kerria or the Japanese-rose. The plants are taller, more leggy, and the flowers are double, resembling little roses in form, although yellow in color. Var. *picta*, the Silver Kerria, has green leaves, edged white. It makes a lower growth and has finer twigs. It is constantly sporting to the green form.

USES. Splendid for foundation plantings, for masses of twiggy shrubs for Winter display, as a shrub to dress down the taller, more leggy sorts. The single form thrives in quite dense shade.

SOIL. Circumneutral pH 6.0–8.0.

PRUNING. So tiny are the twigs of many sorts that they become a trifle winterkilled, in which case it may be necessary to shear the shrubs in early Spring, but even when this is not done, the foliage soon covers these bare twigs. Some pruning is advisable for another reason: it causes the production of branches in various stages of development and thereby increases the length of the flowering season.

PESTS. At present Kerria is seriously troubled with a canker on the branches. This appears in the form of brown spots on the leaves and upon the branches, causing whole shrubs to die, as it spreads

The familiar double flowers of the Kerria

rapidly. Cutting out the branches to the soil is advised. It seems to have periods of virulence; some years it is bad and others the plants thrive nicely.

PROPAGATION. 1. *Softwood cuttings inserted in frames root nicely in the Summer.

2. *Hardwood cuttings, choosing good sized wood, are successful.

3. The plants lend themselves to division very nicely.

4. Seed of the single sort may be sown in Spring.

KOLKWITZIA (Beautybush)
(Named after R. Kolkwitz, Professor of Botany, Berlin)

In recent years we have heard more about the *Kolkwitzia amabilis* than in the past, due to the efforts of several nurserymen to push this handsome shrub. It is allied to the Weigela and the Honeysuckle and resembles each a little. It grows 6 feet tall and is an arching shrub with the center always quite upright. The flowers are somewhat lipped and bell-shaped, pale pink with orange veins in the throat, the buds are deeper colored. The flowers bloom in June and are produced in

Spray of Kolkwitzia amabilis
Shows the formation of the flowers described so graphically by E. H.
Wilson in the accompanying text. Photo E. H. Wilson, courtesy
Arnold Arboretum

pairs, forming a cluster (cyme) of about twenty-five flowers. The leaves are opposite, ovate, long-pointed, soft, hairy above and below; the ends of the branches are reddish leaved. The young Winter twigs are very woolly; the older twigs are brown and flaky barked. The flower stalk and the ovaries are brown and so bristly as to appear cobwebby.

Regarding its history, E. H. Wilson writes:

"It is, indeed, a most graceful, pleasing and floriferous hardy shrub, and the only fault to be found with it is the uncouth generic name for which neither the plant nor its introducer, myself, can be held responsible. On account of its peculiar charm and fascination, I suggest as a common name for this shrub that of *Beautybush*.

"This monotypic plant was discovered sometime between 1890 and 1895 in Shensi by Pere J. Giraldi, on whose herbarium specimens the genus was founded by Graebner. In the Summer of 1901 I found it on the high mountains of northern Hupeh and in the Autumn secured seeds for Messrs. Veitch, who succeeded in raising a stock of plants. Neither Giraldi nor I saw the wild plant in blossom and it was not until June, 1910, when it flowered for the first time, that the flowers were known.

"I met with the plant but once, about a score of bushes growing among rocks at an elevation of between 9,000 and 10,000 ft. on the high range which forms the watershed between the Yangtsze and Han Rivers in the Fang magistracy. With it on the windswept ridge grew *Rhododendron fargesi* and *Clematis montana* var. *rubens*, making a choice and valuable trio."

USES. Attractive shrubs, such as Kolkwitzia, are always welcome in the garden where the true garden lover is ever anxious to make new friends. Although found in 1901, it is as yet not as much planted as it deserves.

SOIL. Soils of good drainage should make for perfect hardiness. W. H. Judd, of Arnold Arboretum notes, "To be successful Kolkwitzia must be grown where the air circulates freely during the Winter, otherwise the previous year's wood is liable to get winterkilled."

PROPAGATION. 1. Much of the American grown seed is thought to be infertile. Good seed germinates readily.

2. Ripe or half-ripe wood cuttings in August root well.

LABURNUM—Goldenchain (Beantree)

Native to Southern Europe, the Goldenchain, or Beantree, has been cultivated since 1560. The long pendulous clusters of yellow flowers in May and June are always attractive and appear to advantage over the tops of the masses of the lower shrubs. M. H. Horvath has used them to splendid advantage at Severance Gardens in Cleveland, where they are planted at regular intervals in a formal planting of evergreens.

Laburnum anagyroides (*vulgare*) attains a height of 20 ft. when trained to tree form. The racemes of bloom are often 12 in. long. The leaves are three-parted, elliptical, rounded at the tip and abruptly bristle-pointed, grayish-green, silky beneath when young. The pods are 2 in. long, hairy, with a thick keel; the seeds are black. The branchlets are grayish-green and covered with appressed hairs.

Left, Laburnum vulgare with its long, pendulous racemes of golden flowers; *right*, showing the profusion of bloom borne by Leucothoe catesbaei

Laburnum alpinum, the Scotch Laburnum, is a native of Southern Europe and Scotland. Unlike the former sort, the branchlets, leaves and pods are not hairy. It is usually of a lower growth, hardier, later flowering by two weeks and has longer, more slender racemes, 15 in. long.

A strange form, originating near Paris in 1825, is *Laburnum adami*. This is one of the so-called graft hybrids. Mons. Adam grafted *Cytisus purpureus*, a low shrubby sort, with purple flowers, upon *Laburnum anagyroides*, with the result that a shoot sprang from the union of the stock with the cion and continues to produce its own characteristic parental branches besides certain branches which are hybrid in appearance. In other words, the plant produces yellow, purple and pink flowers, some in long clusters like *Laburnum*, others in short clusters as in the *Cytisus*. The leaf characteristics are rather intermediate. The plants are of a bunchy growth lacking in beauty.

Uses.   Goldenchains may be used against panels of walls, as tall accents in shrub borders or as specimens. They endure shade. All parts of the plant, particularly the young fruits, are poisonous. The wood was once used for bows. It takes a heavy polish.

Soil. Well-drained, especially in limestone. Circumneutral pH 6.0–8.0.

Pruning. Avoid pruning unless necessary as the wounds do not heal well.

Pests. Subject to aphids. Spray with Black-Leaf 40.

Hardiness. Summer heat with strong daily variations in temperature cause these plants to suffer. It is generally believed that they do not stand cold, but it is dry air that limits their value.

Propagation. 1. Sow seeds in Spring. Seedlings are apt to be less profuse flowering. Often self-sow.

2. Graft the good sorts upon seedlings.

3. Suckers may be used.

LAGERSTROEMIA—Crapemyrtle
(Named for Magnus von Lagerstroem, a friend of Linnaeus)

Travelers to the Winter resorts of Florida are most inquisitive about this lovely plant, often seen as a tree. It is hardy as far North as Philadelphia. *Lagerstroemia indica* produces crinkled, crepelike flowers, usually of a magenta-purple, sometimes pink or white. The flowers are produced in huge clusters (panicles), 8 in. long, from August to October. The leaves are generally opposite, although the upper ones may be alternate, elliptical, less than 3 in. long. The bark is smooth, brown and the branchlets are four-angled.

Use. Trained as a tree, it is used as a specimen for lawn decoration.

Pruning. Frequent pruning causes the production of new wood which soon blooms profusely.

Culture. It is possible to store the plants in a cool cellar, even in regions normally too cold for the Crapemyrtle. Pruning even to the soil in this case is not detrimental to bloom.

Propagation. 1. Blooms the first year from seed. Sow the seeds in Autumn in greenhouse. In the Spring they germinate.

2. Softwood cuttings root nicely in Summer in greenhouse.

3. Hardwood may also be used.

LAUROCERASUS (Prunus) — Laurelcherry
(From *Laurus*—Laurel and *Cerasus*—Cherry)

By many botanists the Laurocerasus is considered a species of Prunus or the Cherry. These are all evergreens with the flowers produced in long clusters, or racemes. The group includes some valuable shrubs and trees used as shrubs in the warmer regions of the country.

Laurocerasus caroliniana, the Carolina Laurelcherry (Wild-orange), (Mockorange in the South), (Laurier-amande). This shrub is found growing wild from South Carolina to Texas. It attains a height of from 20 to 30 ft. The flowers are creamy white with a small, brownish calyx, and are borne in dense racemes 1 in. long. The bark is rather smooth, gray, with black blotches. The leaves are oblong-lanceolate, sharp pointed, 2 to 4 in. long, narrowed at the base, seldom with a few teeth, glossy, the margin rolled a trifle. The fruit is short, oval, pointed, black, and shining.

Laurocerasus lusitanica, the Portuguese Laurelcherry, is a native of the Canary Islands, Spain, and Portugal. Really a tree, it grows to a height of 40 ft. The flowers are white, small, in racemes 5 to 10 in. long. The leaves are thick, leathery, glossy, oblong, 2 to 4 in. long, sharp pointed, with rounded teeth, lighter green beneath. The fruits are dark purple, without pulp.

Laurocerasus officinalis, the English Laurelcherry (Englishlaurel), is a native to Southeastern Europe and Asia Minor. It grows as far North as Washington, D. C. The white flowers are borne in spikes 2 to 4 in. long. The evergreen leaves are oblong, pointed, lustrous dark green. There are numerous varieties with broad, narrow, round, small, and variegated leaves.

Uses. The various species are valued as tub plants for trimming into formal shapes. In the Southern States and along the Pacific Coast they are unexcelled specimens, are also used for hedges, and untrimmed they are splendid background shrubs. They are quite free from disease. It is said that the foliage of the Carolina Laurelcherry is poisonous when eaten by cattle. For best results the shrubs should have a rich soil.

Propagation. Long, hardwood cuttings root readily.

LAURUS—Laurel
(Laurus is the ancient name)

The true Laurel of history, *Laurus nobilis*, properly called the Greek Laurel to distinguish it from the other and numerous plants also known as Laurels, is a native to the regions around the Mediterranean Sea. It attains a height of 40 ft. The stiff, evergreen leaves are dull green, lanceolate to oblong normally but there are many varieties which have narrow, curled margins and variegated leaves. The white flowers are not very showy but are followed by dark purple fruits. As commonly seen, the Greek Laurel is sheared to form globes, pyramids, and pillars and used as tub plants.

CARE OF THE TREES IN THE NORTH. Prune them in early Spring, shearing the young growth. They will need larger tubs every three years, but their beauty will depend upon keeping them in as small containers as possible, so that it is well to remove some soil each year and replace it with well fertilized rich soil. Water the tubs freely in Summer, and if possible, plunge them in the soil to keep them from drying out. Syringe the foliage daily. Take the plants indoors at the approach of cold weather, although they are known to endure zero temperatures. Winter the plants at a low temperature near the freezing point in subdued light. For this purpose cellars are satisfactory. Merely water the tubs enough so that they do not become bone dry.

PROPAGATION. 1. Seeds.

2. Layers.

3. Root cuttings.

4. Cuttings of ripened wood in a closed frame.

LEDUM—Labrador-tea

The Labrador-tea, *Ledum groenlandicum* (*latifolium*), is an unusual little shrub which is a native of the true northern regions through Canada and the mountains of Pennsylvania. Seldom over a foot tall, it will attain a height of 3 ft. under favorable conditions. The flowers are white, produced in May or June, crowded in terminal clusters (umbel-like) of 12 or more flowers. It is the leaves which are unusual. They are 1 to 2 in. long, narrow, rolled at edge and rusty, thick, woolly beneath and evergreen. The branches are also rusty woolly.

USES. It can be used combined with *Andromeda calyculata* and such like plants in semi-wild places. For rockeries in cold regions, where snow covers the soil in Winter, the Labrador-tea is splendidly adapted. During Colonial days, it is reputed to have been used for tea.

SOIL. It is said to like a cold, damp soil. Mediacid pH 4.0–5.0.

TRANSPLANTING. Move the plants with a ball of earth.

PROPAGATION. 1. Layer in peat with a little sand.

2. Seed may be sown and treated like Azaleas (See page 150).

3. Many plants are collected from the wild.

Leiophyllum, a rare gem for rockeries

LEIOPHYLLUM (DENDRIUM) (AMMYRSINE)—Sandmyrtle

(Named from *leios*—smooth, *phyllum*—leaf)

The *Leiophyllum buxifolium* is a low growing shrub with small box-like leaves, evergreen, oval, rolled at the edges, $\frac{3}{8}$ in. long, lustrous above, pale beneath. The flowers are white with pink tips, produced in May and June, and borne in umbel-like clusters. The flowers are five-petaled and bear ten purple anthers. Var. *prostratum* (*lyoni*) is a prostrate form of the above, growing 6 to 12 in. tall. The leaves are mostly opposite, whereas those of the type are mostly alternate. Native to the Carolinas, it is known as the Allegheny Sand-myrtle.

USES. The Sandmyrtle is good as a ground cover or for patches in the rockery, but after all, its use must be confined to the gardens of specialists. It grows in sun or shade.

SOIL. Peat is preferred. Mediacid pH 4.0–5.0. (See acid soils page 21.)

PROPAGATION. 1. Seeds sown as for Azalea (see p. 150).
2. Cuttings under glass.
3. Layers in Autumn.

LESPEDEZA (DESMODIUM)—Bushclover

(Named for Lespedez, a Spanish governor of Florida)

Confusion of names ahead, take care! Generally our catalogs have awed us with the name *Desmodium penduliflorum* with no common name generally given. Now we know this plant as *Lespedeza formosa*, although some catalogs infer that *L. racemosa* and *L. sieboldi* are different shrubs, but no, they are one and the same. However, *L. japonica* is a white variety of *L. formosa* and not a different species. Whether or not you are more confused than ever, the fact remains that this is a desirable shrub, the reason for which will be stated later for fear that this paragraph has been read by botanically inclined persons only.

The Purple Bushclover, *L. formosa*, is a half shrub which behaves not unlike a herbaceous perennial. It has long, arching branches, grows usually 3 ft. tall but attains a height of 10 ft. where it does not freeze to the soil each Winter. The pealike flowers are rosy purple, produced in long drooping clusters 2 ft. long, (really a panicle of racemes, each of which is 3 to 9 in. long). The flowers come at a welcome season—late Summer, September. The three-parted leaves are hairy beneath; the leaflets pointed, 1 to 2 in. long. The branchlets are lightly hairy and grooved. Seed is seldom produced. Var. *albiflora* (*japonica*) Japanese B., has smaller leaflets, white flowers marked violet.

The Shrub Bushclover, *L. bicolor*, native of Northeastern Asia, differs from the former species by its blunt, oval leaflets, which are bristle-tipped, gray-green beneath. The flowers are rosy-purple, not the usual bicolor effect. Flowers in August and September.

Uses. Plant these shrubs for specimens; with age they are often broader than high. Late Summer and early Autumn flowering shrubs are rare, so that these Bushclovers are greatly appreciated. *Horticulture* advises planting them against a wire fence. In front of taller shrubs they show to advantage. M. H. Horvath suggests their use to tone down the Peegee Hydrangea, the two making a good color combination.

Soil. Deep rich soils are best, although they do thrive in real dry soils. Circumneutral pH 6.0–8.0.

Pruning. The tops must be pruned each Spring.

Propagation. 1. Seed is not usually produced on *L. formosa* but *L. bicolor* seeds freely. Keep dry and sow in Spring.

2. *Summer cuttings may be rooted and kept in the greenhouse for the first year. If taken in the soft stage in early Spring, they root readily and live over Winter when planted out.

3. *Large plants may be divided.

LEUCOTHOE—(ANDROMEDA)
(Named for the Greek daughter of Orchamus, King of Babylon)

Through Virginia, Georgia and Tennessee the beautiful evergreen, *Leucothoe catesbaei*, the Drooping Leucothoe, is found wild. It usually grows 2 to 3 ft. tall but occasionally attains a height of 6 ft. The waxy, fragrant, bell-shaped, white flowers are borne on the tips of frondose branches in April and May. The leaves are 3 to 6 in. long, shining, dark green, leathery, bristle-tipped teeth, long sharp-pointed. They change in Autumn to bronze and claret. The branches are reddish.

Unlike the above *L. axillaris* has leaves which are abruptly sharp-pointed and leaves which are nearer oval. The young twigs are hairy. The leaves do not turn color in Autumn. It makes larger clumps of growth.

Uses. Leucothoes are splendid for undergrowth among Rhododendrons and for bordered paths or roads in naturalistic plantings. *L. axillaris* spreads more than the more handsome species, *L. catesbaei*. Both sorts may be used in city plantings for bordering conifers. Florists use quantities of the leaves for wreaths and other floral decorations.

Soils. They are native of the moister soils, peaty in nature, although they grow in any acid soil. Subacid pH 5.0–6.0.

Transplanting. Set these shrubs in Spring, moving with a ball. They may be planted 2 to 4 ft. apart, or closer in soils not adapted to them.

Propagation. 1. Sow the seeds in sphagnum moss and sand under glass, treating as Azalea, page 149.

2. *They lend themselves to division.

3. *Most commercially sold plants are collected in the young state and grown in the nursery for several years.

4. Softwood cuttings will root with bottom heat. Use a mixture of sand and peat moss.

LEYCESTERIA—Himalaya-honeysuckle
(Named for W. Leycester, a chief justice at Bengal)

A shrub, allied to the Snowberry, *Leycesteria formosa* grows 3 to 4 ft. tall. It is not very hardy, dying to the soil North of Philadelphia. The white flowers are tinged purple, produced in whorls in the axils of leafy purple bracts upon pendant racemes. The leaves are opposite, oval, entire or toothed, heart-shaped base. The branches are quite soft-wooded, gray-green, hollow, bloomy when young, smooth at maturity. The red fruit gives an attractive effect in Autumn.

Uses. As stated above, it is not hardy north of Philadelphia, but in its range it is showy for the flowers, bracts and fruits. It prefers shaded places.

Pruning. It is of straggling habit unless pruned.

Propagation. 1. Half-ripe cuttings in August, softwood cuttings in Spring.

2. Seeds may be sown in Spring in moss and sand.

3. Divide plants in the Fall.

4. Layers.

LIGUSTRUM—
Privet

(From *ligare* — to tie, refers to the use made of certain kinds)

What home owner does not know the Privets, called Prim in old gardens ? These favorite hedge plants of diverse habit and form in foliage are often interesting in flower. They can usually be depended upon to succeed in adversity.

The European or Common Privet is unexcelled for its lovely black fruits

There are many sorts of Privet, each one resembling the next so closely that it is difficult to tell them apart, especially when grown from seed collected where they have hybridized one with the other.

KEY TO COMMONER PRIVETS

1. Slender-flowered Privets, tube two or three times as long as the four lobes or spreading parts............................2

1. Short-flowered Privets, tube shorter than the four lobes or spreading parts..5

2. Branchlets hairy..3

2. Branchlets smooth, leaves half-evergreen. California P.*L. ovalifolium*

3. Flowers in erect clusters, 1 to 2½ in. long. Amur P....*L. amurense*

3. Flowers in nodding clusters 1 to 1½ in. long...................4

4. Habit of plant horizontal branching. Commonly called Regel P.
L. obtusifolium var. *regelianum*

4. Habit of plant more erect. Commonly called Ibota Privet but truly
L. obtusifolium

5. Leaves half evergreen..................................6
5. Leaves very thick, truly evergreen.........................8
6. Branchlets more or less hairy..........Chinese Privet, *L. sinense*
6. Branchlets smooth.......................................7
7. Flowers pedicelled (with stalks)...........Common P., *L. vulgare*
7. Flowers sessile (stalkless).................Quihou P., *L. quihoui*
8. Branches smooth..9
8. Branches hairy.......................Nepal P., *L. nepalense*
9. Leaves 3 to 5 in. long, tapering at base, tips long pointed (acuminate)
Glossy P., *L. lucidum*
9. Leaves 2 to 3½ in. long, rounded at base, tips short pointed or obtuse
Japanese P., *L. japonicum*
9. Leaves 1½ to 2½ in. long, blunt or notched at tip. Thickleaf P.,
L. japonicum var. *rotundifolium*

Evergreen Privets. *Ligustrum lucidum.* the Glossy Privet, is
one of the handsomest for foliage. The branches are spreading. The
foliage is thick, shining, ovate, 3 to 5 in. long, acute or long pointed,
tapering at base, with six to eight pairs of veins, petioles reddish. The
branchlets are dotted. The flowers are white, borne in long clusters,
8 in. long, in August and September. Hardy in Philadelphia but sometimes injured. Other names for it are *L. sinense latifolium robusta*,
L. macrophyllum, L. spicatum.

L. japonicum, the Japanese Privet, is similar to *L. ludicum*, but
smaller leaves, 1½ to 3 ins. long, rounded at base, darker green, more
obtuse. Var. *rotundifolium* (also called *L. coriaceum*) has glossy leaves
which are crowded, and more broadly ovate or orbicular than the type.

Ligustrum nepalense, the Nepal Privet, is an evergreen which differs
from the California Privet in having hairy twigs and underside of the
leaves. The leaves are oblong, 2 to 5 in. long, sharp pointed and hairy
beneath. The flowers are produced in broad clusters interspersed with
petioled bracts. They have short corolla tubes and are no longer than
the limb of the petal. They bloom in July and August. This Privet is
tender and grows only in the South.

Nearly Evergreen Privets. *L. vulgare*, Common P. (Prim),
grows 15 ft. tall, is very hardy, upright in growth. The leaves are
oblong-ovate to lanceolate, 1¼ to 2½ in., smooth. The flowers are
white, produced in June and July, in large, dense, erect terminal clusters (panicles), 1¼ to 2½ in. The fruit is large, black, borne on the
tips of the upright branches. This is the Polish Privet of catalogs,

according to Rehder. Var. *lodense* is a new form, growing 12 to 18 in. tall, with smaller leaves than the type. Great faith was placed in the value of this form but blight affects both the type and this variety so that in many sections it cannot be depended upon for low hedges, a use for which it was intended. There are many other garden forms: var. *aureum*, golden leaves, and var. *sempervirens*, nearly evergreen, as well as yellow and green fruited sorts, pendulous sorts and a pyramidal variety.

L. ovalifolium, California P., the most used of all Privets, is gradually losing popularity for northern planting because it freezes to the soil so often. This Privet grows 15 ft. tall, has a great profusion of yellowish-white flowers, of unpleasant odor, produced in July. The leaves are dark glossy green, yellowish beneath, and smooth. Var. *variegatum*, Golden California P., has leaves variegated with yellow. It is constantly reverting to its green form.

Ibolium Privet, a hybrid between *L. ovalifolium* and *L. obtusifolium*, is hardier and differs in having a few hairs on the midrib and branchlets.

Ligustrum, one of the most common plants for hedges

This is without doubt the most useful hardy Privet, resembling the California Privet in appearance.

L. sinense (villosum) (fortunei), the Chinese P., is a slender branched spreading shrub, a little less hardy than California P. The plants grow 8 ft. tall. The flowers are very attractive, white, produced in July in pendulous clusters, 4 in. long. The leaves are glossy, dark green, 1¼ to 2½ in. long, softer and thinner than the above, oval to elliptical. The branches are hairy, green or brown. The fruit is black, ripening in September, and remains until January.

L. quihoui, the Quihou Privet, is a rigid spreading shrub growing to 6 ft. tall which produces long clusters of sessile flowers late in the Summer, September to October. The leaves are dark, shining, elliptical or narrow, 1 to 2 in. long. The branchlets are purplish, pubescent when young. The fruits are shining, purplish, ripening in October.

L. amurense, Amur P., is an upright nearly pyramidal shrub, growing to 15 ft. tall. The leaves are oval, 1 to 2½ in. long, rather blunt, pubescent on midrib below. The flowers are produced in clusters, 1 to 2½ in. long; calyx smooth or slightly hairy at the base. It resembles the Ibota but may be distinguished by its upright, rather than spreading habit. The lateral branchlets are erect, and the terminal flower clusters larger. It is very hardy.

Privets which lose leaves early. Ibota Privet, so-called, is not truly named according to Rehder. The true Ibota is very irregular in growth and one of the least ornamental species. What we have called Ibota is *L. obtusifolium*, which has very hairy branchlets, petioles and veins of the leaves. The branchlets are spreading at a wide angle and curved, clothed with small dark green leaves which turn purplish in the Fall. They bear a great profusion of small, black bloomy fruits in small clusters. Var. *regelianum*, Regel P., has horizontal branches, is dwarfer, denser and more hairy than the type. The margins of the leaves are wavy. One of the best shrubs for foundation planting because of its graceful frondose branches, free from insects or disease. Very drought resistant. They produce the same profusion of black berries as the type.

HARDINESS. In range of hardiness the so-called Ibota is very hardy. Ibolium has stood 36 degrees below zero in Michigan. Amur and the Common (*L. vulgare*) are also perfectly hardy. Then come Regel,

Quihou, California, Chinese, Japanese and, lastly, the Glossy and the Nepal, which are hardy only south of Washington, D. C.

USES. Privets are not to be considered as hedge plants exclusively for they are of use in many other ways. For example, the following are profuse flowering: Amur, California, Chinese, Common, Glossy, Ibota, Regel and the Quihou.

Black fruits are borne heavily by the Common, the Ibota and the Regel. *L. vulgare* var. *leucocarpum* has white fruits.

SOIL. Circumneutral pH 6.0-8.0.

PROPAGATION. 1. Seeds may be sown of such sorts as the Ibota and the Common Privet but most of the others do not freely produce seed in the North. The Regel P. does not breed true. From seed the plants vary greatly in habit. Privet seed may be sown in the Fall or else stratified until Spring. It may not germinate the first year.

2. *Cuttings.* Few plants root more readily from hardwood cuttings than the California Privet. These may be taken in Winter or even in Summer or Spring. The prunings from a hedge in Spring will even root.

3. Many lesser known sorts are best propagated from softwood cuttings in Summer. Regel P. will root if long canes are cut up and used in late Summer.

4. Rare sorts, as well as Lilacs, are grafted on the Common and California Privets.

LONICERA—Honeysuckle
(Named for Adam Lonitzer, German physician and botanist)

When Honeysuckles are mentioned the garden lover, who has not looked widely over the available plants in the landscape, thinks of the climbing sorts. Among the bush species there are many lovely fruit, flower and foliage sorts.

Flowers two-lipped, branches with solid white pith. 1. *Lonicera fragrantissima.* Winter Honeysuckle (Fragrant H.) This is the first of the Honeysuckles to bloom; the tiny fragrant flowers coming in March before the leaves are expanded. They are creamy-white and if it were not for their fragrance would not be seen except where they are very abundant on the plants. The leaves are quite evergreen, stiff, leathery, dark green above, gray beneath. The branches are reddish, smooth.

2. *Lonicera standishi (fortunei)*, Standish H., also blooms early but differs from *L. fragrantissima* in that the branchlets are covered with reflexed bristly hairs. The habit is more upright. The leaves of the first named species end in a sharp, abrupt point. Both sorts bear red fruits but the Standish H. is usually not as showy as some sorts.

Flowers two-lipped, branches hollow. Flowers white or pink, do not change to yellow. 3. *L. tatarica*, Tatarian H. This is one of the most commonly planted Honeysuckles. It varies greatly, so that the horticulturist could pick out many varieties if they were outstanding enough. It is a native of southern and eastern Russia to Siberia and is, of course, perfectly hardy. The plants grow 10 ft. tall, have rose, light pink or white flowers in May which do not change yellow as do those of some other species. The tubular part of the flower is short and swollen. The young twigs are often a little hairy. The old branches are grayer in landscape effect than most shrubs. Fruit red, Summer, July and August.

Var. *grandiflora*. Larger flowers, double the size of the type, white. Leaves also large.

Var. *discolor*. Flowers rose inside, dark red outside.

Var. *lutea* (*xanthocarpa*). Flowers white; fruit dark yellow.

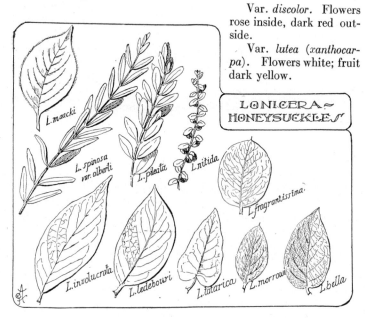

LONICERA~
HONEYSUCKLES

L. maacki

L. spinosa var. alberti

L. pileata

L. nitida

L. fragrantissima

L. involucrata

L. ledebouri

L. tatarica

L. morrowi

L. bella

Var. *latifolia* (*splendens*). Flowers l a r g e, pink; leaves large. The best form for cultivation.

4. *L. korolkowi*, Blueleaf H., has slender spreading branches and grows 12 ft. tall. The leaves are a grayish blue-green, v e r y showy, very densely hairy beneath, ovate or elliptical, acute tips. Botanically related to *L. tatarica* but not similar in appearance. In *L. korolkowi* the flowers are rose-colored; the lobes of the bloom are divided to the middle but not to the base as in *L. tatarica*.

Flowers two-lipped, branches hollow. Flowers white or pinkish, changing yellow with age. 5. *L. maacki*, Amur H., grows 12 to 15 ft. tall, u p r i g h t and spreading.

Showing the flowers of the latest fruiting Honeysuckle, Lonicera maacki var. podocarpa

The flowers are white, fragrant, borne in great profusion in axillary pairs on stems shorter than the stems of the leaves. The leaves are 1½ to 3 in. long, downy on the veins. Branchlets hairy. Fruit red, ripens in September. Var. *podocarpa*, Late H., is more evergreen, the last to ripen fruit, more spreading and more hairy, darker green leaves. This species is very hardy.

6. *L. morrowi*, Morrow H., grows 8 ft. tall, wide spreading growth. Flowers on axillary stems, (pedicels) longer than the leaf stems (petioles), therein differing from *L. maacki*. The flowers are white, appearing in May and June. The leaves are gray, hairy beneath and the branches are also hairy. Berries translucent, blood red, July and August. Var. *xanthocarpa* is a yellow fruited form.

7. *L. bella*, Belle H., is a cross between *L. tatarica* and *L. morrowi*. The plants grow 8 to 10 ft. tall. Like the parent, *L. morrowi* the white or pink flowers change yellow; the branches are slightly pubescent.

The smooth grayish leaves resemble its parent, *L. tatarica*. Berries red, produced abundantly.

8. *L. ruprechtiana*, Manchurian H., attains a height of 10 ft., has white flowers, changing yellow. Leaves are dark green, paler and gray, hairy beneath. Branchlets are slightly hairy. Fruit is coral or orange-red. Bailey says that the hybrids with *L. tatarica* are common in gardens; such forms with pink flowers show *L. ruprechtiana* blood. Var. *xanthocarpa*, flowers yellow, smaller; fruit yellow.

9. *L. xylosteum*, European Fly H., attains a height of 10 ft. The flowers are yellowish-white or pinkish tinged, changing yellow, and are in pairs. The leaves are finely hairy beneath. Young shoots are downy. Fruits dark wine color, August to September.

Flowers equally tubular or bell-shaped (by which is meant that the flowers are *not* two-lipped, neither are they swollen nor provided with pouches which bulge from the flower.) 10. *Lonicera spinosa* var. *alberti*, Albert H. This is not like the usual Honeysuckle in appearance, being a slender arching or procumbent sort with leaves ½ to 1¼ in. long, very narrow, smooth, bluish-green, with several teeth at the base. The flowers are purplish or rose, fragrant and produced in the axils of the leaves. This variety is not spiny; the spiny type is not in cultivation. The fruits are purplish-red, covered with bloom (like a grape).

11. *Lonicera syringantha*, the Lilac H., is a slender, irregularly branched, upright, twiggy sort which has elliptic to oblong leaves, not linear as above, sometimes in whorls of three, and grows 4 to 5 ft. tall. The leaves are bluish green, smooth, not hairy. The flowers are pale lilac rose, fragrant, rather hidden by the leaves and produced in May. The fruits are scarlet in August. Var. *wolfi* has carmine flowers, partly prostrate branches, pointed, narrower leaves. This is more often grown than the type.

12. *Lonicera thibetica*, the Thibetan H., resembles the above. The leaves are shining green above and white, felty beneath. The branches are partly prostrate. The flowers are pale purple, produced in May and June. The fruits are red, ripening in August and remaining until October.

Flowers tubular or bell-shaped but swollen and with small sacs at the base. 13. *L. nitida*, Box H., is of upright growth, 6 ft. tall, not as hardy as the next species, with leaves ¼ to ½ in. long. It has such tiny leaves that one does not believe it to be a Honeysuckle. They are quite evergreen, oval, glossy and present four regular rows of foliage when seen from above (called decussate). Branches purple. The fruit is bluish-purple, transparent, but seldom fruits in the East. A splendid plant, 3 ft. tall, is hardy at Brooklyn Botanic Garden.

14. *L. pileata*, Privet H., is prostrate, has evergreen or semi-evergreen leaves, glossy above, pale green beneath, ¼ to 1¼ in. long, tapering at the base. The flowers are white, opening in April, fragrant but not showy. Fruits purple, translucent with bractlets at the base. Splendid plants at Brooklyn Botanical Garden.

15. *L. ledebouri* is an upright shrub 8 or 9 ft. tall, bearing orange-yellow flowers, tinted red, surrounded by two large reddish-purple bracts, which enlarge to persist upon the purplish-black fruit. The leaves are dull green above, downy beneath, oblong, long-pointed. The branchlets are four-angled. Handsomer than *L. involucrata* to which it is related, darker foliage and showier display of flowers; leaves more hairy beneath.

USES. Many of the Honeysuckles are unexcelled fruit shrubs, although so far as the writer has heard, none of the common ones have palatable fruit. Any desire to attempt to sample these delicious appearing fruits is dispelled by the first taste. *L. tatarica* and *L. bella*, produce scarlet fruit; *L. morrowi* and *L. xylosteum*, deep crimson fruit; *L. ruprechtiana*, orange-red fruit, and *L. maacki* var. *podocarpa* is the latest to bear its dark red fruits. Yellow fruit is produced by *L. tatarica* var. *lutea*, *L. morrowi* var. *xanthocarpa* and *L. ruprechtiana*. Purple fruit is characteristic of *L. thibetica*.

Evergreens for the rockery are *L. nitida*, *L. pileata*, and *L. spinosa* var. *alberti*. Nearly evergreen of a taller growth are *L. fragrantissima*, *L. standishi* and *L. maacki* var. *podocarpa*. The first two sorts may be used near conifers to harmonize them with the more deciduous shrubs; the latter sort is of giant size and needs a lot of room.

The contrast between the gray-blue leaves of *L. korolkowi* and its pink flowers or red fruits is most pleasing.

As flowering subjects most sorts are splendid, so that it might be well to point out those which are not as showy in flower but which are grown for other purposes. In *L. fragrantissima* the flowers are yellowish-white, and although not showy, they are so fragrant as to attract our attention in early April. *L. xylosteum* flowers are rather hidden but the fruits make up for this fault. *L. ledebouri* is most unusual; the flowers are surrounded by large russet or mahogany-red bracts. Tiny leaves are borne by *L. nitida*, making it appear more like a perennial of some sort.

PRUNING. With such Honeysuckles as produce both handsome flowers and fruits, the tendency to avoid pruning is strong. Prune out some of the oldest branches, thereby renewing the vigor of the bush. This is best done in Spring, or with the early fruiting sorts, prune just after the fruit is shed.

SOIL. Circumneutral pH 6.0–8.0.

PLANTING. Some of the Honeysuckles, notably *L. tatarica* and *L. morrowi*, start growth early in the Spring so that orders to nurseries are often so late that these shrubs are in full leaf when received. This exhausts the shrubs to some extent. Place orders for Fall delivery or insist upon early Spring planting. The rarer sorts, *L. nitida*, *L. pileata* and *L. spinosa* var. *alberti*, should be purchased pot grown or balled and burlapped. Severely prune any late planted Honeysuckles, otherwise the foliage will be thin and at the top of the shrubs only.

PROPAGATION. 1. *Most species may be grown from stratified seed. Remove the pulp as soon as seeds are ripe.

2. Softwood cuttings may be used for most sorts but especially for *L. nitida*, *L. spinosa* var. *alberti* and *L. pileata*. These sorts are rooted in the greenhouse during the Summer.

3. *Hardwood cuttings of most sorts are very successful. Few cuttings root as readily as *L. tatarica*, *L. morrowi* and *L. bella albida*.

LYONIA (XOLISMA)—He-huckleberry (Maleberry)
(Named for J. Lyon, American collector of plants)

The He-huckleberry, *Lyonia* (*Xolisma*) *ligustrina* (*paniculata*), is not a shrub of great ornamental value. The glossy leaves resemble the Andromedas but they are not evergreen. The young branches are hairy. The bark is smooth and greenish-brown. The nodding white flowers are produced in dense terminal clusters (panicles) 2 to 6 in. long, flowering from June to July. The plants grow from 4 to 10 ft. tall.

USES. They serve as under shrubs or fillers for naturalistic plantings of Azaleas, Kalmias and Rhododendrons but the various Andromedas would be preferable for this purpose.

SOIL. Acid soil required. Subacid pH 5.0–6.0.

OBJECTIONS. A straggling growth; the annual growth does not cover the bare branches.

PROPAGATION. 1. Seed. (See Azalea page 150).
2. Layers.
3. Divisions.

MAGNOLIA
(Named for Pierre Magnol, director of botanical garden at Montpelier)

The late John Dunbar says of Magnolias: "I think if these Magnolias had never been introduced from Asia, what a serious blank would have occurred in our parks and gardens today." It is not the province of this book to take up the most glorious tree Magnolias, but the few that will be mentioned forthwith are surely in the front rank of garden merit.

Naming these Magnolias in order of season of bloom we start with the Star Magnolia (*M. stellata* or *halliana*) It is slow growing and becomes wide spreading and treelike in time. Plants over 30 years old are not over 12 ft. tall. The flowers are white, or rarely streaked pink. There are twelve or more petals which are long and narrow, thereby differing from the other species. The leaves are obovate and rather wavy margined, dull green above, lighter beneath. The flowers open before the leaves, sometimes in March, are about 3 in. in diameter and have a very delicate fragrance. They bloom at a young age and it is curious to see plants hardly 2 ft. tall with six or eight flowers. The buds and branches are densely hairy in Winter.

Magnolia stellata is a slow growing shrub which starts to bloom when very young

The Anise M. (*Magnolia salicifolia*) is but little known. It is as early as the Star Magnolia but has narrow leaves and petals. Leaves white beneath.

One of the most gorgeous of small trees or large shrubs is the Saucer Magnolia (*Magnolia soulangeana*), resulting from a cross between *M. denudata* and *M. liliflora*. The flowers vary from white to rose and deep purple; they are 4 to 6 in. across, and open before the leaves. The flowers are often upright bell-shaped, although some varieties open flat. The large leaves, often 7 in. long, are obovate and hairy beneath. Magnolias have curious cone-like seed pods, the orange seeds or fruits being suspended by threads. Differs from parent, *M. liliflora*, which is always purple, with sepals that are small, greenish, not petal-like, and from its other parent, *M. denudata*, which is white, with the sepals and petals alike, nine in all.

Since the quarantine against importing these plants, the names of the varieties have not been stressed. The following list may assist in identifying your variety:

Var. *alexandrina*.   Big white flowers, tinged purple outside toward the base. Large bush; early.

Var. *lennei*.   Bushy habit. Late flowers; often blooming a second time. Flowers rosy purple outside, white inside. Sepals narrower and paler. The lateness of the flowers often allows them to be less damaged by late Spring frosts.

Var. *norbertiana*.   Vigorous, regular in outline. Late flowers, white, shaded light purple.

Var. *purpurea*.   Stout branches. Flowers purple outside, creamy white inside.

Var. *speciosa*.   Smaller and lighter than the type; week later, remaining in good condition longer than others.

Var. *spectabilis*.   White flowers, merest tinge of purple outside toward the base.

Var. *rustica*.   Flowers light, more rose-red; vigorous growth.

The Sweetbay, *Magnolia glauca* (*virginiana*) does not make a glorious display as do the other species. A few fragrant, creamy white flowers open every day or so from June to August. The flowers are 2 to 3 in. across, solitary, with nine to twelve petals. In the South this species is evergreen. The leaves are glossy, distinctively whitish beneath, 3 to 6 in. long, elliptical. Due to its preference for wet soil, it is also known as Swampbay and Beavertree.

The Oyama Magnolia *M. parviflora*, is a sort which is treelike, bearing white flowers rather constantly all Summer. The plants as seen in cultivation are often shabby in appearance unless growing in a moist, light loam. The leaves are often 6 in. long, broadly elliptical, sharp-pointed, but round at the base.

Uses. The Magnolias here mentioned are especially valuable as lawn specimens and show to advantage with evergreens as a background. The Sweetbay is well used in clumps in the moister soils.

Soil and culture. *Horticulture* remarks,

"It is also important to remember that the Magnolias, like the Rhododendrons, should have a somewhat acid soil. Lime and fresh manure should never be given them. The best fertilizer for them is decayed leaves and peat. They like a somewhat moist location, or at least a situation where water can be given them at intervals."

The soil then should be subacid pH 5.0-6.0 and for *M. glauca* mediacid pH 4.0-5.0.

The late John Dunbar says that they love an abundance of light, sunshine and air. They cannot fight for existence or succeed when their roots are crowded among trees. Neither can Magnolias flourish in partial shade, as does the Flowering Dogwood. Magnolias need a deep, cool, moist, well-drained, medium light loam to be at their best.

As mentioned above, the Sweetbay prefers moist conditions. In *Country Life*, Wm. Macfarland relates that it is well to dig a deep hole, filled with the richest soil procurable, plant the shrub in this, water well and leave a deep pit about the plant as a rain collector or for watering in time of drought. Before Winter, fill up the hole level, or nearly so, but do not pack the soil too much. After this first season the Sweetbay will grow because its roots are cool and there will be plenty of food available.

Pruning. Pruning is rarely done with Magnolias because the branches do not heal very readily. Do not prune except to shape up a very bad specimen, and in this case prune after flowering when growth is active. The unruly shoots—those having a tendency to grow unsymmetrically—can be pinched or cut back at the tips to make for greater formality.

Transplanting. The roots of the Magnolia are very soft and are destroyed either by exposure to the air or injury when the plants are dug in such a way that the roots are pried. The outer layer of the root then peels. Let the plants be dug by cutting the roots, not prying them in the slightest degree. Careless digging results in the roots dying back.

Transplant when in full flower. The roots are then active and will heal over and not die back.

Move them with ball and burlap always.

Never tramp the soil about the roots in planting for fear that the roots will be injured. Water the soil in around the roots. If your soil will not stand this, it needs drainage, and if this is not provided, the Magnolia will not succeed anyway.

OBJECTIONS. "With all their faults, we love them still." The Sweetbay is untidy as soon as the flowers fade, inasmuch as the old blossoms are held upon the plants instead of dropping.

The main fault with the Star Magnolia is that, in comparison with the Cup Magnolia, many persons are disappointed in it, first because the flowers are white, and second because they are smaller and have pointed, narrow petals.

The objection to *M. stellata* and the *soulangeana* varieties is that they often open their flowers so early that they may be in bloom only a day before a heavy frost overtakes them. This is especially true in central Ohio where they are provoking every few years.

PROPAGATION. 1. Seed. Magnolia seed is enclosed in a fleshy fruit which is gummy inside. It is dangerous to let the pulp rot away as the fungus which causes the pulp to decay spreads through the seed-coat and into the seed. Soak the seeds for a few days in pure water or water to which a little washing soda or wood ashes is added; then remove the pulp by rubbing the seeds with the hands through a sieve. Do not store them dry but keep them in moist sand.

Sow the seed in a frame or flats in the Fall. When the second leaf appears pot them up and carry them in frames.

Stocks for grafting, as well as the true species are rasied from seed.

2. *Layers.* Use last year's growth in Spring, notched or tongued. Sever them a year from the following July, when the new growth has ripened. Plant in pots and keep in a close frame until they are well established. If severed the Spring following layering, they usually die.

Some persons layer plants, which have been cut down in early Spring, as soon as new growth is large enough. This is done by mounding.

3. *Grafting. Magnolia acuminata*, Cucumbertree, and *M. tripetala*, Umbrella M., are raised from seed and used as the commoner stocks for grafting the varieties of *M. soulangeana* and *M. stellata*. The side or veneer graft is used upon potted seedlings kept in the greenhouse. This would usually be most successfully done after the "turn of the year," possibly February or March. Arthur Grube has used cions 2 ft. long upon strong seedling stocks and has found them as successful as short cions. See discussion on grafting, page 72.

4. *Cuttings.* It is reported that certain Holland nurserymen place bands of paper around the twigs of Magnolia to shut out the light. This is intended to promote rooting when the branchlets are used for making cuttings.

MAHONIA—Hollygrape

(Named for Bernard McMahon, American horticulturist, 1775-1816)

The Mahonias are evergreens with leaves which remind one of the Christmas Holly. The commonest species, *Mahonia aquifolium*, the Oregon Hollygrape, is the state flower of Oregon. The plants grow 2 to 3 ft. tall. The leaves are three- to nine-parted, shining, leathery and spiny toothed. The young leaves are bronzy; the mature leaves turn red in the Autumn. In localities with much sun in Winter, they are not evergreen. The flowers are yellow, produced in dense spikelike clusters at the ends of the branches, flowering in April and May. The fruits are purple-black, ripening in September.

Mahonia pinnata, the Cluster Hollygrape, grows 12 ft. tall, resembles the above but has seven- to thirteen-parted leaves which are duller.

Mahonia bealei, the Leatherleaf H., is the species usually cataloged as *Mahonia* or *Berberis japonica*. It is a stout, upright shrub to 12 ft.

A, n asset to your home planting the Oregon Hollygrape has a wide range of adaptability

tall. The leaves are very thick and rigid, with nine to fifteen roundish-oval leaflets each of which has two to five long, spiny teeth. The leaves are dark blue-green above and grayish beneath. The leaves do not change color in Winter. The flowers are yellow in bunched clusters. The fruits are bluish-black. The true *Mahonia japonica* is not in the trade.

Mahonia repens (*nana*), the Creeping Hollygrape or Ash-barberry, spreads by underground stems. It grows but 7 to 10 in. tall. The leaves are duller than the Oregon Hollygrape, three- to seven-parted, leathery, broad ovate, leaflets 1 to 2 in. long. The flowers, as with the other sorts, are yellow, and the black fruits, produced in clusters at the ends of the branches, are bloomy.

Mahoberberis neuberti is a hybrid between *Mahonia aquifolia* and *Berberis vulgaris*. This is often sold as *Mahonia aquifolia* but the leaves are simple, or some may be three-parted. It is spineless and the leaves are solitary. In general it may be considered interesting as a hybrid, but of little ornamental value, in that the branches are too stiffly upright. It has been cataloged as *Berberis ilicifolia*.

Uses. The Oregon Hollygrape is truly a beautiful shrub, being nearly evergreen. It is splendid for massing in semi-shaded places where it retains its foliage better than in the sun. It is useful for Rhododendron beds. The striking foliage may be cut for house decoration or used for combining with cut flowers.

Soil. Mahonias thrive in any soil (Circumneutral pH 6.0–8.0), even dry and sandy. Feeding with manure or bonemeal will prevent the plants from becoming straggly.

Transplanting. Plants are more easily moved if taken with a ball of earth, although this is not really necessary.

Pruning. Cutting back the plants in Spring will keep them from being leggy.

Objections. They burn in sunny places. Both *M. aquifolia* and *M. bealei* are apt to be too upright and bare of foliage at the base.

M. repens has a dull foliage. It should be good for a ground cover but it seldom makes a good growth, regular throughout the area where it is desired.

The faults of *Mahoberberis neuberti* have been dwelt upon.

Propagation. 1. Clean seed of pulp and sow as soon as ripe. Vilmorin says that it takes 2 years to germinate.

2. Suckers.

3. Layers.

4. Softwood cuttings will root under glass.

MALUS—Apple, Crab Apple

The Apple blossom of Springtime is one of our choicest flowers representing the embodiment of the hope for a season of abundance and the symbol of Spring.

In Persia the Apple is the fruit of immortality. A weird tale relates how Anashindhu, a holy man and wise, was given an Apple as a token that he should live forever. He placed it to his lips but suddenly thought of his discontented wife. He would give anything to satisfy her,

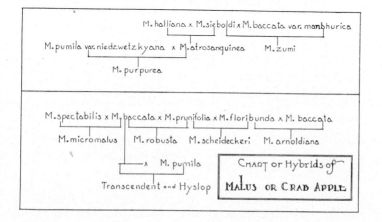

so he gave her the Apple. She refused the fruit, imploring him to sell it that they might both enjoy a better home, a golden carriage and the accompaniments of luxury. Her pleas led Anashindhu to sell his Apple to the king. But the king also aspired to holiness and sacrificed by giving it to his queen. The queen retired to her garden and there in a trysting place beneath the moon bestowed it upon the captain of the guards. Now, the captain of the guards loved a serving maid more dearly than his queen. To her he gave the fruit, happy in the idea of making her a goddess and immortal. The next day the serving maid, in humble dress, offered the king a withering Apple. When the king saw the Apple he was astonished and demanded to know from whom the girl had received the Apple. The king beheaded his queen, burned his captain, commanded that his goods be divided with the poor, and decided to become a beggar along the roadsides. One day Anashindhu passed, dressed in brocades of silk and in a golden litter. "Here," said the king. "eat of the Apple and live." As Anashindhu raised the Apple to his lips, it was jolted from his hand. A passing dog, gulped it at a mouthful. Thus was immortality denied to man, but in the East, a dog is wandering from place to place unable to die.

The Apple has been endeared to many races of people, the fruit of health and the flower of Springtime. But the flowers of many of the oriental Crabs is even more exquisite than that of the common Apple. In many of the ornamental sorts the branches are wreathed with bloom so thick that leaves cannot be seen and with fruits of great beauty as well.

The Flowering Crabs are small trees which are so much associated with good shrub planting that a few outstanding sorts are here discussed. There is a constantly growing interest in these incomparable plants.

Species According to Season of Bloom*

Malus angustifolia (late 3)	*Malus micromalus* (1)
arnoldiana (1)	*parkmani* (1)
atrosanguinea (1)	*prunifolia* var. *rinki* (1½)
baccata var. *mandshurica* (1½)	*pumila* var. *niedzwetzkyana* (1½)
coronaria (1½)	*robusta* (1½)
floribunda (1)	*sargenti* (1½)
halliana (1)	*spectabilis* (1½)
ioensis var. *bechteli* (3)	*theifera* (1)

1. Arnold Crab (*Malus* or *Pyrus arnoldiana*) (*M. baccata* x *M. floribunda*). This beautiful sort originated at the Arnold Arboretum. It has rose-colored flowers, larger than *M. floribunda*, which fade white. The flowers are produced on long drooping stems. It is a low spreading tree with long arching branches. The fruit is yellow.

2. Bechtel Crab (*M. ioensis* var.) This a natural sport producing double flowers, found by Bechtel, a nurseryman near Staunton, Illinois. Its large double pink, roselike flowers, its round buds, and its great profusion of bloom year after year has endeared this small bushy tree to the hearts and gardens of America. The foliage is shallowly lobed and always attractive. There is a feeling that this sort should not be grafted or budded upon the Common Apple as the trees are shorter lived. Seedlings of *M. ioensis*, or some other native sort, are best.

3. Carmine Crab (*M. atrosanguinea*) (*M. halliana* x *M. sieboldi*). This sort has redder buds than *M. floribunda*, purplish in tone, opening red instead of white. Fruit reddish-yellow. Hicks suggests it as a substitute for the pink Magnolia which is rare. It blooms about the same time.

---

*To A. E. Wohlert, of Narberth, Pa., I am indebted for the facts as to season of bloom. He writes, "Indicate them as 1 and 1½ for earliness, and 3 as late, as there is a gap between the early and late and really no midseason."

4. Cherry Crab (*M. robusta*) (*M. baccata* x *M. prunifolia*). Very early. Flowers white, fragrant. A handsome tree. Fruits 1 in. across, dull red.

5. Chinese Apple (*M. prunifolia* var. *rinki*). Large white flowers. Fruit red, yellow and green, 1½ in. in diameter. Cultivated in China for fruit. Fruit remains for a long period of time.

6. Chinese Flowering Crab (*M. spectabilis*). A tall shrubby sort. Flowers pink, fragrant, semi-double. Fruit not showy, pale yellow, not large. Leaves smooth and shining.

7. Japanese Flowering Crab (*M. floribunda*). One of the handsomest and most reliable. A small tree, round topped, with single flowers. The buds are carmine but change to pink, then white. The fruit is the size of a pea and red. Stands cold and drought. Tremendously profuse blooming.

8. Manchurian Crab (*M. baccata* var. *mandschurica*). Early. Flowers pure white, large and fragrant. Fruit dark purple on long stems.

9. Midget Crab (*M. micromalus*). Early. Flowers pale pink, buds tiny, deeper color. Fruit yellow. Habit pyramidal. Also called Kaido Crab. (Hybrid between *M. spectabilis* x *M. baccata*.)

10. Parkman Crab (*M. halliana*). Small, dark green leaves remaining until late. Flowers very double; bud dark rose opening rosy white. Fruit size of pea, reddish. Favorite in Japanese gardens.

11. Redvein Crab (*M. pumila* var. *niedzwetzkyana*). The variety name is one of no beauty and great length. The leaves are brownish red, smooth and shining. The fruit, flowers, twigs and all parts have a cast of red.

12. Sargent Crab (*M. sargenti*). A low, hardy sort. Flowers white, stamens golden. Fruit scarlet, hanging until Spring. The fruit alone serves to make this one of the most desirable.

13. Scheidecker Crab (*M. scheideckeri*). Flowers semi-double, pink; buds red. Fruit yellow. Small tree of pyramidal habit. The flowers are in "bottlebrush formation along the stems." This sort may be forced in the greenhouse.

14. Siberian Crab (*M. baccata*). Very hardy, tall narrow tree. Flowers white, Fruit red or yellow, size of a cherry.

15. Southern Crab (*M. angustifolia*). Open tree, 30 ft. tall. Bright pink flowers, latest to bloom. Branches rigid and spiny. The fruit is flattish, yellow-green. The leaves are slightly lobed.

16. Tea Crab (*M. theifera*). Lovely tree bearing numerous clusters of flowers which are rose-red in bud and pale when expanded.

The yellow fruits serve to make this plant appear to be in bloom in Winter.

17. Wild Sweet Crab (*M. coronaria*). Flowers blush-colored, fragrant. Branches thorny. Fruit yellow, hard. Native Canada to Maryland. Not as profuse blooming but fragrant.

Uses. Such small trees as the Crabs are always more useful for home grounds than the larger trees. Among flowering trees, the Crabs are the largest group, giving a glorious succession of bloom. They serve as specimens or for the background of extensive shrub borders.

A. E. Wohlert recommends the Crabs for tall hedges, pointing out that the foliage is good, that there are few insect pests to contend with, that they will flower and are hardy. It is suggested that the pruning for hedge purposes may be done in May or early June and again a month later. This assures a crop of bloom. For this purpose *M. atrosanguinea*, *M. floribunda*, *M. arnoldiana*, and *M. scheideckeri* may be used. The hedge may be kept at 4 ft. or allowed to attain a height of 20 ft.

Soil. Most sorts will thrive in the stony, poorer soils. Circum-neutral pH 6.0-8.0.

Pruning. Except to start them in the way they should grow, there is little difficult pruning necessary. See that the first few branches are evenly spaced around and up the trunk, pruning as little as possible. Most sorts bloom when quite young. The pruning of mature trees should be for the purpose of retaining a good form and attempting to renew the wood.

Propagation. 1. These Crabs are all budded (See page 79) on Apple stock in July or August or root grafted (See page 78) in Winter. It might be wise to graft or bud upon tall stocks.

2. The species, not hybrids, may be raised from seed; namely, *M. spectabilis*, *M. theifera*, *M. floribunda*, *M. sargenti*, *M. coronaria*, and *M. baccata*.

MELALEUCA—Bottlebrush

(From the Greek *black* and *white*, from the black branches and white bark of one species)

These plants resemble the Callistemons with their unusual flowers which resemble a bristly bottlebrush. They are commonly planted on the Pacific Coast and in the Gulf States but are not hardy North.

Melaleuca decussata, the Lilac M., is of a graceful, drooping habit with pendulous branches. The shrubs grow 20 ft. tall. The flowers are lilac, produced in cylindrical spikes 1 in. long. The flower spike continues in a leafy shoot. The leaves are bluish green, opposite, lanceolate to oblong, ¼ to ½ in. long and less than a ¼ in. wide.

Melaleuca armillaris (alba), the Drooping M., is a large shrub ranging from 15 to 30 ft. tall, with graceful, pendant branches. The bark is gray and sheds in narrow strips. The leaves are needlelike, light green, ¾ in. long and 1/16 in. wide. This is the best of the whiteflowered species with the spikes 2 in. long.

Melaleuca hypericifolia (oppositifolia), the Dotted M., is tall but resembles a St. Johnswort (Hypericum) with its mostly opposite leaves, less than 1½ in. long and ¼ in. wide. The flowers are rich red in dense spikes 2 to 3 in. long. This sort is one of the best.

Melaleuca has its stamens united in bundles opposite the petals and in that differs from the Callistemon, which see (page 170) for brief cultural notes.

MERATIA (CHIMONANTHUS) (CALYCANTHUS) —Wintersweet (Chinese-allspice)

(Named for Francois V. Merat, French physician and botanist)

Related to the Sweetshrub, this Wintersweet, *Meratia praecox* (*Chimonanthus fragrans*) is one of the earliest flowers to bloom, coming on mild days in January. Obviously such a shrub is not perfectly hardy in Northern regions. It will stand zero weather and opens its flowers in Philadelphia and Cincinnati. The plants will grow to a height of 9 ft. but as usually seen, 4 ft. is more characteristic. The outer petals, or sepals, are pale lemon; the inner are purplish brown with a group of white stamens at the center. The flowers are delightfully fragrant. The foliage is not unlike that of the Sweetshrub, opposite, pointed at the tip and wedge-shaped or rounded at the base.

Uses. Branches may be cut and placed in water in which case the flowers will open and scent a whole room in Winter.

Soil and culture. It is wise to plant in a sandy soil in a position facing south against a wall. In such situations the flowers can be protected.

Pruning. The plants should be pruned rather severely after flowering.

Objections. Too tender for cold climates; the buds refuse to open.

PROPAGATION. 1. Cuttings may be rooted under glass during Summer.

2. Layers are successful in Spring.

3. Sow seed in early Spring in warm greenhouse or outdoors when the soil is warm.

MICHELIA (MAGNOLIA) — Banana-shrub (Brownflower-Magnolia)
(Named for Peter A. Michel, a Florentine botanist, 1679-1737)

These evergreen shrubs are related to the Magnolias which have flowers at the tips of the branches, whereas these flowers are borne in the axils of the leaves. *Michelia fuscata* is a branchy shrub from China which grows from 10 to 15 ft. tall and is a popular favorite in the South. The flowers are yellowish brown, edged reddish maroon, appearing in Spring and Summer. They are 1 to 1½ in. across and have a decided banana odor. The leaves are oval, bluntly pointed, glossy above. The twigs are brown, hairy.

PROPAGATION. 1. Seeds.
2. Ripe wood cuttings.

MYRICA—Bayberry, Waxmyrtle (Candleberry)

These interesting shrubs bear the gray berries which yield the wax for making Bayberry candles.

Myrica carolinensis is the Northern Bayberry. It grows 8 to 9 ft. tall. The leaves, though not truly evergreen, hang upon the plants until Spring. The oblong-lanceolate leaves are shallowly toothed at the tip and are golden dotted beneath. The dots are glands which exhale the familiar bay rum odor. The fruits are grayish and produced in clusters upon the branches and are not showy until the leaves are removed.

Related to this last species is *M. cerifera*, the Southern Waxmyrtle which becomes more treelike. The leaves are sharp-pointed, and sharply toothed.

Myrica gale, the Sweetgale (Baybush), (Bogmyrtle) (Sweetwillow), grows 3 to 4 ft. tall. The leaves are dark green, smooth above and hairy beneath, 1 to 2½ in. long, narrowly wedge-shaped. The fruit is produced in dense catkins ¼ in. long, is resin dotted but not wax covered. It is compressed and three-pointed.

Uses. Myrica is at home among Rhododendrons. It grows well on slopes. It is a splendid seaside shrub, tolerating salt spray.

The berries of *Myrica cerifera* and *M. carolinensis* are boiled, in which case the wax melts from the fruit and comes to the surface. This is cooled and skimmed over to be of use for making Bayberry candles, the latter giving off a pleasant odor as they burn. In early American homes the boiled roots produced a tea for headaches; the bark was used for poultices and for jaundice. The Scottish people use the leaves in place of hops for brewing, which increases the intoxicating effect.

The Myrica or Bayberry

1. *M. carolinensis*; 2, the leaves of *M. cerifera* are sharply pointed and sharply toothed; 3, the Sweetgale, *M. gale*, are narrow and small

Sweetgale is the emblem of the Scottish clan Campbell. The English people place branches among clothes to give them an agreeable odor, and as well to banish moths.

SOIL. Dry and sterile soils, sandy or peaty soils are those in which *Myrica carolinensis* thrives naturally. Sweetgale is more of a moisture loving subject. Subacid pH 5.0-6.0.

TRANSPLANTING. Nurserymen furnishing good plants of these shrubs usually ship them balled and burlapped as they are rather difficult to establish.

PROPAGATION. Most Myricas are collected from the wild and are not propagated.

1. Seed may be sown as soon as ripe or stratified until Spring. Remove the pulp by rubbing with a brick. Seedlings develop slowly the first year.

2. Layering.

3. Suckers. *Myrica gale* suckers freely.

MYRTUS—True Myrtle
(The ancient Greek name is Myrtos)

The True Myrtle, *Myrtus communis*, is a shrub 3 to 10 ft. tall. The flowers are tiny and white. The shrubs are everflowering in Southern California and in other less favored locations they open in July. They possess numerous stamens. The opposite, simple leaves are lanceolate, sharp pointed, glossy and aromatic. The fruit is a black berry. There are variegated varieties, small leaf sorts and ones with double flowers. The Myrtle is used for hedges, specimen shrubs and in masses.

CULTURE. The culture is simple, growing as they will in any soil, but the plants should never be allowed to dry out.

PROPAGATION. 1. They are easily increased by short ripe wood cuttings.

2. Seeds.

NANDINA—(Heavenly-bamboo)(Chinese sacred-bamboo)

The reedlike, upright growth has given *Nandina domestica* the strange common name of Heavenly-bamboo. The unbranched stems grow 3 to 6 ft. tall. The leaves are evergreen, shining, clustered at the tip of the branches, pinnately compound into 9 to 27 divisions. The leaves stay on the plants about three years. They turn scarlet in the Fall and are red also when first unfolding. The individual flowers are not showy, but are produced in great profusion. They are white, opening in June and July, produced in terminal spikes, often a foot long. The fruit is purplish-red, edible, $\frac{1}{4}$ in. across. The Nandina is related to the Barberry.

Uses. Its tenderness prohibits the use of Nandina farther north than Washington, D. C., but where hardy, it is prized for its brilliant Autumn foliage and large clusters of red fruits. Commonly cultivated in California as a dooryard plant or useful for tubs.

Soils. Waterer (Eng.) says that they prefer warm spots, light peaty loam. A little shade suits them.

Objections. Slow growth when young. The bare stems are unsightly unless the base is covered.

Propagation. 1. The van Lindley Nursery Co. says, "Sow the seed in April in flats and leave in shade all Summer. Move to greenhouse in the Fall." From seed it takes several years to make salable plants, although the seeds germinate in three months.

2. The plants may be divided but this would spoil their appearance.

NEILLIA

(Named for Patrick Neill, Edinburgh botanist)

Related to Stephanandra and Physocarpus, *Neillia sinensis* resembles both genera. The plants grow 5 to 6 ft. tall. The flowers are pink, produced in terminal nodding racemes, in June, and are rather bell-shaped. The leaves are oval but long-pointed, lobed by being deeply toothed. There are many zigzag, slender, drooping branchlets, which are reddish-brown. The bark sheds on old branches.

Uses. For the shrub border this pretty flowered and graceful foliage plant is just another different and rarely seen subject. It is perfectly hardy at Rochester and at Boston. *Horticulture* comments: "It is a shrub which is bound to take an important place in American horticulture when it becomes better known."

Soil. Prefers moderately moist soils.

Propagation. Same as for Spiraeas, page 370.

Neillia is an uncommon shrub resembling the Ninebark

NEMOPANTHUS—Mountain-holly

(Name from *nemo*—thread, *anthos*—flower, refers to flowers on long stems)

A rare shrub, noted for its beautiful fruit in the wild, is *Nemopanthus mucronatus*, called Mountain-holly because of its relation to the true Hollies. It is wild from Nova Scotia to Ontario, Wisconsin and Virginia. The plants grow 6 to 8 ft. tall. They are apt to bear but one sex, in which case they produce no fruit unless plants of both sexes are present. The berries are red, ¼ to ⅜ in. long.

USES. One would desire this shrub after seeing it in the wild, but at the Arnold Arboretum and at Highland Park, Rochester, it has a burnt appearance, although it was early Summer when observed.

SOIL. Prefers the moister soils and a little shade. Subacid pH 5.0–6.0.

PROPAGATION. See Ilex, page 269, for propagation.
1. Divide the plants. 2. Greenwood roots under glass (N. M.).

NERIUM—Oleander

(Ancient name, supposedly from the Greek word *neros*—wet places, alluding
to the habitat where it is found wild)

Few readers will need an introduction to the Oleander, *Nerium
oleander*, for it is known from one end of our country to another and
since horticultural history has been grown as a tub plant in cold regions
and planted out in the open in the balmier climates. The plants grow
to a height of 15 ft. The flowers are white, light and dark rose pink,
scarlet and buff. They are funnelform and borne in bouquets at the
tips of the branches. The leaves are opposite or whorled, evergreen and
long narrow. When the plants become leggy they need to be cut back
severely in the early Spring but that will defer blooming for a year.
They are often troubled with scale in the open soil.

CARE IN TUBS. Oleanders may be kept in a cool greenhouse of a
temperature of 40° to 45° during the Winter months. In the Spring
they should be repotted if rootbound; if they are so large that repotting

The Oleander (Nerium) is a popular hedge plant on the West Coast

is out of the question, 2 or 3 in. of the top soil should be taken off and replaced by the same amount of good rich loam. When danger of frost is past, the plants should be plunged out of doors level with tops of the pots, first putting a large handful of ashes at the bottom of the hole to ensure good drainage and to keep worms out. They usually begin flowering early in July and continue until frost.

The dropping of the buds is probably caused by drying at the roots and insufficient ventilation in the Spring. Give plenty of air and water when weather is suitable.

PROPAGATION. 1. Root rather mature twig cuttings, even in bottles of water.

NEVIUSIA—Snow-wreath
(Named for Rev. R. D. Nevius, its discoverer)

The Snow-wreath, *Neviusia alabamensis*, is a spirealike shrub bearing flowers without petals. It was found along the sides of Sand Mountain, near Tuscaloosa, Alabama. It is hardy in Columbus, O. The plant grows 4 ft. tall and bears white or yellowish-green flowers in May and June. The flowers are composed of hundreds of stamens and they are ranged along the long-arching branches, producing a most pleasing effect. The leaves are like small Ninebark leaves, doubly toothed, alternate.

USES. It may be used among other shrubs as the plants are not very attractive after they have flowered.

SOIL. Loose, well drained soil makes for hardiness.

PROPAGATION. 1. Softwood cuttings root quickly.

2. Plants may be divided as they sucker somewhat.

Neviusia or Snow-wreath
Little known relative of the Spireas

ONONIS—Restharrow

So few shrubs are available for the rockery that it is well to speak here of *Ononis fruticosa*, a small shrub, rarely 18 in. tall, bearing terminal clusters (panicles) of pink pealike flowers produced from June until August. The leaves are distinct, about 1 in, long, three-foliate, the leaflets long, narrow and coarsely toothed. The bark is gray, almost silvery.

USE. As seen at the Brooklyn Botanic Garden the clump of Ononis is a thing of great charm. Mr. Montague Free of that institution considers it one of the most reliable blooming shrubs for the rockery. Most of the species of Restharrow are perennial. This sort is not cataloged in America.

PROPAGATION. 1. Seeds may be obtained in Europe.

2. Dividing established plants is possible.

A dainty rockery shrub, Ononis fruticosa, the Restharrow, is rare in cultivation

OSMANTHUS—(Holly-olive)

(From *osme*—smell, *anthos*—flower; in some sorts the flowers are fragrant)

Many persons believe this to be a Holly. The leaves are similar to the English Holly, but Hollies are alternate-leaved, whereas this has opposite leaves, which are smaller and thicker. *Osmanthus aquifolium* (*ilicifolium*) is a shrub 7 to 8 ft. tall, although sometimes becoming tree-like and 20 ft. high. The plants are not hardy north of South Carolina, although with protection some are growing in Washington. The leaves are lustrous, evergreen, 1 to 2½ in. long with two to four large teeth on each side. The flowers are white, fragrant, not showy, and are only produced upon old plants. The fruit is a bluish berry ½ to ¾ in. in diameter. Var. *variegata*, leaves splashed gold. Var. *myrtifolia*, leaves not spiny margined.

USES. Protected places sheltered by evergreens would be the

This appears to be a Holly but is truly Osmanthus, the Holly-olive. Note that the leaves are opposite whereas those of Holly are alternate. See page 82 also

ideal place to plant Osmanthus out of its range of real hardiness. It is good near the sea.

TRANSPLANTING. More easily transplanted than Hollies.

SOIL. They prefer a peaty soil, according to *Le Bon Jardinier.*

PROPAGATION. 1. Meehan advises, half-ripe wood under glass, also cuttings made in August when wood is firm.

2. Layers.

3. Grafting. As these plants are related to Privet, it might be used as a stock for grafting.

4. Seeds are rarely obtainable and rest a year before germinating.

PARROTIA—(Irontree) (Persian-ironwood)
(Named for F. W. Parrot, German naturalist)

The *Parrotia persica* is a large shrub, 10 to 15 ft. tall, which resembles the Witch-hazel. The flowers are purplish with pendulous stamens, open in March and April. The leaves are oval with coarse, round teeth and turn in Autumn to glorious tints of yellow and orange-scarlet. The bark is smooth and the branches are tortuous. The flowers are charming to the observer of dainty gems.

Use. Specimens may be used as a background for lower subjects.

Soil. It requires well-drained places, perhaps on a slope, where it gets sun.

Propagation. 1. Seed.

2. Softwood cuttings in greenhouse.

3. Layers.

Parrotia persica, a good background for lower subjects

PERNETTYA—(Prickly-heath)

(Named for A. J. Pernetty, who accompanied Bougainville and wrote
"A Voyage to the Falkland Islands" 1716 to 1801)

Related to the Heathers, the Broadleaf Pernettya, *Pernettya mucronata*, is a native of Chile. The showy fruits are the chief reason for growing this shrub. The plants are only 18 in. tall. The flowers are white, tinged pink and appear in June and July. The leaves are evergreen, alternate, small, in two rows (2-ranked), spiny pointed, and finely toothed. The fruits are globose berries, white to dark purple but usually red. They should be grown in the sun.

SOIL. They prefer a peaty, porous, moist soil.

PROPAGATION. 1. Seeds.
2. Cuttings in Summer.
3. Layers.

PEROWSKIA—(Silversage) (Azuresage)

(Named for M. Perowsky, Russian botanist)

A mintlike shrub from Afghanistan, *Perowskia atriplicifolia* resembles a herbaceous perennial. It is hardy in Massachusetts and Ohio, although protection for Winter is advisable. The plants grow 3 to 5 ft. tall. The deep lavender-lipped flowers are borne in whorls to form a panicle, flowering in August and continuing until freezing weather. The leaves are longish oval, gray, unequally and coarsely toothed, and minty scented. The stems are hairy.

USES. The gray leaves and late flowers would serve to make this desirable to the lover of rare and unusual shrubs. It dies to the soil in Winter.

SOIL. Prefers light, well drained soil.

PROPAGATION. 1. Seed from European nurseries.
2. Summer cuttings.
3. Division.

PHILADELPHUS—Mockorange (Syringa)

(Philadelphus is from Ptolemy Philadelphus, who reigned in Egypt
about 280 B. C.)

Such a lovely flowering shrub as the Mockorange should not bear a name which infers that it is mocking anything. The name under which it is known throughout the Eastern States is Syringa, but this name is confusing, being the botanical name for the Lilac.

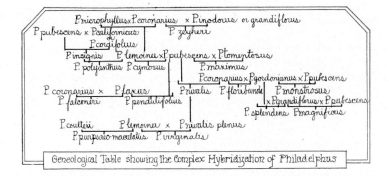

Geneological Table showing the Complex Hybridization of Philadelphus

There are about 40 species of Philadelphus, each of which has certain characteristics definite to botanists, but generally rather uninteresting to the gardener. The genealogical table showing the evolution of the good types of Philadelphus (above) will be of interest only to show how wonderfully Victor Lemoine, the great French hybridist, has combined the characteristics of many forms into varieties with a combination of good characteristics.

VARIETIES AND SPECIES

(S—single. D—double. SD—semi-double)

Albatre. SD. 2 in. across; June 20; 8 to 10 ft.

Avalanche. S. Small flower; 4 to 5 ft.; "an avalanche of bloom."

Banniere. SD. Early.

Belle Etoile. S. Purple blotch; fragrant.

Boule d'Argent. D. Free flowering.

Bouquet Blanc. SD. Arching plant; low growth; bouquet-like clusters.

Candelabre. S. Large flower; good bush.

Conquète. D. Broad clusters; arching bush.

coronarius. S. Good species; beautiful enough without improving.

Dame Blanc. SD. Creamy white; cut petals; fragrant.

Etoile Rose. S. Rosy pink.

erectus. S. Upright habit; fragrant.

falconeri. S. Narrow leaves and long, narrow petals.

Fantasie. S. Rose center.

floridus. S. Large flowers, 8 ft.; resembles *P. laxus*.

Girandole. SD. More profuse and like Virginal; tall.

Glacier. D. Dense clusters of creamy white flowers; small leaves; 4 ft.

gordonianus. S. Large, 1½ in. in diam.; cross-shape; leaves light green.

grandiflorus. S. Scentless; blooms week later than *P. coronarius;* 2 in. in diam.; flowers four-cornered, solitary.

hirsutus. S. Early; "one of smallest flowered sorts;" not good for garden.

incanus. S. 6 to 10 ft.; one of latest to bloom (July); leaves woolly; profuse flowering.

inodorus. S. 4 to 6 ft.; solitary, cup-shaped; not fragrant.

insignis. S. Latest (Mid-July); slight fragrance.

latifolius. S. Tall; 20 ft.; trifle fragrant.

laxus. S. Large flowers, 1½ in. in diam.; leaves pendulous.

lemoinei. S. Small flowers and leaves; a group of lovely hybrids.

lewisi. S. Medium sized flowers; 8 ft.; slight fragrance; leaves but slightly toothed. Later than most.

magdalenae. S. Mid-June; 6 to 8 ft.; broad shrub; drooping one-sided panicles, 6 to 10 in.

Manteau d'Hermine. S.D. Small flowers; small leaves.

Maximus. S. Tallest, 10-15 ft.; large leaves; upright.

microphyllus. S. Small flowers; 3 ft.; slender stems; pineapple fragrance.

monstrosus S. 10 ft. tall; upright; fragrant.

Mont Blanc. S. 4 ft.; upright; fragrant; strong growth.

nepalensis. S. 5 ft.; upright; slight fragrance.

Norma. S. or D.

Oeil d'Pourpre. S. Spotted blackish-purple; arching habit.

Pavillon Blanc.

pekinensis. S. Flowers with yellow center; broader than high.

pubescens. S. Flowers rather hidden by foliage; 15 ft. tall; leaves gray, hairy beneath.

purpureomaculatus. S. Low, open, purple spotted; drooping stalks.

Rosace. SD. Flowers 2 to 3 in. in diam.; upright; fragrant.

sericanthus var. *rehderiana.* S. Tall; blooms July; fragrance of garden Heliotrope.

Sirène. S. Center rosy; large flower.

splendens. S. Scentless; large. "The showiest in Philadelphus group at Arnold Arboretum." Arching habit.

subcanus. S. Early; plaited foliage; odor of Hyacinth.

Voie Lactée. S. Large flowers; attractive stamens; leggy; 8 to 10 ft.

Virginal. D. Large flowers, 2½ in. in diam.; sweet; tall; leggy. Perhaps best of all.

Left, Typical of the Lemoine Mockorange this picture was taken in Highland Park, Rochester, N. Y., where one of the finest collections of shrubs may be found; *right*, few shrubs are so fragrantly lovely as the Virginal Mockorange.

With the large array of varieties mentioned above, do not be confused. Without doubt Virginal is the finest large flowered, semi-double. Girandole, lesser known, may be a trifle more profuse. For beauty of arching shrubs loaded with bloom such varieties as Avalanche, Bouquet Blanc, Glacier, Candelabre, and Manteau d'Hermine should be chosen. These are generally lower growing as well and are the Lemoinei type, which means that the leaves are small, the twigs slender and the fragrant flowers, though not large, are produced in great profusion. Those with a purple or rose center belong to the group *purpureomaculatus* and include Etoile Rose, Fantasie, Oeil d'Pourpre and Sirène.

Philadelphus microphyllus, Littleleaf Mockorange, is useful for the rock garden. The Golden Mockorange, a variety of *P. coronarius*, has bright yellow leaves early in the season which in sunshine become green. It will, therefore, appreciate a little shade. It may be used as a hedge clipped to formal outlines. It is a lower growing shrub than its type species.

SOIL. Philadelphus is supposed to be lime-loving but it seems to grow in any soil. Circumneutral pH 6.0–8.0.

PRUNING. Prune after flowering. Remember that if one does not desire a big shrub, he should purchase the lower growing varieties and should not attempt to slaughter the taller sorts in the hopes of keeping them low in growth.

PROPAGATION. 1. Most of the named varieties, of course, being hybrid in nature, will not grow from seed. The species are easily raised. Sow in Spring as early as possible.

2.*Softwood cuttings root readily in Summer. The Golden Mockorange is more difficult so that some growers are only successful by taking cuttings from plants forced in the greenhouse.

3.*Hardwood cuttings may be stored through the Winter in a cold pit and planted out in Spring or else short cuttings may be inserted in sand bench of greenhouse in late Winter and almost buried. Oliver emphasizes that it is wise to gather the cutting material as soon as the leaves drop in Fall.

4. Suckers are freely produced so that the plants may be divided.

PHOTINIA—Christmasberry (Chinese-hawthorn)

(Named from *photeinos*—shining, refers to leaves being lustrous)

Although introduced many years ago to Parsons Nurseries, *Photinia villosa* has not been widely distributed. It is hardy on Long Island but needs some protection in Massachusetts. The plants are often 15

Photinia arbutifolia, the Christmasberry, is commonly grown
in the South for its bright red fruits and shining evergreen
leaves

ft. tall. The white flowers resemble those of a Hawthorn and are produced in May in rounded clusters (panicles). The leaves are oval, hairy
beneath, sharply toothed and lustrous. The branches and young parts
are hairy. The charm of this shrub lies in the fruits—red berries which
are $\frac{1}{3}$ in. long, ripening in Summer and persisting until Winter. Var.
laevis has narrower, smaller leaves, smooth beneath.   This species is
sometimes cataloged as *Crataegus*, *Pyrus*, *Heteromeles*, *Mespilus* or
Eriobotrya.

The Low Photinia, *P. serrulata*, is less hardy but is evergreen,
growing 15 to 20 ft. tall. It stands 10 degrees of frost. The fruits are also

attractive. It is cataloged as *Crataegus glabra*. The young growth is chocolate. The white flowers are rose tinted.

USE. As a flowering and fruiting subject, we have already spoken of its merits. Added to this the foliage of *P. villosa* changes in Autumn to a glorious red.

Birds like the fruits so that they do not persist as long as desired.

P. serrulata is a good seaside plant, according to Waterer (England).

SOIL. Needs perfect drainage. A light sandy, loamy soil with plenty of leafmold suits it best. It prefers sun.

OBJECTIONS. Tender in North. Very susceptible to San José scale.

PROPAGATION. 1. Seed should be stratified after washing from the pulp.

2. Softwood cuttings in Summer.

3. Layers.

4. *Grafted on Apple or Hawthorn, it develops plants faster.

PHYSOCARPUS (OPULASTER) (NEILLIA) (SPIRAEA)—NINEBARK

(Named from *physa*—bladder, *karpos*—fruit, refers to inflated fruit)

A large, spreading shrub to 10 ft., *Physocarpus opulifolius* bears clusters of about 25 blooms, pinkish or greenish white in color, in early June or late May. These are followed by conspicuous, five-lobed, reddish capsules which are changing color all Summer. The leaves are five-lobed, coarsely toothed. The bark peels in narrow, threadlike strips. Var. *luteus* (*aureus*) has bright yellow leaves at first, becoming bronzy green.

USES. Very fastidious persons who despise yellow foliage will not like the golden variety of Ninebark but it is, without doubt, one of the very attractive shrubs producing the red capsules to contrast with the foliage. The writer has found no substitute for use in large flower arrangements during June and early July. The branches, cut long or short, are gracefully arching.

SOIL. A native of the lowlands, it likes a cool moist soil. It is not drought resistant.

OBJECTIONS. The peeling bark appears rather shabby in Winter.

PROPAGATION. 1. Hardwood cuttings.

2. Softwood cuttings should be taken which are quite mature.

3. Seeds. A large percentage of the seeds of golden sorts come green.

PIERIS (ANDROMEDA) (PORTUNA)—
(Lily-of-the-valley-shrub)

(Name from Pieria, a district of Macedonia, the home of the Muses)

The Andromedas here noted are of unusual charm because of foliage and flowers. The most attractive one is *Pieris japonica*, the Japanese Andromeda, which has deep green, leathery foliage which becomes reddish and bronzy in Winter.

The flowers are white, bell-shaped, produced in drooping terminal clusters (panicles or reduced to racemes) during April and May, a week earlier than the native sort to be mentioned below. The buds are formed in the Fall.

The Mountain Andromeda, Mountain Fetterbush (*P. floribunda*) is a native sort growing from Virginia to Georgia. It differs in having upright clusters of bloom, branches covered with stiff, straight hair. (The branches of the foregoing sort are without hair.) It is more widely adapted to American gardens than the Japanese sort.

Perfect sprays of Pieris japonica, the Japanese Andromeda

The Japanese A. could be forced as a pot plant to bloom before Christmas.

USE. These shrubs are incomparable for an evergreen planting, especially as a foreground for taller Rhododendrons. The arrangement of foliage and branching is all that could be desired.

Never overcrowd the plants; let them develop their characteristic graceful form. Partial shade suits them.

SOIL. Being members of the Heath family, they want an acid soil. (See page 20.) Sandy peat, well drained, or at least a loamy, loose soil is preferred. They, therefore, dislike lime and clay. Mediacid pH 4.0-5.0.

OBJECTIONS.   The flower buds of the Japanese sort freeze in coldest regions.

PROPAGATION.   The propagation is considered difficult.

1. The Mountain A. is collected from the wild and divided.

2. Layers are slow.

3. Seed should be sown as advised for Azaleas, page 150. They germinate in two months.

4. Cuttings from forced plants would root more readily. Some take August cuttings inserted in greenhouse propagating frames.

PITTOSPORUM
(From the Greek *pitch* and *seed*, refers to the coating of resin on the seed)

Attractive evergreen shrubs for tub specimens and for hedges along the Gulf Coast and the Pacific States. *Pittosporum tobira* is the commonest species which is seen in its green and its variegated form. The fragrant flowers are white, produced in clusters at the tip of the branches during the Winter. The leaves are alternate, thick, leathery, clustered to appear at the tips of the branches. This species is adapted to seaside planting. It is a common subject in the gardened homes of Florida and California. The plants tolerate severe pruning so that they may be kept at any height.

The Narrowleaf Pittosporum, *P. phillyraeoides*, has pendent twigs. The leaves are narrow with a hooked point. Miss Kate Sessions says that it resembles an evergreen Weeping Willow. The seed pods are large and bright yellow on long, pendent stems. It is advised for use in a narrow place and for the margins of pools. It is a native of the deserts of Australia and consequently is very drought resistant.

PROPAGATION.   1. Soft wood cuttings is the common method.

PLUMBAGO—(Leadplant)
(Name derived from Latin for the metal lead)

In writing of the Plumbago, Caroline Elizabeth Strong facetiously remarks that "this is neither a fruit nor a rheumatic trouble." *Plumbago capensis*, the Cape Plumbago, is a native of South Africa. It is more or less climbing in habit and is commonly seen as a part of most plantings in Southern Florida. In the Northern States it is grown as a pot plant. This plant attains a height of 15 to 20 ft. The flowers are pale blue and

Plumbago capensis is one of the loveliest of blue, semi-climbing shrubs and is grown in tubs or in the open soil in regions where Winters are not severe

resemble those of a Phlox, being salverform and produced in terminal clusters.

Less commonly seen, the Rose Plumbago, *P. rosea* (*indica*), and its variety the Scarlet Plumbago, *P. coccinea*, has larger leaves clasping at the base.

SOIL. A fibrous loam, sand, and peatmoss is the advised soil.

PROPAGATION. 1. Cuttings of nearly ripe wood are used.

2. Old plants may be separated.

3. Seeds are sometimes used.

POLYGALA—Milkwort

(The name means "much milk." Some sorts are said to increase the flow of milk)

Many Eastern wild flower lovers are familiar with a tiny woods flower with Orchidlike flowers which is known as the Fringed Polygala, *P. pauciflora*. This wild flower is related to a lovely shrub grown in the semi-tropics. It is known as *Polygala dalmaisiana* and is of hybrid origin, being a cross between *P. myrtifolia* var. *grandiflora* and *P. oppositifolia* var. *cordata*. This shrub has slender twigs. The flowers are bright purple red, almost always in bloom. The lower petal is concave and fringed. The leaves are either opposite or alternate. The neat habit of growth commends this shrub for planting at the foundations of the house.

PROPAGATION. Cuttings may be taken in Spring.

POTENTILLA—Cinquefoil

(From Latin *potens*—powerful; refers to medicinal properties of some species)

For sandy soils, the evergreen Wineleaf Cinquefoil, Potentilla tridentata, is a charming ground cover

The Shrubby Cinquefoil, *Potentilla fruticosa*, is one of the most widely distributed plants in the North Temperate zone. A low, dense plant, it grows 3 ft. high and normally has golden-yellow flowers which open for four months, beginning in June. The flowers are not unlike yellow Strawberry blossoms. The leaves are three- to seven-parted, silky hairy above and silky gray hairy beneath. The bark is shreddy. There are a number of varieties, the best of which are:

Var. *friedrichseni* (*P. fruticosa* × *P.* var. *dahurica*). A larger flower, paler yellow and better habit.

Var. *veitchi*. White flowers; the leaves are not silvery above, but glaucous beneath.

Var. *micranda*. Dwarfer; lemon-yellow flowers.

Var. *vilmoriniana*. Leaves silvery on bronze-red branches; therefore, showier than the type.

The Wineleaf Cinquefoil, *Potentilla triden-*

tata, grows but 8 to 10 in. tall. It has dark, shining green leaves, three-parted, each leaflet with three teeth at the apex. The flowers are white, borne in tiny clusters (cymes). It has good foliage all Summer and is quite evergreen.

FAULTS AND USES. The continuous bloom of *Potentilla fruticosa* serves to make it a shrub which is useful but not completely satisfactory. The seed vessels hang a long time and are shabby. The growth is a little irregular. It is good in adverse situations where a low shrub is desired. It spreads fast and has been a weed in certain places.

Potentilla tridentata is most desirable for the rockery and as a ground cover in dry soil. It is a common roadside and woodsplant in the sand of northern Michigan.

SOIL. *P. fruticosa* is often a native of boggy places but also grows in dry soil.

P. tridentata, mediacid pH4.0–5.0.

PROPAGATION. 1. Softwood cuttings are used for *P. fruticosa*, taken in Summer.

2. Seeds. Sow when ripe.

3. Layers.

4. Division.

PRUNUS, (includes AMYGDALUS)—Peach, Almond, Cherry, Plum

Many of the most exquisite flowering Peaches, Almonds and Cherries are shrubby by nature, whereas there are many other sorts which become large trees.

PEACHES

The Peaches, of course, are trees, but several sorts are generally grown as shrubs. For foliage effect, the Bloodleaf or Purpleleaf Peach (*Prunus* or *Amygdalus persica*), produces shiny, deep reddish-purple leaves upon long branchlets. Such branches are ornamental when cut for use in flower combinations. These plants should be pruned severely each Spring. This will encourage the leaf coloration.

There are also double red, pink and white-flowered varieties which are very attractive in the garden in May, the red variety being so intense in color as to be seen for great distances. It is best combined with white varieties of Cherry, Apple or the Pearlbush, as the color does not harmonize with soft pinks. The success in growing these Peaches is hampered by their susceptibility to Peach borers. They are propagated by budding upon Peach seedling stock. Sometimes they bear fruits which are reputed to breed rather true to color and doubleness.

ALMONDS

Well known, because often grown, is the Flowering Almond, varieties of *Prunus g'andulosa*. The flowers which are rosy pink, or white, generally fully double, are set close to the wandlike branches. The leaves are ovate or oblong-lanceolate, acute at the tip, 2 to 3 in. long. The plants sucker freely so that as seen they usually form large clumps. They are quite hardy in the cold climates and persist in old gardens under gross neglect. They serve as low shrubs for beds or for use in front of taller sorts. They are best propagated by divisions, the budded plants being susceptible to Peach borers. (See also *Prunus trikta*).

Closely resembling the above is the Russian Flowering Almond, *Prunus nana*, which differs botanically in having a tubular, not bell-shaped, calyx and sessile flowers, not pediceled. It is used freely at the South Dakota Agricultural College where Professor Hansen has planted it for its great hardiness. It can be propagated from root cuttings or division, or budded on the Plum.

PLUMS

Unlike the above sorts the Flowering Plum (*Prunus triloba*), with flowers like the Flowering Almond, double, roselike, and hugging the naked branchlets, has leaves which appear later and have a tendency to be three-lobed. This variety has not the great tendency to sucker but forms a miniature, treelike growth. It is not so long-lived nor so persistent as the above. This is a worthy shrub and useful for gardens, for forcing and for its cut branches. It is hardy at Minot, North Dakota. Its Chinese name refers to the fact that its leaves are Elm-like.

The Purpleleaf Plum (*Prunus cerasifera* var. *pissardi*) has leaves which are not quite as purple as some other so-called purpleleaf plants, but the color is lasting. The flowers are produced early, almost the first of the small flowering trees, except *Cornus mas*. The flowers are small but produced in great profusion In cold regions this variety freezes back and at Mackinac Island, Michigan, is used as a shrub growing

3 ft. tall. In Ohio, it grows treelike. This Plum is a most useful contrast plant. It is budded or grafted upon common Plum stocks. Another purpleleaf Plum is Othello, a variety of the Burbank Plum which has larger leaves of a deeper purple and early fruit of a deep crimson color. Prune both of these sorts heavily in early Spring to induce long growth, which is more attractively colored. They are propagated by budding upon Plum stocks.

Henry Hicks exclaims so loudly about the Beach Plum, *Prunus maritima*, that it is necessary to include it. He writes:

"Those who have a family to feed are enthusiastic over the Beach Plum. There seems no limit to the amount of fruit they can pick or make into jam and jelly. It forms a big, round bush, 8 ft. high, covered with healthy, dark green foliage which withstands the drought on sand dunes, pine barrens, or the caustic salt spray of the beach. Use it for any of these places. Try it for a hedge for underplanting of Pines and Oaks or edging to or replacing part of your present shrubbery. It should be possible to improve the value and size and to establish Plum culture where the European Plums have not become established. You can help in this work both by selecting and grafting. It may be grown from seed although most plants sold by nurserymen are collected from the wild. The flowers appear in mid-May; the fruit ripens at the end of August."

CHERRIES

Although most Cherries are trees, there are several smaller growing subjects that are desirable to plant among shrubbery, the most outstanding being the Nanking Cherry, *Prunus tomentosa*. It blooms at the end of April, each joint producing a flower, pink in the bud, but white when open, with a red calyx. The fruit is highly decorative for garden or for indoor display. It is red, ½ in. across, and edible. The leaves are crowded, obovate to elliptical, unequally toothed, rough, densely hairy beneath. It is hardy even in Wisconsin and Canada. It is resistant to disease and insects. It grows about 5 ft. tall and spreads wider than high. It has been cultivated for over 40 years in America, but has taken a long time to become known as a perfectly hardy desirable shrub. It may be propagated from seed or by softwooded cuttings. See page 56.

The Western Sand Cherry, *P. besseyi*, is a low, rather prostrate sort growing 3 ft. tall, worthy of a place in the shrub border for front ine planting. The dark glossy leaves, 1 to 3 in. long, are attractive. The white flowers and black fruits are produced in great abundance. The fruits are astringent, but edible.

Commenting upon the Yoshino Cherry, *Prunus yedoensis*, the Bulletin of the Arnold Arboretum says:

"This is the Cherry so generally planted in the parks, cemeteries and streets of Tokyo, and its flowering heralds an annual national holiday decreed by the Emperor. It was believed that over 250,000 trees were growing in the precincts of Tokyo before the destruction of a large part of the city a few years ago by fire and earthquake. The oldest authentically known trees were in the Imperial Botanic Garden at Koishikawa and were planted less than fifty years ago. This Cherry is a quick growing and apparently short-lived tree with wide spreading and slightly drooping branches forming a wide, flattened head. The bark is pale gray and smooth, becoming darker and somewhat rough on old trunks. The slightly fragrant flowers are produced in clusters of two or several, usually before the leaves, but occasionally at the same time, and vary in color from white to pale pink. It is this tree which was presented by the Government of Japan to our Government and is the principal Japanese tree which has been planted in the streets of Washington. This Cherry produces seeds abundantly now in the Arboretum and in Washington, and it ought to be much more generally planted a little farther south than Massachusetts where the flower buds are too often injured by severe Winters. It grows perfectly well in New York, and thousands of trees might well find a place in Central Park, where so many of the original plants have disappeared, and in all the regions south of Washington."

CALIFORNIA EVERGREEN CHERRIES. There are several species of Cherries which are found wild in California that are widely used for hedges and specimen broadleaf evergreens.

Prunus ilicifolia, Hollyleaf Cherry (Islay) (Evergreen Cherry) (Mountain-holly). A native of San Francisco region and Lower California, this sort grows as a tree 30 ft. tall. The flowers are white, produced in slender racemes. The leaves are hollylike, broad, the margins spiny toothed. The fruit is purple, nearly black.

Prunus lyoni (*P. ilicifolia* var. *integrifolia*). Catalina Cherry. The plants are found wild on the islands off the coast of California. The sort is similar to the above but the leaves are longer and more pointed, and the plants are more compact so that it is considered superior. It is extremely drought resistant.

FORCING PRUNUS TRILOBA. The Flowering Plum is an exquisite plant for forcing in a greenhouse. Young plants should be procured in the Fall, potted in a good soil, sandy loam, and stored in a sheltered spot until New Year's Day or later. They should be taken into an intermediate house for a week or so before being introduced to the forcing house. A temperature of 65 degrees is suitable (in a higher temperature the plant will not give its best), and constant syringing is necessary until the flower buds begin to open. It is well then to cool the plants down at this stage, and if this is done carefully, the flowers will remain for three weeks or a month in perfection. After flowering it is well to encourage the development of growth by placing the plants in a warm Peach house, when, after the severest frosts are over, they may be placed out of doors in a sheltered situation.

PTELEA—Hoptree (Wafer-ash)

This aromatic shrub or small tree has fruits not unlike large Elm seeds. *Ptelea trifoliata* grows from New York to Florida. The greenish flowers are not attractive but are followed by the fruits which hang in dense clusters. The leaves are three-foliate, and are seen to be dotted when held to the light. The golden sort is attractive, not burning as does Golden Elder.

Another species, which is apparently not cataloged is *P. baldwini* (*P. angustifolia*). The leaves are smaller, very shining, three-parted, gray beneath. It has an irregular, but interesting habit, growing 8 ft. tall in Highland Park. The bark on the young twigs is warty and silvery. The whole plant has a pleasant odor and is very airy and graceful.

Ptelea or Hoptree
At the left is the Common Hoptree, *Ptelea trifoliata*; at the right, the Baldwin Hoptree *Ptelea baldwini*, a gray twig and leaf sort

Uses. An interesting, treelike shrub with attractive foliage, the Hoptree is further interesting because of the hoplike odor of its branches, leaves and fruits. C. C. Deam writes, "The odor is akin to that of a polecat." How opinions differ about a hoplike odor! The golden sort is considered one of the best of yellow-leaved plants.

Soil. Prefers a moderately moist, well-drained soil, in a little shade.

Propagation. 1. Seeds grow readily when sown as soon as ripe or stratified until Spring.

2. Layers may be made.

3. Golden form grafted on the type.

PUNICA—Pomegranate
(The ancient name of the plant is *Malum punicum*, the Apple of Carthage, so that the Romans no doubt grew to know this fruit during their contests with the Carthaginians)

The Pomegranate is now known as *Punica granatum* and is a native of Southeastern Europe to the Himalayas. The small trees or shrubs are grown for their flowers and their fruits. Pomegranates are hardy as far north as Washington. The flowers are scarlet and the calyx is purple. They bloom from May to June and the petals have a crumpled appearance. The leaves are opposite and rather shining. The twigs are angled. The fruit has a leathery rind which encloses a pulpy mass of seeds. Var. *nana* is commonly grown as a pot plant for it is a dwarf sort.

Propagation. 1. Cuttings should be rooted under glass.

2. Leonard Vaughan writes of the culture of the dwarf Pomegranates from seed as follows:

"These plants can be easily grown from seed; in fact, they can be grown better from seed than from cuttings. The seeds should be planted about December in flats in the greenhouse and when they are of suitable size to prick off, they should be planted in 2 in. pots and a little later in 4 in. pots where they will get established. As soon as the weather warms up sufficiently, they could be shifted to coldframes in the full rays of the sun and brought back into a forcing temperature about the last week in August and 'forced' in a temperature of 60° to 65° for the Christmas trade. They come into flower early, but the first flowers, which are a brilliant orange scarlet, should be kept 'nipped' until well on in September when they will begin to take on a general crop which will make them salable in December and for several months following. Another point of advantage may be mentioned here: the plants which may be left on your hands can be carried over and brought into flower the next year and a much larger blossom will be produced."

The Dwarf Pomegranate, Punica granatum nana, has recently
become popular for a pot plant

PYRACANTHA—Firethorn (Everlastingthorn)
(From *pyr*—fire, *acanthos*—thorn)

Resembling Cotoneasters and Hawthorns is *Pyracantha coccinea*
(*Crataegus pyracantha*). It grows 6 ft. tall. The leaves are evergreen,
dark, glossy, 2 in. long, and have fine, rounded teeth. The young
branchlets and leaves are hairy. The branches are thorny. The
flowers are white, in many-flowered clusters (corymbs), but it is for
the orange-scarlet fruit that we admire the Firethorn. These last
until December and in favorable places until Spring.

Laland Firethorn, var. *lalandi*, is of more vigorous growth with slenderer and longer branchlets; the leaves are less deeply toothed. As this is a hardier form, it is more often cultivated.

The Nepal Firethorn, *P. crenulata*, has the branchlets and petioles rusty hairy. The teeth of the leaves are bristle-tipped. The stems of the flowers are smooth, not hairy, as in the above species.

The Gibbs F., *P. gibbsi*, is more vigorous and freer fruiting than others, and perhaps hardier, in the opinion of Alfred Rehder, although not cataloged often. Differs from *P. crenulata* in having obovate leaves with round-pointed teeth, the leaves of that sort being wider above the middle and with bristle-pointed teeth. It differs from *P. coccinea* in having smooth-stemmed flower clusters.

Uses. Firethorns are very desirable shrubs on account of their evergreen foliage, their attractive fruits which hang for a long time, and for their flowers. They would make attractive hedges though they might not be hardy enough for some climates.

Soil. Well drained soils, especially limestone. Circumneutral 6.0–8.0.

Pruning. Some shearing is necessary to keep the plants shapely.

Propagation. 1. Seed. No doubt it needs treatment similar to Cotoneaster (See page 50).

2. Cuttings from forced plants or ripened wood in greenhouse in late Summer.

3. Grafting. Graft on Cotoneaster or Crataegus.

4. Layers.

RAPHIOLEPIS—Yeddo-hawthorn and India-hawthorn
(Name derived from *rhaphe*—a needle and *lepis*—a scale, referring to the bracts of the flowers)

These shrubs have evergreen leaves and stand 10 degrees of frost without injury. They are popular in the South and on the Pacific Coast. One sees them most commonly planted as filler shrubs for foundation planting.

Raphiolepis umbellata (*japonica*) (*ovata*). Yeddo-hawthorn. A native of Southern China, this shrub attains a height of 8 to 12 ft. The flowers are white with a reddish brown calyx; they are very fragrant and are borne in loose racemes. The leaves are leathery with a few teeth, long oval, rather rusty hairy beneath when young. The fruits are black with a slight bloom.

Raphiolepis indica. India-hawthorn. The plants are of lower growth. The leaves are regularly toothed. The flowers are pinkish.

SOIL. A loam mixed with peatmoss and sand is advised.

PROPAGATION. 1. Cuttings of ripe wood should be taken in late Summer.
2. Seeds.
3. Layers.
4. May be grafted upon Hawthorn.

RHAMNUS—Buckthorn

(From *rhamnos*—a thorn bush)

Although there are about 100 species of Buckthorn, only a few are known. *Rhamnus cathartica* is the commonest sort, known variously as Hartsthorn, Waythorn and Rheinberry. It is a stiff, twiggy, spiny shrub, of irregular habit, growing 12 ft. high. The greenish, four-petaled flowers are not showy. The leaves are dark green, elliptical to ovate, with only three to five pairs of veins, deeply impressed.

Another species, *R. dahurica*, the Dahurian B., is similar but more spreading and with larger, yellower green leaves.

The Alder Buckthorn, *R. frangula*, is much more attractive. It also has several names—Berryalder, Glossy Buckthorn, Persianberry, and is the Black-dogwood of England. It is an erect shrub, 12 ft. tall, although it grows even taller. As it ages it spreads out. The flowers are pale yellow, produced all Summer, followed by red fruit which changes to black. This is one of the chief things of beauty about the shrub, for there are berries in all stages of development. The leaves are not toothed and are glossy, pale green.

Var. *asplenifolia* is often seen but seldom does one associate it with being a variety of the Alder Buckthorn. The leaves are very narrow, linear, with a wavy margin. It is curious and not very handsome.

One of the best sorts seen at the Arnold Arboretum is the Veiny B. (Carolina B.), *R. fallax*, which has large, glossy, deep green leaves, 3½ in. long, oval-elliptical, abruptly pointed, rounded or heart-shaped, alternate, with 12 to 20 pairs of prominent veins. It had a splendid, upright habit and grew to a height of 10 ft. It resembles *R. libanotica* and *R. imeretina*, both of which are somewhat hairy beneath, whereas this is perfectly smooth.

USES. The Common Buckthorn is commonly used for hedges; it stands shearing and is thorny, two features of advantage. For taller hedges the Alder B. is useful, although it is also a very handsome specimen or background shrub on account of its glossy leaves and fruits of three colors—green, red and, when ripe, black. The foliage of the Veiny B. is large and almost blue-green. Its regular growth would make it a specimen shrub or for combinations it would offer good contrasts. The berries of *R. cathartica* are, as the name implies, powerfully laxative. The wood of *R. frangula* is used in England for the manufacture of gunpowder.

SOIL. They seem at home in sand or clay. Circumneutral pH 6.0–8.0.

PRUNING. The Common B. is irregular unless pruned often. The leaves of the Alder B. are glossier and borne on strong shoots which are encouraged by vigorous pruning.

TRANSPLANTING. It is often said that the Common B. would be more widely used for hedges if it were easier to transplant. It is not difficult but the plants cannot be thrown about as is California Privet or Japanese Barberry.

PROPAGATION. 1.*Seeds should be stratified or sown in the Fall.
2. Hardwood cuttings.
3. Rarer sorts may be grafted on *R. cathartica*.

RHODODENDRONS—Rosebay
(From the Greek for *Rose tree*)

Botanically, the genus *Rhododendron* includes also the Azaleas. The group is one of the most aristocratic of shrubs. Rhododendrons are the most gorgeous of all flowering woody plants grown in temperate climates. (See illustration, page 351.) Invariably they require acid soils, and a high peat content is a general horticultural prescription for their soils. Those commonly known as true Rhododendrons are broadleaved evergreens. In America, they occur wild in the mountains and forests of the Appalachian chain and on the mountain slopes of the West Coast. The great natural concentration of species occurs in Western China and in the Himalayas, where hundreds of new kinds have been discovered within recent times. It is difficult to grow them in arid regions or where temperatures are excessively cold or hot. They are shallow-rooted, and wherever they occur in limestone regions, it is always upon an organic, acid-testing layer above the calcareous rock and not in an alkaline soil.*

*Clement Gray Bowers was good enough to supply the discussion of Rhododendrons, for he is an expert. See also Azalea, page 147.

SPECIES. Nearly one thousand species have been named, but relatively few of these are of horticultural importance. In the Pacific Northwest, scores of species from the Orient, as well as a fine array of British-bred hybrids, can be successfully grown and new sorts among them are constantly appearing. Along the East Coast, on the other hand, few oriental species can be considered reliable, and American species and their hybrids predominate. There is great variation among individuals within a species. With regard to hardiness, certain superior clones are occasionally found among groups that are otherwise unhardy, and these may eventually extend the use of various exotic species considerably. Besides this significance of the individual clone or variety, great importance is attached to local conditions of site, soil, exposure, air-drainage and temperature in determining the success of these plants. The different kinds are quite specific in their preferences and one should plant only those which are compatible with the local climate.

Ordinary Rhododendrons are shrubs, frequently as broad as they are tall, and range from large sizes (20 feet) down to dwarfs suitable or rock-gardens.

Rhododendron catawbiense, the Catawba Rhododendron, and its hybrids, is recognized as the best all-around species for hardy culture in the Eastern United States, although in some other areas it has been replaced by newer sorts. The wild color is lilac-purple, with flowers about 2 inches or more across, borne in round trusses of 20 or so, early in June. The leaves are thick and leathery. In hybrids, the flowers range from white, through pink and rose, to crimson, purple and dark lilac. Yellowish, greenish or brownish markings frequently occur on the upper lobe of the flower. The plant is hardy to temperatures of −20 degs. in the North, at which temperature the flower buds begin to freeze.

Rhododendron maximum covers vast areas in the Eastern mountains. It blooms about three weeks later than *R. catawbiense* and is less showy, but no hardier. Its flowers are somewhat smaller and are commonly Apple-blossom-pink or pure white; they are borne in trusses up to 6 inches across. The plant is upright in growth. Few hybrids are available, but these are generally superior to the wild type.

Rhododendron carolinianum is dwarfer and blooms earlier than either of the above. Its flowers, borne in trusses 4 to 5 inches across, are pale rose-pink and its leaves are rusty-dotted underneath. It blooms about May 20th at New York City. A related species, *R. minus*, blooms six weeks later and generally bears flowers which are pale lilac. Both species are hardy at sub-zero temperatures.

Of lesser importance is *R. smirnowi* which, in one form, equals the Catawba Rhododendron in beauty. A very small-leaved species, with insignificant flowers, *R. micranthum*, is hardy but is of little merit. The Alpine Rose, *R. ferrugineum*, and its hybrids are hardy, dwarf and compact, making a good dense evergreen plant for foliage effects, but slow of growth and not showy. Many other alpine and arctic species exist, but, for gardens in the Northeast, they are difficult to grow in cultivation and are not recommended except for experimentation in that climate. Several of them are on the market.

The kinds discussed above are mainly hardy in New England to –20 degs. A new race of large-flowered hybrids, based upon *Rhododendron fortunei* and its allies, known generally as the Dexter group, has proved promising for regions in the East where temperatures do not descend below –5 degs. or –10 degs. Also certain forms of *R. racemosum* and other dwarfish species which as yet are not widely grown. Persons interested in experimenting with these rarer sorts should consult publications of the American Rhododendron Society for information relative to the adaptability of new introductions, of which hundreds are presently being offered. No "rules of thumb" can be given for guidance, but the results of temperature tests as published from time to time can assist in making judgments. At low altitudes in the South, warm Summer temperatures seem to discourage the evergreen Rhododendrons, and in other places they have been inadequately tested as yet. Around Long Island and Philadelphia many new sorts are being tried, and encouraging reports are made concerning some British hybrids and oriental species. For the most part, such reports come only from places where temperatures rarely go below zero. On the West Coast, the San Francisco region supports some rare species from Burma and the Himalayas, while farther North, in Oregon and Washington, the best Rhododendron conditions on this continent are to be found and most of the English sorts grow there beautifully. Generally, nurserymen in these geographical regions are informed concerning the outstanding Rhododendrons for their specific areas, so that no attempt will be made to list them here. The lists are constantly changing as new materials become available. Although ordinarily unsuited to regions of hot, dry Summers, some of the hardier Rhododendrons are being grown successfully by a few vigilant gardeners in such places as Missouri and Texas, using rather special methods to overcome the climatic obstacles. For what it may be worth, we reproduce an old list of Catawba clones considered to be the best of the "ironclad" sorts for New England:

Red or Crimson

Atrosanguineum
Charles Dickens
Caractacus

Rose

Roseum Elegans
Lady Armstrong

White

Catawbiense Album
Album Grandiflorum
Album Elegans (slightly tinged)

Deep Rose

Mrs. Charles Sargent
Henrietta Sargent

Purple

Purpureum Elegans
Purpureum Grandiflorum

Lilac

Everestianum

For milder regions, there are many others that may be better, yet the above have withstood the test of time and are generally unexcelled for difficult places.

USE. Rhododendrons prefer to grow upon uplands or slopes, and usually dislike valley bottoms, especially where frost pockets prevail. They object to heavy clay soils without adequate drainage and aeration. They are admirably adapted to semi-shade in gardens, cities and woodland. They will survive total shade, but do poorly and bloom sparsely. "High shade" from tall trees, preferably Oaks, is considered best, but such trees as Maples and Elms, which produce root competition, should be avoided. Rhododendrons may be placed in open sun in the North, provided the site is not on a windswept, dry or southern slope and provided that they are standing in a deep moist (but not wet) peaty soil, well mulched with Oak leaves, peatmoss, Pine needles or sawdust.

Besides naturalistic use in the border or edge of a woodland, or as a foundation planting, Rhododendrons may also be used effectively in formal beds or plantings in architectural courtyards or around public buildings. Because their leaves curl and droop at low temperatures, the large-leaved sorts should be kept away from light-colored walls and white backgrounds. Dark conifers serve as good backgrounds-also dark walls and heavy masonry, although, in the latter, care must be taken to see that lime from the mortar does not drain with rain; water into the Rhododendron bed. Mixed plantings with deciduous Azaleas are often successful, especially where yellow or orange Azaleas are used to enliven the somber purplish tones of *R. catawbiense*. They may also be used with many other Heaths.

CULTURE. In the Northeast, transplant in the early Spring and move only with a carefully undisturbed rootball, usually wrapped in burlap. Make a hole considerably broader than the rootball and be sure there is good underdrainage. Set plants at the same depth as they were previously growing. A light soil is preferred, and it should contain organic matter, such as peatmoss, in sufficient quantity to give it a fibrous and spongy structure—one that will retain moisture and still admit oxygen, like a moist sponge. Nothing is better than sphagnum moss, either alone or with half soil. A peat bed is excellent for mass plantings. The soil reaction should be acid, testing between pH 4.5 and pH 5.5. Some "hard" water contains alkaline salts which will quickly neutralize an acid soil; this is a common condition with well-water and is often a cause of non-success in certain regions. Avoid the use of such water by applying a leafy mulch in Autumn, up to 6 inches deep, and allowing it to remain throughout the year. Oak leaves or Pine needles are excellent. This mulch will protect the roots and keep them uniformly moist. There are a number of other reasons, chemical, physical and biological, why a mulch is desirable. Thin leaves, such as Maple and Elm, quickly turn alkaline and should be avoided. Sawdust is often used as a mulch and as a substitute for peatmoss. It is successful, but must always be accompanied by an application of nitrogen in the form of ammonium sulphate or as an organic fertilizer (but never as nitrate of soda, which is toxic). If a commercial fertilizer is used, it should be such as is prepared especially for acid-soil plants; ordinary garden fertilizers are risky. As an acidifier, flowers of sulphur, not exceeding one pound to each 100 square feet of area per application, is recommended. Aluminum sulphate, widely used, may have a toxic reaction in time. Planting in acid peat will generally obviate the necessity of acidifying the soil, but the site should be such that surface drainage from nearby alkaline areas will not run into the planting. Rhododendrons are responsive to fertilizers in the soil or applied as foliar feeding, but these should not be given after June. Periodic soil testing is desirable to insure that acidity is maintained. The soil should never be cultivated because Rhododendron roots are very delicate and are near the surface. Weeds may be pulled by hand. Rhododendrons will bloom more consistently from year to year if the flower-trusses are removed immediately after blooming each season.

PROPAGATION. 1. Seed may be sown soon after it ripens, but a peaty soil and a temperature of 70 degrees is required for satisfactory germination. Propagation by such means is generally not practicable for amateurs unless familiar with greenhouse techniques.

2. Grafting, done in early Winter, on stock of *R. ponticum* or *R. maximum*, is not usually feasible unless professionally equipped. (See page 73.)

3. Outdoor layerage is feasible when stock plants are growing in peat where branches may be pegged down for 18 months after being notched and buried at the point of notching. (See page 81.) Air layerage, using a bandage of moist sphagnum inside a plastic wrapper, is possible on the upper stems of a growing plant. In May a slit is made on a stem of the previous year's growth and a small quantity of indole-butyric acid is inserted into the wound. Moist sphagnum is squeezed dry and placed about the stem. Then the whole is wrapped around with an 8 in. x 10 in. sheet of plastic (polythene) and tied at top and bottom with rubber bands. Roots form the whole is removed and potted in August without removing the sphagnum.

4. Cuttings are not easily made by amateurs. Careful timing, nursing and feeding is necessary, and greenhouse techniques are employed. Considerable difference exists between varieties in their ability to root from cuttings.

PESTS. Sucking insects, such as the lace bug, aphis or mealy bugs, may be controlled by standard contact insecticides, such as nicotine sulphate or some of the newer materials such as those containing DDT or hexaethyl tetraphosphate, the latter to be used only with extreme caution. Lace bug, the more serious, is decidedly worse on plants growing in the sun than those in the shade. Chewing insects, such as inch-worms or beetles, are controlled by a stomach poison, such as arsenate of lead or some of the newer insecticides. Bordeaux mixture or dusting sulphur are standard remedies for fungous diseases on the leaves, such as leaf spots, blight (on leaves or stems) and molds. Diseases of young seedlings will not be dealt with here. Azalea galls are not serious. Sun-scald and Winter injury appear as leaf discolorations, usually due to the withdrawal of water from certain tissues, and are not caused by insects or diseases. Yellowing of the leaves may be caused by any kind of unthrift and is often a chlorosis due to insufficiently acid soil. It may be temporarily remedied by spraying the foliage with a solution of 1 ounce of ferrous sulphate to 1 gallon of water

RHODOTYPOS—Jetbead (White-kerria)

(From *rhodon*—rose, *typos*—form or shape, resembles, perhaps, a single white Rose)

The shrub known commonly as the White-kerria, *Rhodotypos kerrioides* (*scandens*), resembles the Kerria, but its leaves are opposite, the branchlets are black, not green, and it produces black fruit. It is a native of Japan and China, grows 4 ft. tall. The flowers are white, four-petaled, solitary, blooming intermittently from May throughout the season. The leaves are doubly-toothed, silky underneath, and appear plaited. The fruits are like four black nutlets clustered together surrounded by the persistent calyx.

USE. For its flower and black fruits which hang all Winter, this shrub is attractive, but it is also useful as it thrives in adverse places.

SOIL. Thrives in heaviest clay soil, even crowded, shaded and in smoky cities. Circumneutral pH 6.0–8.0.

TRANSPLANTING. A trifle difficult to transplant, the plants should be pruned back at planting time.

PRUNING. Prune back the plants severely from time to time to make them more compact.

PROPAGATION. 1. Seeds often self-sow under the plants. Sow seed when ripe or stratify until Spring. If dry, seed must be soaked several days before sowing.

2. Softwood cuttings in Summer root slowly, often eight to ten weeks.

3. Hardwood cuttings in Winter.

Left, Jetbead, Rhodotypos kerrioides, adapted to adverse conditions, and whose white flowers are produced all Summer, followed by black, nutlike fruits; *right,* Rubus odoratus which delights in rocky, shady places

RHUS—Sumac, includes Cotinus (Smoketree)

The Rhus is a varied group of good plants and some poisonous ones, ranging from trees to vines and ground covers, from wonderfully beautiful sorts to some of little value ornamentally.

The late Mr. Jack of the Arnold Arboretum believed that *Rhus canadensis* (*aromatica*), the Fragrant Sumac, was one of the best plants to connect the larger shrubs with the lawn area; consequently, it is extensively used there for that purpose and borders many of the drives. It is native from Vermont and Ontario to Minnesota, Florida and Louisiana. Its growth is half-trailing, growing 2 to 6 ft. high, but always wider than high. The flowers are inconspicuous, except when seen in masses, catkinlike and yellow. The leaves are three-parted, pubescent when young, and have an odor when crushed. The leaves like those of many other Sumacs, change to glorious Autumn tints. The fruits are hairy and red.

The Shining Sumac, *Rhus copallina*, although wild from Maine and Ontario to Florida, is a shrub of great beauty because of its lustrous leaves. It usually grows 3 to 5 ft. in the North, but becomes almost a tree in the South. The tiny flowers are yellowish-green and open later than the other wild Sumacs in mid-August. The compound leaves have 9 to 21 leaflets, winged between the leaflets; they are usually hairy beneath. The fruits are hairy, red. It suckers freely.

Another sort with wings between the leaflets is the Java Sumac, *R. javanica* (*osbecki*) (*semialata*). This sort comes from Japan, China and Southern Asia. It grows to a height of 25 ft. and stands a temperature of 25 degrees below zero at the Massachusetts Agricultural College. The flowers are white, borne in large, very showy clusters, produced in August and September. The leaves have 7 to 13 leaflets and, unlike the above species, are deeply toothed. They are brownish hairy beneath. The fruits are orange hairy. The branches are smooth and yellowish.

The two common Sumacs are *R. typhina* (*hirta*), the Staghorn S., and *R. glabra*, the Smooth Sumac. The chief distinction is that in the former species, the branches are covered with dense velvet hairs while in the latter they are smooth. Of both sorts there are cutleaf varieties of great beauty. The glorious Autumn color of these two species makes them unrivaled among shrubs. If they were rarer we would prize them more highly.

Totally different from the Sumacs are the Smoketrees. One species, variously called *Rhus cotinus* or *Cotinus cotinus* or *Cotinus coggygria*,

Rhus glabra, a wild Sumac that is useful because of its fruit display

is a European or Asian species; the other is a Southern United States sort, *Rhus cotinoides* or *Cotinus americanus*.

Rhus cotinus has been known as the Purple Fringetree, the Venetian Sumac, the Wigtree or the Common Smoketree. The plants grow 15 ft. tall and bear huge, plumy masses of green or purple flower stems, so numerous as to be highly ornamental. These are developed in August and last for a month or more. The leaves are oval, smooth, somewhat bloomy. A few fruits are scattered through the mass of sterile flower stems. It is said to have been cultivated for 2000 years.

Rhus cotinoides, the American Smoketree, is not generally recognized as being different, but the leaves are wedge-shaped at the base, generally broader above the middle and 2½ to 5 in. long, with a more pleasing tint of green, whereas the leaves of *R. cotinus* are rounded at the base, broadest at or below the middle, sometimes notched at the apex, 1¼ to 3¼ in. long. Both have beautifully colored leaves in the Autumn, but our American sort has a poor "smoke" display.

Uses. Sumacs, even the common roadside Staghorn Sumac, are prized for large shrub beds because of the wonderful color displays in the Autumn. They generally change color early in the Fall and become gloriously colored yellow, orange, crimson and scarlet. *R. copallina* becomes purple and because of its glistening leaves is the most ornamental of the various sorts.

The fruit display of *R. typhina* and *R. glabra* is splendid and these varieties are useful for railway banks, steep slopes, large parks and semi-wild places.

The Java Sumac should be used as a specimen, displaying a large head of bloom in the Fall. The plant is often trained to treelike form in which case it attains a height of 25 ft.

The general usefulness of a low sort such as the Fragrant Sumac will be readily recognized; it provides an undergrowth shrub, even in the shade, a foreground shrub of refinement and yet thrives under the worst conditions.

For specimens or grouping in the background, the Smoketree is admirable. At Highland Park a group surrounds a seat. Each one is

Glorious masses of the Smoketree (Rhus cotinus) surround this bench in Highland Park, Rochester, N. Y.

a trifle different in the color of its plumy masses of seed heads, for although there are supposedly only two colors, green and purple, there is much variation in the tints.

> There's the mist o'er the mountain and the mist o'er the vale,
> There's the mist o'er the ocean where ships must sail,
> But the mist in the landscape most delightful to see,
> Is the billowy mist of the old Smoke-tree.

The bark of the Staghorn Sumac is used for the production of tannin, used in dressing leather. Several species, especially *R. vernicflua*, are used as a source of lacquer by the Japanese.

Soil. Sumacs grow in the driest, most barren soil. Circumneutral pH 6.0–8.0. At the top of steep banks and in very arid, sterile places color display is better. No color change in low soil. *R. cotinus* prefers light soil.

Pruning. To keep the shrubs low, the Staghorn, the Shining and the Smooth Sumac can be cut to the soil each year. This also makes for denser growth, although they fruit better and appear beautiful when grown naturally. The Winter effect of these sorts is not good because the branches are large and irregular. On the other hand, these sorts, together with the Java Sumac, may be trained as trees by removing all the shoots from the soil except one.

Objections. *R. copallina* suckers so freely that, even though beautiful, it is a nuisance except upon dry, barren banks.

Propagation. 1. Many of the sorts are collected from the wild.

2. Most sorts can be raised from seeds sown as soon as ripe. Some believe that potash is desirable for seedlings; it may be that potash softens seed coat.

3. The suckering sorts, *R. typhina* and *R. copallina*, may be propagated from root cuttings. Cut the pieces 3 in. long and plant shallow in the nursery rows in Spring.

4. Layers are successful.

5. Hardwood cuttings are sometimes used, especially for *R. cotinus*.

6. *Rhus canadensis* is merely divided.

RIBES—Currant

Several species of Currant are splendid for landscape use. Especially useful is *Ribes alpinum*, the Mountain (Alpine) Currant. This is a dense, shapely shrub growing 6 ft. high eventually, but generally considered a low growing shrub. The flowers are greenish and tiny, produced in April, and are not very showy. The leaves are deeply toothed, three-lobed. The shrubs leaf out very early and are usually much broader than high.

A very commonly planted sort is known as the Golden Currant, *Ribes odoratum*. Similar and confused with it is *Ribes aureum*, the Slender Golden C. Superficially they are almost the same, shrubs 6 ft. tall, irregular in growth with deeply three- to five-lobed leaves and yellow, clove-scented flowers, produced in clusters very early, generally April. The fruits are purplish-brown.

In *R. aureum* the flowers are more numerous, and less fragrant and the sepals are more than one-half as long as the calyx tube. The young branchlets are smooth but slightly hairy. The leaves are not heart-shaped at the base. In *R. odoratum* the flowers are larger and the sepals are less than one-half as long as the calyx tube. The young branchlets and petioles are densely hairy. The leaves are often heart-shaped at base. It has a more spreading habit and is the commoner of the two. These sorts color a beautiful purple and gold in sterile soil.

The Winter Currant (Redflower C.) *R. sanguineum*, is a red-flowered Currant growing 10 ft. tall, not as hardy as the others, a native of British Columbia to California. An interesting bit of history is related by C. P. Halligan:

"The Winter Currant is one of the interesting native plants of America whose discovery is closely associated with the story of the early explorations to Northwestern America. Dr. Archibald Menzie, a doctor in the Royal Navy of England, on a voyage around the world, first found it in 1787 near Nootka Sound. On a later expedition in 1795, sent out by the British Government to ascertain the existence of any navigable communication between the North Pacific and the North Atlantic oceans, he found it growing all along the coast of California and Oregon and sent specimens back to the British Museum. The beautiful qualities of this bush, however, still remained unknown to the people of England until it was again seen in 1822 by that venturesome plant explorer, David Douglas, whose services are commemorated in the naming of the Douglas Fir. Greatly impressed with its beauty, he sent seeds of it to the Horticultural Society at Cheswick, England. There they were planted in the open border in 1828, the first of the myriad Winter Currant bushes to deck the gardens of England. Though entering England as an alien, it has since found its way there into the gardens of every rank, while here in America, its native country, it is still scarcely known and seldom cultivated."

The flowers open in April and are produced in drooping clusters with colored bracts. The leaves are three- to five-lobed, whitish beneath. The young growth is hairy. The fruit is bloomy blue-black. *Var. gordonianum* (*R. sanguineum* x *R. odoratum*), the Gordon C., has yellow flowers tinged red outside, hardier, and with the spreading habit of the Golden C. As an ornamental shrub, it is preferable to the Winter Currant.

USES. The Mountain Currant is an excellent shrub for the shade and succeeds well, even in the dense shade of trees. The branches come down to the soil and serve to connect taller shrubs to the lawn.

The main value of the Golden Currants is their ability to grow where almost any other shrub refuses to grow. They are useful for fillers, for railway embankments and such places. They tolerate shade.

SOIL. Never particular about the soil, although they grow better in soil which is moderately fertile. Circumneutral pH 6.0–8.0.

PRUNING. The Golden Currant will need pruning after flowering if it is to be kept in a refined form as it usually spreads in all directions.

In pruning the Winter Currant, it must be known that flowers are produced on previous season's growth.

OBJECTIONS. The Golden C. suckers freely, has an irregular habit, is not refined, and is subject to scale. Nurseries have difficulty in supplying these because of interstate quarantines.

PROPAGATION. 1.*Hardwood cuttings of all sorts root easily.

2. Softwood under glass in Summer.

3. The Golden Currant may be propagated from suckers.

ROBINIA—Locust

(Named for J. Robin and Vespasian Robin, herbalists to the King of France)

In the group of Locusts, most of them are trees but there are several shrubs of great beauty.

Most popular is *Robinia hispida*, the Rose-acacia (Moss Locust). This shrub has a bad, suckering habit and makes an irregular growth but its flowers are so lovely that in spite of its faults, "we love it still." The flowers are rose-pink, pealike, produced in three- to five-flowered racemes in June. The leaves are soft green, 7 to 13 parted. The branches are covered with long red bristles. The wood is very brittle. The pods are densely purple, hairy, produced in Summer.

R. hartwigi (*R. glutinosa*) is a tall shrub or small tree, 12 ft. high. The branchlets, petioles and peduncles are clammy or sticky, hairy. The flowers are white to rosy purple, produced in 6- to 16-flowered upright racemes. The leaves are 13- to 23-parted, oval leaflets, often abruptly bristle pointed, grayish beneath.

Left, **Spray of Robinia (Locust) bloom;** *right,* **characteristic spray of Sorbaria**

R. kelseyi, from the mountains of the Carolinas, has prickly twigs. The leaves are nine- to eleven-parted; the leaflets are smooth, pointed. The flowers are rose, in five- to eight-flowered clusters. The seed pods are showy with purple, glandular hairs.

USES. All three of these Locusts are extremely beautiful small trees or large shrubs because of their showy flowers. They would be best used as specimens. The Rose-acacia is frequently grafted on the Black Locust, in which case it is greatly improved in habit and is prevented from suckering. The brittle branches are broken easily in exposed places.

SOIL. Locusts do not seem particular but being legumes improve the soil where planted. Light soil is preferred by Rose-acacia. Good in sterile places where they are allowed to roam at will and serve as undergrowth for trees.

PRUNING. The Kelsey and the Rose-acacia are improved by heading-in to improve their form.

OBJECTIONS. As stated above, the Rose-acacia spreads widely by suckers and often sends up so many shoots that the strength does not go to one branch but is carried to many. Prune out the suckers and stake one shoot up. Meehan says, "Two forms are found, one upright, another sprawls; the sprawly sort does not seed, but suckers."

PROPAGATION. 1. Seeds sown in Spring. Soak in hot water, or scald the seeds before sowing.

2.*Suckers.

3. Grafted upon the Black Locust, *Robinia pseudo-acacia*, these sorts become treelike. Best grafted at a height of 5 or 6 ft. in early Spring.

4. Softwood will root readily.

ROSA—ROSES

The Rose is strictly a garden flower, apart from the general group of shrubs, and requires a book to extol its merits. Nevertheless, we shall discuss here certain shrubby Roses, not for the small Rose garden, but adapted to the shrub border.

YELLOW SORTS

1. The commonest early yellow which has been planted about the homes of thousands of persons because it propagates readily by

Rosa xanthina has yellow flowers and the branches have prickles but no bristles

A valley of Rhododendrons at Highland Park, Rochester, N. Y.

suckers is the Persian Yellow, a form of *Rosa foetida* (*lutea*). The branches are very thorny. The flowers are sulphur-yellow and semi-double. Desirable because of its earliness, but less beautiful than species No. 3.

2. The Scotch Briers, *Rosa spinosissima*, are lower growing but with yellow or white flowers and small leaves. They are also very thorny. Seldom are they more than 3 ft. tall and useful for bordering other sorts. This sort may be confused with species 4, 5 and 6, but the flowering branchlets of this sort have both bristles and larger spines. The fruit is black, whereas it is red in the other species.

3. When *Rosa foetida* was crossed with *Rosa spinosissima*, Harison's Yellow was produced. This blooms later than Persian Yellow, has coarser but fewer thorns and bears yellow flowers deeper in color and with an orange or reddish glow. This is not so popular because it blooms when other garden Roses in June are open.

4. Three species resemble each other greatly so that they are frequently confused in the trade. The first, *Rosa hugonis* or Hugo Rose, has of late been widely advertised and sold. It blooms earlier than the Persian Yellow, coming in May. The single flowers are sulphur-yellow, produced solitary. The shoots are covered with thorns mixed with finer bristles, straight, and compressed.

5. The second of this group is *Rosa xanthina*, the Korean Rose, which has yellow, frequently double, flowers but the shoots have prickles all of one kind and no bristles. The leaves are slightly hairy beneath, especially when young, and more deeply toothed than species Nos. 4 or 6 and with rounder teeth.

6. The third species, *R. ecae*, the Eca Rose, is easily distinguishable from Species Nos. 4 and 5 in that it has spicy, aromatic foliage. The prickles are wide at the base. By many this is considered the choicest of the three species.

Roses Not Yellow, but Pink or White

7, 8, 9, 10. Four species of native Roses resemble each other so closely that they may be distinguished by botanists only. They are: *R. carolina*, *R. lucida* (*virginiana*), *R. nitida* and *R. palustris*. They are sentimentally associated with our roadsides and beautiful because of their simple, single flowers and red fruits.

Rehder distinguishes them as follows:

A. Stipules more or less rolled longitudinally; prickles hooked, leaflets round-toothed . . . . *R. palustris*

AA. Stipules flat; leaflets coarsely toothed.

   B. Leaflets 5-7 . . . . *R. carolina*

   BB. Leaflets 7-11.

      C. Leaflets 7-9, elliptical; prickles below the stipules usually curved . . . . *R. lucida (virginiana)*

      CC. Leaflets 7-11, elliptic oblong to narrow; prickles below. the stipules usually straight and slender. Plants 18 in tall . . . . *R. nitida*

11. *Rosa rugosa*, Rugosa R., is the well-known everblooming Chinese and Japanese Rose with rough leaves and bearing pink, carmine and white, single and double flowers at the same time that fruits are reddening. It is perfectly hardy. The flowers are large, the fruits are handsome, it has few pests and serves as one of the most desirable landscape Roses. The many hybrids are gradually being planted more and more. Blanc Double de Coubert is a good double white, hedge Rose. F. J. Grootendorst has rose-colored flowers with fringed petals so that it is often called the Carnation-flowered Rose. Lady Duncan and Max Graf are trailing sorts with lovely pink flowers.

12. The Japanese Rose, *R. multiflora*, is a sort with long, reclining branches, white flowers and small fruits in large, pyramidal clusters.

A well-known everblooming Rose with thick, rough leaves and rugged habit is
Rosa rugosa

It is valued mainly for its red fruits which are very ornamental in Winter. It may be confined to good form by trimming back the shoots which become too wayward. It is a parent of the Rambler Roses.

13. The Prairie Rose, *R. setigera*, is the common wild sort along the roadsides from Canada to Nebraska, Texas and Florida. It has three leaflets, or rarely five, often dull, appearing dusty. The flowers are pink fading white in clusters. It often climbs into trees or rests itself upon shrubs and fences. Highly admired by many because it is native, although many hybrids are more beautiful. The fruits are decorative along the roadside in Fall and Winter.

14. The Penzance Briars, *R. penzanceana*, result from a cross between *R. rubiginosa* (*eglanteria*) the Sweetbrier and *R. foetida*, the Austrian Brier. The Sweetbrier is familiar to most residents of the Eastern States because it has naturalized itself, having been brought here by the English settlers. It has sweet, apple-scented leaves, but the flowers are small and not as beautiful as the varieties now known as the Penzance Briers which were produced by Lord Penzance, a Scotch lawyer. The colors are lovely—pink, salmon, and such colors as are known as ecru, fawn, and pearl-pink. They are tremendous growers and are only useful for backgrounds of shrubbery where they may send their long arching branches as a canopy for a tall Philadelphus or Lilac. The foliage of these hybrids is also delicately scented. Because of sentimental associations and its daintier habit, the Sweetbrier will continue to be admired and cultivated.

15. The Redleaf Rose, *R. rubrifolia* (*glauca*) (*ferruginea*), is unusual, having leaves which are purplish tinged bluish-green. The flowers are worthless but the foliage is good, not being a brilliant red, but one rather pleasing in contrast with other foliage.

Uses. *Rosa hugonis* and *R. ecae* are truly lovely additions to the garden because of their admirable early yellow flowers, their clean, fresh foliage and their charming, arching habit.

The Sweetbrier and its hybrids is especially delightful after a rain, when its foliage is more fragrant than most flowers.

The luxuriant foliage, freedom of bloom, abundance of large fruits and lack of insects and diseases commend the Rugosa Rose.

Soils. Most of these sorts are not particular as to soil but they thrive best in a heavy clay. In hot, dry, limey soils the Rugosa is apt to become yellow and the growth to become irregular.

Pruning. The shrubby Roses should be pruned in early Spring and then only enough to remove some of the old deadwood and shape the plants.

PROPAGATION. The complete propagation of Roses is discussed in the author's *How to Increase Plants*.   1. *Seeds are commonly used for the species.   See page 50 for information about after-ripening of seeds.

2. Softwood cuttings are usually made indoors in Winter by specialists.

3. Suckers of the Persian Yellow and others.

RUBUS—Flowering Raspberry

(From the Celtic *Rub*, red)

A charming native shrub, the Flowering Raspberry, *Rubus odoratus*, grows 3 to 6 ft. tall and has odoriferous, rosy-purple flowers produced in many-flowered clusters (panicles) from June to September.   The fruits and flowers are upon the plants at the same time.   The flat, light red berries are slightly edible.   The leaves are large, three- to five-lobed, hairy on both sides.   The leaves have a woodsy odor.   The branches are yellowish-brown; the bark is shedding.

USES.   They are at home on the margins of ponds, and on woodsy hillsides.   The Flowering Raspberry likes shade but it also grows in the sun in wet places.

SOIL.   Rich, rocky, shady places are best.

PRUNING.   As the canes flower but once, the old ones may be cut out.

OBJECTIONS.   As a refined shrub it suckers too freely and appears shabby, due to shedding bark, but it is charming in wild spots.

PROPAGATION.   Suckers are plentiful.

SAMBUCUS—Elder

(Named from the Sambuca—a musical instrument made from the Elder)

Nancy S. delightfully remarks of the Elder:

"It is said to be the dwelling place of many mischief working elves, offspring of witches, and abandoned by them under its branches.   I have as yet detected no workings of the sly creatures in my Elder ! So many nice, helpful qualities are assigned to the Elder, too, and they are so amusing that I must set them down. It is said to cure toothache; protect the house from attack; fend off snakes, mosquitoes and warts; quiet nerves; interrupt fits, and guarantees that he who cultivates it shall die in his own house.   A bouquet of the flowers in the house indicates that the women dwelling therein shall never marry, and if one carries a walking stick made of elder wood, one invariably makes oneself an object of slander.   (I have decided against those two practices !)   If a cross made of the wood of the

Elder is planted on a grave, as it is in the Tyrol, it is generally believed that if the cross-bush opens into leaf and blossom the soul of the departed is in some heavenly fairyland; if it fails to do so one must draw his own conclusions. '

The juice of the Elder was used by the Romans to paint the statues of Jupiter red. The stems are used for troughs when Maple trees are tapped.

Several species of Elder are cultivated for fruit and flower; their rounded bushes, tall and vigorous are known to us all.

The American Elder, *Sambucus canadensis*, grows from Nova Scotia and Manitoba to Florida and Texas. The shrubs are generally 5 to 8 ft. tall and as broad as high. The fragrant flowers are white, produced in flat clusters (cymes), often a foot across, being in full glory in June and July. The leaves are pinnate with seven leaflets. The fruits are black and edible. There is a cutleaf variety of this.

The European Elder, *Sambucus nigra*, has black fruits, also but five-parted leaves. There is a golden form of this and another variety with finely cut foliage. Both sorts have white pith in the branches.

Less commonly cultivated is the European Red-berried Elder, *Sambucus racemosa*, which blooms in April and May, and hastens to

The American Elder, Sambucus canadensis is a wild sort that produces flat cymes of white flowers and edible, black berries

ripen its red berries at the time when the Common Elder is in bloom. *Sambucus pubens* is our native Red-berried Elder, which has hairy branchlets and yellowish-brown bark. Both sorts have five to seven leaflets and the branches have brown pith. It is magnificent on rocky, shaded slopes.

USES. The flowers and fruits of the Common and the European Elder are attractive. The birds like the fruits. It is only fair to say that Europeans use the flowers and fruits to make wine; the American merely admires the blossoms and fruits, according to law. The red-fruited, the golden leaved, and the cutleaved sorts each are used where large, showy shrubs are wanted. Some sun must be given the Golden sorts, otherwise they become green; on the other hand, too hot sun burns the edges of the leaves.

SOIL. The Elders grow in low, swampy soil, although the red-berried sorts grow on rocky hillsides and all sorts tolerate adverse soil.

PRUNING. Each branch is but short-lived, making pruning desirable. To keep the plants shapely, the older wood is cut out each Spring.

SOIL. Circumneutral pH 6.0–8.0.

OBJECTIONS. The suckering habit is provoking in a cultivated planting. The golden sorts burn badly in bright sun. Of course, all these Elders lack the refinement which is demanded of closely inspected plantings.

PROPAGATION. 1. Seed stratified for Winter and sown in Spring.

2.*Hardwood cuttings root very easily.

3. Softwood cuttings of golden sorts root readily when very soft, in early Spring.

4. Division of plants because of suckering habit.

SHEPHERDIA (LEPARGYRAEA)—Buffaloberry (Rabbitberry) (Beef-suet-tree)

(Named for J. Shepherd, curator of Liverpool Botanic Garden)

These shrubs, related to the Oleasters, have scaly leaves and branches also.

Shepherdia argentea is wild in Northern United States and Southern Canada. The shrubs are very hardy and grow 12 ft. tall. The flowers are inconspicuous, yellow, produced in April and May. The leaves are opposite, differing from *Elaeagnus* and *Hippophae* which are al-

The Buffaloberry (Shepherdia argentea) has silvery leaves, spiny branches and showy, scarlet fruit

ternate. The leaves are silvery on both sides. The branches are spiny, and silvery when young. The fruits are scarlet and showy.

A second species, *S. canadensis* has leaves which are not silvery, but green, above and brownish scurfy beneath, although silvery. The twigs are not thorny. The plants are of lower growth, seldom more than 3 to 7 ft. tall. The fruit is yellowish-red, but tasteless.

Uses. They are splendid shrubs for the banks of streams, although seldom seen in cultivation. The fruits are highly ornamental as they are produced in great profusion. Like their relatives, the Elaeagnus, the flowers are of one sex only; therefore, they must be planted in clumps, making certain to include both male and female plants.

The fruit of the Buffaloberry, *S. argentea*, is edible and is used for jellies.

Soil. Cool soil is desired. They like shade. Circumneutral pH 6.0–8.0.

Propagation. 1. Sow seeds as soon as ripe or stratify. Seedlings are sensitive to strong sun.

2. *Le Bon Jardinier* says, "Root cuttings are used."

3. In grafting, to get both sexes on the same plant, the Russian-olive (*Elaeagnus*) may be used as a stock.

SKIMMIA

(Japanese name *Skimmi*, meaning hurtful fruit)

This evergreen shrub is hardy in sheltered places at Philadelphia. *Skimmia japonica* grows 3 to 4 ft. tall, has entire, alternate, elliptical leaves clustered at the tip of the shoots, bright or yellowish-green above and yellowish-green beneath. The flowers are fragrant, white, produced in May in terminal clusters (panicles), rather tiny, but are followed by bright red berries in late Summer which stay upon the plants until the next year. The leaves have translucent spots, as in Hoptree. The plants are unisexual.

USES. An ornamental evergreen with red berries is always admired. This is one sort commonly used farther south than Philadelphia.

SOIL. Sandy or peaty soil. Dislikes limestone. Likes shade. Endures smoke and is therefore, advised for city planting.

PROPAGATION. 1. Cuttings in early Spring under glass from forced plants. Use rather mature cuttings.

2. Seeds sown in peat. One must wait until they flower to determine whether they are male or female plants. Best sown under glass with bottom heat.

SORBARIA (SCHIZONOTUS) (BASILIMA)
(SPIRAEA) False-spirea

(Named from resemblance of leaves to the Sorbus or Mountain-ash)

These plumy-flowered shrubs with compound leaves are often known as Spireas. Were they better known, they would be popular.

The commoner sort, the Ural False-spirea, *Sorbaria sorbifolia (foxi)*, attains a height of 3 ft. occasionally 6 ft., and because of its suckering habit grows in large clumps. The branches are not very woody and are crooked. It bursts into leaf early in the Spring, before most other shrubs. The leaves are pinnate, 13 to 23 parted; the leaflets are irregularly doubly and deeply toothed, furnished with 20 pairs of veins. They are hairy when young, as are also the branches. The flowers are white, in long (4 to 12 in.) upright clusters (panicles), borne in June and intermittently until August. Because of the similarity of species it is necessary to add that the flowers have 40 to 50 stamens; *S. assurgens* has only 20, but 25 or more pairs of veins in the leaves. It is similar in habit to *S. aitchisoni* which has simply-toothed, not doubly-toothed leaves.

The Kashmir F., *S. aitchisoni*, differs from the other sorts by the narrow, nearly simply toothed leaves and the red twigs when young. It grows 6 to 8 ft. tall and blooms in September. The flowers are produced in compact, terminal panicles 12 in. or more long. The leaves are not so deeply cut as the last species, and are narrow, ⅝ in. broad. It has a better habit than *S. lindleyana*.

The Tree-spirea, *S. arborea*, is very hardy. It will attain a height of 18 ft. The branches are hairy. The leaves are 13 to 17 parted, a trifle hairy beneath or in the variety *glabrata* sometimes smooth. It is similar to *S. lindleyana*, taller and hardier. The hairs of *S. lindleyana* are not starlike and the stamens do not protrude from the flower, whereas in this species the hairs are starlike and the stamens are long. They often produce blooms in the Fall, especially if faded flowers are cut.

Uses. It would seem that all these species are good and that such sorts as *S. arborea*, being treelike, would have great usefulness for backgrounds of shrub borders, and that the lower growing clumpy sort, *S. sorbifolia*, would be valuable for beds.

Soil. They prefer rich soil, well supplied with moisture. They enjoy a little shade. Circumneutral pH 6.0–8.0.

Objections. *S. sorbifolia* suckers, as do some other sorts. Most sorts hold their faded flowers which should be removed.

Propagation. 1.**S. sorbifolia* suckers freely and can be divided. The other sorts may be propagated most easily by this method also.

2. Hardwood cuttings are successful.

3. Seeds.

4. Softwood cuttings are successful.

SPIRAEA—Spirea (Includes Bridalwreath and Meadowsweet)

(Name derived from *speira*—anything wreathed; the flowering branches were used as garlands)

Every home owner is familiar with some one of the vast company of Spireas. This is a group of splendid shrubs of many uses. It is our intention to include only such sorts as have undoubted merit.

It will be advisable for the reader to classify the various kinds of Spireas in his mind so that when new ones are seen, he will be able to place them into certain classes. It is not our purpose to present a key but only a scheme showing a few typical sorts:

I. Spiraeas with White Flowers in Umbels or Umbel-like Clusters.

Umbels close to stems, that is, almost sessile.
  1. *S. prunifolia*
  2. *S. thunbergi*
  3. *S. arguta*

Umbels on short, leafy shoots.
  a. Leaves toothed, stamens short.
    4. *S. vanhouttei*
    5. *S. cantoniensis*
  b. Leaves toothed, stamens longer than the petals
    6. *S. chamaedryfolia*
  c. Leaves not toothed or with only a few at the tip.
    7. *S. gemmata*
    8. *S. trichocarpa*

II. Spiraeas in More Branchy Clusters, Flat-topped, Arranged Along Arching Branches, Not Terminating the Growth.

  a. Leaves toothed near apex only.
    9. *S. henryi*
  b. Leaves not toothed, entire margined.
    10. *S. veitchi.*

III. Spiraeas with Flowers in Terminal Clusters, Flat-topped.
  a. Flowers rose-colored.
    11. *S. japonica*
    12. *S. margaritae.*
    13. *S. bumalda*
    14. *S. superba*
  b. Flowers white.
    14. *S. superba*
    15. *S. albiflora*

IV. Spiraeas with Flowers in Long Clusters (Elongated Panicles), Much Longer Than Broad.
  a. Leaves smooth beneath,
      (1) Flowers white
    16. *S. alba*
    17. *S. latifolia*
      (2) Flowers rose
    18. *S. salicifolia*
  b. Leaves hairy or woolly beneath, flowers rose.
    19. *S. billardi*
    20. *S. tomentosa*
    21. *S. douglasi*

Species

1. *Spiraea prunifolia*, Bridalwreath (Plumleaf S.). A very upright shrub, but slightly arching even when in bloom. It grows 4 to 6 ft. tall. The flowers are white and as usually seen are fully double, buttonlike. They are produced at the end of April in small, sessile (stemless) clusters. Each flower has a short pedicel but the cluster itself is stemless. The leaves are oval, 1 to 2 in. long, smooth above, turning bronze, then orange and scarlet in early Fall. Its value lies in its early

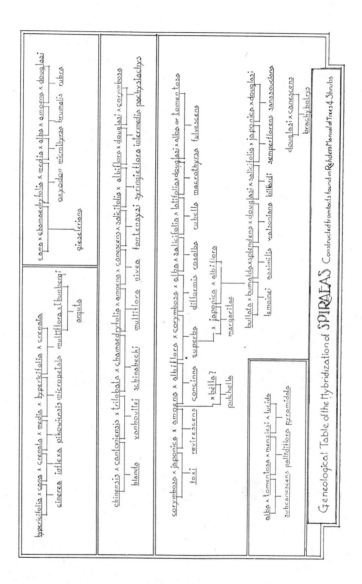

Genealogical Table of the Hybridization of SPIRAEAS Constructed from facts found in Rehder's Manual of Trees & Shrubs

bloom and brilliant foliage. Its leggy, stiff growth is its objectionable feature. It needs a background of evergreens and some other shrub in front of it to cover its bare legs. Sometimes the tips freeze.

2. *Spiraea thunbergi*, Thunberg Spirea. A bushy, slender branched, tiny-leaved shrub of arching habit. The plants grow 3 ft. tall. The flowers are white, produced in March or April before the leaves; later than *S. arguta*. The flowers are produced in three- to five-flowered clusters, the cluster being stemless. The leaves are very small (¾ to 1½ in. long), very narrow, pointed, toothed, yellow-green, changing early to red and orange. Its light, airy growth, small foliage, and early flowers testify to its value. Its faults are that it becomes yellow in Summer and has many dead twigs as the result of Winter injury.

3. *Spiraea arguta*. Garland Spirea (Snowgarland). A hybrid sort, *S. thunbergi* x *S. multiflora*. It grows 4 to 5 ft. tall and has the same sort of slender, arching, twiggy branches as *S. thunbergi*, but more profuse flowering, wider leaves, with several leaves at the base of the flower clusters which are short-stalked at the base of the branches. Has same (or greater) value and same faults as *S. thunbergi*.

4. *Spiraea vanhouttei*. Vanhoutte Spirea. It is a cross between *S. reevesiana* x *S. trilobata*. This wondrous fountain of bloom has been more extensively planted than any other shrub, except Privet and Japanese Barberry. It grows 5 to 6 ft. tall, blooming in May. The flowers are white, produced in clusters on short, leafy shoots, and are so numerous as to wreath the branches. The leaves are dark green, rhombic-ovoid, deeply toothed, small and attractive. Its value is for hedges, partial shade, lawn subjects, adverse situations, foundation plantings and cut flowers.

With the catalog of its virtues, we must also mention its faults: 1, too many of these Spireas are to be seen throughout the cities and countryside, typifying the trite old saying, "it is too much of a good thing"; 2, it remains in bloom for too short time, the rains washing the flowers from the plants almost as soon as they are open; 3, it is used where dwarfer shrubs and evergreens are needed for foundation planting.

5. *Spiraea reevesiana* (*cantoniensis*) Reeves S. This is an arching shrub, much like its offspring, *S. vanhouttei*, but less hardy, with larger, more lasting, often double flowers, and leaves which are narrower and longer (more rhombic-lanceolate than rhombic-ovate). If it were hardier, it would be preferable to *S. vanhouttei*. The double form is known as var. *lanceata*; it also has narrower leaves than the single.

6. *Spiraea chamaedryfolia*, Germander S. This is a shrub of stout, erect habit, becoming 4 or 5 ft. tall. The white flowers are rather

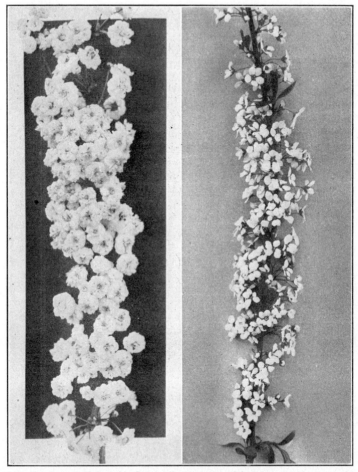

Left, the true Bridalwreath Spirea (Spiraea prunifolia) has double buttonlike flowers and tiny, oval leaves; *right*, Thunberg Spirea, characterized by its tiny leaves, early white flowers, low growth and profusion of bloom

large and produced on leafy shoots. The stamens are longer than the petals. The leaves are 1½ to 3 in. long, ovate or narrowly ovate, irregularly and doubly toothed, slightly bluish-green. Var. *ulmifolia* is taller, less spreading, with stouter branches; the leaves more rounded at the base. The branches are smooth, angular and somewhat zigzag. It uc kers freeiy.

7. *Spiraea gemmata*. Mongolian S. This sort grows 6 to 9 ft. tall and has slender, angled, red-brown branches. The buds are elongated, long-pointed, longer than the petioles of the leaves. The leaves are narrow elliptical, often with a few teeth at the apex, grayish-green beneath. The flowers are white in small umbels. Attractive because of its small, handsome leaves.

8. *Spiraea trichocarpa*. Korean S. This shrub at Highland Park is 4 to 5 ft. tall. It has the same graceful, arching form as *Spiraea vanhouttei*. The blooms are very profusely borne, larger than *S. vanhouttei*. The pedicels are hairy. The leaves are oblong to oblonglanceolate, 1 to 2 in. long, dark green, quite lustrous; the teeth are confined to the upper third of the leaf. It blooms later than *S. vanhouttei* and makes a good specimen.

9. *Spiraea henryi*. Henry S. This is one of the taller Spireas, often 6 or 8 ft. tall, very upright and arching at the top. It is not as graceful as *S. veitchi*, being too open and a trifle leggy in growth. The white flowers are produced in loose, flat-topped clusters (corymbs), 3½ in. across. The leaves are longish oval (oblong to oblanceolate), sometimes 3 in. long, coarsely toothed toward tips, a little hairy above and very much so beneath. Campbell says it is not hardy in Detroit, although it succeeds in Boston.

10. *Spiraea veitchi*. Veitch S. This sort is the tallest of all and has an arching habit. It grows 9 ft. high at Rochester. The branches ere reddish-brown. The leaves are elliptical and are without teeth, grayish beneath. The white flowers are produced in dense clusters (corymbs), often 3 in. across. It blooms in June and July. It is useful for the background of other shrubs, as it towers and arches umbrella-like above them.

11. *Spiraea japonica* (*callosa*). Japanese S. (This should not be confused with *Astilbe japonica* which is called *S. japonica*, but is really a herbaceous perennial). It grows about 4 ft. tall. The leaves are oval to narrowly ovate, 2 to 4 in. long, deeply toothed, paler beneath. Close inspection shows that the teeth are really in two rows. The flowers are pink to rose or white, in flat-topped, loose, terminal clusters (corymbs). The fuzzy stamens give a distinctive effect. The branches

are round, light brown. Var. *fortunei* is taller, hairy when young and with narrower leaves.

12. *Spiraea margaritae.* Margarita S. This Spirea grows 3 to 5 ft. tall, bearing rose-pink flowers in July and again in August and September. They are arranged in leafy, flat clusters (corymbs), with stamens twice as long as petals. The leaves are elliptical, narrow, coarsely and doubly toothed. Botanically, it differs from *S. japonica* by having larger flowers, the sections of the fruit not spreading, the branches are purple-brown.

13. *Spiraea bumalda.* Bumalda S. This resembles *S. japonica* but is of lower growth, more strictly upright, with slightly angled branchlets. The young growth is often pinkish tinged. It is most commonly cultivated in its two varieties:

A popular, low growing shrub, Spiraea bumalda, var. Anthony Waterer, with rosy crimson flowers and rather narrow leaves

Var. Anthony Waterer. This is one of the most popular Spireas, seen next often to Vanhoutte S. It has rosy-crimson flowers and rather narrow leaves. The stems of the new growth are light in color. Difficult to tell from *S. japonica* but has more strictly upright flowers, a better and deeper color and angled branches.

Var. *froebeli* is taller, has broader ovate-oblong leaves. The branchlets even when young are dark brown. It is generally considered superior to Anthony Waterer because the new growth covers the old seed heads of the first crop of flowers. It blooms two weeks earlier.

14. *Spiraea superba.* Striped S. The branches are striped dark brown. The cluster of bloom is a single corymb, there being no tendency for short side clusters to develop. The flowers are whitish-pink or light rose. The leaves are oblong, elliptical, acute at the ends, single or doubly serrate. Generally cataloged as *S. callosa superba.*

15. *Spiraea albiflora.* Like the foregoing four species, but with white flowers, angled, smooth branches, long, narrow leaves, long-pointed at apex, wedge-shaped base, 2 to 2¾ in. long, singly or doubly, toothed with callous teeth. The main cluster (corymb) of bloom large with many smaller ones beneath. A very upright shrub.

By reference to the diagram of hybrids it will be seen that *Spiraea japonica*, *S. albiflora* and *S. corymbosa* have been hybridized together to produce the types listed under species 11 to 15. All of these sorts, therefore, resemble each other very closely. Nurseries often raise these from seed. In that case, we get plants of types which cannot be named. Such sorts have been sent out as true Anthony Waterer, Superba, Froebeli or with other coined or imagined names. These forms are something, but what?

16. *Spiraea alba.* Meadow S. (Meadowsweet). Cataloged as *S. lanceolata* or *S. salicifolia paniculata.* The plants grow 6 ft. tall, upright. The flowers are white in leafy, pyramidal clusters (panicles), broad at the base. The leaves are smooth, oblong to narrowly lanceolate, sharply notched but not lobed. The branches are reddish-brown, slightly hairy when young.

17. *Spiraea latifolia.* Pink Meadow S. (Meadowsweet) (Queen-of-the-meadows). (Also called *S. canadensis* and *S. salicifolia var. latifolia*). This shrub grows 4 to 6 ft. tall. The flowers are whitish or pinkish-white, produced in broad, smooth, pyramidal panicles, very branchy. The stamens are pink, longer than the petals. The leaves are broad elliptical, generally acute at the ends, coarsely and often doubly serrate. The branches are smooth, bright or dark red-brown, angled, springing

directly from the soil. (In *S. alba* the panicle is hairy; in this the pedicels are smooth).

18. *Spiraea salicifolia.* Willowleaf S. (The name *salicifolia* has been applied to *S. alba* and *S. latifolia* in the trade). This sort grows 4 ft. tall. The branches are slightly angled, yellowish-brown. The leaves are long and narrow, acute at the ends, sharply and closely toothed, light green beneath and smooth. The flowers are rose, borne in slender, hairy panicles with ascending branches. This sort suckers freely. It is a European and Asiatic form.

The Billiard Spirea bearing bright rose flowers produced in long panicles during July and August

19. *Spiraea billiardi.* Billiard S. The Spirea, being a cross between *S. douglasi* and *S. salicifolia*, has hairy, brown branchlets. The leaves are narrow, acute at both ends, doubly toothed except on lower third, usually grayish beneath. The flowers are bright rose in narrow, long panicles, 4 to 8 in. long, the stamens nearly twice as long as the petals. A splendid, compact sort with good foliage, profuse in flower and good in rather shaded places. Blooms in July and August. Pruning heavily delays the bloom and keeps the plants more sightly in appearance.

20. *Spiraea tomentosa.* Hardhack (Steeplebush). A native sort in the Eastern States from Nova Scotia to Georgia. It grows 4 ft. tall. The flowers are pinkish-purple, borne in narrow, dense, hairy panicles produced in July and August. The leaves are ovate or oblong, pointed, unequally and often doubly toothed, wrinkled above, yellowish or grayish hairy beneath. Branches reddish-brown, hairy, angled.

21. *Spiraea douglasi.* Douglas S. This species grows 3 to 4 ft. tall. Resembles *S. tomentosa*, but is white hairy beneath, also *S. billiardi*, the flowers of which are in broader panicles and the leaves being less white beneath. The leaves are broader and rounded at the ends. The

branches are reddish-brown, woolly, striped. This species is used for naturalizing but is seldom valued for cultivated planting.

USES. Reference to the species will suggest many uses for the diversity in bloom, habit and foliage of these Spireas. We group a few outstanding sorts:

FOR TALL BACKGROUNDS
Spiraea henryi
S. trichocarpa
S. vanhouttei
S. veitchi

DAINTY FOLIAGE
Spiraea arguta
S. bumalda
S. gemmata
S. prunifolia
S. thunbergi
S. vanhouttei

LOW GROWTH FOR FOUNDATION PLANTING
Spiraea billiardi
S. bumalda
var. Anthony Waterer
var. Froebeli
S. japonica
S. superba

FOR SPECIMENS
Spiraea reevesiana
S. trichocarpa
S. vanhouttei

SOIL. Circumneutral pH 6.0–8.0.

PRUNING. A glance at the species shows that certain of the Spireas are Spring-flowering, producing their bloom upon branches of last year. Spring pruning for these would destroy the bloom for that year. Such sorts should be pruned after flowering. The late-flowered Spireas may be pruned in early Spring, their profusion of bloom depending upon fewer but stronger shoots.

PRUNE AFTER FLOWERING, NOT IN EARLIEST SPRING. All those numbered 1 to 10 which include the Spireas in umbels and the sorts which have flat-topped clusters arranged along the arching branches:

S. arguta
S. reevesiana
S. chamaedryfolia

S. henryi
S. prunifolia
S. thunbergi

S. trichocarpa
S. vanhouttei
S. veitchi

PRUNE IN EARLIEST SPRING BEFORE GROWTH STARTS, and later, after flowering, to remove seed heads which often makes them more everflowering:

S. alba
S. albiflora
S. Anthony Waterer
S. billiardi

S. bumalda
S. corymbosa
S. douglasi
S. froebeli

S. japonica
S. margaritae
S. salicifolia
S. superba
S. tomentosa

In this latter group, the plants may be cut down quite severely. Anthony Waterer may be cut to the soil or sheared back one-half; when so treated the plants are more compact and regular in outline.

PROPAGATION. 1. Except for the hybrid sorts, such as *S. arguta*, *S. billiardi*, Anthony Waterer, Froebeli and *S. vanhouttei*, most sorts may be raised from seed. *S. thunbergi* is especially successful from seed, because the cuttings are so very slender, difficult to make and touchy to handle. Seedlings are produced in great quantity and grow quickly. The seed ripens in April or May, long before you expect it.

2. Hardwood cuttings taken in Autumn root readily. Vanhoutte Spirea may be grown from hardwood inserted in early Spring, just before the buds burst.

3. Softwood cuttings may be taken in late Spring or Summer of most sorts. *S. bumalda* var. Anthony Waterer is usually propagated by this method. Rare sorts are propagated during late Winter from forced plants. *Spiraea prunifolia* is best propagated when the shoots are still soft; must be cut at proper stage.

4. Many sorts, such as *S. bumalda* var. Anthony Waterer, *S. tomentosa* and allies, and *S. salicifolia* and allies may be divided easily.

STAPHYLEA—Bladdernut

(Name derived from *staphule*—a bunch; flowers are in clusters)

The large, inflated pods give the common name to these shrubs, some of which are beautiful in flower and foliage.

THREE-PARTED LEAVES. *Staphylea trifolia*, the American Bladdernut, is not as beautiful as some of the other sorts, but is our native one. The leaves are three-parted, slightly hairy beneath, although often smooth at maturity. The flowers are white with greenish-white sepals, produced in nodding clusters. The fruits are inflated, three-lobed. This species flowers in April and fruits in September.

FIVE- TO SEVEN-PARTED LEAVES. *Staphylea pinnata*, European B. (Jobs-tears) (St. Anthony-nut). This species grows 15 ft. tall, and is very upright in growth. It is reported to freeze in Arnold Arboretum, but seems to thrive splendidly in Rochester. The leaves are five- to seven-parted; the leaflets are oval, finely toothed. The flowers are greenish- white, produced in May in drooping clusters. The bladders are ½ to 11 in. long.

Staphylea colchica or Bladdernut
The yellowish-white flowers and large, inflated seed pods commend this shrub for culture

Staphylea colchica Colchis B. (Caucasian B.), is dwarfer than *S. pinnata* with showy, upright clusters of yellowish-white flowers opening in May and June. The leaves are five-parted, except on flowering shoots, where they are three-parted. They are pointed, sharply toothed, lustrous beneath. The fruits are 3 to 4 in. long, three-lobed, produced in September. It is not the hardiest, but where hardy, it is one of the most desired species.

Uses. The Bladdernuts are of interest in a shrub border because of their fruits. They rather like shade. The Colchis B. has attractive flowers and in Europe is forced as a pot plant. It is said that the flower buds may be used like capers to season food. The seeds are sometimes eaten.

Soil. The American Bladdernut is native to low ground, near the water, and, therefore, enjoys rich, moist soil. Circumneutral pH 6.0–8.0.

Objections. Generally subject to oyster shell scale and foliage is often shabby.

PROPAGATION. 1. Seeds sown when ripe or stratified.

2. Hardwood cuttings root readily.

3. Softwood from forced plants in early Spring.

4. Layers.

5. Suckers.

STEPHANANDRA

(Named from *stephane*—a crown, *andros*—stamen; refers to a crown of
stamens)

From Japan and Korea has come a graceful, wide spreading shrub
related to the Spireas, *Stephanandra flexuosa* (*incisa*). It will grow
to a height of 6 ft. but generally remains at a height of 3 ft. The
white flowers are small, opening in June and produced in panicle racemes. The flowers are not very showy but the leaves are attractive
and dainty. The leaves are deeply toothed, produced in two rows,
¾ to 2½ in. long; they turn red in the Autumn. The branches are
zigzag.

Another species *Stephanandra tanakae*, the Yeddo S., has larger
leaves, 3 in. long, three-lobed and deeply doubly toothed. The clusters
of bloom are larger, blooming in June and July. It is a more vigorous
shrub. The leaves turn orange, scarlet and yellow in the Autumn.

USES. The common Stephanandra is a splendid low growing shrub
for dressing plantings of taller sorts. The foliage is dainty and commends these plants for plantings in small areas where everything is
in scale. If shrubs are permitted in the perennial border, this should
be one of them. *S. tanakae* would serve much the same purpose. It
seems to be at home in Rochester, N. Y. and appears fresh when many
other shrubs are shabby in July. Give both of these sorts a sheltered
place, on northern slopes. Subject to drought injury.

SOIL. Waterer says, "Peaty soil."

PRUNING. The slender twigs are subject to Winter injury in the
North, so that Spring pruning is generally necessary.

PROPAGATION. 1.*Half-ripe wood in Summer generally in greenhouse.

2. Hardwood.

3. Root cuttings of *S. flexuosa* may be made in Spring and given a
warm place in the greenhouse.

STYRAX—Snowbell (Storax)

The Snowbells are really grown as trees but they are so attractive that the writer could not resist the temptation of including one species.

Styrax japonica, the Japanese Snowbell, is a native of Japan and China. It is a shrublike tree, 10 to 12 ft. high, with horizontal, very twiggy branches. It is hardy in Rochester. The branches in mid-May or June are lined on the underside by fragrant, white, pendant bells, in three- to six-flowered clusters on short branches. The leaves are oval, sharp-pointed, shiny. The fruits are ovoid. The young branchlets are hairy, but this soon disappears, the twigs then becoming reddish. The bark of the trunk cracks in a netted fashion and has a contrasting lighter layer beneath.

Uses. Styrax is well planted on a slope so that the observer can walk under the tree and thereby, see the flowers to better advantage. It may be planted among a group of taller trees, where it is protected from the sweep of the wind.

Soil. Styrax likes a lot of water, but should be in a well-drained place. They prefer slight shade from full exposure. Subacid pH 5.0–6.0.

Objections. The tips winterkill. The trees are a trifle too compact. They are difficult to transplant. Nurserymen grow them so that they can be shipped with ball and burlap.

Styrax japonica is a tree that has attractive, white, pendant bells which are very fragrant. It may be planted among taller trees

PROPAGATION. 1. Grows readily from the abundantly produced seed which should be sown as soon as ripe. Usually wait a year before germination.

2. Sometimes grafted on *Halesia carolina*.

3. Only a small percentage of cuttings usually root.

4. Layers useful.

SYMPHORICARPOS—Coralberry, Snowberry

(From *Symphoreo*—to accumulate, *carpos*—fruit; fruits are clustered)

The Coralberry, *Symphoricarpos vulgaris*, is one of the most popular red-berried shrubs for steep banks to hold the soil. The leaves are gray-green, elliptical to oval, hairy beneath, opposite. The flowers are not showy, produced in July and are followed by purplish-red fruit, ⅙ to ¼ in. in diameter, clustered together, ripening in October and in shaded places staying red until Spring. The branches are hairy when young. Bailey and Rehder call this species *S. orbiculatus*. Other common names are Indian-currant, Buckbush, Snapberry and Turkeyberry. There is a variety with variegated leaves.

The Snowberry, *S. racemosus* (*albus*) has white fruits ½ in. or more in diameter, ripening in September and persisting until Spring. In this case the flowers are pink, not very showy but at the same time dainty. The leaves are oval, elliptical, downy beneath. If you examine the leaves of a Snowberry, it will be noted that they may not be hairy, but smooth beneath; this then is var. *laevigatus*, which has larger fruit clusters and is taller. This latter form is the most frequent in cultivation. Var. *pauciflorus* is the Low Snowberry which is lower in growth, has smaller leaves, white beneath and smaller berries.

The Western Snowberry or Wolfberry, *S. occidentalis* is low-growing and more upright than *S. racemosus*; it has hairy branches and larger leaves. The stamens protrude from the flower, which is not true of the Common Snowberry. The berries are dull, not so waxy.

Another sort with hairy branches, but white fruit is *S. mollis*. In this the stamens do not protrude from the flower. This is a more profuse berry producer and superior to the common Snowberry.

Symphoricarpos chenaulti is a hybrid between *S. microphyllum* and *S. vulgaris*. It is of a neater habit. The fruits are red, spotted white. The leaves are small and hairy beneath.

Left, Stephanandra, a slender branched shrub with dainty foliage, useful in foreground planting; *center*, Symphoricarpos albus, unequalled for shady places; *right*, Symphoricarpos vulgaris, a red fruited, suckering shrub

Uses. Whenever the question is asked, "What shrub grows in the shade?" the first thought is Snowberry and Coralberry. They will both grow in dark corners near the house. They are splendid in the wild garden and are ideal, especially the Coralberry, for holding steep banks that wash. The Coralberry sends down hundreds of shoots which root where they touch the soil.

The Ojibwa Indians used a decoction of the berries of Coralberry for sore eyes. The fruit is apparently not of good flavor as birds do not eat it.

Soil. Generally natives of limestone and clay. Circumneutral pH 6.0–8.0.

Pruning. It may be necessary to thin out the growth as the bushes become a wilderness of branches.

Faults. The Coralberry is not refined; it is a tenacious squatter which comes to stay and hold as much space as is available, but it is useful for adverse situations.

Propagation. 1. Divide the plants because they sucker freely.

2.*Hardwood cuttings root very easily.

3. Softwood cuttings are very easy to root.

4. Seeds grow readily.

SYMPLOCOS—Sweetleaf (Sapphireberry)
(From *sumploke*—a connection; the stamens are united)

Ernest Wilson writes: "A plant so hardy and so beautiful is deserving of a place in every garden. Indeed, the fact that it is rarely seen is a reproach to those who make a business of distributing good shrubs."

Symplocos paniculata is a well-shaped, slender-branched, spreading shrub, eventually 15 ft. tall. It is perfectly hardy in Massachusetts. The flowers are white or cream colored, fragrant, opening in May and June, some flowers bearing only one sex, others being fertile. The flowers are borne in panicles and have numerous stamens. The leaves are alternate, elliptical to oval, 1 to 4 in. long, with deeply impressed veins. The fruits are sapphire colored, ⅓ in. long, ovoid and ripen in September.

Uses. These shrubs are valued for their white flowers and clusters of unusual colored fruits. The starlings and other birds eat the fruits as soon as they are ripe.

SOIL. The Bulletin of the Arnold Arboretum says that they will not grow in limestone soil, but N. E. Spingarn reports that he has plants in an alkaline soil. Minimacid pH 6.0–7.0.

PROPAGATION. 1. Seeds germinate the second year.

2. Softwood cuttings under glass.

3. Layers.

SYRINGA—Lilac

Even prosaic persons become reminiscent and sentimental at the sight of Lilacs. To each person's mind, when Lilacs are mentioned, there come thoughts of school desks laden with bloom, perhaps an old, neglected farm or maybe billowy masses above a high board fence and out of reach. As some poet once wrote:

"In an old-fashioned garden where children once played,
There's a spot by the gate, where the Lilacs have stayed.
They glisten and rustle, in Springtime—all green—
They surely are tended by fingers unseen.

"When the lights of the village are twinkling gold,
And the peace of the twilight seems earth to enfold,
They tap on the roof of the tumble-down shack,
Just wondering—When will the children come back?"

Lilacs are ever popular, having been cultivated for years throughout the gardens of the world. Washington planted Lilacs at Mount Vernon and the settlers of Manitoba took them to Canada. Through the years the fragrance of Lilacs has arisen from thousands of otherwise barren homesteads. The fact that the plants improve year by year is a desirable feature.

HISTORY. They are believed to have reached Europe in 1597 by way of Constantinople and Vienna. Until recent years it was believed that the Lilac was a native of Persia, but it is found in the mountains of Bulgaria.

At Highland Park, Rochester, and at the Arnold Arboretum, Cambridge, are extensive collections so that Lilac Sunday is observed in these cities.

Prof. C. S. Sargent tells us:

"The improvement of the Lilac dates only from 1843 when a nurseryman at Liege in Belgium raised a plant with small double flowers. Nothing is now known of the origin of this plant, but as it was called *Syringa vulgaris azurea plena*, it was probably a seedling of the common Lilac and not a hybrid. It was this plant that Victor Lemoine chose as the first plant in his initial attempt to improve the garden Lilacs, fertilizing it with the best Lilacs of the day and with *Syringa oblata*, which was found by Fortune in a Shanghai garden. The crossing of these sorts produced a plant known as *S. hyacinthiflora*, characterized by early and very fragrant flowers. By fertilizing the flowers of *Syringa vulgaris azurea plena* with the pollen of varieties of the common Lilac, Lemoine produced the first important double-flowered Lilac, *S. lemoinei* and others, and by again crossing these with forms of the common Lilac the double flowered Lilacs of recent years have been made. By the crossing of varieties and by careful selection the flowers of the common Lilac have been gradually changed in size and in color in the last thirty years, but unfortunately the flowers of many modern Lilacs have lost a good deal of the fragrance of the old-fashioned Lilac, which, once enjoyed, is never forgotten. There are too many varieties of the common Lilac now cultivated. Some of them with different names given to seedlings in different nurseries and often in different countries are identical, and others are so much alike that they can only be distinguished by close comparison."

SPECIES. 1. Common Lilac, *Syringa vulgaris*. The Common Lilac needs no description as it is known to all. It differs from *S. villosa* and *S. josikaea* by having two end buds, both of which flower, whereas in these two species there is one terminal bud which blooms or else continues the growth of the stem. From the other species which have

attenuate or acute bases to the leaves, *S. vulgaris* differs in having rather heart shape or blunt base leaves. The best varieties are listed on pages 380 to 383.

2. Rouen Lilac, *Syringa chinensis* (*dubia*) (*S. persica* var. *laciniata* × *S. vulgaris*) (*S. rothomagensis*). This is often confused with its *persica* parent, but differs in its longer, ovate lanceolate leaves and panicles of bloom 3 to 6 in. long. (See *S persica*, page 379.) It is superior, being more profuse flowering, more compact, and blooms at a young age. It grows 10 to 12 ft. tall. The flowers are

Syringa chinensis, a profuse, compact flowering shrub

reddish-purple, dark red or

Syringa villosa, one of the privet-flowered, pinkish Lilacs blooming in July

white. Although the flowers are smaller than those of the Common Lilac, they are borne in greater profusion and give a greater display.

3. Persian Lilac, *Syringa persica*. Often the leaves show a tendency to be lobed and in one variety, *laciniata*, they are pinnatifid. The leaves are long, narrow, lanceolate; the branches are drooping and willowy; the flower clusters seldom over 2 to 3 in. long. The flowers are lavender or white. It grows 8 ft. tall. Less desirable than *S. chinensis*.

4. Manchurian or Amur Lilac, *Syringa amurensis*. This upright shrub has ovate leaves tapering at the base, smooth beneath. The flowers are yellowish-white, produced in June. Unlike the above species, the corolla tube is very short.

Var. *japonica*, Japanese Lilac, is an upright tree with bark not unlike that of Cherry. The leaves are oval, rounded at the base and more or less hairy beneath. The inflorescence is often a foot long, and slightly hairy. The tiny flowers open in June and July. The odor of the flowers is rank, not unlike that of the Privets to which these sorts are related. This is a superior sort noted for its misty long clusters of bloom.

Var. *pekinensis* has a shrubby, spreading habit, is 20 to 30 ft. tall, and as broad. The bark is yellow-brown, peeling like that of the Birch. The leaves are smaller than the type, oblong, pointed, narrow at the base. The flowers are borne earlier than the Japanese Lilac. More graceful with slenderer branches than the type.

5. Late or Himalaya Lilac, *Syringa villosa* (*bretschneideri*). This sort blooms later than the Common Lilac and has broadly oblong leaves, often 7 in. long, shortly pointed. The name *villosa* would lead one to think that this species was very hairy but such is not the case, inasmuch as the veins only are hairy. The flowers are pale lilac or pinkish-white, strangely scented.

6. Hungarian Lilac, *Syringa josikaea*, is similar to the above but without hairy veined leaves; the panicles of bloom are denser and the color is deeper lilac. Difficult to say whether this is superior to *S. villosa*. Its flowers at least have more color.

Varieties (Recommended by the Late John Dunbar)

Dark Purple-Red. Chas. Joly has dark purple-wine blossoms with silvery reverse; De Saussure produces numerous thyrses of violet-red to purple-red blossoms with clear mauve reverse; Paul Hariot is a free bloomer with dark red-violet flowers and silvery reverse; Violetta with semi-double, cucullate, very dark violet flowers, is a very beautiful variety. Adelaide Dunbar* has semi-double flowers in large clusters; the blossoms when opening are maroon or dark crimson, and when fully open turn violet-red. It is perhaps the darkest double flowering lilac in cultivation. The unfolding leaves are slightly copper colored.

Double Bluish-Lavender and Azure-Lilac. Condorcet with deep blue mauve blossoms; Emile Gentil, with cobalt blue, imbricated flowers in large clusters; Hippolyte Maringer, with clusters that stand up well of deep bluish-lavender; Jean Mace, most distinct with very large clusters of bluish-mauve; Julien Gerardin, with prominent thyrses of bright cobalt blue; Marechal Lannes, a most beautiful sort with flowers $1\frac{1}{4}$ in. across, semi-double, in large clusters, bluish-violet; Marc Micheli, displaying large clusters of tender azure lilac; Olivier de Serres another beautiful variety, with immense clusters and large blossoms tinted delicate azure-lavender; Rene Jarry Des-loges, with bold clusters of clear, azure-lilac, much imbricated blossoms; Tournefort, with bluish-lilac blossoms; and Victor Lemoine, whose enormous clusters that weigh down the branches are of delicate azure-mauve. General Kitchener* bears numerous dense thyrses of semi-double flowers, bluish-lilac with a tinge of violet. General Pershing* with semi-double blossoms tinged a very delicate light azure-lilac, flowers freely and is a remarkably beautiful Lilac.

*Originated at Highland Park by the late John Dunbar.

Double Silvery-Lavender and Pinkish-Lilac. Carmen, silvery-mauve; Henri Martin, lilac-mauve and large, handsome clusters; Leon Gambetta, a beautiful variety with pinkish-lilac thyrses; Linne, with rosy-lilac blossoms in long-pointed clusters; Louis Henry, rosy-lavender clusters; Montaigne, pinkish-mauve blossoms in large clusters; Paul Thirion, upright clusters of rosy-lavender tinged with claret; President Carnot, very pale silvery-lavender; and President Fallieres, pale lavender with immense clusters, causing the branches to droop.

Double White. Edith Cavell is a magnificent form with bold, handsome clusters, which might be described as cream-white; it always attracts attention. The Lemoines paid a fine tribute to this distinguished woman when they named this Lilac in her honor. Madame Casimir Perier has been

Descartes, a representative of the early-flowering race produced by Lemoine by crossing S. affinis var. giraldi with S. vulgaris. This variety has an erect-branching, rapid-growing habit, and bears showy, pinkish-mauve flowers

in cultivation for many years, but is still in the first rank of double white flowering Lilacs. It is a free bloomer, has an excellent habit, and is a good variety for forcing. Madame de Miller is a compact, low growing bush with numerous clusters of pure white flowers; Miss Ellen Willmott has large clusters of imbricated white blossoms and flowers late; Princess Clementine is said to be a cross between Marie Legraye and Madame Lemoine and has prominent clusters of handsome, pure white flowers; Taglioni is a free bloomer and displays pure white flowers. General Sheridan* produces freely numerous large clusters of pure white, double flowers. The individual blossoms are not as large as in some double flowering white Lilacs, but the clusters stand out boldly. General Sherman* has immense, many-shouldered, upright clusters of single flowers of which the color might be described as creamy lavender. This is perhaps one of the most beautiful Lilacs in cultivation.

Single Purple-Red, Deep Claret-Violet. Diderot with very large blossoms 1⅛ in. across of rich claret-purple; Dr. Charles Jacob, dark wine-red when fully open; Laplace, with much reflexed flowers of a claret-violet shade; Marceau, with remarkably large, purple-violet flowers with round, curved lobes, but, unfortunately, a very thin branching habit. Monge is a free bloomer with very graceful, reflexed, dark purple-violet flowers; Milton has pure violet flowers with a silvery reverse; Negro, which has been in cultivation for many years, has very beautiful, deep purple flowers; Pasteur has a very thin growing habit, but the blossoms are very distinct, shading from purple-red to claret-red; Reamur is a very free bloomer with purplish-carmine flowers; Tombucton has blossoms somewhat cucullate and might be described as a violet Wallflower; Vesuve has very large, very handsome regular flowers of rich claret-purple, but the plant seems to have a poor constitution. Alexander Hamilton,* in which the flowers are remarkably large (measuring 1 5-16 in. across), violet-lavender, borne in large, dense clusters, slightly cucullate. President Roosevelt* bears claret-red to purple-red single flowers in numerous thyrses, and is a most attractive variety; it produces a charming effect when the buds are opening. Thomas Jefferson* with single flowers, might be described as violet-lavender, it blooms freely.

Single Bluish Tints. Bleuatre, deep bluish-lilac with a faint tinge of violet; Cavour, with upright clusters of large blossoms, tinged slate blue; Crampel, a low growing variety, with bluish-lilac flowers and light centers; Decaisne, very handsome with both thyrses and individual blossoms, very large, and of pale azure-lilac; Gilbert, a most beautiful Lilac with its handsome bold clusters and individual large flowers of delicate bluish lavender; Melide Laurent, which might be described as bluish-lilac splashed with a faint rosy tinge; President Lambeau, a very free bloomer, with clear bluish-lavender clusters; and Ronsard, an early, very free bloomer, with clear bluish-lilac flowers and whitish center. Hiram H. Edgerton* has single, many-flowered thyrses, the individual flowers being large and of a deep bluish-slate color; the variety has an excellent, compact habit. Henry Wadsworth Longfellow* bears clusters of semi-double flowers, light bluish-lilac; President Harding* produces many clusters of single purple-red to reddish-lilac blossoms. President Lincoln* blossoms early bearing many large clusters of wedgwood blue, single flowers. In our opinion it is perhaps the bluest of single flowering Lilacs in cultivation.

---

*Originated at Highland Park by the late John Dunbar.

Single Pinkish to Silvery-Lavender. Christopher Colomb has large flower clusters, with a tender, silvery-lavender tinge; Jacques Callot, a very old variety, but still in the front rank, has large, silvery-lavender or silvery-mauve blossoms; Lavoisier is a free bloomer with a rosy-mauve to pinkish-lavender tint; Lovaniensis, long in cultivation has individual flowers that are not large, but of a decidedly pinkish-lilac; Lucie Baltet is in a class by itself as there is no other Lilac with a similar tint, which is a most attractive pink salmon; Macrostachya flowers freely, has clear pinkish colored blossoms and is very popular; Rosea grandiflora is an old variety with rosy-lavender to silvery-mauve blossoms; and Schermerhorn, an old form, has very dainty pink blossoms in which, however, the individual flowers are small.

Single White.—Kate Harlin, with pure white blossoms of large size, is a free bloomer; Madame Florent Stepman which, we understand, was originated by Stepman De Messemaeker of Brussels, Belgium, and which has an excellent growing habit, producing numerous large clusters of pure white flowers that stand out boldly, is one of the best; Mont Blanc is also a highly meritorious Lilac, its large clusters being well branched and the individual flowers with round, wide and prominent lobes being very large and pure white. Princess Alexandra, raised and named in Windsor, Ont., between 40 and 50 years ago, is an excellent white flowering variety in which the clusters stand up boldly; Reine Elizabeth is a very distinct form, the large pearly white flowers having undulating lobes and presenting a charming appearance. Vestale is a very floriferous variety with large, pure white panicles that stand out prominently.

Early Flowered Lilacs. The Lemoines of Nancy, France, produced a most valuable race of early flowering Lilacs by crossing *Syringa affinis* var. *giraldi* with an early flowering *S. vulgaris* variety. The resulting forms flower from a week to ten days ahead of the *S. vulgaris* forms, and are therefore very important. They are all erect branching, rapid growing shrubs. Berryer has double clear mauve flowers; Claude Bernard is semi-double with bright lilac-mauve blossoms; Descartes has single, showy pinkish-mauve flowers; Lamartine is a very strong grower displaying large clusters of single rosy-mauve flowers; Mirabeau is similar to Lamartine with single flowers, lilac-mauve to rosy-lavender; Pascal is a remarkably free bloomer with single flowers of a typical lilac color; Vauban is similar to Berryer, with double, tender pinkish-mauve blossoms.

Uses. Lilacs may be used as tall screen hedges, for massing, for specimens and for their abundant display of bloom. They are unexcelled by any other shrub, blooming even under adverse city conditions.

Lilacs make desirable cut flowers, but some varieties wilt soon after cutting. Remove some bark from the stems and plunge the stems deeply in almost boiling water, and leave them until they have revived. This will also prevent wilting.

Soil. Many growers in acid regions apply liberal quantities of lime to Lilacs when they are not as healthy as desired. They prefer a circumneutral soil pH 6.0–8.0 and it would seem wise to try the experiment of using lime upon such plants as are not thriving. It might be what they need.

PRUNING. Pruning of Lilacs consists mainly of thinning out the interiors and preventing congestion. Lilacs, some varieties especially, will throw up a mass of suckers, and this should not be permitted. It is important to prune the plants when young, so that several stems will branch close to the ground. If a bush is grown to one stem and serious trouble develops from the ravages of uncontrolled borers, the entire plant is liable to be lost; whereas, if there are several stems, there is a good chance to preserve the variety. It is good cultural practice to remove all flower clusters when they are through blooming, not only for appearance sake but also to prevent weakening the shrubs by the formation of seeds.*

If Lilacs are cut with rather long stems, this will serve as a method of pruning.

WHY LILACS FAIL TO BLOOM

1. When pruned too heavily.
2. When the old flowers are not removed.
3. In shade they do not produce properly.
4. Too many suckers.
5. Sometimes plants must be 10 years old.

INSECTS. *Scale.* Oyster shell and San José scale are both bad on Lilacs. The former is only controlled by spraying when the scales are moving, generally in June, using a miscible oil, 1 part to 15 of water, to which a spoonful of Black Leaf 40 is added per gallon. It may take three sprayings, three days apart, to destroy a heavy infestation. San José scale is usually well controlled by a dormant Winter spray of some miscible oil.

Borers. The Lilac borer is especially destructive to those sorts trained to tree form. Squirt carbon bisulphide into the channels by means of a medicine dropper or hyperdermic syringe. After using, plug the holes with mud or grafting wax. The borer work is in evidence in June and July.

PROPAGATION. 1. *Seed.* Except for *S. pubescens*, according to John Dunbar, all species produce seed freely. When sown as soon as ripened and carried over in frames or sown in Spring, they make good plants in three years.

2. *Softwood Cuttings.* Early, rather softwood cuttings root readily. According to climate they are taken about June 15 to July 1. They are not the easiest of cuttings to root and will benefit by bottom heat.

---

*Advice of the late John Dunbar.

3. *Hardwood Cuttings.* Some growers are successful, but usually they root very poorly.

4. *Layers.* To obtain varieties or hybrids on own roots, layering is a very good method, if the plants have been prepared for it by low branching. Of course this is a slow process and perhaps does not suit the grower who wants quantity rapidly.

5. *Budding.* The various Privets are used as stocks for budding. California Privet is considered too tender. *Ligustrum ibota, L. vulgaris* and *L. amurensis* are preferable. This is done in August and is a common method with nurserymen. For quick results in the growing of Lilacs to be forced in pots, there is no better method. For permanent plantings, however, it is not desirable, as the plants are apt to be short-lived. It is a good plan in budding Lilac on Privet to get stock for permanent planting, to bud low down; then, after one year's growth has been made, transplant, placing the union 4 to 5 in. below the surface. The plants will quickly get on their own roots.

6. *Grafting.* Grafting on Privet or Lilac piece roots in late Winter, placing the grafts in a cool cellar, and planting them out in Spring (when care is taken to plant the union at least 4 in. beneath the surface, so as to give the cion an opportunity to root) is a good method. We know from personal experience that, if deep planting is rigorously followed, in two to four years' time such plants will be on own roots. It is true, though, that some varieties will root more readily above the graft than others. Sometimes Lilac stocks are used for grafting or budding. This is highly undesirable, because Lilac stocks are sure to sucker freely. In the hands of amateurs or private gardeners the suckers will go unobserved and cion be crowded out and the plant ruined before anything is done. In the case of Privet, if it should sucker (which it may occasionally do during the first year or two even in deep planting) any amateur can readily detect the sucker and dig down and remove it immediately.

There is an urgent demand for Lilacs on own roots for permanent planting, and whatever method nurserymen adopt, the aim should be ultimately to establish them on their own roots.

TAMARIX—(Tamarisk)

(Named from Tamaris, a river in the Pyrenees)

The fine, graceful foliage and the airy heads of bloom of Tamarix are greatly admired. There are many kinds which are superficially very similar, and with names that are hopelessly mixed.

The Tamarix with its fine graceful foliage and pink flowers

April- and May-Flowering Sorts

1. *Tamarix parviflora* (called *T. tetrandra purpurea*). This sort grows 15 ft. tall, is of slender, spreading growth. The pink flowers are produced in April, in racemes, lateral on last year's branches. The sepals, petals, stamens are four; the petals are persistent. The leaves are ovate, dry at the tip. The bark is dark purple. (Confused with *T. africana* and *T. tetrandra*.) (Offered in catalogs as *T. africana* which is rarely seen.)

2. *Tamarix tetrandra* (*taurica*) (*speciosa*), the Fourstamen Tamarisk, is another tall sort, growing to 15 ft. The light pink flowers are produced in April, on short side branches of last year's growth. The sepals, petals, stamens are four; the petals are erect and drop as soon as the flowers are mature. The leaves have a thin margin. The bark is purplish, almost black.

3. *T. juniperina* (*japonica*) (*plumosa*), Juniper T. A slender spreading, densely branched sort; the branchlets are very thin. Grows 15 ft. tall. The flowers are pink, produced in May. Unlike species Nos. 1 and 2, the petals, sepals and stamens are five, wilting but persisting. The racemes are 2 in. long, on old branches. Leaves are dry at the edge.

Late or Summer Flowering Sorts—Parts of Flower Five, Branches and Leaves Hairy

4. *T. hispida* (*kashgarica*), Kashgar T. A slender, upright sort. 4 ft. tall. The pink flowers are produced in August and September in dense racemes forming a terminal panicle. The leaves are bluish-green, finely hairy.

Branches and Leaves Not Hairy

5. *T. pentandra* (*hispida* var. *aestivalis*) (*amurensis*), Five stamen T. "A variable species," says Rehder. Very hardy. A small but distinctive characteristic is that the disk at the base of the flower has ten lobes (other common species, except *T. chinensis*, have five). The foliage is pale or gray-green as in species 4, but is not hairy. One of the best sorts, hardy and good habit, producing flowers in profusion.

6. *T. odessana*, Odessa T. (Caspian T.). Upright slender growth. The racemes of bloom are 1 in. long on naked pedicels. The petals are persistent, wilting. The leaves are awl-shaped, decurrent (have lines which extend down the stem).

7. *T. gallica*, French T. Often very spreading, to 12 ft. tall or even 25 ft. Blooms in July, often again later. Leaves dull to bluish-green, dry margins, triangular. A trifle tender.

Uses. They are adapted to the seaside where they tolerate salt air and wind. They serve as tall background plants for the shrub border. As foliage for florist or home use the Tamarisk is splendid.

Apparently *T. pentandra*, *T. odessana* and *T. parviflora* are the hardiest ones.

Soils. "Most soils, except too much lime," *Le Bon Jardinier*. (Circumneutral pH 6.0–8.0.) They like humidity. They thrive in sandy soils, being a little less hardy in heavy clay.

PRUNING. The late-flowered sorts, if they become straggling, can be cut to the soil in the Spring, the others after flowering.

PROPAGATION. 1. Seed is fine and must be carefully sown.

2.*Hardwood cuttings. Use long cuttings which root along their entire length.

3. Softwood under glass.

4. Layers.

ULEX—Gorse (Furze) (Whin)

A very spiny, branchy shrub, related to the Brooms is the Gorse, *Ulex europaeus.* It is hardy from Washington southward. It grows only 2 to 4 ft. tall. The flowers are pealike, yellow, with a hairy, yellow calyx, being brilliant in effect, fragrant and crowded at the ends of branches in April or May and again later in Summer. The leaves are scalelike, often reduced to a spiny petiole. The fruit is dark brown, ½ in. long, hairy. The branches are evergreen.

Ulex or Gorse
Extremely spiny, green-branched shrubs with brilliant yellow, pealike flowers

Uses. Good for seaside planting. Naturalized at Vancouver and in Middle Atlantic States.

Soil. Gravelly or sandy. They serve as sand binders for dry banks. Subacid pH 5.0–6.0.

Transplanting. Rehder comments on their difficulty of transplanting and suggests sowing seed where the plants are to stand permanently.

Propagation. 1. Seed sown in Spring as late as May. Plants from seed bloom in two years.

2. Green wood rooted under glass.

3. Ripe wood in early Summer under glass.

VACCINIUM—Blueberry, Cranberry

Although there are many sorts of Blueberries with edible fruits and ornamental foliage, the ones best known are the Highbush Blueberry for wet soil, the Lowbush Blueberry for dry soil, and the Cranberry for bogs.

The Highbush B., *Vaccinium corymbosum*, attains a height of 12 ft. The young branchlets are yellow-green, warty. The leaves are elliptical, without teeth, attractive. The flowers are white or pinkish, urn-shaped, in dense clusters. The fruit ripens in July. The plants bloom when the leaves are half developed.

The Lowbush B., *V. pennsylvanicum*, grows 2 ft. tall. The flowers are smaller than those of the Highbush B. and are greenish-white; they open from April to May. The leaves are bristle-toothed, narrow elliptical. The fruit is blue-black.

The American Cranberry, *V. macrocarpon*, is well known for its edible fruit. The stems are creeping, often 3 ft. long. The leaves are ½ in. long, whitish beneath. The Cranberry found in the mountains of North America is smaller and is *V. vitisidaea*, a charming little ground cover.

Uses. The Highbush B. is a splendid ornamental shrub. Its foliage is good, changing to yellow, orange and red in the Autumn. The flowers and fruits are also attractive. The grace of the fine branchlets is ever attractive. The two other sorts mentioned here are not worthy of cultivation for ornament.

SOIL. *V. corymbosum* prefers an acid marsh but will grow in ordinary acid soil. *V. pennsylvanicum* is adapted to dry, sandy soil, growing often in the wild in very barren places. Note that they want acid soil; it would seem that the sourer the better. Subacid pH 5.0–6.0.

PRUNING. Prune severely at planting time.

PROPAGATION. 1. Suckers freely. 2. The propagation of commercial Blueberries is interestingly described in great detail in U. S. D. A. Professional Paper Bulletin 334 by Dr. F. V. Coville and quoted in *Practical Plant Propagation* by the writer. Most sorts used ornamentally are collected from the wild and not propagated.

VERONICA (HEBE)—Shrub Speedwell

(From *vera*—true, and *ikonika*—face, referring to the legend of St. Veronica who received the true face of Jesus on her napkin. Certain species have the resemblance of a face in their flowers)

The Shrub Veronicas are natives of New Zealand. They are evergreens which are commonly grown in the warmer regions of the country for their glossy leaves and lovely flowers.

There are many species but we can note only a few. Perhaps the most important is *Veronica speciosa*, the Showy Speedwell, which grows to a height of from 2 to 5 ft. The oval leaves are from 2 to 4 in. long, dark green and glossy. The reddish purple flowers are borne in axillary racemes near the tips of the branches.

V. andersoni, Anderson Speedwell, makes strong growth. The flowers are violet purple. This is a hybrid between *V. salicifolia* and *V. speciosa*.

V. buxifolia, Box S. Dwarf; leaves are small; the flowers are white.

V. carnea, the Flesh S. Slender growth; leaves long, narrow; flowers lilac purple; good for shade.

V. cupressoides, the Cypress S. Dense, compact; leaves are scale—like a Cypress; flowers lilac; leaves scented.

V. decumbens. Low, spreading; leaves dark green; flowers in dense spikes.

V. elliptica (decussata), the Seacoast S. Grows 5 to 20 ft tall; flowers violet in bud but white when open.

V. imperialis, the Imperial S., is of the same parentage as the Anderson S.

V. formosiana. Tall; leaves bright green; flowers white.

Veronica imperialis is amaranth red and one of the most desirable hybrids

V. pimeloides. Low, compact growth; leaves tiny; flowers creamy lilac.

V. pinquefolia. Spreading, decumbent; leaves silvery gray margined red; flowers white.

V. traversi, the Bush S. Shrubs are 3 to 5 ft. across; leaves long, narrow; flowers pure white.

PROPAGATION. Cuttings in Summer under a bell jar.

VIBURNUM

No group of shrubs is so generally desirable as is the vast array of Viburnums. We may search widely to find serious objections to many of the sorts, except the common Snowball. They have splendid foliage and contrast with one another so that an entire planting might be made of Viburnums alone. To show their further usefulness, they have been arranged in lists.

RED FRUITS

V. dilatatum
V. opulus
V. sargenti
V. suspensum
V. theiferum
V. trilobum
V. wrighti

BLACK FRUITS

V. acerifolium
V. affine
V. alnifolium
V. dentatum and allies
V. lentago
V. tinus

EDIBLE FRUITED SORTS

V. affine
V. lentago
V. prunifolium
V. sargenti
V. trilobum

SHADE LOVERS

V. acerifolium
V. alnifolium
V. dentatum
V. lentago
V. molle
V. sieboldi
V. suspensum

FOR DRY PLACES

V. acerifolium
V. dilatatum
V. lantana
V. opulus
V. prunifolium
V. pubescens
V. tinus

LEAVES CHANGE COLOR IN FALL

V. acerifolium
V. alnifolium
V. cassinoides
V. lentago
V. molle
V. prunifolium
V. pubescens
V. pubescens var. *canbyi*
V. sargenti
V. trilobum

FOR WET PLACES

V. cassinoides
V. dentatum
V. lentago

ATTRACTIVE FLOWERS

Snowballs

V. macrocephalum var. *sterile*
V. opulus var. *sterile*
V. tomentosum var. *plenum*

Not Snowballs

V. dentatum
V. dilatatum
V. lentago
V. prunifolium
V. rufidulum
V. pubescens
V. sieboldi
V. tomentosum

TENDERER SORTS

V. carlesi
V. macrocephalum
V. rhytidophyllum
V. suspensum
V. tinus

EVERGREEN

V. rhytidophyllum
V. suspensum
V. tinus

FRAGRANT

V. carlesi

GROUPING THE VIBURNUMS

I. Shedding leaves in the Fall.

  a. Flowers all sterile (snowballs) or a row of sterile flowers on the outside with fertile flowers in the center.
      (1) Leaves not three-lobed...........1. *V. tomentosum*
          2. *V. macrocephalum*
          3. *V. alnifolium*
      (2) Leaves three- or five-lobed.......4. *V. opulus*
          5. *V. trilobum*
          6. *V. sargenti*

  b. Flowers all uniform in shape and bisexual
      (1) Leaves three-lobed..............7. *V. acerifolium*
      (2) Leaves not lobed, principal veins straight, ending in teeth.

8. *V. lantana*	13. *V. molle*
9. *V. carlesi*	14. *V. pubescens*
10. *V. sieboldi*	15. *V. dilatatum*
11. *V. dentatum*	16. *V. theiferum*
12. *V. affine*	17. *V. wrighti*

      (3) Leaves not lobed, principal veins not reaching the margins because they branch freely.18. *V. lentago*
          19. *V. prunifolium*
          20. *V. rufidulum*
          21. *V. cassinoides*
          22. *V. nudum*

II. Evergreen leaves
    a. Leaves roughly embossed, entire margined (not toothed).
                       23. *V. rhytidophyllum*
    b. Leaves not roughly embossed, round toothed.
        (1) Twigs scurfy hairy.................24. *V. suspensum*
        (2) Twigs and leaves quite smooth........25. *V. tinus*

1. *Viburnum tomentosum*, Doublefile V., Japanese Snowball. The branches are quite horizontal. The plants grow 10 ft. tall. The white flowers open in May or June. The flat clusters of sterile and fertile flowers are 2 to 4 in. across and so placed that they are opposite and face upward, making a flat, wandlike branch. The fruit is small, oval, red, changing blue-black. In the Japanese Snowball, var. *plenum* (*plicatum*) (*sterile*), the clusters are made up of sterile flowers entirely. They bloom a week later than the type. The leaves are long, oval, prominently toothed, 1½ to 4 in. long, abruptly sharp-pointed, smooth above, hairy beneath, veins very prominent. The leaves of the Japanese Snowball are less hairy beneath. The branches are hairy when young. Var. *rotundifolium*, not the Snowball type. Leaves rounder than the type, with red veins. Flowers in fewer, larger heads, two weeks earlier, more spreading growth than the type. "Not so hardy and less valuable north of Philadelphia," says Meehan. Handsomer

Japanese Snowball (Viburnum tomentosa var. plenum)

A sterile form of the Doublefile Viburnum. The white snowball-like blooms are produced in May or June

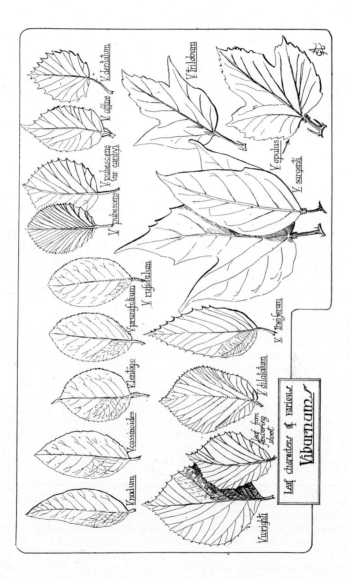

Leaf characters of various Viburnams

Autumn color. Var. *mariesi*. Foliage more elongated, more downy, plants more spreading and more dwarf. Flower clusters and flowers larger.

2. *V. macrocephalum*, Chinese V. A spreading shrub to 12 ft., less hardy than *V. tomentosum*, flowers often injured. A variety with all sterile flowers is the one generally grown; it is the Chinese Snowball and much larger than the others, sometimes 7 to 8 in. across. The flowers develop normally in late Spring, but the buds, which are formed the previous Summer, often open in Fall when the weather is not favorable to holding them back. The leaves are semi-evergreen, oval, 2 to 4 in. long, toothed. The leaves are coarser, more oval, less heart-shaped than *V. lantana*. The Chinese Snowball is var. *sterile* and is often cataloged as *V. fortunei* or *V. macrophyllum*.

3. *V. alnifolium* (*lantanoides*), Hobblebush (American Wayfaring-tree), (Witch-hobble), (Moosewood V.). This shrub grows 5 ft., or rarely 10 ft. tall; some branches are procumbent and rooting. The flowers are greenish, changing white, opening in May. The leaves are very large, almost round, often 4 to 8 in. across, heart-shaped, the upper surface rich green, brownish beneath. They turn deep red in the Fall. The branches are scurfy. The fruits are bright red, turning black, egg-shaped, ⅜ in. in diam., palatable, ripening in September.

4. *V. opulus*, European Cranberrybush (Highbush Cranberry), (Pimbina). The leaves, unlike those of the above species, are three, often four or five-lobed, 2 to 4 in. long, hairy or smooth beneath with disklike glands at the sides of a narrow grooved petiole. They do not turn red in Fall. The white flowers are produced in May or June. The sterile form of this is the Common Snowball or Guelder-rose, var. *sterile*, a very popular shrub for many years, but losing favor because plant lice cause the leaves to curl badly. In the type scarlet berries are produced on upright stems in August and September which remain all Winter as they are too sour to be eaten by birds. Var. *nanum*, the Pigmy Snowball, grows 6 to 18 in. tall and never flowers.

5. Similar to the above is the American Cranberrybush, *V. trilobum* (*americanum*) (*oxycoccos*). In this species the lobes of the leaves are more entire, less coarsely toothed, smoother beneath, hairy only on the veins; petioles with a shallow groove and small stalked glands. It is usually a more open, spreading bush than *V. opulus* and the fruits are large, orange-scarlet, edible, remaining upon the plants all Winter and produced on drooping stems.

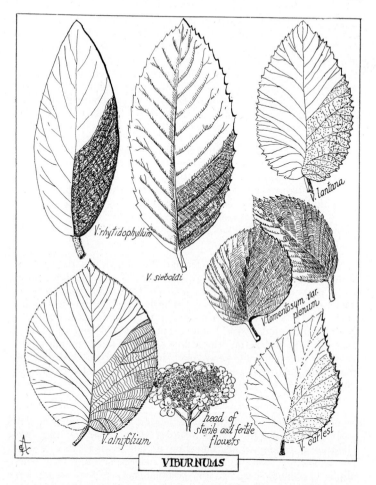

V. rhytidophyllum

V. sieboldi

V. lantana

V. tomentosum var. plenum

V. alnifolium

head of sterile and fertile flowers

V. carlesi

VIBURNUMS

6. There is yet a third similar sort, the Sargent Cranberrybush (Manchurian C.), *V. sargenti*, which has darker, more corky branchlets with prominent dots. The leaves have an elongated middle lobe, almost without teeth; the lateral lobes are spreading and short. Sometimes the leaves are not lobed. The anthers are purple, in the two other sorts they are yellow. This sort does well in the West. It does not fruit as freely.

7. *V. acerifolium*, the Maple-leaf V. (Dockmackie), has also three-lobed leaves but the flowers are all fertile flowers. The fruit is black. The Maplelike leaves are 2 to 5 in. long, coarsely toothed, rounded or heart-shaped at the base, slightly hairy above and densely so beneath, with minute black dots. The flowers open in June and are white. The branches are slender, downy at first, becoming glabrous. The leaves change in the Fall to purple and crimson. It is found wild from New Brunswick to Minnesota and south to North Carolina. It is useful under trees in drought and shade.

8. *V. lantana*, Wayfaring-tree. This upright, treelike shrub has very stout, scurfy young branches. It often grows 15 to 20 ft. tall. The flowers are white, produced in June and July in flat-topped clusters, all flowers alike and fertile. The fruit ripens in July and August, is red, changing to black. The leaves are wrinkled, rough, coarsely toothed, 2 to 4 in. long, heart-shaped base, hairy beneath, turning red in the Autumn. Var. *rugosum* has larger, more wrinkled leaves and larger heads of bloom.

9. *V. carlesi*, Fragrant V. (Korean V.). This is a round-topped bush, seldom more than 4 to 6 ft. tall. In this case the flowers are a lovely pink, fading to white; the buds are tinted orange-pink. As the cluster does not open all its flowers at once, there are flowers of various tints. The flowers are in dense cymes, 2 to 3 in. in diameter, with a fragrance not unlike the Trailing-arbutus. The season of bloom is early April at which time the leaves have not fully expanded. The leaves are long-pointed to almost circular, irregularly toothed, dull blue-green, hairy above and below. The branchlets are also hairy. The fruits, ripening in September, are blue-black, ½ in. long.

10. *V. sieboldi*, Siebold V. This is a large-leaved, tall sort with peppery-scented leaves. The plants become 10 ft. tall and sometimes treelike. The flowers are in a longer cluster (panicle) than most Viburnums, creamy-white, flowering in late Spring, May or June. The leaves are lustrous, prominently veined (seven to ten pairs), elliptic to oblong, sharp or blunt pointed, sharpely toothed and large (6 to 8 in. long). The leaves drop at the early frosts without change of color. The branches are stout; hairy when young.

11. *V. dentatum*, Arrowwood. This very attractive shrub grows from 5 to 15 ft. tall and is native from New Brunswick to Minnesota, south to Georgia. It is of upright habit. The flowers are white, in umbel-like cymes, 2 to 3 in. broad. The leaves are round or oval, coarsely toothed, lustrous above, only hairy in the axils of the veins

beneath. The branchlets are gray. The leaves change to purple and red in the Autumn. The fruits are black, small, glaucous, ripening in August and September. The birds eat them. Resembles *V. affine,* which has two prominent stipules at the base of the leaf.

12. *V. affine (pubescens),* Missouri V. Grows 3 to 6 ft. tall. Blooms profusely in June and July, in cymes on stalks ½ in. to 1 in. long. The leaves are rounded, heart-shaped, coarsely toothed, tapering to a point, smooth or hairy on the veins, four to six pairs of veins. Fruit oval, slightly flattened, bluish-black, sweet, edible. The birds are fond of the fruit. Resembles *V. dentatum* but with stipules on petioles and with shorter petioles. Resembles *V. molle,* but the leaves are less heart-shaped at base, with shorter petioles and with close bark which does not shed. Resembles *V. pubescens,* but leaves have four to six pairs of veins whereas that species has seven to nine and no stipules at the base of the leaf.

13. *V. molle,* Kentucky V. (Silky V.). Grows 12 ft. tall. The flowers are produced in late May, later than many others, the cymes on long stems, 3 in. or more. The leaves are ovate or round, 3 to 5 in. long, coarsely toothed, deeply heart-shaped at the base, hairy beneath. The young branchlets are glabrous, becoming gray. The old bark peels from the branches. Stipules at base of leaf as in *V. affine.*

Resembles *V. affine,* see above.

Resembles *V. dentatum,* but with finer and more closely set teeth and hairy.

Resembles *V. pubescens* which has smaller leaves, more densely woolly, seven to nine pairs of veins.

14. *V. pubescens (venosum) (nepalensis),* Downy V. A compact shrub, often 12 ft. tall. The cymes are 2½ to 4 in. across, on long stalks. The flowers are white, opening during June and July. The bark is reddish-brown. The leaves are ovate to round, 2 to 4 in. long, sharp-pointed, rounded at base usually, thickly toothed, woolly beneath. Branchlets scurfy, gray-brown. The fruits are blue, ¼ to ⅓ in. in diameter, ripening in September. Var. *canbyi* is attractive, blooms late, July, with less hair beneath, thinner, larger, broader leaves. Splendid glossy foliage.

15. *V. dilatatum,* Linden V. (Japanese Cranberrybush). A shrub of spreading habit, growing 10 ft. tall, it has creamy-white flowers in a hairy stemmed cyme. The fruits are red, small but abundant, and hang for a long time. They ripen in September. The leaves are broadly ovate, abruptly short-pointed, rounded or a little heart-shaped at the

base, shallowly toothed, hairy on both sides, veins prominent, five to eight pairs. Branches hairy when young.

16. *V. theiferum*, Tea V. A long, narrow-leaved sort growing 12 ft. tall. The white flowers have a purple calyx and are produced in five-branched cymes. The leaves are ovate-oblong, 3 to 5 in. long, sharp pointed, broadest below the middle, six to nine pairs of veins with silky hairs on them beneath. Branches smooth. Fruits are oval, red and attractive. The Autumn effect is very charming, the orange-red fruits contrasting with the red stems. Resembles *V. wrighti*, but with narrower leaves, shorter stamens; in *V. wrighti*, the stamens are longer than the corolla.

17. *V. wrighti*, Wright V. (Oriental V.) This upright sort grows 6 to 8 ft. tall. The cymes of white flowers are very short stalked, five-branched, very slightly hairy. The leaves are blue-green, prominently veined, smooth below, except on the veins, rounded to broad-obovate on the flowering shoots, abruptly pointed, coarsely dentate. The scarlet fruits are abundant, but small, ¼ in. long. The branchlets are nearly glabrous, red; the old branches are dark brown. Resembles *V. theiferum* but leaves are wider at or above the middle. Resembles *V. dilatatum* but less hairy leaves.

18. *V. lentago*, Nannyberry (Sheepberry) (Sweet V.). This large shrub or tree grows to a height of 30 ft. with slender branches. It is common from Hudson's Bay to Mississippi. The fragrant white flowers are produced in large cymes, 4 to 5 in. across. The leaves are oval or elliptical, 2 to 4 in. long, sharp-pointed, rounded or wedge-shaped at the base, finely toothed, often scurfy on veins beneath; petioles with wavy wings. The branchlets are slightly scurfy. The terminal Winter buds, are long-pointed and gray. The fruits are delicious, mealy, black, oval flattened, ripe in September; the clusters droop. Resembles Nos. 19 and 20.

19. *V. prunifolium* (*pyrifolium*), Blackhaw (Sloe) (Stagbush). Like the last, a treelike shrub. They flower a little earlier in April. The leaves are less abruptly sharp-pointed or even rounded at the tip. The petioles lack the wavy wings. The branchlets are smooth. The terminal Winter buds are short-pointed. The branching is more twiggy, horizontal. The fruits are edible, black, oval, flattened.

20. *V. rufidulum*, the Southern Blackhaw, resembles the two species above (Nos. 18 and 19). It grows 30 ft. tall and is less hardy. The leaves are shining, veins rusty beneath, especially on leaves at base. Winter buds scarcely pointed and reddish woolly. Flower clusters smaller than species No. 19.

21. *V. cassinoides*, Withe-rod (Appalachian-tea) (Wild-raisin). It grows 6 ft. tall, occasionally 12 ft. The leaves are elliptic or long oval, 1 to 4 in. long, sharp-pointed or bluntly long-pointed, wavy, shallow teeth, nearly smooth. The flowers are creamy white, produced in cymes on short stems, thereby differing from species Nos. 18, 19 and 20, in which the clusters of blooms have no stems (peduncles). The fruits are borne in drooping clusters, green at first, changing to pink, and then to black, with a bloom. The leaves turn purple, then orange-red.

22. *V. nudum*, Smooth Withe-rod (Possumhaw). This shrub resembles *V. cassinoides*, but the leaves are not toothed, only a little wavy or smooth at the edge. The edges of leaves are slightly turned over (revolute). The young leaves are somewhat scurfy on both sides when young, but become smooth. The flowers are yellowish-white, produced in large, convex clusters, followed by large fruits in drooping clusters, changing from green to black, with a glaucous bloom.

23. *V. rhytidophyllum*, Leatherleaf V. This stout-branched evergreen sort grows 10 ft. tall. The flowers are yellowish-white, borne well above the foliage in cymes 4 to 8 in. across. The buds are developed in the Fall and open in May or June. The leaves are ovate-oblong to oblong-lanceolate, 3 to 7½ in. long. The upper surface is dark green, shining, wrinkled; the lower surface is covered with gray or yellowish hairs. The branches are stellate hairy when young. The fruits are red changing black.

24. *V. suspensum* (*sandankwa*), Sandankwa V. This tender species is a splendid shrub for the Pacific Coast and the Gulf regions. It is a native of the Liu-kiu Islands. The twigs are slender and warty or scurfy. The leaves are evergreen, oval, pointed, with a few round teeth. The flowers are white, sometimes opening in February and in the cooler regions in June and July. The fruits are red. It likes partial shade in Summer.

25. *V. tinus*, Laurustinus. The twigs may be hairy but are not scurfy. This species grows to a height of 10 ft. The leaves are downy on the veins only, oval, sharp pointed, dark green, shining above. Flowers pinkish in bud and white when open. Fruit black. Useful in dry and shaded places, they succeed in adversity. Var. *lucidum* has arger and more glossy leaves. It is less hardy and less compact.

Soils. Most Viburnums are not particular as to soil but *V. alnifolium* and *V. nudum* seem to prefer a subacid soil (pH 5.0–6.0); the others seem to grow in the circumneutral soils (pH 6.0–8.0).

Faults. The Common Snowball is very subject to attacks of plant lice, which cause the leaves to curl, thereby giving a poor appearance in the planting. *V. trilobum* is not subject to aphis.

The European Cranberrybush should not be used for foundation plantings about homes as the fruits have a sour odor during the mild days of Winter.

The Japanese Snowball transplants with difficulty.

Propagation. 1. *Seed Sowing.* Most of the sorts, such as *V. opulus* and allies, *V. lentago* and allies, and *V. lantana* and allies grow readily from seed. Wash the seed from the pulp as soon as ripe.

The time usually required for Viburnum seed to germinate is two years, but Opal Davis at the Boyce-Thompson Institute has studied *V. opulus* and has found briefly that there are three stages in the development of the seeds.

(a) The first development takes place at 68 deg. or higher in approximately 60 days. During this period the embryo of the seed grows from 1-32 in. long to much larger and is ready to germinate; that is, break through the seed coat. A low temperature for even a few hours at this stage retards development.

(b) During the second stage, the rootlet starts out through the seed coat and develops the root system, but the seed leaves (cotyledons) remain in the seed. This stage requires 60 days and goes on at a temperature of from 40 to 50 degrees F. At higher temperatures the root system does not become as extensive.

(c) The third stage takes place when the seeds are removed from the cool storage to a higher temperature such as 68 degrees. It is now that the seedlings develop properly.

This sounds very complicated and impracticable but it is not so. Gather the fruit early so that the seed is sown early and will have 50 days to 60 days of warm weather in the Fall. The second stage then develops in Winter when the seed bed is mulched. Remove the mulch in Spring, whereupon the seedlings develop their third stage as the weather becomes warmer.

If the seed does not ripen early enough, merely sow in boxes and keep in rather warm place for two months, then place in coldframes, a cool basement or outside storage cellar. When moved outside in early Spring, the seedlings develop while the nights are rather frosty. Before putting outside, examine them to see that the seeds have mostly germinated.

Perhaps the other species of Viburnum behave the same way.

2. *Cuttings.* Most of the sorts, except *V. carlesi,* root from hard-wood cuttings.

3. Softwood cuttings are used for *V. opulus sterilis, V. o. nanum, V. tomentosum* and varieties, *V. carlesi. V. tomentosum* cuttings must be in growing condition. Cuttings of *V. molle* and *V. pubescens* decay easily because stems are woolly and hold too much moisture.

4. *Graftings.* Some growers graft *V. tomentosum* var. *plenum* the Japanese Snowball, upon pieces of root of the species or else they use *V. lantana* or *V. dentatum* seedlings and graft by veneer graft during the Winter. *V. carlesi* is also grafted on these stocks and may be budded in July. When *V. sieboldi* is budded upon *V. dentatum* it makes a larger cion growth than the roots and seems short lived.

5. *Layers* are extensively used in Europe for growing the Japanese Snowball and Common Snowball.

6. *Root cuttings. V. dentatum* cuttings come freely.

VITEX—Chaste-tree (Hemptree) (Monks-pepper-tree)

(From *vieo*—to bind; named from the flexible branches)

These bushy shrubs are related to the Verbena and grow 10 ft. tall. *Vitex agnus-castus* is hardy north but kills back to the soil in severe Winters. The flowers are pale lilac-blue, or white, fragrant, produced in one-sided, panicled spikes 5 to 7 in. long. The flowers open in late Summer and continue through the Autumn. The leaves are opposite, five- to seven-parted, velvety, dark green above, hairy beneath. The leaflets are like the fingers of the hand, unequal in size, entire margined or with but a few teeth. The branches are four-angled. *Vitex negundo* var. *incisa* is hardier but less showy because the racemes are not as long. The leaflets are deeply cut, even pinnatifid.

Uses. They are good specimen plants.

Soil. A deep, moist but well-drained soil suits Vitex, especially when a trifle acid. Minimacid pH 4.0–5.0.

Pruning. The floral display is improved by cutting the plants back severely, even to within 6 in. of the soil. This is best done in early Spring.

Objections. As sold by nurserymen, the plants are very poor appearing shrubs, so that the buyer often believes them to be worthless unless he knows otherwise. They are not perfectly hardy.

Propagation. 1. They seed freely. Sow in Spring.

2. Summer softwood cuttings root easily but must be Wintered in the greenhouse when young.

Left, Weigela, a profuse-flowered shrub of which many varieties are cultivated; *center*, Vitex agnus-castus, related to Verbena, its pale lilac flowers appearing in late Summer; *right*, Vaccinium, flowers white or pinkish, urn-shaped, produced in May the fruit blue-black, produced in July

3. Hardwood cuttings also root but should not freeze.

4. Layers.

5. Suckers.

WEIGELA—(Diervilla)

"In the garden of an old mandarin on one of the most beautiful islands of the world, the Island of Chusan, off the coast of Northern China, the common pink Weigela of our gardens was first found. There, in 1843, the eyes of an English plant explorer, Robert Fortune, first fell upon it, loaded with its tubular rose-colored flowers, the pride of the old mandarin and the admiration of the adventurous discoverer. Declaring it to be one of the most beautiful shrubs of Northern China, Robert Fortune sent specimens back to England where it was enthusiastically received and named to honor the German botanist, Weigel."

Thus writes C. P. Halligan so romantically.

We are interested in a few species because of their outstanding characteristics, namely:

W. florida, called also *W. amabilis*, *W. rosea*, *W. pauciflora*, the Rose W., one of the commonest in cultivation. It grows 6 ft. to 9 ft. tall. The branches have two rows of hairs. The leaves are long-pointed, toothed, except at the base, hairy on the veins beneath. The flowers are deep rose outside, paler within, blooming in May and June, on short, lateral twigs.

W. praecox is not as handsome as the above but is the Early Weigela; it has contributed earliness to hybrid sorts. The leaves are hairy above and below.

W. floribunda, the Crimson W., has dark crimson flowers. The branchlets are hairy.

In 1865, Victor Lemoine, made his first crosses and produced a good share of his splendid varieties. At a later date he crossed these varieties with *W. praecox* and obtained a group of earlier sorts which are hardier because their wood matures. For reference we are including a list of varieties of which there are no standard descriptions.

Abel Carrière. Rose carmine, yellow throat, fading purple.
Auguste Wilhelm. Rose.
Avalanche. Pure white.
Avante-garde. Pink; early.
Bouquet Rose. Satiny rose; throat striped yellow; early, large.
Bousson-fleuri. Deep rose.
Candida. Best white; light green leaves.
Chamaeleon. Rose; profuse.

Congo. Crimson.

Conquérant. Dark pink, reverse carmine; early.

Conquête. Rose-p'nk; large.

Dame Blanche. Blush.

Desbois. Crimson; small.

Dr. Baillon. Dark red.

Duchartre. Oxblood red outside, purple within.

Emile Galle. Carmine.

Esperance. Salmon.

Eva Rathke. Crimson; more dwarf than some; very popular.

Fleur de Mai. Purplish buds, pinkish red flowers; early.

Floreal. Rose, mauve reverse; early.

Gracieux. Sulphur, salmon reverse; early.

Gustave Mallet. Rose pink, bordered white; medium large.

Groenewegeni (Greenway). White, striped red, red reverse; tall.

Henderson. Deep rose; robust.

Incarnata. Deep red.

Lavalle. Bright crimson.

Luteo-marginata. Leaves bordered yellow.

Le Printemps. Flesh; free flowering; early.

Messager. Rich pink.

Mme. Couturier. Creamy white, tinted pink.

Montesqieu. Fuchsia red.

Nana variegata (rosea nana fol. var.) Leaves variegated white; flowers blush; dwarf.

Othello. Maroon.

Pavillon Blanc. Flesh; large.

Perle. Creamy white, bordered pink; large spikes.

Purpurea. Purple.

Rubra. Crimson; good foliage.

Saturne. Carmine red, darker than Eva Rathke.

Sieboldi argenteo-marginata. Silver edge; leaves outlined white; flowers pale pink.

Steltzner. Dark rose, much like rosea.

Vanhoutte. Carmine, spotted rose.

Variegata. Several sorts with yellow or white variegations.

Venosa. Carmine, throat orange-pink.

Verschaffelt. Pale pink, bordered white; long sprays.

Vestale. Creamy white; early.

Waterer's Ruby. Crimson. Improved Eva Rathke.

USES. The exquisite flowers of the Asiatic Weigelas are admired in all gardens. The foliage is often a little coarse, but the spreading habit and superb flowers of the varieties redeem this feature.

SOIL. Give good soil for healthy growth. It likes full sun, becoming straggling in shade. Circumneutral pH 6.0–8.0.

PRUNING. If pruned immediately after flowering and if the strong growths are shortened from time to time, Weigelas will bloom intermittently throughout the Summer.

DISADVANTAGES. Coarse foliage. It is rather tender in northern regions, where it is planted only in protected places. It needs room for development and resents crowding.

PROPAGATION. 1.*Softwood cuttings root readily. Bailey says that the tip of cutting should not be removed. Eva Rathke must be forced and cuttings taken from greenhouse grown plants.

2. *Hardwood cuttings* are easily rooted, especially taken short and inserted in late Winter in greenhouse where bottom heat is available.

3. *Grafting.* *Weigela florida* or Henderson W. makes good stock for whip grafting in Winter for propagating the variegated, dwarf and Eva Rathke. Nurserymen often use the roots of such variegated leaf sorts which have run out.

ZANTHORHIZA—(Yellowroot)

(From *xanthos*—yellow, *rhiza*—root)

This ground cover shrub has celerylike leaves and spreads by underground stems. *Zanthorhiza apiifolia*, the Yellowroot, is so named because its inner bark and its roots are yellow. The plants are very hardy, grow 1 to 2 ft. high. The leaves are usually yellowish-green, deeply toothed and cut into five leaflets. The flowers are dull purple and so tiny that the casual observer believes that the Yellowroot does not bloom. The leaves turn gold in the Fall.

USES. Good for covering bare spots under shrubs, for use under trees and steep banks. A yellow dye is made from the roots. Good in moist, shaded places.

SOIL. Damp. Partial shade. Banks of streams in the Alleghenies are covered with it.

PROPAGATION. 1. Division of plants is easiest as they sucker freely.

2. Seed may be sown in Autumn or early Spring. The young plants are quite weak.

ZENOBIA—(Andromeda)
(Named for Zenobia, the Empress of Palmyra)
The lovely gray-leaved shrub, *Zenobia pulverulenta*, of the Heather

Zenobia pulverulenta
A lovely, gray-leaved shrub of the Heath family

family, usually grows 2 or 3 ft. high, but is reputed to attain a height of 6 ft. It has upright, arching branches. The leaves are gray, oval to oblong, 1 to 3 in. long, alternate, with shallow, round teeth. The flowers are large white bells, twice the size of a Lily-of-the-valley, produced in racemes. It has had an abundance of names, some of which are: *Andromeda dealbata, A. glauca, A. candida, and Z. speciosa.*

Var. *nuda* (*cassiniflora*) is devoid of the grayish cast of the leaves and is, therefore, not as attractive.

USES. The grayish leaves and large flowers make this a splendid contrasting plant for beds of Rhododendrons.

SOIL. Being a Heath relative, it wants peaty or acid soil (See pages 21 to 25).

PROPAGATION. 1. Seeds.

2. Softwood in July or from forced plants.

3. Layers.

Explanation of Terms

Every effort has been made to avoid technical terms in the body of this book, but in many cases there are but small points of distinction between one species and another, and it is therefore unavoidable to remark that the leaves are stipulate or that they are obovate with a mucronate tip. The author hopes that the reader will make the little effort necessary to refer to the diagrams on pages 411, 412, 413 and 414 so that he may better identify his specimens. The plates and explanatory material are taken from *The Home Gardener's Pronouncing Dictionary*, by the author.

PLATE 1:

The difference between *acute* and *acuminate* is that *acuminate* is more narrowly pointed. An *obtuse* leaf is blunt; a *truncate* leaf is cut off rather straight at the apex; however, if the tip is somewhat drawn in, it is *emarginate* or *notched*. There is an essential difference between a *mucronate* leaf, which has an abrupt, short, sharp point; and a *cuspidate* tip, which has a sharp, stiff point, but less abrupt.

Shape of Leaves. A *linear* leaf is a long-narrow one with rather parallel sides; when a trifle wider it is called *lanceolate*. *Ovate* means almost *oval*. *Spatulate* is the opposite of a lanceolate leaf; that, is, wider at the apex. *Obovate* is the opposite of an oval leaf; that is, an almost oval leaf wider at the apex. When the base is heartshaped it is called *cordate*. A wedge-shaped leaf is called *cuneate*. When the petiole is attached toward the center, away from the margin, it is known as *peltate*.

If the leaf margin has no teeth, it is known as *entire;* if small teeth, *serrate;* if very small teeth, *serrulate;* coarse teeth, *dentate;* rounded, coarse teeth, *crenate;* if wavy with rounded dentations, it is known as *sinuate;* if merely wavy without decided teeth, *undulate;* if almost lobed because of the large and irregular teeth, it is known as *incised*.

PLATE 2:

Leaves are arranged on the stem *opposite*, *alternate*, or *whorled*. When two leaves are grown together and encircle the stem, they are called *perfoliate*.

They are *simple* or *compound* (with at least several leaflets). *Compound* leaves are known as *pinnate compound* when the leaflets are arranged along a petiole; *palmate compound* when the leaflets arise like the fingers of the hand; *pinnatifid* when they are apparently compound but in which the divisions do not actually reach the midrib and make separate leaflets. When the petiole branches so that the leaf is several times compound it is known as *decompound*.

Sessile leaves have no petiole but sit upon the stem. *Stipules* are leafy growths at the base of a leaf.

PLATE 3:

Flowers without petals are known as *apetalous* (ex. Elm); when the petals are more or less grown together it is known as *gamopetalous* (ex. Morning-glory); flowers made up of distinct and separate petals, 3, 4, 5, or more, are known as *polypetalous*.

A *salverform* flower has a long tube which expands at the top into a flat perianth (ex. Phlox).

The *Rose* family has numerous stamens and pistils (ex. Apple, Raspberry, Spirea, and Plum). The *bell-shaped* flowers are those like Foxglove, Campanula and Platycodon. *Catkins* are the long, tail-like flowers of the Willow, Alder and Oak. *Lipped* flowers are represented by such flowers as Snapdragons, all the Mints, and Salvia. The *papilionaceous* flower is pea-like, represented by most leguminous plants, such as Sweet Pea, Clover, Vetch, Colutea, and Laburnum. In many cases the stamens are attached at their base, with the pollen-bearing parts, or *anthers*, separate. The aroids, such as the Calla, the Jack-in-the-pulpit, and the Skunk-cabbage have a large leafy sheath known as the *spathe* which is associated with a club-shaped body bearing stamens or pistils, known as the *spadix*. The Buttercup family has numerous stamens and usually numerous pistils. A *rotate* flower has a regular corolla which is wheel-shaped. A *mallow* has the stamens and pistils grown together upon a column which stands in the center of the flower.

PLATE 4:

Types of Inflorescence. A *spike* differs from a *raceme* in that in a *raceme* the flowers have stems or *pedicels*. An *umbel* and a *corymb* are both flat topped, but in the *umbel* all pedicels are of equal length, and arise from a common point. In the *cyme* the central flower opens first and the other flowers spring from beneath a regular order in branching. In a *panicle* the branching goes on irregularly.

A *head* is characteristic of the Daisy family in which there are long, strap-shaped flowers on the outside, known as *ray florets;* and tubular flowers at the center, known as *disk florets*. These are enclosed by a scaly *involucre*.

Types of Fruits. Fruits are all of two types: *dehiscent* fruits split open when ripe, and *indehiscent* fruits do not split open.

A *dehiscent* fruit which splits along one line is known as a *follicle;* along two lines, a *legume;* along more than two lines, a *capsule*.

Of the indehiscent fruits, we have the dry, one-seeded fruits, known as *achene* (ex. Buckwheat). Most others are fleshy. A *berry* is a many-seeded, fleshy fruit (ex. Grape and Tomato). A *drupe* or *stone* fruit is one-seeded (ex. Cherry, Viburnum). A *pome* is a core fruit (ex. Apple).

Aggregate fruits are fruits formed by the union of a number of pistils each section of which is called a *drupelet* (ex. Mulberry, Blackberry). An accessory fruit is formed from parts of the flower besides the ovary.

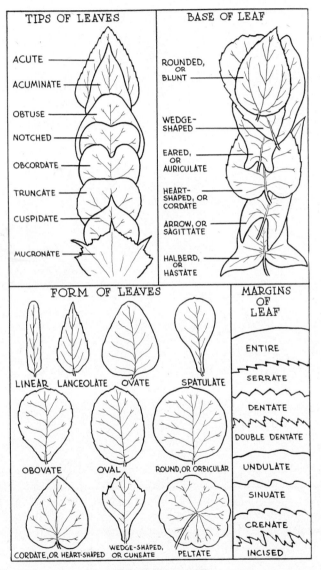

TIPS OF LEAVES

ACUTE
ACUMINATE
OBTUSE
NOTCHED
OBCORDATE
TRUNCATE
CUSPIDATE
MUCRONATE

BASE OF LEAF

ROUNDED, OR BLUNT
WEDGE-SHAPED
EARED, OR AURICULATE
HEART-SHAPED, OR CORDATE
ARROW, OR SAGITTATE
HALBERD, OR HASTATE

FORM OF LEAVES

LINEAR   LANCEOLATE   OVATE   SPATULATE
OBOVATE   OVAL   ROUND, OR ORBICULAR
CORDATE, OR HEART-SHAPED   WEDGE-SHAPED, OR CUNEATE   PELTATE

MARGINS OF LEAF

ENTIRE
SERRATE
DENTATE
DOUBLE DENTATE
UNDULATE
SINUATE
CRENATE
INCISED

Plate 1—See page 409

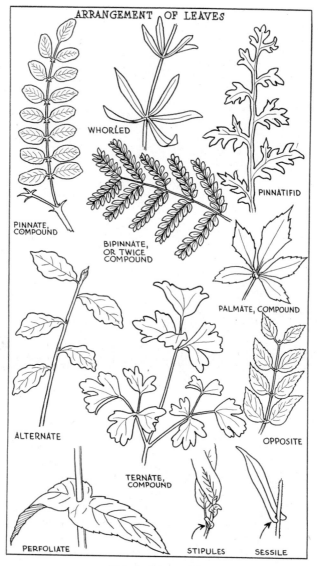

Plate 2—See page 409

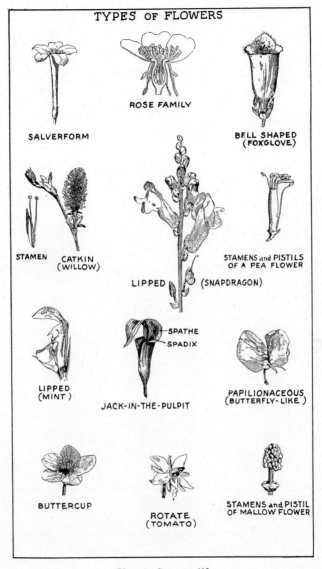

TYPES OF FLOWERS

SALVERFORM

ROSE FAMILY

BELL SHAPED
(FOXGLOVE)

STAMEN   CATKIN
(WILLOW)

LIPPED   (SNAPDRAGON)

STAMENS and PISTILS
OF A PEA FLOWER

LIPPED
(MINT)

SPATHE
SPADIX

JACK-IN-THE-PULPIT

PAPILIONACEOUS
(BUTTERFLY-LIKE)

BUTTERCUP

ROTATE
(TOMATO)

STAMENS and PISTIL
OF MALLOW FLOWER

Plate 3—See page 410

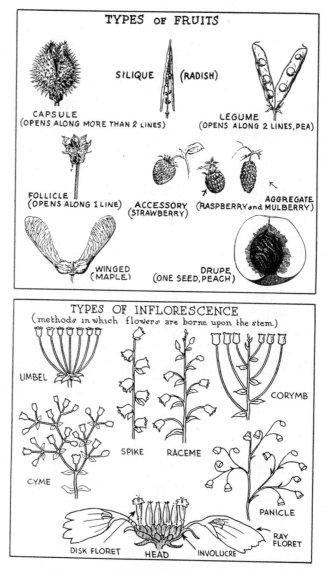

Plate 4—See page 410

TABLE OF SHRUBS

S—Sun. Sh—Shade. O indicates that flowers or fruits are unimportant.

Name	Height (in feet)	Exposure to plant	Soil	Color of flowers	Season of bloom	Color of fruit	Remarks
Abelia chinensis	4–5	Protect	Light, peaty	Pink	June-Nov.	O	Not as hardy
floribunda	4–5	Protect	Light, peaty	Rosy-purple	June-Nov.	O	Not as hardy as A. grandiflora
grandiflora	3–6	Protect	Light, peaty	White, flush pink	June-Nov.	O	Hardiest
Acanthopanax pentaphyllum	4–6	S	Rich, heavy	White	O	O	For adverse conditions
Acer campestre	–36	S	Ordinary heavy	O	O	O	Corky bark; leaves yellow in Fall
ginnala	–20	S	Ordinary heavy	O	O	O	Leaves turn red
palmatum	–20	S	Ordinary heavy	O	O	O	Leaves turn from green-yellow to crimson-scarlet
pennsylvanicum	–25	S	Acid	O	O	Salmon pink	Gray, striped green bark
tataricum	–25	S	Ordinary	O	O	O	
Aesculus parviflora	3–10	S	Rich, damp loam	White	July-Aug.	O	Forms large clumps
pavia	4–20	S Sh	Slight acid	Dk. red, pur.	June	O	Treelike
Alnus incana	–20	S Sh	Wet	Brown	March	Brown	
rugosa	–25	S Sh	Wet	Brown	March	Brown	
Amelanchier alnifolia	15	S Sh	Limestone, loamy, or leaf	White	May	Black	
canadensis	30	S Sh		White	May	Maroon-pur.	Young leaves quite purple
laevis	36	S Sh		White	May	Black	The best sort for fruit
oblongifolia	–20	S Sh	Sandy	White	May	Black	A soilbinder
stolonifera	3–8	S Sh	Sandy, chalky	White	May	Purplish-blk.	Gray leaves
Amorpha canescens	2–4	S		Bluish-purple	June-July	O	Locust-like leaves
fruticosa	6–18	S	Well drained	Purple	July	O	For rockeries
microphylla	–1½	S	Acid	Rosy purple	June-July	O	Little known, but dainty
Andrachne phylianthoides	–3	S	Acid	Green	June	O	Leaves gray beneath
Andromeda glaucophylla	½–1	Sh	Moist, rich, heavy	White	May-July	O	
polifolia	½–1½	Sh		Pink, white	May-July	O	
Aralia elata	–40	S or partial Sh		White	August	Black	Treelike
chinensis	–24	Sh		White	August	Black	Suckers freely
spinosa	–30	Sh		White	August	Black	
Arctostaphylos manzanita	1	Difficult in cultivation	Sandy, acid well drained	White to pink	May	Brownish-red	Evergreen; trailing
tomentosa	1	Difficult in cultivation		White to pink	May	Brownish-red	Hairy
uva-ursi	tr. 1	S or partial Sh		White to pink	April-Aug.	Red	Evergreen leaves turn bronze in Fall

Name	Height (in feet)	Exposure to plant	Soil	Color of flowers	Season of bloom	Color of fruit	Remarks
Ardisia crenulata	2–3	Half Sh	Neutral	White	Spring	Red	Grow in Florida for berries
Aronia arbutifolia	—9	S Sh	Moist	White pinkish	May	Red	Leaves turn red in Fall
floribunda	12	S Sh		White	May	Black	
melanocarpa	2	S Sh	Rocky slopes	White	May	Black	Undershrub
var. elata	6	S Sh		White	March-April	Green-black	The form usually cultivated
Asimina triloba	20	Half Sh	Rich, moist	Purple	0	0	Rarely cultivated
Aucuba japonica	3	S	Clay	0	April-May	0	Tub plant
Azalea amoena	4–15	Half Sh	Acid	Magenta	June-July	0	Half evergreen
arborescens	3	Half Sh	Acid	White	June	0	Leaves turn red
calendulacea	9–12	Half Sh	Acid	Yel. to scarlet	April-May	0	Very hardy
canadensis	12	Half Sh	Acid	Rosy-purple	May-June	0	The Rhodora Evergreen
indica	3	Half Sh	Acid	Various	May	0	
lutea	6	Half Sh	Acid	Yellow	May	0	
kaempferi	12	Half Sh	Acid	Orange-red	April-May	0	Lovely colors
mollis	15	Half Sh	Acid	Yellow	April-May	0	Flowers before leaves
nudiflora	3–4	Half Sh	Acid or lime	Pink	May	0	
rosea	6–8	Half Sh	Acid or lime	Pink	April-May	0	
schlippenbachi	9	Half Sh	Acid	Pink	June-July	0	Rosettes of leaves
vaseyi	15	Half Sh	Acid	Various	April-May	0	Early
viscosa	15	Half Sh	Moist	Pink, white	June-July	0	
Baccharis halimifolia	4–7	S	Sandy and salty	White	Aug.-Sept.	White, fluffy	Good for seashore
Benzoin aestivale	4–8	S Sh	Wet	Greenish-yel.	March	Red	Leaves turn yellow in the Fall
Berberis aggregata	6–15	S	Neutral	Yellow	April	Coral	Small leaves
buxifolia	3	S	Neutral	Yellow	May	Purple	Evergreen, spiny
darwini	6	S	Neutral	Yellow	April	Dark purple	Tender evergreen
julianae	10		Neutral	Yellow	April	Bluish-black	Evergreen
sargentiana	5		Neutral	Yellow	April	Bluish-black	Evergreen
thunbergi	6	S Sh	Neutral	Yellow	April	Red	
vernae	3–6		Neutral	Yellow	April		Varying leaf size
verruculosa	5	Protected spot	Neutral	Yellow	April	Violet-black	
vulgaris	2	S Sh	Neutral	Yellow	April	Red	New growth red
wilsonae	10+	S	Neutral	Yellow	April	Salmon-red	Harbors wheat rust
Buddleia asiatica	1½	S	Well drained	White			Leaves brilliant Fall. Slow growing
davidi	12	S	Well drained	Lilac	July till Autumn		Not hardy. Profusion of bloom. Twigs 4-ridged, hairy. Rockeries
globosa	8	S	Well drained	Orange-yel.		0	Half evergreen
lindleyana	8	S	Well drained	Purplish-red		0	Flowers not as profuse as davidi

Name	Height	Exposure	Soil	Color of flowers	Time of bloom	Fruit	Remarks
Buxus sempervirens	20	S Sh	Rich	O	O	O	Leaves broad below middle. Branchy, dense evergreen.
microphylla	Prostrate to 3	S Sh		O	O	O	Leaves broad above middle
Callicarpa americana	6	S	Rich	Bluish	June	Reddish-viol.	Leaves densely rusty, downy beneath
giraldiana	9	S	Well drained for hardiness	Pink	July	Violet	Leaves sparsely hairy beneath
japonica	4	S		Pink	August	Violet	Leaves 2½ to 5 in. long
purpurea	4	S		Pinkish	August	Lilac-violet	Leaves 1 to 3 in. long
Callistemon lanceolatus	12-30	S	Light	Red	Jan.-June	O	Specimens for Florida and California
rigidus	8-12	S	Light	Red	Jan.-June	O	
speciosus	40	S	Light	Red	Jan.-June	O	
Calluna vulgaris	½-2½	S	Peat	Pink	May-July		Scotch Heather
Calycanthus fertilis	8	S	Moist loam	Purplish-red brown	June-July	Brown	Leaves not so shiny above, not hairy beneath as is C. floridus. Seeds freely
floridus	8	S	Moist loam	Purplish-red brown	June-July	O	Leaves shiny above, hairy beneath
Camellia japonica	45	Half Sh	Any	Various	Oct.-June	O	Hundreds of sorts
Caragana arborescens	20	S preferably	Sandy	Yellow	June	O	Tall hedge. Shelter plantations in the Northwest
chamlagu	4	S preferably	Sandy	Yellow to red brown	May-June	Green pod, profuse but not showy	
frutex	9	S preferably	Sandy	Yellow	May-June		
maximowicziana	3	S preferably	Sandy	Golden-yel.	May		
Carpenteria californica	6-10	Sheltered from sun & high winds	Dry, sandy	White with yellow stamens	June to August	O	Not hardy nor useful for a general shrub collection. Flowers large and fragrant
Caryopteris incana	2-6	S	Well drained	Violet-blue, rarely white	September	O	Here used in the perennial border
Ceanothus americanus	2-4	Partial S	Dry	White	June to Oct.	Silver line cup	In nature found on hillsides
delilianus	3	S	Dry	Blue	Spring	O	Pacific Coast shrubs with blue flowers
prostratus	Prostrate	S	Dry	Blue	Spring	O	
thrysiflorus	30	S	Dry	Blue	June-July	O	
Cephalanthus occidentalis	10	S Sh	Wet, swampy	White, pink pistils	July to Aug.	Globular heads	Foliage too coarse
Cercidiphyllum japonicum	15 to 30 to 100	S	Deep, rich damp soil	O	O	O	Transplanting is difficult
Chaenomeles japonica	3	S	.....	Brick red	April	Yellow	Fruits fragrant
lagenaria	4+	S	.....	Brilliant scarlet	April	Yellowish-green	Autumnal foliage, most attractive
sinensis		S		Light pink	April	Golden-yel.	Leaves rusty beneath, nearly evergreen
Chamaedaphne calyculata	Prostrate 1-3	S Sh	Wet (peaty or acid)	White	April and May	O	
Chilopsis linearis	30	S	Well drained	Lilac	All Summer	O	Specimens, long season of bloom

Name	Height (in feet)	Exposure to plant	Soil	Color of flowers	Season of bloom	Color fruit	Remarks
Chionanthus retusa	18	S	Moist, sandy loam	White	June-July	Blue	More profuse flowering
virginica	10-30	S	Moist, sandy loam	Greenish-white	May-June	Blue	Profuse flowering
Choisya ternata	9	S	Loose, gravelly lime	White	Spring	O	Pot plant, house, for forcing
Cistus ladaniferus	4	S	Limestone	White	June-July	O	Semi-tropical shrub
Citrus trifoliata	10+	S	Neutral	White	April	Orange	Flowers not fragrant
Clerodendron foetidum	3-6	S	Rich	Lilac-rose	August	O	Not hardy
trichotomum	10	S	Rich	White	September	Blue, crimson calyx	
Clethra acuminata	18	Sh	Wet, peaty or acid sandy	White, purple anthers	July-Sept.	O	Unfavorable environment, straggling growth
Clethra alnifolia	3-8	Sh	Wet, peaty or acid sandy	White, pink tinge	July-Sept	O	
tomentosa	9	Sh	Wet, peaty or acid sandy	White	Aug., Sept.	O	Leaves hairy beneath; distinctive feature
Colutea arborescens	12	S Sh	Dry	Yellow	June-Sept.	Bronze-red	Fr. inflated bladder-like pod
orientalis	6	S Sh	Dry	Orange	July-Sept.	Purple	
Comptonia asplenifolia	2-4	S Sh	Peaty, sandy or sterile	O	O	O	
Coprosma baueri	20-25	S	....	O	O	Bright yellow	Don't tolerate a rich, limey soil Evergreen for Florida and Pacific Coast
Cornus alba	5-10	S Sh	....	Creamy white	May or June	Bluish-white	Red twigs
alternifolia	-20	Sh	....	Pale yellow	May	Bluish-black	Branches in tiers
amomum	5-10	S	Wet	White	June	Blue	Purple twigs
baileyi		S	Dry	White	May	White	Red twigs
brachypoda	-15	S	Dry	Yellowish-white	July and August		
florida	15+	S Sh	Acid	White	May	Black	Rather tender
kousa	15+	Sh	....	White	June	Red	Brown twigs
mas	10+	S Sh	....	Golden-yel.	March	Pinkish	Brown twigs
officinalis	10+	S	....	Golden-yel.	April	Scarlet	Green twigs
paniculata	3-15	S	Wet	Creamy-white	June	Red	Green twigs
rugosa	10	S	....	White	June	White or pale blue Light blue or green-white	Green twigs
sanguinea	10+	S	Wet	White	May-June	Green	Hard to transplant Green branches
stolonifera	8+	S	Wet	Dull white	May	White	Suckers freely
Coronilla emerus	3-4	......	Well drained	Yellow	May-Sept.	O	Rather tender

Name	Height	S / Sh	Soil	Flower	Time	Berry	Remarks
Corylopsis pauciflora	4–6		Peaty and sandy	Primrose-yellow	April	Black	Fragrant
spicata	4–6		Peaty and sandy	Yellow	March	Green	Purple leaves
Corylus avellana	15	S	Moist	Catkins	March	Purplish	
maxima	30	S	Moist	Catkins	March	Beaked green	Long nutlets
rostrata	9	S	Well drained	Catkins	June	Red	
Cotoneaster acuminata	8–12	S	Well drained soils preferred	Pinkish	May–June	Black	
acutifolia	12	S		Pinkish	June	Red	
adpressa	Creeping	S		Pink	June	Red	
apiculata	3	S		Pink	June	Red	Tender species
dammeri	Prostrate	S		White	June	Scarlet	
dielsiana	–6	S		Pinkish	June	Red	
divaricata	–6	S		Pink	June	Black	
foveolata	9	S		Pink	June	Orange	
francheti	6	S		Pink	June	Red	
frigida	–10	S		White	June	Red	Almost a tree, tender
horizontalis	Trailing	S	Well drained soils preferred	Pink	June	Red	Leaves turn yellow in Autumn
hupehensis	6	S		White	May	Scarlet	
microphylla	3	S		White	May	Scarlet	
multiflora	10	S		White	June	Red	Tender; grayish leaves
pannosa	8	S		White	May–June	Scarlet	
racemiflora	8	S		White	June	Scarlet	
rotundifolia	9	S		White	June–July	Red	
simonsi	30	S Sh		White	May	Red	Hardy
Crataegus cordata	25	S Sh		White	May	Red	Horizontal growth
crusgalli	25	S Sh		White	June and July	Red	Horizontal growth
oxacantha	–30			White	June	Red	Horizontal growth
Cyrilla racemiflora			Sandy loam	White	June–August		Popular hardy species
Cytisus albus	1½	S	Limey	Yell'ish-white	May	O	
canariensis	6	S	Limey	Yellow	Winter	O	Tender; grown in semi-tropics
glabrescens	3	S	Limey	Yellow	May	O	Hardy, splendid for rockeries and edging other shrubs
hirsutus	2	S	Limey	Yellow	June–July	O	
nigricans	6	S	Limey	Yellow	June–July	O	
purgans	3	S	Limey	Yellow	May	O	
purpureus	1½	S	Limey	Purple	May		Trifle tender
supinus	3	S	Limey	Yellow	June		
scoparius	–10	S	Peaty or sandy alkal.	Yellow	May or June		
Daphne blagayana	1½	S	Peaty or sandy alkal.	Creamy white	April	O	
cneorum	1–1½	S	Peaty or sandy alkal.	Pink	April and Sept.	Yellowish-brown	Less hardy
genkwa	–3	S	Peaty or sandy alkal.	Violet	April	O	Most desirable

Name	Height (in feet)	Exposure to plant	Soil	Color of flowers	Season of bloom	Color of fruit	Remarks
Daphne mezereum	—3	S	Alkaline	Pink, rose purple	April	Scarlet	Flowers as soon as Winter is over
Deutzia gracilis	3-6	S	Well drained for greater hardiness	Pink-white	May	....	
lemoinei	3	S		White	May	....	
parviflora	4	S		White	May	....	
scabra	4-6	S Sh		Pinkish-white	May	....	Not as hardy
Diervilla sessilifolia	3	S Sh		Yellow, red	June, July	....	
trifida	3	S		Yellow, red	June, July	....	
Diosma ericoides	2-4	S Sh	Peaty	White	Spring	O	Tiny, heathlike
Dirca palustris	2-4	S	Moist	Yellow	March-April	Red	Rarely cultivated
Dombeya wallichi	30	S	Peaty sand	Yellow	Winter	O	Snowball-like flowers; Tropics
Duranta plumieri	15	S	Well drained	Pink	Aug.	Orange	Native of Mexico
Elaeagnus angustifolia	20	S	Sandy, clay	Blue	June	Yellowish	Flowers fragrant
argentea	6-12	S	Sandy, clay	Yellow	June	Silvery	Leaves silvery
longipes (multiflora)	9	S	Sandy, clay	Yellow	June	Red	
pungens	6-12	S	Sandy, clay	Yellow	June	Red-brown	Evergreen
umbellata	12	S	Sandy, clay	Silver-white	June	Scarlet	Fruit showy
Elsholtzia stauntoni	3-5	S	Well drained	Yellow	September	O	Prune to soil
Empetrum nigrum	Creeper	S Sh	Peat	Red-purple	April, May	Black	Good ground cover
Enkianthus campanulatus	6	S Sh	Acid	Purple	May		Leaves turn scarlet
subsessilis	4	S	Acid	Pink	May	Drooping capsules	
Erica carnea	½	S	Acid	Pink	Feb-April	...	Bronze leaves
Escallonia montevidensis	9	S	Any	White	Fall-Winter	O	See pages 225 and 226 for others
rubra	3-6	S, Sh	Any	Red	Fall-Winter	O	Splendid in semi-tropics
Eugenia myrtifolia	12	S		White	Spring	O	Southern hedge
Euonymus alatus	6-8	S	Well drained, not particular except E. japonicus which is acid	Yellowish	May	Violet O	Fall coloring
americanus	5-8	S		Greenish-pur.	June	Purple O	Treelike growth
atropurpureus	15-25	S Sh		Purple	May	Light scarlet	
bungeanus	18	S Sh		Yellowish	June	Crimson	Tree grower
europaeus	20	S		Yel'ish-green	May	Yellowish or pinkish	Treelike growth
japonicus	10-12	S		Greenish	May O	Pink O	Evergreen
latifolius	21	S		Greenish	June		Fall coloring
patens	9-10	S		White	May	Bright red	
planipes	Spreading, 14-16	S Sh		Greenish	June		
fortunei (radicans)	Climber	S Sh				Pink	Evergreen
radicans var. acutus	Climber	S Sh				Bright red	Handsome fruit
radicans var. argen. margin.	Climber	S Sh					Ground cover; Leaves bordered white

Name	Height	Light	Soil	Flower	Time	Fruit	Remarks
Euonymus radicans var. carrierei	Shrubby	S Sh	hardier in dry or sandy soil.	Greenish	June	Orange	Profuse fruiter
radicans var. colorata	Climber	S					Fall coloring
radicans var. kewensis	Climber	S Sh					Small leaves
radicans var. picta	Climber	S Sh					Leaves small white on veins
radicans var. rosea	Climber	S Sh					Leaves bordered pink
radicans var. vegetus	Climber	S Sh					Not upright
yedoensis	15	S	Sandy and limey soils	Greenish	June	Orange	Fruit retained into Winter
Exochorda giraldi	10	S		Greenish	June	Rose-colored	Handsomer than commoner ones
korolkowi	10	S		White	April-May	○	
macrantha	15	S		White	April-May	○	
racemosa	10	S		White	April-May	○	
Fatsia papyrifera	5–15	S Sh	Moist	White ○	○	○	Grown as tropical foliage shrub
Fontanesia phillyreoides	15	S	Dry	Yellow	April	○	Drought resistant
Forsythia europaea	6	S Sh	Unimportant	Yellow	April	○	
intermedia	9	S Sh	Unimportant	Yellow	April	○	
ovata	5	S Sh	Unimportant	Yellow	April	○	
suspensa	9	S Sh	Unimportant	Yellow	April	○	Less showy
vividissima	9	S Sh	Unimportant	White	April	○	
Fothergilla gardeni	4	S Sh	Light	White	April or May	○	
major	6	S	Light	White	Summer	○	
Fremontia californica	20	S	Dry	Yellow	June–Sept.		A California shrub
Fuchsia magellanica	20	Semi-Sh	Acid	Violet, red	Winter	Purple	Graceful, semi-tropical pot plants
Gardenia florida	2–6	Sun	Resents lime	White	Spring	○	Fragrant tropical white flower
Grevillea thelemanniana	5	S	Dry soil	Red	Spring	○	Valued in semi-tropics
Hakea pugioniformis	8–10	S	Dry soil	White			Strange, semi-tropical shrub
Halimodendron halodendron	6	S	Salty or limestone soil; dry	Pale purple	May	○	
Hamamelis japonica	–30	S	Indifferent	Lemon-yel.	Feb. or Mar.	⎫ Ripen in Fall	
mollis	–30	S	Indifferent	Golden yel.	Feb. or Mar.	⎬	
vernalis	–6	S	Indifferent	Light yellow		⎭ Black seeds	
virginiana	10–25	S	Indifferent	Yellow	Oct. or Nov.		
Helianthemum chamaecistus	2½	Sh	Limestone, dry	Yel. to rose, crim., white	June to Aug.	○	
Hibiscus rosa-chinensis	25	S, Sh	Rich	Reds		○	Popular in South
syriacus	20	S Sh	Not too sandy	Wht, red, pur.	August	Brown	Good for city conditions
Hippophae rhamnoides	30	S	Limey	Yellow	April	Orange	Treelike
Holodiscus discolor	20	S	M	White	July	○	Good shrub border
Hydrangea arborescens	3	S Sh	In acid soils the pink sorts remain pink, but in limey or neutral soil they become blue	White	June	○	
bretschneideri	12–15	S Sh		Blue, white, or pink	July	○	Cold regions freeze to 2½ ft.
cinerea	3	S Sh		White, pink, or pink	June		
opuloides	8	S Sh		gr'ish bronze	July	○	
paniculata	25	S Sh		P'kish-white-purplish	July		
quercifolia	10	S Sh		White	June	○	
radiata	3	S Sh		White	July	○	
xanthoneura	8	S Sh		Pinkish		○	

Name	Height (in feet)	Exposure to plant	Soil	Color of flowers	Season of bloom	Color fruit	Remarks
Hypericum aureum	3	Sh	Sandy	Yellow	July-August	O	Evergreen in Summer
calycinum	1	Sh	Sandy	Yellow	July-Sept.	O	
densiflorum	6	Sh	Sandy	Yellow	July-Sept.	O	
kalmianum	2-3	Sh	Sandy	Yellow	August	O	
moserianum	1½	Sh	Sandy	Yellow	Aug.-Sept.	O	Large flowers
patulum	3	Sh	Sandy	Yellow	July-Sept.	O	Large flowers
prolificum	4	S, Sh	Sandy	Yellow	July-Sept.	O	
Ilex cassine	30	S	Well drained	White	July	**Red**	Superior Southern berried shrub
cornuta	9-15	Partial Sh	......	White	June	Red	Rather less hardy
crenata	5-10	S	......	White	July	Black	Evergreen
geniculata	8-15	Partial Sh	Wet	White	July	Black	
glabra	8	S	......	White	July	Orange-red	Evergreen
laevigata	8	S	Wet	White	July	Red	
serrata	8	S	Wet	White	July	Red	
verticillata	8	S, Sh	......	White	July	Red	
vomitoria	25	S	Sandy or peaty soils	White	July	Red	Superior Southern berried shrub
Indigofera decora	1-1½	S	} Sandy or peaty soils	Pink	July-August	O	
gerardiana	2+	S		Purple	June	O	
kirilowi	3+	Sh		Rosy-purple	June	O	
potanini	3-8	Sh		Rosy-purple	June	O	
Itea virginica	3	S Sh	Wet	White	July	O	Twigs green
Jamesia americana		Sh	Acid or sand	White	May-June	O	
Kalmia angustifolia	6-24 in	S Sh	Sandy, acid	Pink, white	June	O	Evergreen
latifolia	8	Sh	Sandy, acid	White, pink	June	O	Evergreen
polifolia	1	Sh	Sandy, acid	White, lilac	June	O	Evergreen
Kerria japonica	4-6	S Sh	Good drainage	Golden-yel.	June-Sept.	O	Green twigs
Kolkwitzia amabilis	6	S Sh	Well drained	Pink and orange	June	O	Woolly, flaky bark
Laburnum adami	10-20	Protected spot	Well drained limestone	Yellow, purple, pink	June	O	Trifle tender in North
alpinum	10-15	Protected spot	Well drained limestone		June	O	Trifle tender in North
Laburnum anagyroides	20	Protected spot	Well drained limestone	Yellow	May	Pods 2 in. long seeds black	Trifle tender in North
Lagerstroemeria indica	15-20	S	......	Pur. to white	Aug.-Oct.	O	Tender
Laurocerasus caroliniana	20-40	S, Sh	Rich	White	Spring	Black	
lusitanica	40	S, Sh	Rich	White	Spring	Purple	} Southern evergreen cherries
officinalis	30	S, Sh	Rich	White	Spring	Purple	} Southern evergreen cherries
Laurus nobilis	40	S, Sh	Good	O		Purple	Tub plant
Ledum groenlandicum	1	Partial Sh	Wet	White	May-June	O	

Name	Height	S/Sh	Soil	Flower	Time	Fruit	Remarks
Leiophyllum buxifolium	1	S Sh	Acid	White	May-June	○	Evergreen
var. prostratum	½-1	S Sh	Acid	White	May-June	○	Evergreen
Lespedeza bicolor	3-6	S		Rose-purple	September	○	
formosa	3-10	S		Rose-purple	September	○	
Leucothoe axillaris	3-10	Sh	Acid	White	April-May	○	Evergreen
catesbaei	2-3	Sh	Acid	White	April-May	○	Evergreen
Leycesteria formosa	3-4	Sh		White	Aug.-Sept.	Red	Rather tender
Ligustrum amurense	15	S Sh	Indifferent	White	June-July	Black	
ibolium	15	S Sh	Indifferent	White	July	Black	
ibota	15	S Sh	Indifferent	White	August	Black	Evergreen
japonicum	15	S Sh	Indifferent	White	Aug.-Sept	Black	Evergreen
lucidum	15	S Sh	Indifferent	White	July	Black	
obtusifolium	15	S Sh	Indifferent	White	July	Black	Horizontal growth
var. regelianum	15	S Sh	Indifferent	White	August	Black	
ovalifolium	6	S Sh	Indifferent	White	Sept.-Oct.	Purplish	
quihoui	8	S Sh	Indifferent	White	July	Black	
sinense	15	S Sh	Indifferent	White	June-July	Black	
vulgare	8-10	S Sh	Indifferent	White, pink	May	Red	
Lonicera bella	4-5	S	Indifferent	Rose	March		
fragrantissima	12	S	Indifferent	White	May	Purple	Quite evergreen
korolkowi	8-9	S	Indifferent	Orange-yel.	June	Red	Blue leaves
ledebouri	12-15	S	Indifferent	White	May	Blood-red	Strange bracts on fruit
maacki	8	S	Indifferent	White	May, June	Blue, purple	Fragrant
morrowi	6	S	Indifferent			Purple	Gray, hairy leaves
nitida	Prostrate	S	Indifferent	White	May	Orange-red	Almost evergreen
pileata	10	S	Indifferent	White	June	Purplish-red	Semi-evergreen
ruprechtiana	Procumbent	S	Indifferent	White	March		
spinosa var. alberti	4-5	S	Indifferent	Rose	May	Scarlet	
standishi	4-5	S	Indifferent	White	May	Red	Fragrant flowers
syringantha	10	S	Indifferent	Rose, white	May, June	Yellow	Like L. fragrantissima
tatarica		S	Indifferent	Rose, white	June	Red	
var. lutea	4-5	S	Indifferent	Purple	April	Dark red	Most commonly planted
thibetica	10	S	Indifferent	Yellow-white	All season	○	
xylosteum	4-10	S Sh	Indifferent	White	May	○	
Lyonia ligustrina	10	S	Acid	White	June	○	Not very ornamental
Magnolia denuda'a	50	S	Moist, somewhat acid	White	April	○	
glauca	10-15	S	Moist, somewhat acid	White	All Summer	○	
liliflora		S	Moist, somewhat acid	Purple	May	○	
parviflora	4-10	S		White	May	○	Fragrant
salicifolia	12-15	S		White-rose	March	○	
soulangeana	12	S		White	May		
stellata	2-3	Sh		Yellow	March		
Mahoberberis neuberti	2-3	Sh	Dry, sandy	Yellow	April	Black	
Mahonia aquifolium	2-3	Sh	Dry, sandy	Yellow	April	Black	

Name	Height (in feet)	Exposure to plant	Soil	Color of flowers	Season of bloom	Color of fruit	Remarks
Mahonia bealei	2–3	Sh	Dry, sandy	Yellow	April	Black	
pinnata	12	Sh	Dry, sandy	Yellow	April	Black	
repens	Prostrate	Sh	Dry, sandy	Yellow	April	Black	
Malus angustifolia	30			Pink	May	Green	
arnoldiana	10			Rose	May	Yellow	
atrosanguinea	15			Purple	May	Reddish yel.	
baccata	40		Well drained neutral soils best	White	May	Red, yellow	
var. mandschurica	40			White	May	Purple	
coronaria	30			Blush	May	Yellow	
floribunda	30			Carmine	May	Red	
halliana	15			Rose	May	Red	Double
ioensis var. bechteli	30			Pink	June	O	
micromalus	15			Pink	May	Yellow	
prunifolia var. rinki	20			White	May	Red, green	
pumila var. niedzwetzkyana	30			Red	May	Red	
robusta				White	May	Dull red	
sargenti	6			White	May	Scarlet	
scheideckeri	20			Pink	May	Yellow	
spectabilis	24			Pink	May	Yellow	
theifera	24			Rose	May	Yellow	
Melaleuca armillaris	15–30	S	Light	White	Jan. to June	O	Specimens for South and Pacific Coast
decussata	20	S	Light	Lilac	Jan. to June	O	Specimens for South and Pacific Coast
hypericifolia	10	S	Light	Red	Jan. to June	O	
Meratia praecox	4	South	Sandy	Purp.-brown	January	......	Fragrant flowers
Michelia fuscata	10–15	S	Moist	Yellowish brown	Spring to Summer	O	Good in South
Myrica carolinensis	8–9	S	Dry	O		Gray	Fragrant leaves
cerifera		S	Dry	O		Gray	
gale	3	S	Moist	O		Gray	
Myrtus communis	3–10	S Sh	Any	White	Ev flowering	Black	The True Myrtle
Nandina domestica	3–6	S	Peaty loam	White	June–July	Red	Leaves turn scarlet
Neillia sinensis	5–6	S Sh	Moist	Pink O	June	O	Related to Spiraeas
Nemopanthus mucronatus	6–8	S	Acid	O		Red	Splendid in wild
Nerium oleander	15	S	Damp	Scarlet to white	Spring	O	Common tub plant and shrub for warmer sections
Neviusia alabamensis	4	S	Well drained	White	May, June	O	A Spiraea without petals
Ononis fruticosa	–1½	S	Well drained	Pink	June–August	O	Bark gray-silver
Osmanthus aquifolium	7–8–20	Protected places	Peaty	White	O	O	Evergreen
Parrotia persica	10–15	S	Well drained	Purplish	March–April	Bluish O	Leaves turn from yellow to orange-scarlet in Fall

Name	Ht. (ft.)	Exposure	Soil	Flower	Blooms	Fruit	Grown in South for fruit
Pernettya mucronata	1½	S	Peat, Light, well drained	White	June to July	Red	
Perowskia atriplicifolia	3-5	S	Lime-neutral	Lavender	Aug.-freeze	O	See page 317
Philadelphus	3-20	Limey	Light, sandy, loamy	White	June	O	
Photinia serrulata	15-20	S	perf. drain.	White, rose-tinted	May	Red	Evergreen
villosa	—15	S	Cool, moist	White	May	Red	Leaves turn red in Fall
Physocarpus opulifolius	10	S Sh	Acid	P'kish-greenish-white	May-June	Reddish	
Pieris floribunda	3-5	Sh	Acid	White	April-May	O	Leaves reddish bronzy in Winter warmer regions
japonica	3-5	Sh	Any	White	April-May	O	Foundation plant in warmer regions
Pittosporum tobira	10	Sh		White	Winter	O	Semi-climbing
Plumbago capensis	15-20	Semi Sh	Light	Pale blue	Constant, Everbloom'g	O	Splendid shrub for semi-tropics
Polygala dalmaisiana	4	S Sh		Purple red	May	O	
Prunus besseyi	3	S	Good, well drained loam	White	May	Black	Hardy
cerasifera var. pissardi	20	S	Good, well drained loam	White	May	Red or yellow	
glandulosa	6	S	Good, well drained loam	Rosy pink to white	Spring	Red	
ilicifolia	30	S	Good, well drained loam	White	Spring	Purple	Very hardy
lyoni	25	S Sh	Good, well drained loam	White	May	Purple	Evergreen for South
maritima	8	S	Good, well drained loam	White	May	Purple	Evergreen for South
nana	6	S	Good, well drained loam	Pink, white	April	O	Very hardy
persica	18	S	Good, well drained loam	Red, pink, or white	May	Yellow	Very hardy
tomentosa	5	S	Moderately moist but well drained	White	May	Scarlet	Purple leaves
triloba	10	S	Moderately moist but well drained	Pink, white	April	Red	Hardy
yedoensis	45	S	Moderately moist but well drained	White to pink	May	Black	Good for forcing
Ptelea baldwini	—8	Sh	Dry or wet	Greenish-white	June	Green	Hardy
trifoliata	—24		Dry or wet	Greenish white	June	Green	
Potentilla fruticosa	3	Partial Sh	Dry, Acid, Indifferent	Yellow and white	June to Oct.	O	Shabby
tridentata	8-10 in.	S	Dry, Acid, Indifferent	White	June, Sept.	O	Evergreen
Punica granatum	15	S	Limestone, well drained	Scarlet	May to June	Orange red	Hardy as far north as Washington, D. C.
Pyracantha coccinea	6	S	Limestone, well drained	White	May-June	Orange-scar.	
crenulata	6	S Sh	Limestone, well drained	White	May-June	Scarlet	Splendid fruit display
Raphiolepis umbellata	8-12	S Sh	Light	White	Spring	Black	Splendid fruit display
Rhamnus cathartica	12	S Sh	Sand or clay	Greenish	June	Black	Tender in North
fallax	10	S Sh	Sand or clay	Yellowish	June-Aug.	Black	
frangula	12		Sand or clay	Pale yellow	June, July, August	Black	
Rhododendron carolinianum	9	Sh	Subacid	Pink	May	O	
catawbiense	6-18	Sh	Subacid	Red and pur.	May	O	
maximum	36	Sh	Subacid	Pink or white	May	O	
smirnovi	18	Sh	Subacid	Red and pink	April-May	O	

Name	Height (in feet)	Exposure to plant	Soil	Color of flowers	Season of bloom	Color fruit	Remarks
Rhodotypos kerrioides	4	S Sh	Indifferent	White	May to Fall	Black	Tolerates adverse conditions
Rhus canadensis	2-6	S Sh	Dry	Yellow	March-April	Red	Leaves turn in Fall
copallina	3-5	S	Dry	Yell'sh green	August		
cotinoides	30	S	Dry	Yellowish	June-July		
cotinus	15	S	Light soil	Green, purple	August		
glabra	15-20	S Sh	Dry	Greenish	July-August	Purplish	Smooth branches
hirta	30	S	Dry	Greenish	June-July	Red	Dense velvet hairs on branches
javanica	25	S Sh	Dry	White	August and September	Red	
vernicifera	40	S	Dry			Orange	
Ribes alpinum	6	S	Moder. fertile	Brownish	June	Brownish	
aureum	6	Sh	Moder. fertile	Greenish	April	Black	
odoratum	6	Sh	Moder. fertile	Yellow	April	Purplish-br.	
sanguineum	-10	Sh	Moder. fertile	Yellow	April	Purplish-br.	
Robinia hartwigi	12	S	Limey	Red		Blue-black	
hispida	-3	S	Limey	White to rosy purple	July		Tree-like
kelseyi	-9	S	Limey	Rose-pink	June	○	Suckers freely
Rosa carolina	3	S	Heavy clay	Rose	June	○	Fruits red hairy
eœae	6	S	Heavy clay	Pink	June, July	○	
eglanteria	9	S	Heavy clay	Yellow	May, June	Red	Aromatic foliage
Harison's Yellow	8	S	Heavy clay	Pink	June	Red	Sweet leaves
Hugonis	8	S	Heavy clay	Orange-yel.	May	Red	Later blooming
multiflora		S	Heavy clay	Sulphur-yel.		Red	
nitida	1½	S	Heavy clay	White	Spring	Red	Reclining branches
Persian Yellow	9	S	Heavy clay	Pink	June	Red	
penzanceana	6	S	Heavy clay	Yellow		Red	
rubrifolia	6	S	Heavy clay	Pink	June, July	Red	
rugosa	6	S	Heavy clay	Deep red	Spring	Red	Semi-double
setigera	15	S	Heavy clay	Pink, white	June-Aug.	Red	Tremendous growers
spinosissima	3	S	Heavy clay	Pink	June	Black	Purplish leaves
virginiana	9	S	Heavy clay	Yellow, white	June, July	Red	Single and double
xanthina		S	Heavy clay	Yellow	May, June	Red	Common Prairie Rose
Rubus odoratus	3-6	Sh	Rich, well-drained	Rosy-purple	June-Sept.	Red	
Sambucus canadensis	5-8	S Sh	Swampy	White	June-July	Red	
nigra	5-8	S Sh	Indifferent	White	June-July	Black	
racemosa	6-8	Sh	Indifferent	Yellow	April-May	Red	
Shepherdia argentea	12	Sh	Cool	Yellow	April-May	Scarlet	
canadensis	3-7				April-May	Yellowish-red	Five-parted leaves

Name	Height	Type	Soil	Color	Bloom	Fruit	Remarks
Skimmia japonica	3-4	Sh	Sandy and peaty	White	May	○	Evergreen with red berries
Sorbaria aitchisoni	6-8	S	Indifferent	White	June	○	
arborea	18	S	Indifferent	White	June, Sept.	○	
assurgens	3	S	Indifferent	White	June	○	
lindleyana	3	S	Indifferent	White	June	○	
sorbifolia	3	S	Indifferent	White	June-August	○	
Spiraea alba	6	S, but most Spiraeas are tolerant of some Sh	Neutral soils	White	June-August	○	
albiflora	2½			White	July-August	○	
arguta	4-5			White	April	○	
billiardi	6			Rose	July-August	○	
burnalda	3			Pink	June+	○	
Anthony Waterer	2½			Deep rose	June+	○	
froebeli	3			Deep rose	Early June+	○	
cantonensis	4-5			White	May	○	
chamaedryfolia	4-5			White	May-June	○	
douglasi	3-4			Pinkish-pur.	July-August	○	
gemmata	6-9			White	May	○	
henryi	6-8	S, but most Spiraeas are tolerant of some Sh	Neutral soils	White	June	○	
japonica	4			Pink, white	June, July	○	
latifolia	4-6			White, pink.	June-August	○	
margaritae	3-5			Pink	July, Sept.	○	
prunifolia	4-6			White	April	○	
salicifolia	4			Rose	July-August	○	
superba	3			Pink	July-August	○	
thunbergi	3			White	March-April	○	
tomentosa	4			Pinkish-pur.	July-August	○	
trichocarpa	4-5			White	May	○	
vanhouttei	5-6			White	Late May	○	
veitchi	9			White	June-July	○	
Staphylea colchica	10	Sh	Moist, rich	Yel'ish-white	May-June	○	
pinnata	15			Gr'nish-white	May	} Green	
trifolia	10			White	April		
Stephanandra incisa	3-6		Peaty	White	June	○	Dainty foliage
tenakae	3-6			White	June-July	○	Larger leaves
Styrax japonica	10-12	Sh	Well drained, slightly Acid	White	May to June	O	Likes 'ots of water
Symplocos paniculata	15	S		White	May or June	Sapphire	Hardy
Symphoricarpos albus	-3	Sh	Limestone and clay	Pink	August	White	
chenaulti	-3	Sh		Pink	August	Red	Neater habit than others
mollis	-3	Sh		Pink	August	White	Better fruits than others
occidentalis	-3	Sh			August	White	
vulgaris	-4	Sh			August	Red	

Name	Height (in feet)	Exposure to plant	Soil	Color of flowers	Season of bloom	Color fruit	Remarks
Syringa amurensis	20	S	Neutral	Yel'ish-white	June-July	○	Treelike sorts
var. japonica	25	S	Neutral	Yel'ish-white	June-July	○	Treelike sorts
var. pekinensis	20–30	S	Neutral	White	June	○	Treelike sorts
chinensis	10–12	S	Neutral	Reddish-lilac	June	○	Small flowers in large clusters
josikaea	10	S	Neutral	Deep lilac	June	○	Resembles S. villosa
persica	8	S	Neutral	Lav., white	July	○	Willowy growth
villosa	15+	S	Neutral	Lilac	July	○	Flowers resemble those of Privets
vulgaris	12–25	S	Neutral	Various	June	○	List of va-ieties, page 380
Tamarix gallica		Salt air and wind		Pink	July		
hispida	4	Salt air and wind	Not too much lime	Pink	July	○	
juniperina	15	Salt air and wind	Not too much lime	Pink	Aug.–Sept.	○	
odessana	15	Salt air and wind	Not too much lime	Pink	May	○	Gray leaves
parviflora	15	Salt air and wind	Not too much lime	Pink	Aug.	○	
pentandra	15	Salt air and wind	Not too much lime	Pink	April	○	
tetrandra	2–4	Salt air and wind	Not too much lime	Pink	Aug.–Sept.	○	One of best
Ulex europaeus		S	Gravelly or sandy	Yellow	April or May and Aug.	Dark brown	
Vaccinium corymbosum	1	Moist Wet places	Acid	White	April	Purple	Attractive Fall color
macrocarpon	Creeping		Acid	White	April	Red	Not cultivated for ornament but for edible fruit
pennsylvanicum	2	Dry	Acid	White	April	Purple	Common hillside Blueberry
Veronica andersoni	3–4	S	Loam	Violet	Spring	○	} Evergreens for South
imperialis	3–6	S	Loam	Crim-purple	Spring	○	} Evergreens for South
Viburnum acerifolium	5	Sh	Dry	White	June	Black	
affine	3–6	S	Subacid	......	June-July	Black	
alnifolium	5–10	S	Wet	White	May	Black	
carlesi	4–6	S		Pink	April	Black	Fragrant
cassinoides	6	S Sh		White	May	Black	
dentatum	5–15	S		White	June	Black	
dilatatum	10	S		White	June	Black	
lantana	15	Sh	Wet or moist	White	June-July	Red	
lentago	30	Protected place		White	May	Black	
macrocephalum	12			White	April	Black	Largest clusters of bloom
molle	12			White	May	Black	
nudum	8	S Sh	Subacid	White	May	Black	
opulus	10	S Sh		White	May-June	Red	
prunifolium	30			White	April	Black	
pubescens	12			White	June-July	Blue	

		Shaded in Winter					
Viburnum rhytidophyllum	10		Well drained	White	May	Red to black	
rufidulum	30			White	May	Black	
sargenti	10	S Sh		White	May	Red	
sieboldi	10	S		White	May–June	Black	
suspensum	6	Partial Sh		**White**	**February**	**Red**	**Tender**
theiferum	12	S		White	June	Red	
tinus	10	Sh	Dry	**White**	**Spring**	Purple	**Tender**
tomentosum	10	S		White	May or June	Blue–black	
trilobum	10	S Sh		White	May	Red	
wrighti	6–8	S		White		Red	
Vitex agnus-castus	10	S	Slightly acid	Lilac	July–Sept.	O	
negundo	10	S		Lilac	July–Sept.	O	
Weigela florida	6–9	S	Well drained	Various	May–June	O	
praecox	6–9	S	Well drained	Various	April–May	O	
Zanthorhiza apiifolia	1–2	Sh	Wet or dry	Maroon	April	O	Ground cover
Zenobia pulverulenta	2–3	Sh	Acid	White	June	O	Gray leaves

INDEX OF PLANT NAMES

(See also Table of Shrubs, pages 415 to 429)

GENERAL INDEX